Somme Mud

E.P.F. LYNCH

Edited by Will Davies

Somme Mud

The war experiences of an infantryman in France 1916–1919

RANDOM HOUSE AUSTRALIA

A Random House book
Published by Random House Australia Pty Ltd
Level 3, 100 Pacific Highway, North Sydney, NSW 2060
www.randomhouse.com.au

First published by Random House in 2006
This edition published 2008

Addresses for companies within the Random House Group can be found at www.randomhouse.com.au/offices.

National Library of Australia
Cataloguing-in-Publication Entry

E.P.F Lynch
Somme mud

ISBN 978 1 74166 894 0 (pbk.)

Lynch, E. P. F. Australia. Army. Australian Imperial Force (1914–1921). Battalion, 45th. World War, 1914–1918 – France – Personal narratives, Australian. World War, 1914–1918 – France – Trench Warfare – Personal narratives, Australian. Soldiers – Australia – Biography. Somme (France) – History.

940.48194

Cover composite photograph by Frank Hurley, courtesy of the Australian War Memorial, negative no. E0120A
Cover design by Blue Cork
Typeset in 12/15 pt Garamond by Midland Typesetters, Australia
Printed and bound by Griffin Press, South Australia

This narrative is dedicated to the sons of the diggers of the First A.I.F. in the hope that they will strive to recapture and perpetuate the digger spirit of the older A.I.F.

FOREWORD
Professor Bill Gammage

I state something that, after forty-five years of learning about the men of the First AIF, I never expected to say: this book compares with *All Quiet on the Western Front* in what it says, and how it says it. Both are front-line memoirs of men steadily becoming more professional and more disillusioned under the slaughter and stalemate of the Great War. Both are magnificently written. They use the present tense, and in moments of high drama they use short sentences and small words to make the action fast and close. They use detail brilliantly – sharp, vivid, not overloaded, just enough to let readers see the scene, sense being there, feel anxious about what will happen. *Somme Mud* puts you in the trenches, enduring the mud and the cold, smelling the stink of whale oil, following the dogfight overhead, suffering death's randomness. You watch Snow snipe a German half a mile away, then the next day risk his life to save another German and be reprimanded for it. You are brought close up into that war's world, wondering how such men could ever be civilians again, if they got the chance.

There are differences between the books. Remarque wrote a memoir and a literary work. He chooses when his story begins and he has his narrator die on that quiet day in October 1918. This book is a memoir built on a wartime diary and a unit history – the sense of a personal journey never leaves it. It begins as 12th Brigade reinforcements leave Sydney. It ends with the survivors home and facing the post-war world – a rare glimpse, for few narratives do that, published or unpublished, and none do it so well. I wanted the author to go on, but I also pay tribute to how far he has gone, pushing himself to bring such terrible memories to such stark and detailed reality. Scars must have opened, nightmares must have stalked, but he has left a mighty tribute to his mates, an epic of his generation, and a great gift to his country. I wish I had met him.

CONTENTS

PREFACE

Will Davies

What you are about to read is a narrative written by a young Australian soldier, Private Edward Lynch, during the First World War. Like all Australian soldiers at that time, Private Lynch was a volunteer. Like many, he was only eighteen years old when he set sail for France – a mere youth. He was part of a draft of reinforcements that departed Australia on 22 August 1916 on board the ship *Wiltshire*.

In France, the Australian Imperial Force at the time was engaged at Pozières and in taking the Windmill and Mouquet Farm in what was to become the most bloody and costly fighting of the war. In just eight weeks there were 23,000 Australian casualties, but this would not have been known to Lynch and his mates as they steamed westward. Nor would they have known that when winter set in in late November 1916, the war would become one of survival against the elements rather than simply the Germans.

Lynch was repatriated in mid-1919 and wrote about his experiences in pencil in twenty exercise books in the late 1920s and early 1930s, probably in the hope of exorcising the horrors he had witnessed. He claimed that the main character was a friend of his, but it is generally believed that 'Nulla' was in fact based on himself and that Lynch may have used the device in order to try to distance himself from the story.

During his time as Commanding Officer of the Jungle Training School (Lowana), in about 1943, Lynch typed up the book with the aim of having it published and earning some much-needed money.

By then Australia was in the midst of a Depression and Lynch had a young family to support. But the scars and pain of the Great War were too new and too deep for the public to want to be reminded of it, and so, with the exception of some excerpts that were published in the RSL magazine *Reveille*, the manuscript remained with the family, a hidden and untold story.

I became involved by chance in 2002 when I was loaned the typed manuscript – a great heavy tome 9 centimetres thick – by my friend and colleague Mike Lynch, the author's grandson. Mike knew of my interest in the period and of my work on a battlefield guide for the Department of Veterans Affairs in 1998 to commemorate the battle of Hamel, and asked if I would be interested in reading his grandfather's work.

As a friend I was happy to oblige, and to be honest I was intrigued. After reading just one chapter I was captivated, not only by the story and its honesty, but by the detail, and the depiction of an ordinary young Australian in extraordinary circumstances. It soon became clear that this manuscript was an important historical record; it was, in a sense, a literary time capsule.

With the family's permission I set about editing it, mindful of keeping the integrity of the story intact. While this is an abridged version, the turn of phrase, the language and, in today's terms, some very politically incorrect words and racial descriptions, are unaltered. These remain as a record of the attitude and language of the period.

Somme Mud has been for me a labour of love and I feel privileged and honoured to have been able to help it see the light of day.

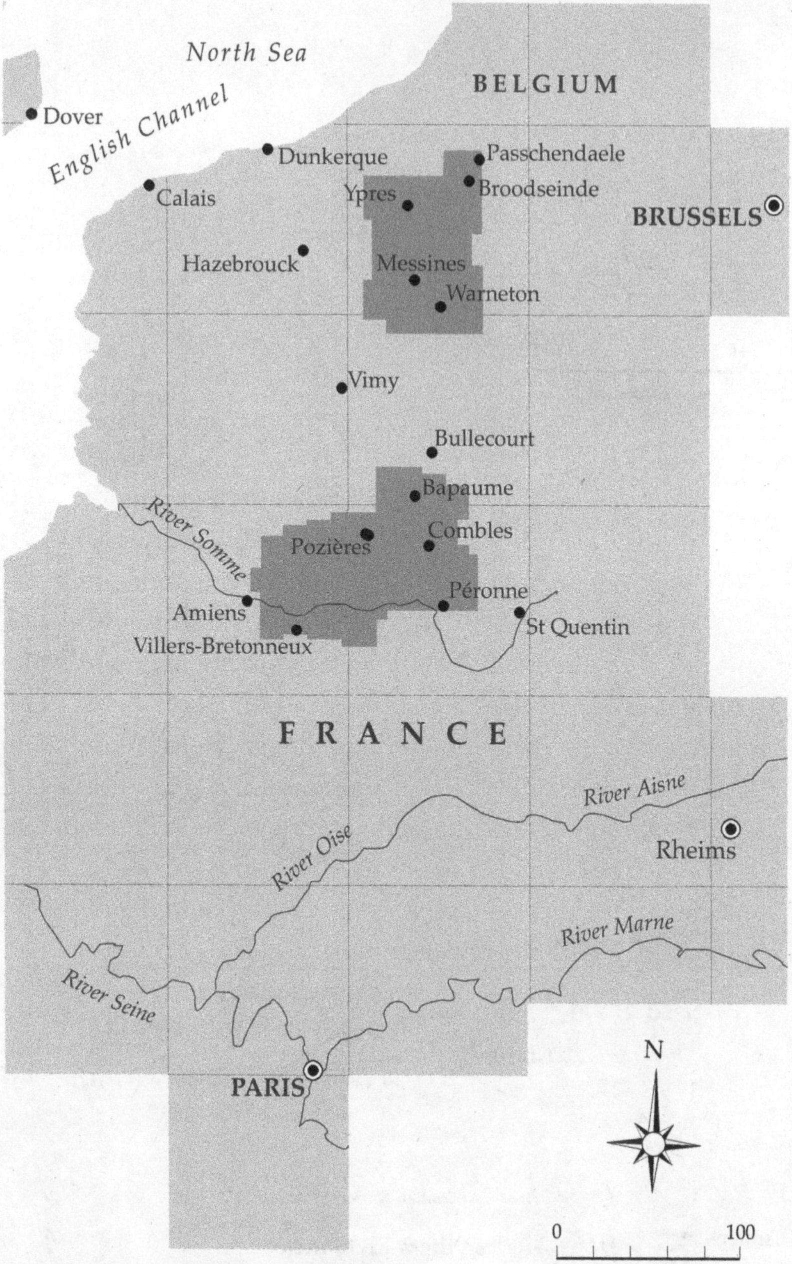

Overview of the Western Front

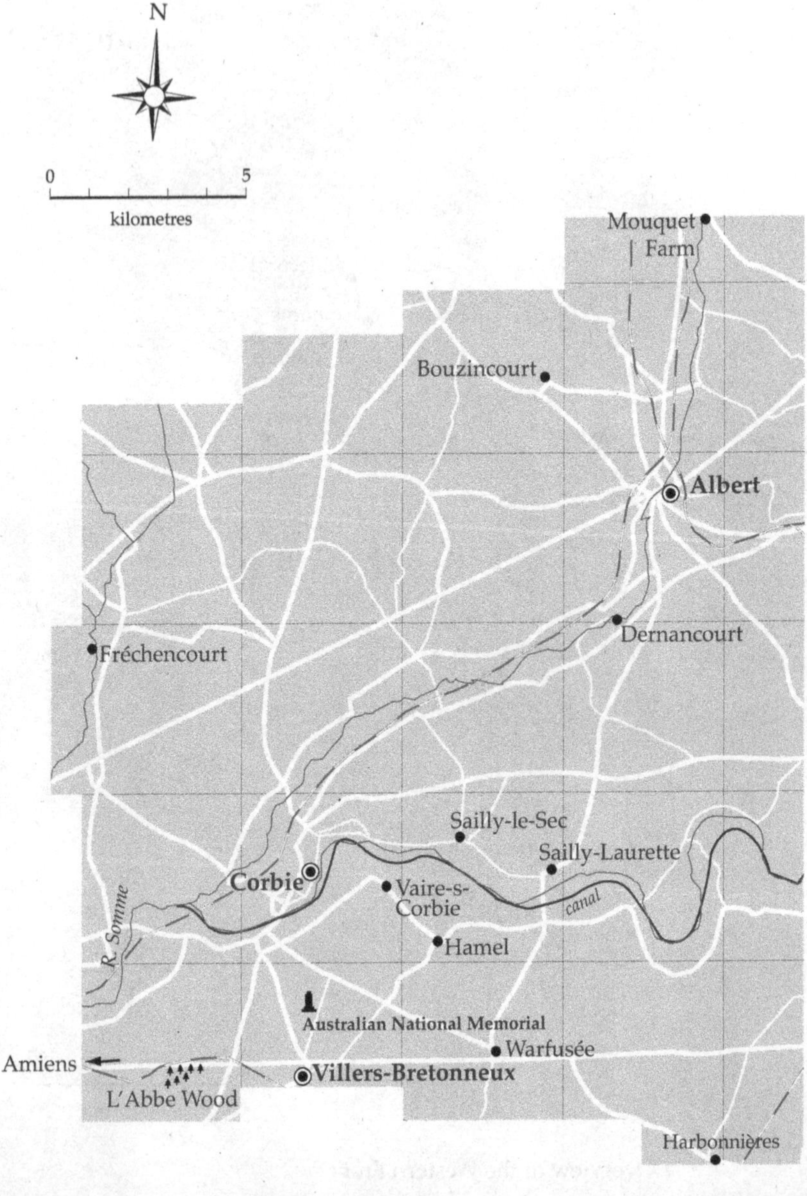
N
0
5
kilometres
Mouquet Farm
Bouzincourt
Albert
Dernancourt
Fréchencourt
Sailly-le-Sec
Sailly-Laurette
Corbie
Vaire-s-Corbie
canal
R. Somme
Hamel
Australian National Memorial
Warfusée
Amiens
Villers-Bretonneux
L'Abbe Wood
Harbonnières

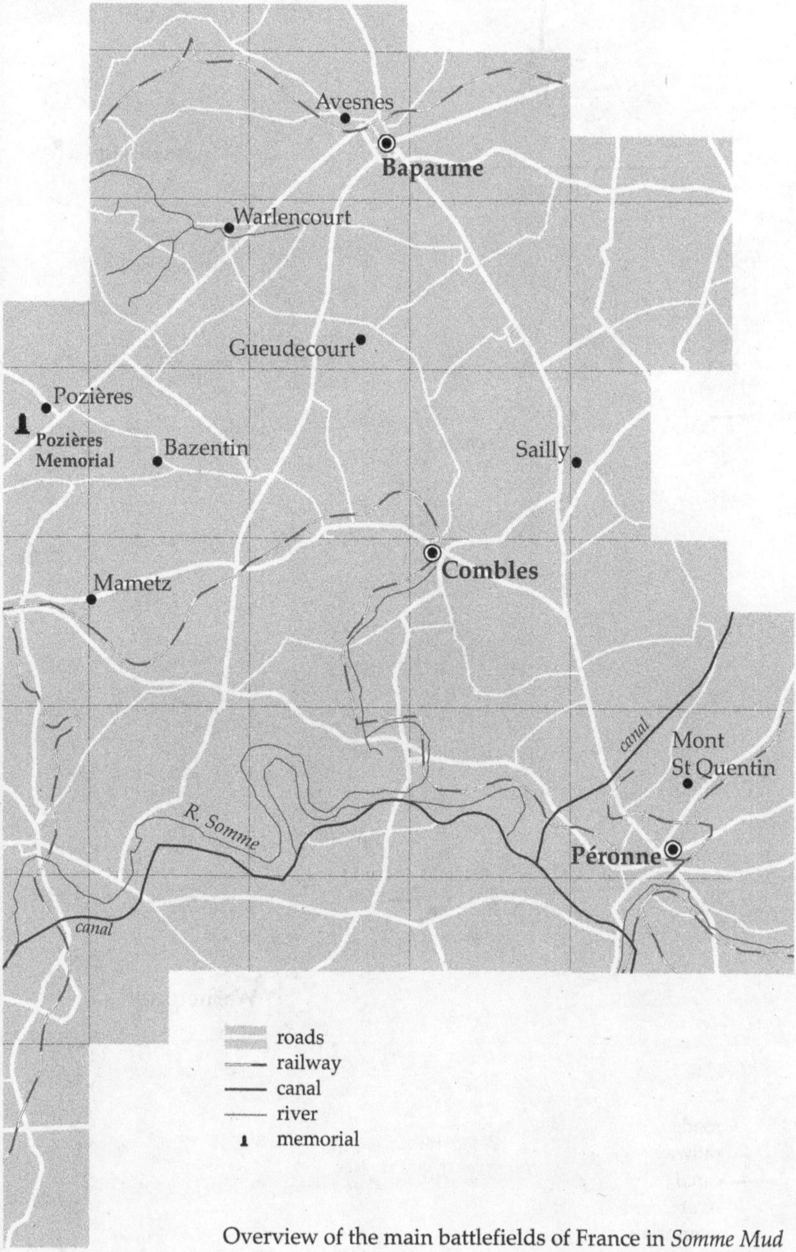

Overview of the main battlefields of France in *Somme Mud*

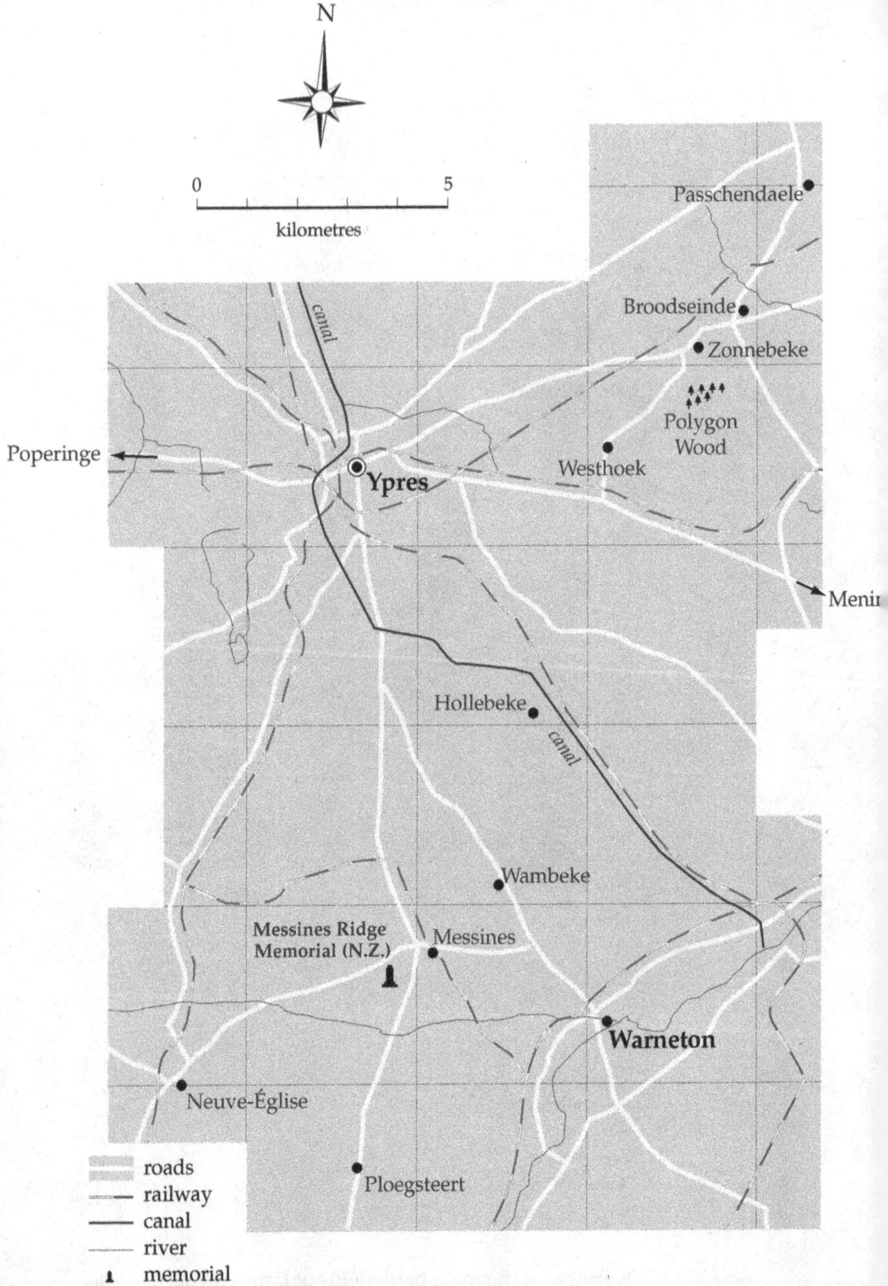

Overview of the main battlefields of Belgium in *Somme Mud*

ONE

Good-bye, Sydney Town, Good-bye

High in the clear morning air rings the lilt of our marching songs as we step out, many of us with our feet just on the first rung of the ladder of manhood.

Through flag-bedecked streets we go ever onward. The windows and roofs of shops are gay with bright flags and pretty, laughing girls. The crowds line the footpaths happy in the *bon camaraderie* of their farewell to us. Here and there are silent women in black, mute testimony to what has befallen others who have marched before. We swing cheerfully on.

A woman breaks from the crowded footpath and arm in arm with her soldier husband marches on with us. She has taken barely a dozen steps when high, clear and laughingly comes another song.

Ping, ping, and the song is cut short as a shower of halfpennies lands amongst us, thrown from the roof of a big verandah. We break step and formation as we battle for those halfpennies, for glued to each is the address of a girl. Most of us collect girls' addresses as a hobby these days. We seize the halfpennies, wave to the roof of girls as we fall into step with our mates and forward again as the girls wave and *coo-ee*.

We swing a corner and are gone from their sight. On to the next corner and an organised farewell from another group of girls. They sing 'Boys of the Dardanelles' as the leading section swings into view. That's all right, girls, but no hero stuff today as 'Boys of the Dardanelles' fades out.

We are nearing the wharves. The crowds march along with us till the big gates loom in front. We pass through, but the crowd is held back as we get our first view of the great liner that is to carry us 'On Active Service Abroad'. Along the wharf: 'Halt'. We come to a stop and answer a roll call, our last roll call in Australia. The Reinforcement is two hundred and fifty men and two officers.

Up the gangway, our officers scrutinise each of us to make sure none has turned into a stowaway or an enemy spy. We're told that we are to be quartered on B Deck and to put our gear there. We don't know where B Deck is nor care much: if it's on the ship we'll find it some day. Just now, we're more concerned to secure a vantage point from which to see all we can of our send-off. Our gear is dropped anywhere and we climb like monkeys all over the ship.

Back through the big gates we see the silent, sober crowd waiting. Suddenly the gates swing open and the crowd charges onto the wharf. We *coo-ee* and call and they answer. Streamers are thrown from the wharf and we catch them. We're a happy-go-lucky, carefree lot. Down on the wharf we see the girls who've caught our spirit. We see two older women with eyes ever searching, searching for a last glimpse of a loved face. They're the mothers and wives, the silent sufferers amongst the seemingly carefree throng. Men are there too, brothers and pals calling and cheering to us and dads proudly erect and calm. Every now and again, a flutter of movement that we try not to see: a mother, wife, sister or sweetheart who couldn't stand the pretence any longer and is being taken away to the rear. A few minutes and she's gamely fought down her sorrow and is working her way steadily forward again, smiling. Brave-hearted women of Australia, playing their part as they've played it from the beginning. You'll do us.

The gangways are removed. Seamen free the great ropes, the streamers straighten, stretch and snap as the lane of be-ribboned water between the ship and the wharf slowly widens. We're on the first stage of our great adventure. Cheers, *coo-ees* and the *cock-a-doodle-do* of harbour craft intermingle in a grand finale. Men, perched high in the rigging, commence to sing and soon the whole ship unites in a last song of farewell to old Sydney . . .

Good-bye, Sydney town, good-bye,
We are leaving you to-day
For a country far away,
Though to-day I'm stony broke
Without a single brown,
When I make my fortune
I'll come back and spend it
In dear old Sydney town.

The transport noses for the Heads and the open sea. Right to the Heads we are followed by small craft loaded with relatives and friends determined upon keeping touch to the very last. We look ever backward to what we're leaving. What's ahead will be taken care of when it arrives. We're interested in the small boats following us and in a school of porpoises racing on ahead. Our eyes turn to the small craft rocking in the wake and our last long *coo-ees* float back over the calm waters of the harbour. Leaving for the first time, most of us; maybe for the first and last time others of us. But that's in the lap of the gods.

A dozen days roll by and we're well on our way – Sydney, Melbourne, Adelaide, Fremantle lie far behind. Each has contributed a quota and now there are two thousand men aboard. Great anticipation as our ship turns from the Suez route and we're making for South Africa. Must be enemy submarines ahead. No, some enemy warships are sinking Australian troopships in the Indian Ocean. No, we're going to Africa to quell a serious rising in German East or German West Africa. Rumours are rife everywhere. Furphies fly right and left. Wash-house wireless.

A quiet night on the ship. Life is one long monotony now. Only relief is mumps or inoculation. 'A black revolving light on the starboard side,' comes a shout from up on deck, and men shove and shuffle up to see it, unthinkingly grasping at anything to break the monotony. Back down they come laughing or swearing at the perpetrators of a well put-over catch.

Days roll on. We run into a heavy swell and into a great storm. Portholes are screwed down. A bit of extra lifeboat drill is given. We are now well up in the 'abandon ship' routine. The sea is heavier and the ship is lurching like a girth-galled brumby. Dinnertime comes and we man the long tables and rattle our knives and forks on tin pannikins because our mess orderlies are late with the scran. A cheer – an ironical one – and one mess orderly is somehow down the bucking gangway and plonking a great bucket of boiling washing-up water against the wall.

The ship lurches, straightens and our other big mess orderly floats down, balancing a great dish of boiling tripe stew on his greasy great stomach. A staggering step as he is about to set the dish down on our table, when 'what-oh, she bumps' and the ship gives another tremendous lurch, making him fight desperately to hold the stew from spilling all over him.

We hoy him up a bit, but the ship does a back-buck, his awkward great feet fly up and his tremendous great seat splashes fair into the bucket of boiling water. Screamed curses rend the air and his meaty part wedges tighter into the bucket of boiling water as he collects the whole dish of tripe, red hot tripe, fair into his lap. He got it fair and square, scalded fore and aft and rises in a tearing hurry and a mighty rage whilst we rock and roar with laughter. The mess orderly can't see the joke, but he does see a long bread knife on the table and grabbing that yells 'Slit ya floppin' yellin' gizzards out, ya flamin' lot'er stinkin' hyenas', as he dives at us murderously.

But we've gone hell-for-leather jumping from table to table, setting and spilling and smashing and splashing everything under foot as we fly for the end gangway and charge up it, still laughing, to lose ourselves from that mess orderly's reach.

We don't get any dinner. Somehow we don't seem to want any, not down on B Deck tables. But we've never enjoyed any dinner like the dinner we didn't have today. Long will the memory of dinnertime on the day of the 'Tripe Storm' sustain and cheer us.

A few more days and the coast of South Africa looms up. Interested in a new land, we constantly watch the changing panorama as we make on down the coast and run into Durban. We're to take in coal here so draw in against a dirty, sooty-looking coaling wharf. The wharf is black with coal dust and niggers. Across the water – Durban. We're interested in it, but more interested in the niggers down below on the wharf.

The niggers yell and call to us. They want pennies so we throw some down and a great struggle goes on. Every time a penny hits the wharf a black, seething, grunting, pushing scrum packs down around it till some coon secures the coin. Then they call for more and we oblige again. Out of a scrummage for a brown, two fellows rise fighting. We cheer them on and they stop fighting, thinking some more pennies are coming.

Someone holds a bob up and signals to the two big coons to fight on again. They understand and tear into each other once more and a good snappy round is staged. A couple of bob pieces are thrown to them, but they're too slow and other coons collect instead. Niggers begin to belt and bash each other everywhere, hopeful of earning a silver coin.

A two-bob piece floats down from the officers' deck and the coons almost tear each other to pieces in their mad haste to get it. They know silver when they see it so we give them silver, plenty of it – pennies wrapped in silver chocolate paper.

'Look out! Let us to the rail.' And a bloke rushes forward with a red-hot two bob in a tobacco tin lid he's been busy heating up to almost white hot. The coons jump for the two bob. One tall nig catches it and, screaming, drops it. Another grabs it, another scream and the coin bounces on the boards. A third fellow thinks his luck's in and lands on it, but jumps back yelling like blazes and the two bob lies there on the wharf with twenty niggers ringed round it, waiting for it to cool. A move, and with one accord they dive together for the coin, the thud of thick skulls meeting in an awful bash brings joy and delight to us.

Out of the scrimmage a long, lean Zulu breaks. Flat out along the wharf he races, juggling the burning coin from hand to hand as he runs and disappears from sight.

A big boss comes on the scene and gets these coons to work, carrying basket after basket of coal up the gangway to be tipped into our ship. We mooch around for a couple of hours watching them and wondering if we're to get ashore.

'There's something doing up on the next deck, Nulla,' Snow calls to me, so we poke up and see a whopper nigger eating plum pudding, blooming good plum duff too. One of our coves has a seven-pound tin from the canteen and is helping the nigger to great junks. Four or five pounds disappear inside the nigger who rubs his fat belly and doesn't want any more.

A man holds up another great lump and a sprat and the coon forces the piece down and is sixpence richer and half a pound heavier. They bribe him with money and he eats and eats that duff till he's as full as a double-yolked egg. He rolls his eyes and rubs his belly, groans and makes horrible noises and we're happy once more. He rolls over with a few mighty moans and seems far worse and we're happier still.

A cove taps the toe of his boot on the fellow's great podgy belly and grins.

'Just a case of a little mild wind on the stomach, Madam. Give the child a little dill water.'

Longun opens the big blade of a jack-knife.

'Oh well, suppose I'd better tap him. Often tapped flamin' blown cows, so suppose there's not much difference between a coon and a cow . . .' giving the blade a few wipes on the seat of his strides.

'You tap coons between the point of the hip and the navel. Doesn't matter to within a foot or two, they're all gut,' Darky informs Longun. The nigger spots the knife blade and attempts to scream, but the scream gets tangled up with plum duff and instead of a scream comes a horrible noise from the depths of the nigger; a noise like Vesuvius getting ready to erupt.

'Come on, he's going to be sick. Goin' to perk.' And Snow pulls me away.

'Well, what's it matter if he does? I don't own him.'

'It matters a flamin' lot if we fall to clean it up, you stupid goat.'

So I drift away after Snow out of the danger zone and we go below to find Farmer and the Prof writing home, telling their people how monotonous it is on a troop ship.

Towards dark our ship leaves the wharf, just as we have it all worked out how we can scale down onto the wharf for a private inspection of Durban. She anchors out in the harbour where she spends the night to our great and profane discontent.

Morning breaks clear. A scorching day ahead. We do a route march through Durban and about ten miles around it. Then we have six hours in the town – the four hours' leave we are given and the extra two hours it takes to round us up afterwards. They find us everywhere, especially in the pubs. We jump in rickshaws to go back to the ship, but change our minds and yell and shout at our Zulu warriors in the shafts as we race each other to the next pub to see who shouts. We're having the time of our young lives; 'Giving Australia a bad name,' the officers call it.

It's getting dark now and every man who has been yarded up has been promoted to military policeman to help land the rest back onto the transport. Eventually we're all back, loaded up with red caps, calabash pipes, Kruger two-bob pieces, African beer and the memory of a good time. After a lot of mucking up and horseplay, we turn in and all's quiet and peaceful again.

Up early next morning ready for another day or several of them in Durban, but the ship pulls out. We *coo-ee* to Durban, wave and signal our *au revoirs* to Miss Campbell who is down near the wharf with her flags and her father to bid us *bon voyage*.

We run on to Cape Town and another route march. We are permitted to visit the town, but in little groups under an N.C.O. armed with a notebook and pencil ready to take the name of any man who breaks ranks. The C.O. isn't risking another Durban, not that we wouldn't oblige him. We'd do that willingly.

Round street after street in the blazing sun, we're well and truly fed up when the sergeant halts us under some nice shady trees, just near a friendly little pub on the outskirts of the town. Brainy sergeant, this bloke.

'Look here, Serg,' Longun puts it to him.

'If you'd like to slip over and have a pint, it's right with us. I'll give you my word I'll stonker the first cove who tries to make a break.'

'Cripes, I could do with a few pints. You chaps can go over when I get back.'

As he makes off, I slip after him and suggest it would look better if a couple of us went over at a time. He agrees and the two of us enter the pub and get our hands shaken and our glasses filled by a dozen civilians, most of whom tell us they saw service in German East or West Africa. We enquire after the fighting there and drink their beer, then head back to the group and wait until all the boys have had a good many. We begin to appreciate Cape Town.

The sergeant then reckons he'd better slip back to the pub to make sure we haven't left anyone there, so I go with him from force of habit or thirst or something. We have a few more beers and he buys a big bottle of whisky, getting the publican to loosen the cork. We set off for the boat. The sergeant sips his whisky at intervals. The sips begin to get longer and the intervals shorter. The sergeant is now rather wobbly.

As we near the ship, we spot half a dozen officers and the C.O. right between us and the gangway. They turn to look at the ship. The sergeant staggers some more and gets ready to sing, but Longun steps up and cracks him on the chin hard and as he falls, Snow rescues the whisky bottle whilst we grab the sergeant and carry him between us. A big khaki handkerchief goes over his face and we approach the officers carrying our knocked-out sergeant.

'What's up with that man? Drunk?' snaps the nasty, suspicious-minded colonel.

'No, Sir. Touch of the sun. Had sunstroke up on the New Guinea expedition and often goes out to it. Will we take him to the ship's hospital?' is Dark's calm reply, and Longun screws the sergeant's face round and shoves a wad of handkerchief in his mouth.

'Yes, men, explain his case to the doctors.' And the guards stand back from the gangway as we carry the heavy sergeant up into the ship. We go straight for the hospital, then straight through the hospital. The doctor doesn't take any notice about sick men. He's too busy helping a pretty little nurse to hold a pair of field glasses to her eyes to bother.

Our luck holds and we pass right through and down into the troop decks where we dump our sergeant, glad to get rid of him. Then we go to our own quarters and polish off what's left of his whisky. Snow pelts the bottle out through a porthole and nearly cuts a nigger's toe off as it bursts at his sprawly feet. That cheers us up quite a lot. These niggers come in handy at times.

Towards dusk our ship moves out into the harbour and we spend the night looking at the town and wishing we were in it.

Morning comes and we are just about to leave. A pretty little motor-boat of the harbour master is *chug-chug-chugging* away over at the wharf. Officials enter it and just as they do, an Australian soldier runs hard across the wharf to climb aboard to get out to the ship; some waif who's been astray in town all night. He gets one foot on the little craft when an official gives him a push and *plonk,* into the water he goes with a splash. A whistle blows on the motorboat and three sailors run up from along the wharf, yank the cove out of the water and march him off to the clink.

We roar at the motorboat, but can't be heard as it comes straight for us. We arm ourselves with everything we can find and wait for the boat. Men rush and get armfuls of spuds from the bags of potatoes on deck. A born soldier jumps up and roars above the din, 'Get quiet! No firing till he's right alongside or you'll spoil everything. Wait till I give the word.'

We wait. The motorboat comes up fast, its engine shuts off and it glides up gracefully with a big head of some sort, clad in a spotless white uniform, all braided, standing on it gracefully waving his cap and smiling at us.

Right under he comes, still smiling when the morning is split with a mighty 'Give it to the floppin' blankard!', and five hundred spuds whistle through the air. Onto the dapper little boat they crash, smashing and breaking all over the men. The bloke in white stops a dozen hard clouts, and water from a hundred splashing spuds drenches him. He dives for the shelter of his glassed-in cabin and reaches it just as a ship's bucket of slop-water, bucket and all, crashes through the cabin showering glass and broken woodwork everywhere.

Whilst the spuds fly in an unbroken stream, the boat gets its engine going, wheels and goes straight out, fifty yards from the ship's side. Then it turns and glides in to the gangway that is out of range of the spud throwers. We see the drenched cove climb up the gangway as the C.O. of our ship, red with rage, descends to meet him. They salute and shake hands, not very friendly like.

'Oh well, he oughta feel at home now; two welcomes – one from us and one from the colonel. Wonder which he'll remember the longest?'

'Look out, here come the officers.' And we charge away down to our troop decks as a whole crowd of officers swoop down to see who 'lowered Australia's name by such outrageous, such unheard-of conduct towards an official of the port'. An officer rushes up to where we're innocently sitting around our table.

'Were you up on deck when those potatoes were thrown?'

'No, Sir. What potatoes? I never saw any potatoes thrown anywhere.'

'Well, what about you?' he fires at another man.

'Me, Sir? Haven't been on deck since breakfast.'

'And what about you? Were you there?' is shot at another cove.

'Where, Sir?' in wondering innocence.

'Up on deck, of course.'

'When, Sir?' real interestedly.

'Just now. Throwing potatoes at a motorboat.'

'A motorboat, Sir?'

'Yes, a motorboat. Are you deaf, or stupid, or what?'

'Don't know, Sir. A motorboat?' And the officer stamps off. He questions a dozen more men without result of course and bounces up the gangway in a horrible temper. We don't know what he'll tell the colonel or care much either.

For days and days we plug northward through the Atlantic. As we are now in submarine-infested waters, we get plenty of practice in what we're supposed to do if we get torpedoed. Early morning and we wake with a start. The ship has stopped and the sudden shutting off of the vibrating *thud, thud, thud* of her engines has roused us. We rush to the portholes and look out to discover we are at a port. That's about as far as our knowledge goes, so we mooch up on deck and learn we're at St Vincent in the Cape Verde Islands.

We are interested in the place, but hear we are not being allowed ashore and then lose interest in it. Soon a swarm of natives' boats come out to us. They have oranges for sale; green-skinned oranges. We put a bob in a bucket and with a rope, lower it to the boats. The natives put a sprat's worth of oranges in the bucket and we haul it up, eat the oranges and get a few more bucketfuls.

Longun sends down money to buy a mat, but the native boatman somehow can't quite understand him, insofar as change is concerned. Longun tries his hand at some homemade pidgin English and when that also fails, he opens up, calling them thievin' black cows. The native hops round, dips the bucket in the water and fills it and Longun has to haul a heavy bucket of sea water right up to the top deck whilst a thousand men and two nurses roar and laugh.

Poor old Longun is grieved, grim and silent. He unties the rope from the bucket, which he pelts, water and all, hard at the native. The bucket looks like knocking a hole clean through the boat, niggers and all, but turns, spills its water and lands with a splash five yards from the boat. The bucket spins, slowly fills and sinks to the floor of the Atlantic.

The ship's bosun rushes up and demands Longun's name and regimental number and tells him that three bob will be put in his pay book to pay for the bucket.

'Right! and if your flamin' bucket'd landed where I wanted it, you could have put three bloomin' quid in the pay book. Been cheap at the price, ya stingy Pommy cow.' And Longun begins pushing his sleeves up and gives his strides a hitch, but the bosun fades away forgetting all about Longun's name and number, whilst Longun ducks away and loses himself in case the bosun's memory returns.

The bosun's memory returns and with a ship's officer. They ask after Longun and we tell them he's a perfect stranger to us and that he must have come from some other deck. They wheel to make off to look for him and as they do so, the bosun stops a hard green orange fair in the butt of the ear, whilst we're all innocently watching the distant town. Exasperated, they wheel on us again and are earnestly assured that the orange must have come from the deck above. None of us pelted it.

'The deck above be blowed. I'll get you fellows for this!' And again they make off, when *bang*, and this time it's the officer who stops an orange – stops it hard and solid on the back of his head. His pretty cap is knocked flying and he grabs at his head to make sure it hasn't gone bowling across the deck with his cap. Then straight for our group he charges and props in front of Dark who stands with his two hands behind his back.

'Here you. Show me your hands. Come on, I saw two oranges in them a minute ago. Come on, show me your hands! You threw it!'

I surreptitiously slip an orange into Darky's empty hand and like a flash he shoves his two hands, with his two oranges, right under the officer's nose and grins hard. That officer comes the biggest gutser he ever came. Speechless, the two merchantmen leave us and climb up the ladder affair that leads to the next deck. As they reach the top rung,

'Them bleedin' Orstralyuns' floats up after them, and we're happier still, but they don't come back to join in our mirth.

A sudden rush to the rail and we join in to see half a dozen boatloads of stark naked niggers coming out to us. They call, 'Money. Me dive.' And as coins are thrown they dive. Beautiful divers and wonderful underwater swimmers, they never lose a coin.

In one boat there's a little chap, a plump joker of four or five. We yell to the men to let us see him dive and they call back 'Him no swim', but grab him by the woolly head and where the seat of his pants should be, and hoist him in. He sinks, rises, desperately treads water and sinks again. When his head comes up the second time, a long nigger leans over and, grabbing the kid by his woolly mop, drops him back in the boat, none the worse for his ducking. We throw some coins and make them understand they are for the little cove so they give him some cash. He grins appreciation with a display of white teeth and white eyes.

Some fancy diving comes next with more coins thrown. The little coon kid is just being hoisted overboard again when from under our ship's stern, a long fast boat appears, rowed by four great coons in trousers. The boat carries three uniformed nigs whom we take to be some kind of police, as the divers row away for dear life, dropping the kid into the water in their fright.

The poor little beggar seems to be in danger of drowning so we yell to the police boat and point and it heads for him. A black policeman pokes a long punting pole at the struggling kid whom we expect to grab the pole, but instead, the pole comes down on top of him and the poor little devil is shoved halfway down to the bottom of the Atlantic. The police take no further notice of him, but row on round the ship, followed by our very lurid opinions.

The little kid is up treading water and bawling like a yearling scrubber under the branding iron. His boat comes back, hoists him on board and sets out for the shore like mad, chased by the police boat which can't catch it. We yell encouragement to the pursued and get much fun out of the little incident.

We leave St Vincent and head for England. A couple of kit inspections and two spare inoculations come our way with two lectures a day from the heads. The colonel tells us how much he has enjoyed the honour of commanding such a fine body of men, then the ship's captain gives us advice should we get torpedoed and instructions about no lights after dark. Next, the senior medical officer has a go and then the chaplain gets in for his cut.

We're earnestly implored to write to our mothers at least once a week, and some cove calls, 'What about our tarts?' but the Sky Pilot doesn't seem to be interested in the question. The chaplain keeps on and on, but we're playing a few hands of poker down behind the backs of those who are paying attention. Then the chaplain asks us to join him in a prayer of thanksgiving for a safe journey. We join in. He shuts his eyes, clasps his delicate white hands and puts great earnestness into that prayer. Then he opens his eyes to give us his blessing and discovers that half the mob has faded away. That gives him a nasty jar and he trails off, forgetting all about bestowing the blessing. Perhaps he thinks we don't need it.

Three days from England now and early in the morning we see away on the horizon ahead three black smudges of smoke. Ships coming our way. After breakfast, we find three British torpedo boats circling about us. One keeps ahead of us, crisscrossing our path and the other two are circling round and round our ship as if we are stationary. Thick black smoke is belching from their funnels. They are speedy – the real greyhounds of the ocean. They don't ride the waves, they cut clean through them.

We're proud of them and cheer as they close in and the sailors wave and cheer back. We're safe from submarines with three watchdogs of our great British Navy guarding us. Good old British Navy. We thrill with unspoken pride of our Empire's Navy and the boys manning it. These Jack Tars'll do us, all right! We crowd the rails to get a good view of the nearest boat. She rushes by close in and we look into her, right into her grey guns and feel sort of glad that we're on her side in the war.

Almost to England now! Night comes down and we go in absolute darkness, a big black smudge gliding through a silent sea of darkness, broken only by the white road of our wake trailing there behind us out in the black night.

Our last day at sea is a busy one. We're kept on the move all day and haven't much time to examine all the ships we pass. Great cliffs of old

England show up ahead and we anchor in Plymouth Harbour. We are mustered on deck and checked over a dozen times in case someone's jumped overboard to walk home. Then we shoulder our kit bags and climb down into a big barge which sets off through the fog towards the lights of a wharf.

The barge drifts into a wharf and we in turn jump on it. With a clatter, our boots land on the decking of the wharf, decking that looks uncommonly like good old Australian ironbark.

Our sea voyage of twelve thousand miles is over and we're in England at last.

TWO

France and Fritz

The white cliffs of Dover are fading astern as our little paddlewheel steamer is *chug-chug-chugging* into the grey misty waters of the Channel carrying us across to France.

England lies behind the mounting cloud of morning mist. England, our country's mother, has been our home for the past few short weeks and now we're on our way to France and the job that lies before us. So long, Blighty, we hope to see you again. Escorted on all sides by warships we steam slowly on.

Our boat rocks and pitches. Faces that a few minutes ago were happy, slowly begin to pale as our poor stomachs pitch and toss to the action of the ship as she bites into the choppy Channel waters. Men, violently seasick, line the rails and the ship reeks with the sour stench of seasickness. We're as miserable as men can be, but there's no escape, no relief; nothing to do but shudder and shiver in our misery and hope that the best or worst will overtake us, and pretty quickly too.

Two or three hours of utter misery and we anchor at Boulogne and we gladly disembark, marching happily from that ship. Marching through the cobblestoned streets, we get our first views of an old land that is new to us. We pack into grimy railway carriages and the train moves slowly on. In the pouring rain of an early darkening evening, we detrain at Étaples and are marched off into a huge camp where we are put into little bell tents. We're at the 'Bull Ring'.

We've heard of it and are now to sample its concentrated training as a final touch-up before facing the foe. After an hour of wandering about the camp, we turn in. We're almost asleep when Longun and Dark rouse us to listen to the faint, dull rumble of the guns coming from fifty miles away. We are not very interested as we know before we're much older we'll hear all the guns we'll ever want to hear.

Morning is upon us with a blast of bugles as reveille rings out over the sleeping camp. An hour's torture from a loud-mouthed physical instructor and we're ready for breakfast, ready for a far better one than we get. A whole morning's route march with full pack and then a whole afternoon of 'hop-overs'. We hop-over and charge trench after trench. For hours and hours we get insulted and abused and sworn at for not doing it better. The hop-over expert leaves us and we're marched back to camp and dismissed.

The second day opens with another big dose of physical jerks. We have a nice quiet morning walking in and out of gas chambers, testing our respirators and ourselves under what is said to be real gas. The jokers in charge here are very earnest in informing us as to what will happen if our respirators are faulty or if we don't adjust them properly. Still none of us seem to die, for as Snow said, 'If we can stand four hours of that flamin' hop-over thing, we can stand all the gas they've got on the Western Front.' Afternoon finds us juggling sheets of iron about in a narrow trench as another maniac squirts liquid flame over us. We don't mind this stunt, it's good fun, especially the part where the flame-thrower specialist burns his fingers.

Our third day sees us marched out to some trenches ringed by red flags. We are handed over to an officer for live bomb-throwing practice. We score an hour's rest whilst the officer talks, mostly to himself, about Mills grenades. Then we spend an hour throwing dud grenades about, with the wrong elevation altogether, so the instructors say.

Next, standing well back, we admire the bravery of the instructor who stands in a deep trench and bursts bombs in a deeper one forty yards away. Our turn comes and we file along the trench, collect a live bomb each, and under the instructor's eye pull the pin, count 'one, two' and fling the bomb to burst with a savage *whang* out ahead somewhere. That over and we march back to the long mess huts to dinner, better soldiers than before.

After dinner we parade with rifles and bayonets and are turned over to a dozen bayonet instructors who lecture us and give demonstrations of how to bayonet bags of straw. Then we charge the bags and fairly murder them as the instructor sergeant stands and roars, 'Hin! Hout! Hon Guard!' It doesn't suit him. We're not savage enough, so we do it again, showing our teeth in ferocity and spoiling half the bags. He is more satisfied.

'Now just get around me and I'll show you how to act if an enemy should charge you with his bayonet whilst you are unarmed.' We get around him. He borrows an entrenching tool handle from someone and says to the Prof, 'Now, my man, just put the scabbard on your bayonet, go twenty paces out and get ready to charge me with your bayonet.' With a sheepish grin, the Prof does as he's told.

The Prof stands with his scabbarded bayonet pointed at the sergeant who stands fearlessly before him, left foot advanced and the short entrenching tool handle held upright in his left hand.

'Now I want you to charge straight at my chest with your bayonet. Are you ready?' And we watch the fun.

'Charge!' roars the sergeant, and the Prof charges up in a half-hearted trot. He's sworn at and sent back four times before he gets any speed up. Finally he does a beautiful charge and props dead with his bayonet point a foot short of the sergeant's chest. The sergeant goes clean raving mad because the Prof won't bayonet him and finally orders, 'Get to blazes back into the ranks!'

Then Farmer has a go. Farmer is a real trier in everything. A very thorough-going, deliberate sort of bloke and when he is told to 'Go hon! Stick yer flamin' bayonet clean through me chest', he takes the sergeant at his word and makes a tremendous charge. Straight for the man's chest flies the scabbarded bayonet with twelve stone of Farmer behind it. The point is almost onto the sergeant's chest when his left hand strikes swiftly sideways and the entrenching handle knocks the bayonet clear of the sergeant. The force of his run carries Farmer forward, and like a flash the sergeant's right foot swings over and trips old Farmer, just as the sergeant's right hand catches him behind the neck with a mighty shove. Farmer with a horrible grunt is sprawled on the ground and the sergeant has grabbed his rifle and is standing triumphantly over him, ready to be admired.

Farmer gets up in a dazed sort of a way and spits out a lot of sand whilst we please the sergeant by laughing heartily.

The sergeant is really happy again, and invites Snow to have a go. 'No good to me,' laughs Snow, and Longun is asked to have a go. To our great delight and surprise he says, 'Righto, I'll give it a go. Pretty poor flamin' circus that hasn't two clowns.' And he gets the rifle and out he goes.

Darky grabs me delightedly. 'Cripes, don't miss this. This'll be worth seein'.'

Longun stands ready. 'Like me to take the flamin' scabbard off?' he asks.

'Makes no difference to me whether the scabbard's on or off, but camp regulations won't allow it,' says the sergeant.

'Oh well, suppose I'll get it in a few inches with the bloomin' scabbard on.' And Longun gets set.

The sergeant gets into position too. 'Charge!' he roars.

Longun fairly flies for him and with a bound is up to him, when *crack!* strikes the entrenching tool handle as the sergeant swings his foot across, but Longun isn't there to be tripped. He's let the rifle go and his two great claw-like hands are flying for the sergeant's throat as one hand almost chokes the sergeant, the other goes a bit wide and his great awkward thumb nearly pokes the beggar's eye out as the pair of them land *bang* into the dust.

To our roars of laughter they rise and separate, the sergeant red with rage and Longun grinning gleefully.

'Reckon that's a bit above Farmer's idea, don't you, Serg?' This Longun is the coolest thing unhung.

The sergeant is fairly spluttering again from rage. He has a handkerchief up to his injured eye and is rubbing his throat with his other hand. He's mad. We just stand and wait. He begins to swear horribly and finally roars 'Fall in!', which we do. Then we hear a lot about ourselves that we never knew before. He's going to put Longun in the clink and have him court-martialled. Suddenly, however, he changes his mind, says he'll send him up to the front line tomorrow morning and says the first Fritz he sees will rip his innards out. He tells him it'll serve him right for not paying attention to the bayonet instruction. Ordering our own sergeant to march us back to camp, he clears out to have his injured eye fixed up.

We march back, wishing we could have bayonet fighting instruction every day. We are late getting in and nearly miss out on the dinner, but it's worth that risk to have seen Longun's demonstration.

The evening is spent having our gear checked before we move to our battalion tomorrow. Late in the afternoon, a doctor lectures on the prevention of trench feet and quotes percentages to show how the Australians have a proud record insofar as trench-feet cases go. Before he's done we almost believe it'd be far better to be killed outright than to disgrace the A.I.F. by getting trench feet. Major Clayton inspects us and wishes us good luck and we are issued with food to last till we find our battalion. Then we're dismissed and warned to be ready to fall in at 4 a.m. tomorrow.

We're not asleep very long when someone trips over the ropes of our tent and nearly brings it down on us. Seven heavy rifles stacked around the tent pole fall with an awful clatter across our shins and nearly maim us for life. We get hunted out at 3 a.m. by a sergeant who carries a hurricane lantern. Swinging the lamp inside the tent flap he shouts, 'Come on, show a leg.' And departs insulted when Dark asks, 'Goin' round your traps, mate?' The base sergeants hate to be called 'mate', or 'cobber', or 'digger'.

We reach the train and get packed into big smoky trucks marked '*40 hommes ou 8 chevaux* (40 men or 8 horses)'. As I'm the French scholar, I have to tell the boys what that means. I tell them, but they don't trust me and ask an English-speaking French railway official who tells them the same.

After a wait of three hours the train pulls out and we spend the day viewing France as we crawl slowly on towards the front. The train stops at every village and the men charge along its streets and buy chocolates and bread and bottles of *vin rouge* and *vin blanc*, which are consumed long before the next village is reached. We hang out of the trucks and watch the horizon till the white-washed walls of another village appear. We jump out of the trucks and race the train to the village estaminet.

For two days we journey slowly towards the Somme. The train stops at night in pouring rain and after marching the wrong way, we arrive just after daybreak at the tumble-down village of Brucamps where our own battalion is billeted. Our little crowd keeps together and we get put into 14 Platoon of D Company. We mix with strange men; happy-go-lucky fellows, chaps who have been through Gallipoli, Fleurbaix and Pozières, and they tell us we move into the Somme in a week's time.

A look at the village and then we return to our billet. Our platoon is in a big shed where fowls once camped before the Australians, part of a large farmhouse. The centre is a great smelly manure pit round which the buildings form a quadrangle. On one side is the residence, whilst barns, stables and sheds complete the other three sides. The pit is fed with every bit of manure dropped on the farm; rotten vegetables, waste straw, potato peelings, feathers and rubbish of all sorts go into it, to be used by the farmer as fertiliser.

A day here and we move on to another village, Vaux-en-Amiénois. The roads are everywhere jammed with streams of traffic. We see miles of motor buses carrying thousands of troops along the road we have to foot-slog. No buses for us. The road is a national military road with tall poplar trees lining each side which appear to meet away in front on the horizon.

Our billet tonight is a disused pigsty, so we 'rat' a lot of hay from a shed to sleep on. The old podgy Froggie farmer pretends not to see us taking the hay. We remark upon this, but a wise-head tells us, 'He sees all right, the lousy cow, but he won't complain for fear that we'll be made to put it back. He'll wait till we're moving out tomorrow and then kick up a shindy and get paid for three times the amount we've used. All these Frogs do that.'

A big sausage-type observation balloon is being sent up nearby. Six or eight men hold each anchor rope as the balloon slowly ascends. Great cylinders of gas are on the ground. From nearby, a big winch is working off the tray of a motor lorry slowly paying out the cable as the balloon rises. Two officers are in the big basket, each with parachutes strapped to their back. They have field glasses, telescopes and a telephone fixed to the side of the basket, a glass frame holding a large-scale map, and a theodolite – a range finder of some sort. Away in the distance can be seen more of these balloons. The men speak of one balloon that recently broke from its moorings, jumping about like a cork in rough water. It was carried high into the sky and drifted across the enemy's lines where the observers jumped out and made successful descents by means of their parachutes.

We come to some crossroads and get put into motor buses and taken to the village of Dernancourt. Dernancourt is the scene of filth, mud and misery. Above, air fights are seen. We watch Fritz aeroplanes chasing our planes home and pity our men sent in their weak little planes against the far more numerous and infinitely more powerful enemy aircraft.

Everything is strange to the men of our reinforcement, so we wander about to see what is to be seen. We climb into lines of old chalky trenches, inspecting and picking up an accumulation of souvenirs. Out to the wire between the trenches we see our first dead man and several half-buried. A man tells us how our wire is removed before we do a hop-over. 'Then,' he says, 'our artillery shells the enemy's wire to blow it away for us to get through to rush the Fritz trenches.'

We wander off and find an anti-aircraft battery. They have two machine-guns pointing into the sky and half a dozen telescopes, range finders and sound detectors all mounted on tripods. On a big Thornycroft motor lorry is an anti-aircraft gun and hidden nearby, hundreds of shells. Fifty yards on each side of the gun are huge search-lights placed in shell holes. The lights have glasses as large as washtubs and revolve on a ball-and-socket arrangement to be turned in any direction to focus their beams on any Fritz planes that come bombing at night.

A terrific explosion is heard and we stand and watch some big guns firing. Their huge barrels slowly rise higher and higher like great snakes' heads. *Bang! Woof!* and the gun kicks back like a living creature as we see the trees on either side sway and bend from the terrific displacement of air. The sound is deafening. We see the barrels slowly rise. *Bang! Woof!* they go again, savagely kick back, lower and rise again; but the firing is over so we make off for fresh excitement.

Some guns of smaller calibre are in the open. Over them is spread wire netting through the meshes of which narrow strips of hessian are threaded to hide the gun from aerial observation. The gunners live in dugouts some distance away, but a gunner stands at each gun ready to fire. We speak to him and he explains that each gun is ranged on our S.O.S. line whenever they aren't firing on a given target.

A clergyman comes along and speaks to us. He is unarmed, but like everyone else, carries a gas respirator. Gas has no respect for padre or private. The padre goes on.

Near a little smashed-up orchard we find many crude graves. The body has generally been placed in a shell hole and earth thrown over it. Some have rough wooden crosses carrying particulars of the man's name and unit with 'K.I.A.' and the date. Others have nothing whatsoever except an old rifle stuck in the ground as a headstone. Some graves have only a stick, a shell or a shell case for a headstone and one little grave is marked by an old weather-worn military boot.

It is almost dark now and we go back to our filthy billet and yarn and listen to the drum-drumming of the gunfire along the front and watch the flash and glow along the horizon as our batteries fire. The discussion turns on the uses of the bayonet. One man speaks of its use as a toasting fork whilst another reckons its chief use is in opening tins of jam. Then they talk of how they fix a lump of cheese on the end of a fixed bayonet and when a rat crawls along the bayonet they press the trigger and the rat is blown halfway across no-man's-land.

Another man is into the argument, but we know full well of a very different use some of these very men put the bayonet to at Pozières and Mouquet Farm not so long ago.

Morning breaks with a regular strafe all along the front. We hear and see enemy shells falling nearby and don't like the war one bit better as a consequence. Soon the casualties come in and we get our first view of the mud-stained, blood-sodden bandages and the frail white faces of seriously wounded men.

Early afternoon sees us moving off for the front line. We march on to Bernafay Wood through absolutely unbelievable conditions. On either side stretches a quagmire, a solid sea of slimy mud. The roads are few and narrow and only distinguished from the surrounding shell-ploughed mud by an unbroken edging of smashed motor cars, ambulances, guns, ammunition limbers, and dead horses and mules.

Along these roads we work our way through a constant stream of traffic. Vehicles of all kinds are bogged and being dug out, patches of corduroy are being placed over the worst places in a road pitted with great shell holes of muddy water, into which mules and horses sink to their bellies and wagon wheels to the hub.

'Well, if this is La Belle France they ought to give it to Fritz.'

'They'd have to pay him to live in it.'

'He should be made to flamin' well live in it as a punishment for starting the war.' And on we slush, mile after mile, towards the front line. For an hour or two we lie in the mud; out in the open with no protection from the pouring rain, but our greatcoats and a few waterproof sheets. Darkness falls and we file on in platoons for the front line. Shells burst about us and we fight down a tremendous desire to get into the big shell holes until the shelling ceases, but the old soldiers move undauntedly onwards and we hide our fear by following them.

Presently, to our nervous ears comes the strangled scream and the rushing air of an approaching shell. Every man of the platoon falls flat on the muddy track, old soldiers and new alike. With a mighty roar the shell explodes, spouting flame and phosphorus fumes everywhere. Mud is showered over everyone as pieces of shell fly over our prone bodies. A man five feet ahead of me is sobbing – queer, panting, gasping sobs. He bends his head towards his stomach just twice and is still.

'Hurry on!' calls the corporal from the front. As we get to our feet he runs back, rolls the hit man over and races on to take his place again at the head of the platoon. One man more whose soldiering days are over! We've had our baptism of fire, seen our first man killed, right amongst us, and hurry on before another shell comes.

'Down!' roars the corporal and we hit the mud as *Bang! Crash!* – it lands behind us, flames leaping from a great fresh hole in the mud, and we're up and running on.

Soon we come to a group of men. One man leads off and following our corporal, we trail after him. A couple of hundred yards through almost knee-deep mud and we are at the front line. Here all is quiet, black and muddy. Some 46th Battalion men are in a trench, standing up though we can see only half of them, the rest in the mud of the trench. They climb out and fade away back into the night and we slither into their muddy trench and are up to our knees in mud. We're in the front line!

Longun looks down towards where his legs and feet have disappeared and snarls disgustedly, 'Thirteen thousand miles for this!' And we agree.

'We're holding Grease Trench and Goodwin's Trench,' the corporal tells us, and Darky, trying to extricate his half-sucked-under legs, rejoins, 'You mean they're floppin' well holdin' *us*.' The corporal sees it his way and laughs. All is very quiet, but even this black quietness is a source of suspense to us, doing our first night in the front line.

Some Fritz trenchmortar shells, *minenwerfers* the old hands call them, land with a terrific bang forty yards away. *Woof! Woof!* they go and the whole ground shakes. Some more *minenwerfers* burst about the position.

We've been in the trench a couple of hours when our company commander comes along and says he wants ten of us for a wiring party, then goes on to collect more from the next platoon. Longun, Darky, Farmer, Snow and I are to go out. We crawl out over the back of the trench and silently follow the corporal. We have our rifles, but are told to get the bayonets off them. Some fifty yards along the trench we are given the wiring material, then out into no-man's-land, sneaking low.

Each man has on his back a coil of barbed wire or a bundle of iron pickets. No one speaks as everyone knows that half a dozen machine-guns are on the enemy parapet just a hundred yards away. Quietly out, our footsteps sound like thunder to our excited minds.

A flare gun goes *Bang! Hiss!* We hear that flare circling up. *Phut!* and we are flooded in an unnatural light under which everything seems strange and unreal. Not a budge, not a move as we stand frozen still, faces turned to the ground. We know that any movement will bring those machine-guns rattling into action. The flare is out and we move on, stringing out along the few strands of wire already erected here.

Silently we twist and turn the long pickets into the ground. Silently men carry the coiled barbed wire to each picket in the row. Silently the coil is twisted round each picket until it has been threaded through the eyes. On to the next move the men with the wire. For half an hour we work and all is very quiet. The job is over and we begin to move back to our trench. The first of the men are in the trench when, from behind us out in the dark desolation of no-man's-land, we hear a sharp clink as two spare pickets meet as the men are coming in. Instantly the silence of the night is shattered as an enemy machine-gun cracks into action, fairly streaming its bullets over our heads as we fall flat upon the muddy ground.

Out in the open behind us we hear an occasional *ping* as bullets strike the wire. The gun is firing through the very wire we finished erecting only a few short minutes ago. A few more bursts and the gun stops. We lie still for a while longer and then get up and silently and quickly hurry for our trench, very relieved to have some protection from the deadly machine-gun bullets whose dreadful *swish, swish* is still running through our ears.

Back to our platoon's post, we feel much more matter-of-fact about this front-line business now we've been beyond it into the muddy mystery of no-man's-land. Our half hour out there on the wire entanglements and our few minutes under the machine-gun have done more to accustom us to front-line soldiering than a whole week of standing in the mud of a front-line trench would have done.

We've made our bow to Fritz and no doubt as time rolls on, we'll better our acquaintance.

THREE

Holding the Line

The battalion is on the move for the front line. We're at Bazentin, now a pulverised brickyard. We moved in this morning from Fricourt, another rubbed-out town, which boasts divisional baths. Had a profitable day being deloused. Half of the battalion has gone on to take over the support trenches of Bull's Run and Pilgrim's Way near Flers. The rest of us are to stay here tonight and to move into the front line at Grease Trench near Gueudecourt tomorrow night.

The evening passes quietly, night settles down and the countryside comes to life with a thick moving stream of transport as we curl up and try to sleep.

Day breaks wet again and as we wait to move off for the front line, a few waterproof capes are issued. We get around in circles and 'sell a horse' to see who gets each cape.

We watch some African niggers on road work. 'Black Anzacs' we call them for they wear turned-up felt hats like ours. They seem as happy a mob as any crowd – doing as little work as they're doing ought to be happy.

A bit of a stir and plenty of howling occurred amongst them half an hour ago. A big nigger dug up a bomb and when our men yelled and showed him by signs to throw it away, he hugged it all the closer. One of our sergeants went over and asked him for the bomb, but the nig pulled the pin out and grinned when the lever flew up. He held the bomb out to the sergeant, but the sergeant wasn't there. He was racing for the shelter of a heap of mud. With a savage explosion it burst in the nig's hand, blowing it off at the wrist. Amid piercing screams from a hundred nigs who weren't injured, the poor black beggar was taken away minus a hand. We reckoned they were lucky half a dozen of them weren't killed.

Evening sets in wet as we march up to the line. Queer how our crowd goes into the line so often on a Sunday, and today is Sunday because Snow who still keeps a diary told us.

We're a strange-looking crowd. Each man wears a wet greatcoat over which is buckled his equipment. Most of us have the breech and the muzzle of our rifle swathed in strips of bagging or blanket to guard against the mud and rain. We don't wear puttees as the weight of the mud pulls them down around our boots, but strips of sandbag instead. Some of the men wear rubber knee-boots, but they are not of much use in the forward trenches as they either get pulled off in the mud or fill with mud and water.

Onto our equipment hangs a water bottle, bayonet, entrenching tool and handle, whilst on our chests we wear our gas respirator bulged out over one hundred and twenty rounds of ammunition. On our backs, our haversacks contain iron rations and odds and ends. Six sandbags are rolled and strapped above the haversack, whilst under it hangs a wet blanket neatly rolled into a heavy ball of dead weight. We are lucky we aren't carrying bags of bombs and picks and spades as well. A few miles of lumping all this stuff along and we realise the truth of Darky's saying, 'A man wants to be strong in the back and weak in the head to make a good infantryman.'

On through the mud. Away in front, enemy flares sweep up, burst, scribe a circular luminous sweep and drop to earth. Some are pretty. Green ones, red ones, all colours, like bar-room snakes. The flares are on three sides of us. We always seem to be approaching the centre of a horseshoe of fireworks. As we near the line, the flares mount higher above the horizon which is marked by the belching sheet flames of firing guns or the quick stabbing flame flowers from bursting shells.

On we trudge, finally reaching the sunken road into the walls of which dugouts have been made to house front area administrative staff and our battalion headquarters, while the front line is less than two hundred yards ahead.

As soon as we hit the cover of the sunken road, a guide calls, 'The relief for Number 12 Post?'

'Here,' answers our corporal and we climb up and make across the mud into a big, wide communication sap nearby. The guide calls it Eve Alley and says it's not used as too many men get bogged in it.

Soon we see men in tin hats below and we're standing on the parados of the front-line trench. In we hop. Half a dozen of the 1st Battalion are here with their gear ready to get out as we take over. This changing over of battalions is a touchy job for if Fritz gets an inkling of when the changeover is taking place, he is sure to shell the position in an attempt to catch in the open either relievers or relieved.

'Where's the enemy?' enquires our corporal.

'Out in front, of course.'

'No "of course" about it. You don't think we suppose he's behind, or up above.' And our corporal waves his rifle skywards. The 1st Battalion jokers give us what information they can and vanish, leaving us to hold the line.

We settle down. Ours is merely a rifle post and along to our right some twenty yards away is a machine-gun post. Our company's to the right, and on our left, we can see nothing but an unmanned, broken-down, water-filled trench. We know we are the left-hand post of our battalion and the 48th Battalion is holding the line on our left, but we can't find out where they are.

'I'm off to get the strength of things about this post. Can't see any 48th down there anywhere.' And our old corporal goes along looking for our company commander to get information.

After a while he comes back with the O.C. who tells us what little he knows. They move very cautiously along trying to establish contact with the 48th men on our left.

Twenty minutes later they're back and tell us the 48th is about a hundred yards away and the trench between the two battalions is smashed away, half full of water and quite uninhabitable. At every odd hour through the night a man from our post is to patrol along to the 48th, and at each even hour a 48th man will visit us to keep hourly contact between the battalions.

'Report to me immediately if the 48th is late in reaching you or if you hear any movement out in front. You've got a pretty touchy post here, Corporal.' And the O.C. goes away while we settle down.

All quiet. Just an odd gun. Now and again the hum of bombing planes overhead. An extra heavy shell high above sounds like a train moving across the heavens. Another, humming from thousands of feet above us is probably a Zeppelin out to bomb distant towns. More shells overhead and every few minutes, enemy flares, but we are used to his fireworks and take little notice. A quiet time can be expected holding the line as it's too boggy for either side to attempt any raiding or fancy stunts.

'Nine o'clock. Who's first patrol?' invites the corporal.

'I'll give it a go, Corp,' I tell him.

'Righto, hero. We'll tell 'em you died game,' laughs Longun, but there's no hero stuff about my offering to do first trip. The offer is prompted more by nervousness than anything else. I'm like that in cricket; can do a better knock if I go in first than after a few wickets are down, and wickets go down quickly here at times.

'You know the password is "Camel", don't you? Don't wander too far from the trench for it's easy to get lost out there. A man disappeared on this patrol the night before last. Must have got lost and wandered into Fritz's trench for no shots were fired. Any rate, he hasn't been seen since. Perhaps an enemy patrol surrounded him.'

Cripes! Aren't I sorry I spoke up so soon, but I'm not waiting for any more, so slipping a bullet in the barrel and with the safety catch off and rifle held ready to fire, I make off.

Along I go listening to the awful noise my boots make in the mud. You can't walk on your toes here. Every time a boot goes to the ground it disappears with a noisy squashy sound and every lift of a foot is accompanied by the loud sucking sound of a cow pulling her leg out of a bog. On I keep going. A flare goes up and I prop still, a lone figure, a flood-lit statue. The flare hits the ground with a flop leaving all blacker than before. I make haste. I hear whispered voices along the trench and by the light of a distant flare just pick out the shape of our steel helmets. I'm okay and hurry on to the 48th post. I'm expected so no challenge or trouble is encountered in getting into their trench.

We pass a few muffled words and they begin to tell me about the man who disappeared. I'm not waiting to hear any more about him. I've heard all I want already so climb out to make back.

'Go back along no-man's side of the trench. It's better walking.'

Off I start.

'Just a minute.' And I stop. A 48th fellow says, 'Don't think we warned your officer about the electric arrows. Intelligence crowd now says Fritz fires steel arrows carrying an electric current. Fires them out of big bows that make no noise except a bit of a *twang*. The arrow hits a man and electrocutes him on the spot and Fritz bowmen carry his body back to their lines for identification. Must be how they got the cove on Friday night, so you want to be ready to step pretty lively if you hear a bit of a swishing sound.'

'Get some brains, you mad goat.' And I go on.

About halfway back, a noise comes to me. I can't interpret it or tell from which direction it comes. I get the breeze up and can't help remembering that man disappearing. A flare gun goes *bang!* and up soars a flare, so I prop still, looking and listening hard. The flare is rapidly descending and great black shadows are galloping unevenly across the broken ground. Out of the corner of my eye I spot two big Fritz crouched in a shell hole not ten feet from me. Together they appear to fly straight for me! Sideways out of their line of charge I bound, crouch low, jab my rifle to my shoulder to fire, but they've slipped back into the hole; as I feverishly lower my rifle muzzle to get one before the other puts me out, there comes the report and hiss of another flare, the place is flooded in light and I'm aiming at two Fritz – dead ones.

What a scare I've had! No six live Fritz have ever given me the awful turn those two dead ones did! I shake. My arms are useless. I'm sick from fear as I crouch in the light of the flare aiming at two dead men! *Flop!* and the flare is down. Up and hurrying along for my post. It's not its protection so much as its companionship I seek. The Prof was right in his psychology when he told us the human being was braver in company. At last I'm back with my mates.

'Well, what sort of a trip did you have?'

'Seen anything interesting on your travels?'

As off-handedly as I can I tell them, 'Nothing much, except a couple of dead Fritz in a shell hole along the trench a bit.'

I'm glad when the corporal tells me to make my report to the O.C. I wander along the trench, my own boots disappearing down to my knees. Half of our O.C. is in a tiny rat of a dugout where a field phone is set up. The bottom half of him hangs out of the dugout. I tell him of the patrol I've made, but don't mention those dead Fritz as I'm ashamed of the scare they gave me.

Back to our post I wade and put in a miserable night standing in the mud. Nowhere to lie or even sit. The best we can do is to lean back against the wet wall of the trench, but that's not comfortable as we slide down as soon as we doze. We stand in the mud. A quarter of an hour's standing and we find we have sunk to our knees so pull our legs out of the freezing bog and stand in a fresh place. No better. Again we sink into the mud, only quicker. A blanket is dropped in the mud and we stand on it. It's a great idea and keeps a man out of the mud – for the first five minutes, then the blanket begins to sink under us. Down the blanket works till our feet have again disappeared under the all-grasping mud. With an effort, we work one leg free and get that foot on a fresh spot. Then we give a heave and up comes the other leg, but the exertion has by now buried the first foot again. We leave it there and grope down a foot or more under the slush and feel about till our frozen fingers secure a grip on the blanket. Then we pull and tug and the blanket with about a hundredweight of mud hanging on it is dropped on a fresh place. The muddy cycle goes on. All night we juggle our feet and struggle with our blanket. It's a great life!

Dawn begins to break. 'Stand to' is passed along and each man looks over the top to keep an eye on no-man's-land as daylight creeps up on us in our world of mud. With daylight we relax our vigil. Just a man here and there on the lookout. An officer comes along with a demijohn of rum and we get about a dessertspoon each and wish for a lot more. Cold food comes to us and we get a couple of cold boiled spuds each, a slab of bacon and some tea that was once hot. Bread and jam are issued, some cheese, a few tins of bully beef and some army biscuits. The biscuits are handy. We spend half the day carving photo frames out of them.

The day passes very slowly. It's no different from the night except that we can see the mud a little better and can light our smokes without having to hold our wet greatcoats over the match to hide the glow.

Another night begins. Not a shot has been fired all day, not an enemy seen, yet we know that in the trenches a hundred yards away are hundreds of men. We most sincerely hope they are as miserable as we are, but we know they're not, for they have deep dugouts. Early in the night, the colonel and our company O.C. visit us and an hour later, the C.S.M. comes along and says the company has to supply a runner as the regular runner has been evacuated. I volunteer for the job. Can't be any worse than standing in the mud all day and night. Going to be pretty crook for me if it is.

'Right, get your gear and report to the O.C.' And I gather up my muddy rifle and sodden blanket and lug them along to the signallers' dugout. Things are no better here. The dugout holds only the signaller on duty at the phone while the O.C. and relief signallers stand outside in the mud. I tell the O.C. that I am to act as his runner.

'Good. Now put your stuff somewhere around here and you can then go along the company's length of the trench and warn all men that rifles will be inspected in half an hour's time. Tell them their rifles must be in working order.'

Away I trudge giving each man the message. Some say 'righto'. An odd man tells me 'Mine's right anyway'. I can see half the rifles are useless as the bolts are caked with mud. Many a bolt won't work as its mechanism is frozen, although non-freezing oil has been issued. A large number of men have yards of blanket to unwind before they can use their rifles. I don't know where they'd be if Fritz came over. We're a pretty casual sort of army all right, yet notwithstanding this, the battalion has never lost a position to the enemy and much of their worth lies in this casual-going attitude. They'll stand amidst a tornado of screaming, crashing death and pump bullets into an enemy attack, or attack the strongest-held enemy position with the same casual air that they'll chuck, or fail to chuck, an off-handed salute to the British staff officers on the Strand.

My job is done and I make back to my O.C. who says, 'I'd like you now to go back to the sunken road and guide up a carrying party. Ever been a runner before?'

'No, Sir.'

'You'll soon get the hang of it. I hope so anyway.'

I climb out over the back of the trench and make back for the sunken road. There's a deep communication sap here, Eve Alley, but I don't use it, remembering that men are continually being bogged in it. At the sunken road I find a party of men to be guided up carrying bags of sheepskin gloves.

I take the carriers up to Grease Trench and the gloves are taken along to the men on the posts. These gloves are fine. Made of sheepskin with the wool on the inside. A long cord passes around the neck so the gloves hang out in front. We can slip our hands out when necessary, like in wading along the trench where we find them such a boon. Before we had them we were continually diving our hands up to the wrists in the muddy trench wall each time we slipped, but now at least we can keep our hands warm and dry.

The carriers go back and I have a quiet hour standing in the mud. I take some men back to carry up some tins of foot oil – whale oil. We make our trip and land back at the trench with some tins which are passed along, and the men somehow get their boots off, pour some oil into each boot and put them on again. The oil is supposed to prevent trench feet, but has an awful smell like nothing we've ever smelt before.

The night passes miserably and another day is upon us. Many men are being evacuated with trench feet or frostbite. The feet swell and sometimes the boot has to be cut off. Huge water blisters appear and when these burst, a painful raw sore is left. Some feet just go numb and appear to die. Others turn black. The men suffering from trench feet endure great agony, can't stand and must be sent out of the line to have their feet amputated.

Our stretcher-bearers are having a gruelling time today carrying out trench-feet cases. Four men can carry a stretcher case, but owing to the dreadful conditions we send ten or twelve with each stretcher as the work is too heavy for four. With a man on the stretcher, the bearers sink to their knees at every step and relief bearers have to take over every fifty yards. Slow, laborious work, but the bearers stick to it like the men they are. From the sunken road the stretchers go back by relays and it's quite common for a stretcher case to take twelve hours from the sunken road to the dressing station about three miles away. Nine or ten relays of bearers handle the stretcher in that short distance. It's bad enough on the bearers, but what a nightmare ride of slow bumping torture to a severely wounded man. A whole day to go three miles, suffering an agony of mind and body, exposed to weather, shell fire, gas and tetanus. No wonder that many men go out to it and the route to the dressing station is lined with the bodies of men who have died along this awful *via dolorosa* of Somme mud.

By night the position is serious. We have been in three days and nights and no relief is yet spoken of. Everywhere men are rubbing whale oil into their frozen feet as cases of trench feet are being reported all along the trench. The stretcher-bearers are worked to a standstill. After the colonel makes another inspection, all C Company men are taken out of the support trench of Bull's Run and sent up to the front line to act as bearers to carry out the sick men of B and D companies now holding this trench. Our A Company is spread out to man the two support trenches of Bull's Run and Pilgrim's Way.

All night the stretchers go from the front line to the sunken road and back to the dressing station in a continual stream. Men put out of action not by the enemy, but by the mud of the Somme. A few runs may come my way tonight, the more the better as movement keeps the circulation going.

Somehow we get through the night and our fourth day breaks upon a poorly manned trench. I decide to walk the length of the trench just to keep warm, but halfway along I prop still, for there, protruding from the trench wall, is a very white hand, palm upwards. Someone, friend or foe, I do not know, is buried in the trench wall and a hand has had the earth broken away from it. A little cardboard square hangs from the hand by a piece of string. Upon the card is written 'Gib it bacca, boss'. And the poor upturned hand is half full of cigarette bumpers. Suppose it is witty, but it's not the brand of wit that appeals to me. Probably we are becoming callous, but wouldn't you be, living among the things we experience? You get hardened to death and the dead when you see them around you all the time.

I look at the hand. It is bleached white from exposure to the weather. A delicate, sensitive hand, long, pointed fingers, straight and well-shaped.

Maybe a musician, a Fritz, as the trench had lately been captured. Perhaps, a little flaxen-headed kid waits for its caress and there it lies protruding from its muddy grave, another trophy of the abominable war. Poor beggar!

I wander on to B Company where there are a few chaps I know. I ask if they've seen the hand.

'Yes, that's nothing. The war must be getting on your nerves if you let little things like that upset you.'

A corporal joins the discussion. He is an elderly man, educated and cultured, every word he says carrying the hallmark of a thinker.

'Look here, lad,' he says. 'You give up thinking too much or this war will get you down. It will beat you. I've been in it since Gallipoli and I know. The man who thinks is done. He'll never know a moment's peace. Don't look too deep and above all don't think too deeply. Try to see the funny side of everything for you will see enough that hasn't any funny side. Take the narrow escapes we all have. Lots of men worry afterwards over them. What earthly good does it do? None at all. They become a misery to themselves and to everyone near them. Take my tip, bring yourself to treat danger as a humorous episode and not as a narrowly averted tragedy, and although I can't say you'll live longer, you'll certainly live happier.'

His advice is sound, I know, and I resolve to do my best to put it into practice, but after four nights and days such as we've had, with barely a wink of sleep, it's much easier to be down in the dumps than cheered up, for as Darky said only this morning, 'If a man can keep himself from crying, this flamin' mud'll keep him from laughin'.'

Towards night the C.O. tells me I am to go back to my old post. The corporal has gone out with trench feet and I'm to take charge of the post. Back I go. The boys are hanging on somehow though we're all far from feeling well. We are craving for sleep and must get some somehow. There's only one way to sleep – standing up.

The men on 'look out' duty must keep looking across no-man's-land and must keep awake, not an easy job after five nights and four days without proper sleep. The man on 'look out' somehow gets his rifle butt on his foot, placing his hand, palm downwards, on the sharp point of his fixed bayonet. Then he rests his chin on the back of that and gazes out into no-man's-land. If he dozes, the nodding of his weighty head on the back of his hand forces the palm down hard on to the bayonet point and he soon wakes up. All night we stay here. Every two hours one of us does the lonely patrol to the 48th Battalion. We've all made it so often that we are now quite used to it. It's a break from standing in the mud.

Extra rum has been on issue for the past two nights and tonight hot stew arrived. Didn't we wade into it. We are not short of food as rations for the whole company are being sent up and almost half our strength has been evacuated.

The fifth night passes and our fifth day dawns. Just after 'stand-down' young Snow sees an enemy soldier a full half mile away. This is the first enemy we've seen on this trip. The man is making back from the line going sideways across our line of vision. In the morning mist he shows up very big. The light of the breaking day is behind him. We see that he has a big pack upon his back.

'Look at him. Off to Berlin on leave,' says Dark, envious of anyone going on furlough.

'Shake it up, boy, or you'll miss the bus,' laughingly advises Longun who is always friendly towards the enemy when they are a long way away.

'Don't you think we oughta have a pot at him?' Farmer wants to know.

'Let him go. Good luck to him,' puts in the Prof. 'Lucky to be getting out of this mud hole.'

'Let him go be blowed. Watch me stir him up a bit.' And Snow is busy getting the cover off his rifle breach. Snow leans half-balanced across the trench and aims. *Crack!* The rifle kicks hard, Snow collects a smack in the jaw from the recoil, slips and nearly falls, whilst Fritz never alters his stride. We laugh and enjoy Snow's mishap.

'Who got hurt the most, Snow?'

'You're a pretty decent shot, Snow. Oughta be a sniper.'

'Fling a clod of mud at him. You might do better.'

'Fritz is pretty safe.'

Snow is a bit rattled. Flat out across the trench he crawls, determined to have a better shot. He seems to forget that he is a wonderful target himself for the enemy manning their trench only a hundred yards away, but his luck is in and he isn't fired at.

We watch Snow. Lying flat in the mud he aims. The rifle moves, steadies, drops a little and steadies again. In unison with Snow we hold our breaths. *Crack!* The rifle kicks back with a sudden jerk and half a mile across the muddy field the enemy soldier jolts upright, falls on one knee, rises hurriedly, takes a few staggering steps and collapses in a heap on the ground. Back into the trench drops Snow. He's looking queer. No one speaks. We don't quite know what to say. Snow gets his pull-through out and gives his rifle a couple of pulls through. He snaps and jerks at the rifle as if he holds it to blame. We all commence talking to relieve the tension for we know Snow is queerly affected by having shot the man.

'Suppose you chaps think I'm a bloomin' mongrel for doing that?' he says, defiantly defending his action.

'No, why the devil would we think that?'

'What else did we come to the war for?'

Snow pelts the rifle up against the trench wall. 'Well, a man's a flamin' mongrel to come at that, whether you think so or not. Poor beggar, probably going on leave too! A man ought to be shot himself for having anything to do with their rotten war.' And he looks at his rifle again.

'The flamin' thing wouldn't hit a house any other time. Low down thing to come at, any rate. Going on leave.'

'What's the sense of going on like that?' Dark puts it up to him.

'Hop out in the open and see if Fritz'll have a go at you or not. For my part, I'll pot a Fritz every chance I get. I didn't come here to be shot at and not hit back.'

Now and again we peep over the top when Snow isn't looking, hoping to be able to tell him that the man has recovered and been carried out wounded after all. No, there he lies still. If his mates would only remove his body we could convince Snow that the man was only wounded. But no, there he lies, a shapeless blue-grey mass upon the muddy shell-torn field, laid low by the bullet of a boy with whom he had no quarrel and who would now give all to undo the effects of that shot.

We think it over – the killer and the killed who probably had never been nearer each other than half a mile of mud and mist which separated them this morning. Undoubtedly the French *c'est la guerre* is the best philosophy to apply to these happenings.

We get through the day somehow. Longun reckons we are getting used to it now and that we'll begin to enjoy it in another week or two. Night, our sixth, sets in with drizzling rain that turns to sago hail.

Wonderful news comes that we are to be relieved. The 2nd Division is to take over from us tomorrow night and already the advance party of the 18th Battalion is in the trench having a look over the position. We hope they'll like the look of things, but more sincerely hope they'll shake it up and relieve us early.

We stand and shiver through the wretchedly cold drizzling rain for half the night. Half dopey from lack of sleep, we don't care much what happens and long for tomorrow night and relief. We are to move back to Gap and Switch trenches for a day or so and then march to some back area.

Suddenly the stillness of the night is broken by a whispered 'stand to' passed down the trench. We're alert instantly. Covers are violently torn off rifles. The clips of ammunition pouches are snapped up as men rip their pouches open to get at their clips of bullets. Men scramble up and line the parapet, eyes peering into the darkness ahead.

'The position must be held!' comes the order.

We hear nothing, but know that there's something doing all right and we're ready for it.

Suddenly three Lewis guns away up on the right are pouring burst after burst across no-man's-land. Pencils of flame stab out as rifles open up with rapid fire. Still we can see nothing. The din of rifle and machine-gun firing is terrific. A man from the next post rushes up to me and shouts, 'Enemy attack on B Company front. Lend assistance. Pass it on!' He races back as the Lewis gun from his post blazes and crackles into action.

I yell to my post of men, 'Fire across B's front! Fritz attacking!'

The boys blaze away for dear life. Above the explosions of their firing, we hear the enemy out in no-man's-land shouting as they attack. We can't understand the shouts but '*ja, ja, ja*' seems to be repeated by man after man as they attack.

Then comes an odd shout from our men and above the din, a big voice booms out, 'Come on, you square-headed bastards! Come on and get us!'

I am firing and watching my men too. The boys are firing like mad and enjoying it. The Prof seems to be shooting erratically; he may put one into our trench next, so I run up and roar at him, 'Stop firing! Watch in front!' And he watches across our front in case Fritz is coming at us too.

Yacob is firing like mad and jabbering away in Russian as he fires. The other men are firing like machines, fast and methodically, without a word. Firing into the black night at moving men who can't be seen.

Longun wheels at me, 'Anyone watching our front?'

'Yes,' I shout, and he is into it again.

Again a man runs down to me. 'No giving ground! Pass it on!'

There's no one to pass it on to as I have the last post. I grab Yacob's arm. He turns and I shout, 'Find all the bombs you can and give them out.' And he runs round and places Mills grenades near each man, drawing his attention to them.

The man from the next post is here again. 'Battalion will hold the trench at all costs! Pass it on!' And away he tears.

'Fix your bayonet and fire on!' And hitting each man in turn I yell, 'Fix bayonets!' Each man does so and resumes firing.

The Prof turns and points along the broken trench to the 48th position.

'Large party moving out there!' And I shout to the boys, 'Cover the broken trench, but don't fire!'

A scramble and five or six men jump down, man the block in the trench and lie waiting and aiming across the block, whilst the Prof gets roared at. 'Bring them blasted bombs here!' And he does so hurriedly.

'Keep your eyes skinned in front, Snow.' And I race along to the Lewis gun on the next post. 'Stand by to lend assistance on the left.'

The gunner grabs his Lewis, races down and mounts it quickly on the block.

'Movement on the left of Number 12 Post. Pass it on!' I shout to one of the gun crew and I hear the message going on to warn the O.C. I race back to the boys just as an officer and two sergeants rush up unconcernedly into the face of five rifles and a Lewis gun. They spot our party aiming at them and prop in a mighty hurry. 'Come on,' I call, and they enter our trench.

'Didn't expect to meet all that aiming at us,' laughs the officer, and asks, 'What's gone wrong up here?' We tell him and the three of them head back to their own battalion. I pass the word: 'All okay on Number 12 Post,' just as a lieutenant races up to take charge. We tell them about the movement we heard coming from the 48th party and he sends Darky to tell the O.C. that the 48th have made contact.

The firing eases off and dies down. Word comes along: 'Enemy attack beaten off.' And a few minutes later: 'Men will stand to till daylight.'

The lieutenant goes back to his post and we remain alert and ready. Darky returns saying a large party of Fritz had got through the wire on a silent raid, but were heard and didn't get within fifty yards of the trench.

Officers are now wading up and down the trench warning that Fritz may come again before morning and may try this end of the trench. A machine-gun has now been mounted on the block at our post and we feel safer.

'Patrol going out,' is passed down, but we can't hear them and don't envy them on their trip.

Some time passes. Lieutenant Breen comes along and says the patrol under Lieutenant Brew rounded up and brought in seven wounded Fritz. The patrol has gone out again and our stretcher-bearers are out gathering up some wounded Fritz still out in the shell holes.

The O.C. visits us and we hear that our bearers collected six more wounded prisoners. The prisoners say that about fifty men attempted the raid and that very few escaped unwounded, but most of the wounded crawled back to their own trench. Just as the O.C. is speaking, we detect movement in front of Mr Brew and his patrol comes in from patrolling no-man's-land and the enemy wire.

'The wire is okay except for a gap Fritz must have opened to let the raiders through. Fritz's stretcher parties are out working the ground on their side of the wire,' we hear the patrol say.

Slowly the day creeps up on us. We are still standing-to, but Fritz doesn't have another go at us. As it gets bright, we can see across no-man's-land and the dead bodies of the raiders who fell in the attack. Late in the morning comes a low moaning from no-man's-land. No need to tell us a wounded man lies out there in the black freezing mud – a broken, tortured, dying body.

The moans shape into words of a foreign tongue, in themselves unintelligible, but piteously clear in their message; the sad, pleading call of a mangled man to his mates. All along the trench our men are asking why Fritz doesn't take him in.

A clatter behind and I hear Darky's anxious shout, 'Hey, get some sense. Where'd you think you're off?' And there's young Snow in broad daylight walking straight out into no-man's-land.

'Come back here, you bloomin' madman!' But Snow doesn't appear to hear and goes on.

'Return to the trench, that man!' a voice of authority orders, but Snow merely looks towards the voice and goes on into seemingly certain death to rescue an enemy wounded.

Straight for the wounded man goes Snow, straight into the sights of dozens of enemy rifles hidden behind their mound of mud. Through the scanty wire he climbs and on again. The wounded man is nearer the enemy lines than we thought. We see Snow walk up to the enemy wire and pause. Then along it he goes and still their rifles are quiet. Surely they must see him, but evidently they know his mission and respect it, though he carries neither flag nor stretcher.

'Give him the protection of a stretcher. Send the stretcher-bearers out to him,' the C.O. calls to Mr Breen. But back comes the answer, 'Not a bearer nor a stretcher in the trench.' Now we know why our bearers haven't gone out. They are all away carrying out wounded prisoners.

'Hey Fritz!' And Snow is standing at the Fritz wire actually shouting at the enemy trench! Surely rifles will crash any minute. No, but an enemy soldier is standing on the trench. We see Snow pointing across their great rows of black, rusty barbed wire. Fritz jumps down into his trench; presently a stretcher is held high up and waved several times, four Fritz climbing out, and head for Snow with it. Snow turns and walks back towards us whilst Fritz place the wounded man on their stretcher and carry him into their own trench.

We can't understand why Fritz didn't come out of their own accord. Surely they don't think that we would fire on stretcher-bearers. Perhaps they have been out and left the man for dead. Hard to say, but their bearers aren't up to much anyway from the way they acted.

Snow is back with us. He has nothing to say except 'I wouldn't hear a bloomin' hurt dog cry if I could help him'. And we know he means it.

The O.C. sends for Snow. We watch him off along the trench. Queer customer. One of those quiet, deep blokes who are hard to fathom. Yesterday all upset and afraid to look at us because he shot an enemy. Today fearlessly walking in the muzzles of a score of enemy rifles to save an unknown foe. The front line lifts the cover off some queer traits of character. Its surprises are many and unexpected.

Snow is back. 'Well, what'd the O.C. say? Promise you a medal?'

'No, he promised me a flamin' court-martial if I ever go out again. Wanted me to become a stretcher-bearer.'

'Are you going to? What'd you tell him?'

'No, told him I came over here to shoot Fritz, not to save 'em.' And he starts cleaning his rifle.

Slowly the day drags by. It gets dark. Rain and sleet fall. Word comes to get ready to move out. We are told that when relieved we are to move independently back to Gap and Switch trenches.

It is very dark now and we're ready to clear out of this slush hole. The O.C. turns up and instructs me to take the relieving N.C.O. along on the patrol to the 20th Battalion, which took over from the 48th last night. I'm not overjoyed, but the boys see some fun in it.

'How do you get these good jobs, Nulla? Must have influence behind you somewhere.'

Ten o'clock comes. No relief here yet so the boys toss to see who will do our last patrol. The last for them, but not for me as I am to take the 18th Battalion N.C.O. along to that 20th Battalion post. Longun loses the final toss and has to go. I tell him to warn those 20th jokers that

I'll be along any minute and Longun fades away into the drizzling mist and mud of the black night.

We wait for the relief and discuss our time here. We've been here for six days and this is our seventh night. Not a man has left our post sick or with trench feet, except the corporal and he is an old bloke anyway. We're proud of our record, but realise our own feet are on the point of giving out. Darky tells the Prof that the itching that he is complaining of in his toes is nothing. 'Only the webbin' startin' to sprout.'

Longun lands back from his patrol. 'Still here? Thought you'd be gone. Waitin' for me?'

Very clearly and distinctly he is given to understand that we're not waiting for him, but for the relief crowd.

Half an hour and dark forms take shape out of the blackness behind us. The first batch of the relief has arrived, late as usual. They tell us that their battalion is in the sunken road and we are very glad to hear that.

Another half hour goes. We are very impatient now, anxious to be gone.

'Here they come!' And a party tramps up across the mud.

Two fellows from the next post come up for a yarn. They are keen to know all about the Fritz raid we stopped last night. They wonder if he'll come over tonight too. We don't know, but hope to be well away if he does, for he'll be pretty sure to come with an artillery barrage next time. An 18th Battalion sergeant and three men come up. The sergeant asks Darky, 'You in charge here?'

The sergeant turns to me.

'I'm taking over and you're to report to our officer. He is down where the phone is. Whilst you're away, could this man show me the strength of the patrol you do from this post?'

Dark and the sergeant make off and I wander down the trench in search of that 18th Battalion officer. The men now in the trench are all strangers to me. Some ask about our time in here. I tell them that until the raid came off we'd seen one Fritz in five days. Already they're growling about the mud and they've been in only an hour or so. Suppose there's nothing strange in that as we were growling good and hard before we'd been in a minute.

Down the trench I go and come to a big group of men. No one is speaking. From their very silence I sense something is wrong. I move closer and get a nasty shock as I see two men with fixed bayonets, and there, standing up against the trench wall not two feet from the business end of the bayonets, is our Yacob.

'Your O.C. here?' I ask.

'Yes.' And an officer moves towards me. 'You the N.C.O. in charge of that left-hand post?'

'I'm a private, Sir, but I've been in charge for the past few days.'

'Ever seen this man before?' And he motions to Yacob. A badly scared Yacob.

'Yes, Sir, he's out of my section. He went out to bring our relief in,' I tell him.

'And he dashed nearly led the relief into the enemy lines. Righto.' His men lower their bayonets and Yacob seems more at home.

The officer turns to me. 'What is he? Foreigner?'

'Yes, Sir. Russian.'

'Well, Russian or not, he's jolly lucky our men didn't shoot him tonight. In guiding your relief in he somehow crossed the trench and, after wandering about a lot, he finally admitted he was lost but kept on asserting he was behind our line. Every time he spoke the suspicion grew stronger that he was an enemy in one of our uniforms.

'Finally he led the relief slap up against the enemy wire and one of our men jabbed a bayonet in his back and ordered him to get his hands up. They took him prisoner and somehow worked back and found the trench. If we hadn't known a relief was lost they probably would have been fired upon for they walked straight into no-man's-land.'

So we disperse. Very down-hearted and grumpy, old Yacob follows me back to our post where we find Dark and the 18th Battalion fellows. The sergeant now knows all he wants to about the patrol and we get ready to move out. The 18th Battalion fellows and Dark are curious about the lost relief, but I'm not showing old Yacob up in front of a crowd from another battalion, so just tell them he was unavoidably delayed.

Yacob climbs into his equipment and gets out of the trench ready to move off. Darky and I gather up our few muddy belongings. I notice

Dark place his great lump of muddy blanket near a nicely rolled up dry one, which lies on top of the trench, and am not a bit surprised when I see him absentmindedly pick up the dry one as we climb out.

Darky doesn't wait. He's got a nice dry blanket and he's not running the risk of losing it. Yacob rushes after Darky. He's not running the risk of getting lost again if he can help it, so he keeps right on Dark's heels as they push out into the night.

'So long, and good luck,' I whisper as I hit out after my two mates on the first stage of our journey back from the line. What a line!

FOUR

Making Back from the Line

Back from the line we three trudge hurriedly across the open. The thought of getting stonkered now lends new energy to our weary legs and we move as fast as the mud will let us. It is pitch black. We're within fifty yards of the old sunken road and feeling happy when *Whizz! Bang! Bang!* and three small shells land all around us. Three flames leap from the black mud and our tired, scared faces gleam white and drawn in the savage glow of the bursting shells. There's no time to get down as we hear the hard *ping* of a piece of flying shell bite into the mess tin on Darky's back.

I wheel to see if he's hit, but he's off for the sunken road as hard as he can run.

'Run for it!' I yell to Yacob, and flat out after Dark we race. *Whizz! Bang!* Three more shells burst behind us. *Whizz! Whizz!* We duck and hear a few more flying overhead and *Bang! Bang!* they explode sixty yards beyond the sunken road, barely clearing the rim. We reach the top to see Dark disappearing into safety, Yacob next and me following. Halfway down I slip and land, head over heels, upside down, at the bottom of the slippery drop.

'Righto, take your time, no hurry, we'll wait.' And I see Darky and Yacob near me. They're amused. I'm not. The shells are falling thickly out beyond the road, right across the track we must take to reach our battalion, now back in Gap and Switch trenches.

'We'll wait till it eases down a bit,' we decide, and wander along to the great dugout.

Many men are grouped about. We hear the dugout is absolutely full of men – sick men, trench-feet cases and a few slightly wounded, all waiting to be carried out tonight. About forty steps lead down to the dugout. Two men are sitting on each step leaving just a narrow space on one side of the steps, along which a constant stream of stretcher-bearers and sick men are moving, grunting and moaning.

Yacob works his way down a few steps and squats down, clean done, poor wretch. Darky and I flop down together on the top step. We're tired, worn out, wet, miserable and at the end of our tether.

'If we told 'em back in Australia that we stood up knee-deep in the mud of a front-line trench in the freezin' cold without a lie down and without sleep, except what we could get standing up, for six days and seven nights at a stretch, s'pose they'd reckon we were tellin' flamin' lies?'

'Suppose they would.' And we must have fallen asleep, for neither of us remembers any more till we wake early next morning when some cove treads on Darky's hand and wakes him and that wakes me. And what a strange changed world we wake into! Gone are the miles of black mud, and before us miles of glittering white snow. Everything is hidden beneath inches of snow. Sleeping here on the top step, Dark and I are almost snowed in, yet we never felt a flake fall, so heavily did we sleep.

Our laps are full of snow. Every crease and crevice of our uniforms holds snow – we're sitting in half a foot of it, it's all over us. We rise, cramped and shivering, and shake ourselves. We search for our rifles and equipment and find them completely snowed under where we dropped them last night near the steps. Men are still asleep on the steps. We're very hungry and know we won't get any food until we reach our own battalion in the support trenches.

The rising sun becomes obscured by more falling snow and we decide we'll make back to our support lines, for no one ventures to cross that great open plain in daylight.

'Come on, we'll make a break and get back to the mob,' suggests Dark, and we follow the road for some distance. We spot a big heap of officers' valises and blankets under the shelter of a few sheets of corrugated iron, so we grab a bundle of dry blankets neatly rolled up and secured by two pack straps, the work of some neat batmen.

'What about you and Yacob leaving your blankets so's there'll be no ill-feeling?' Dark suggests, grinning hard.

'No, come on. Shake it up and get away.' And we set off, but I have time to slip back under the shelter and leave my muddy rifle for a nice clean one, all bound up in oiled rags. What a lot of cleaning it will save me.

We leave the road and make for some scraggy, shell-torn trees three hundred yards ahead. Our progress is slow for Yacob is having much trouble keeping his greatcoat over the big bundle of blankets. We're not risking anyone seeing us carrying them off.

Past the trees we go. It's rough walking, for the snow, which is six inches deep, covers sloppy, unseen shell holes into which we continually stumble. Suddenly the sun comes through and here we are in the centre of the open plain. No shelter anywhere. The nearest is Gueudecourt and we don't venture into that. We are worried and look back towards the sunken road to see where the front line is. Unable to see it, we feel safe Fritz won't machine-gun us from their front line. On we go for another hundred yards when *Whizz! Bang! Whizz-bang! Whizz-bang!* Three more shells land and burst barely twenty yards behind.

We break into a run, glancing back to see black holes in the white snow.

'Swing to the right,' calls Dark, and away to the right we bear and fling ourselves flat in the snow as three more whizz-bangs burst just where we'd have been if Dark hadn't initiated our sudden right wheel.

'Bein' sniped at by a battery of whizz-bang guns,' yells Dark, and we wheel and charge straight on, then suddenly veer to our left and on. Our luck's still holding for the three shells now burst on our left as we flop down into the mud again to escape flying pieces.

'Look!' shouts Yacob, and following his pointed arm we can see about a hundred men under the bank of the sunken road, watching us. They are half a mile away and how we wish we were with them – wish we'd never left.

Cr–up! and a big shrapnel bursts high up just to our right and we see the mud and snow kick up in fifty places where the deadly pellets drive into the ground. Now we're in a serious fix. Shrapnel in the open generally means one thing and well we know it.

'Scatter!' I yell. 'Scatter wide!' And we scatter as we race desperately on, cursing those enemy guns. Hard on we go. The shells still follow us. Further and futher apart we work and are gaining ground. There are old trenches a few hundred yards ahead. The enemy gunners now send a salvo at one of us and then at another. As a man hears the shrieking wail of the shells rushing towards him, he dives flat on the ground and the two runners slacken their pace till he is up unhurt, and then flat out all three race.

Into an old trench I see Yacob jump. Darky further to the right disappears. Its welcome slushy depths open up before me and I too am into it and breathe happily again.

I follow the old disused trench along and find the other two. Yacob still has the blankets, but is looking very scared. Darky is as cool as ever and wants to know what's amusing me.

'Crikey, didn't they stir us up,' says I.

'The stupid owls! Don't know the first thing about gunnery. If they'd kept the shrapnel going they'd have got the three of us. Must have chucked a hundred quid's worth of stuff at us. Anyway we beat 'em, and those jokers back in the sunken road can pay up.'

'Pay up? What do you mean?'

'Pay their bets, of course. I'll wager half a dozen of them were laying odds about which of us would get stonkered first.'

For a few minutes we rest here then work a hundred yards along the old trench and into the open again. Forty yards or so and we are in another trench. The Fritz gunners have given us their best.

Some 48th Battalion men are in this trench. They congratulate us on our lucky escape and say they have been watching the show. Two of their cooks come up and join the discussion. Darky, who always makes a point of cultivating stray cooks, tells them of how our relief was mucked up last night and of our night on the steps of the big dugout, and ends by putting the hard word on them for 'a bit of buckshee tucker, if you've got any to spare, mates'. It works and we make a hearty meal of fried bacon at the 48th cookhouse.

We're told that our battalion went into the trenches two hundred yards behind here last night, and bidding the 48th cooks 'so long' push on. We reach the trench. Not a man to be seen. Just an odd track in the snow. No need to tell us that our chaps are dead to the world behind the old blankets hiding the mouths of sloppy little dugouts.

At the end of the trench we find our own cooks who have dixies of steaming hot Maconochie rations cooked, but no one will come and get any. The boys are far too tired to do anything but sleep. Not so we, for we make a second hearty breakfast standing in the cook's way, our wet backs to the fire.

Our hunger satisfied we decide upon a good sleep so make along the trench. Into dugout after dugout we peer. They are all full of sleeping men. Finally we find an empty one, just a hole about five feet square cut into the wall of the trench. Two sheets of old rusty iron over which an inch or two of mud has been shovelled is the roof. We crawl in and throw out half a dozen bully-beef tins. Though the floor is very wet, we decide to make it our home.

Something is needed to cover the front of it so Yacob wanders about and finds a couple of old torn blankets, which he sews together with some telephone wire for thread, and drapes them down across the mouth of the dugout. We secure them in position by putting plenty of mud on the ends, which overlap the dugout roof. This is slow work as we have to shovel the mud with empty jam and bully-beef tins. Luckily there's no shortage of mud.

That done, we set about fixing up the inside. 'Arranging the interior decorations', as Dark terms it. On the floor we spread my muddy blanket. Our three wet overcoats go down next, then Darky's good blanket and one from our annexed bundle goes on top. The other five blankets are spread for covering, but we take one off and by driving our bayonets through it we fix it along under the roof to catch the drips.

It's going to be really comfortable here. We have a smoke and get our equipment and rifles stacked away in a corner. Then our boots and socks come off for the first time in a week. Of course they are sopping wet and thick with mud. Our tunics come off and get folded for pillows.

As we have no other boots or socks we place them under our tunics, knowing the heat of our heads will dry them whilst we sleep. The sodden strips of bagging used for puttees are shoved under our bottom dry blanket. It's wonderful what the heat of a sleeping body will dry. Next we get out of our pants and they too go down for pillows.

Dark and I get out of our underpants and pull them on again, inside out, to trick the chats. We don't turn our singlets or cardigans, though, as it's too cold. We chance the chats about our upper regions, but can't bear them steeple-chasing around our knees any longer. They've had a pretty fair run now, a whole week of undisturbed freedom in which to play and eat us.

Down we crawl under our dry blankets. We're in luck's way having half a dozen dry blankets. The rest of the men have to make do with an overcoat and one blanket; one they've stood on in the mud for a week. We're lucky all right. Our little dugout is a home from home to us and very soon we drop into a dead sleep, worried by nothing, least of all by the enemy only two miles away.

FIVE

In Support

It's now two days since we arrived back in this support trench with our battalion. All yesterday we slept, except towards dusk when we went to the cookhouse for a hot meal. Last night we just slept – no fatigue and no duties for anyone.

Today is bitterly cold with snow falling. An aerial dogfight commences high up over the enemy's territory. A plane climbs and then swoops down at the enemy plane below, its machine-gun pouring a stream of bullets at the machine it's attacking. This manoeuvring for height and diving goes on for quite a while. Away in the distance we see a plane come down, toppling and rolling like the fall of a dead bird. We think it's a British plane, but it's too far away to be certain.

The fight comes closer. The machine-guns can now be heard plainly. From a Fritz plane we see dark smoke belching as it swings away to retire from the fight. A ball of smoking flame leaves the plane. 'Dropping his petrol tank,' someone remarks. The machine flattens out, trying to glide down to earth. Flames fly from it. A wing blazes and the plane tips towards the burning wing, seemingly out of control. It begins to roll. A few turns and the whole fabric is flaring, and the machine dives nose first straight for the ground, like a falling comet disappearing beyond the horizon, and crashes into the earth. Up in the sky the track of its fiery fall is marked by a vertical column of black smoke; just another plane brought down and another couple of pilots gone to an awful end.

The planes, seven of them, are now almost overhead. Four Fritz machines, all fighters, and three of ours. A Taube is highest. The lowest is one of our observation planes. It flies straight on, not fighting, but continually being attacked, whilst our other two are doing their best to fight four fast enemy fighters and at the same time to keep them away from our observation plane.

Suddenly we see the high Taube dive like an arrow for our old observation plane and from high in the heavens comes the savage barking of his machine-gun. We see tracer bullets streaming straight for our old observer. This will be the end, for the fiercely diving Taube must surely end our old machine. But no, he's swooped down, under and past the slower plane, which has weathered the storm of bullets and flies steadily on.

The Taube flattens out in a fast run and suddenly zooms upwards in a sharp climb. As he does, a little British plane swoops straight by him with its gun barking furiously. The Taube's gun replies, just once, and his nose comes over more and more as the machine momentarily pauses, seems to hang in the air and then he's on his back with his wheels uppermost. Another pause, a wing drops, and over and over the plane rolls, falling, to land over beyond a little hill with a rush of wind and a mighty crash.

Our victorious plane takes a big sweep and comes back, climbing and looking for more trouble, but the three remaining enemy planes have turned and are flying for home, so he wheels and comes flat out after his mate who is still guarding the observation plane. As he flies over we wave and call. The airmen can't hear us, but they see us down below and a hand waves over the side as the machine flashes by.

A crowd of men rush past. They are going over to see the fallen enemy plane. Snow and Farmer are with them. They should know better as the plane may be a mile or two off. A falling plane is very deceptive. More than once have we rushed to where we thought a plane crashed a few hundred yards off only to find it was down a mile away. The last time, we were sent back nearly three miles for stretchers to carry back two dead airmen and bury them. Well do we remember those two young Scotty officers, smashed to pulp, their legs almost burned off as well. We lost a lot of interest in fallen planes after that experience.

Night comes and with it more snow. It's absolutely freezing. The fatigue parties go out to work on jobs and our platoon is sent on a dangerous trip to Gueudecourt to gather up old iron. We gather up what we can and commence our return trip by a different track across a little valley where big bulging lumps show up everywhere in the snow; dead horses, dozens of them, and lying alongside dead Indian cavalry.

Morning breaks clear and cold. A small party of men is coming along the duckboard track from Delville Wood. Suddenly, *Zonk! Bang!* and three or four small shells land around them. The men scatter from the duckboards and race for the shelter of an old disabled tank. Our men shout and wave to them to keep away from it for we know the enemy has its range accurately, but on they rush. A perfect hail of small shells bursts fair amongst them. Flat on the ground they fling themselves. Up and on again, but two khaki lumps remain on the snow. The men run into the tank as we hear the shrapnel pepper its sides.

'A direct hit now and he'll kill the lot!'

'There go the bearers!' And two stretcher parties leave our trench on the run for the fallen men. The shelling has suddenly stopped. The bearers run up to the fallen men. Down beside the first man they drop, and then up, leaving him there, and on to the next man.

'Beyond the need of bearers now, poor beggar!'

The second man is put on a stretcher and his bearers make back towards us. The other stretcher party make for the tank yelling loudly to the men inside, who hear them, rush out and race for the trench behind ours. As soon as they appear on the snow another salvo of shells bursts amongst them. On they rush – all but two. One man has gone a few steps only when he falls. The bearers race through the shelled area, drop their stretcher beside him and he too is on his way to our trench. The other man appears to disregard the shells as he slowly walks over to the dead man. Amidst them he moves slowly, without a duck or a flinch. We see him bend over the dead man for a while, then rise with some things in his hands. He's been collecting the few personal belongings from a fallen mate. Someday, perhaps, a little war-worn wallet and a few faded snapshots will renew the grief afresh in some Australian home. Slowly, through the shell bursts the man walks on, walks where his mates ran, and somehow walks unscathed. The luck of the game.

The first stretcher party enters the trench and we see an ashen grey face turning in pain with blood flowing from a nasty gash across the man's forehead. Dark patches show on the underside of the stretcher, telling us of bleeding from body wounds. The bearers rush him on to the Battalion Aid Post and the second stretcher comes along. On it lies a tall, thin man. Very still he lies, his moustache showing up pitch-black against the pallor of his face. A bandage is on one hand and he appears to have fainted.

We sleep the day away and towards dusk, a party goes off to bury the man with the little black moustache. He had a finger shot off but never rallied from the shock, whilst the other, with a nasty scalp wound, eleven body wounds and a badly smashed arm, was carried back and on the mend already. Matter of constitution or of how much shock is received, we suppose.

A cook has a little fire going in a dugout. We are told to get a drink of tea there, but there's none left, and we begin to go crook again.

'Wait till I get some water boiled and I'll fix you up.' And we watch the cook's off-sider take an axe and an empty sandbag. He finds a big shell hole of frozen water from which he chops a great lump of ice, wraps it in the bag, carries it back and drops it into a dixie. We wait till it melts and eventually boils when we get our drink of tea.

'Hope there aren't too many dead Fritz in the bottom of that hole where he got the ice from,' laughs Dark as he gets a second good issue.

Eventually we're taken off our job and sent up, armed with shovels, to make a communication sap trafficable. The sap leads to the front line, but our work is on this end of it, shovelling out the mud. After an hour an officer comes along and tells us we are to bury an officer who was killed near the sap last night.

Out into the open six of us go, not keen on being in the open only three hundred yards from the front line in broad daylight. We make out carefully, one eye watching the front line, the other measuring the distance back to the sap. The dead officer lies badly smashed, huddled on the edge of a fresh shell hole in the crimson-stained snow – Australian crimson.

'Dig a grave nearby, men,' directs the officer, and we commence digging in the snow and mud.

'Lend me a helmet, someone,' the officer asks, and I give him my tin hat. He opens the dead officer's pockets, gets his belongings and puts them in the helmet; then takes a watch off the man's arm and that too goes into the helmet.

Phit! Crack! and a bullet lands twenty yards short of us as the crack of the rifle comes to our ears.

'Thought we couldn't be seen from Fritz's front line?' Longun puts it up to the officer.

'Neither we can, my man; that's only a sniper some way back.'

'Strike me fat! Can't a bullet from a sniper stonker a man just as well as one from the front line?' Darky asks all and sundry, as he digs like mad to get the job over. The officer doesn't appear to hear him.

Another bullet smacks into the mud, a bit closer, as we dig on.

'This is what I call madness. Why the devil couldn't this be done at night instead of exposing us all here in daylight? No bloomin' wonder we're losing the war,' Snow growls.

'Can't be helped, lad. I'm given my orders to carry out just the same as you, but if you feel bad about it you can slip into the trench. We'll finish here.'

'What, go back and leave the rest here? Not me! There's no one stinkin' sniper can hunt me.'

Twice more the sniper lets go. We hear a bullet fly right amongst us. Snow makes a bite at the air. 'I bloomin' nearly bit that one,' he laughs and Longun warns, 'The next one'll bite one of us.' But it's all lost on the officer who only says, 'We're right. They won't hurt you unless they hit you. Shake it up and get finished, men.' And we shake it up. The sniper is getting more work out of us than fifty brigadiers could.

Two more shots fly by. I'm most uncomfortable and look at my helmet, sincerely wishing my head was in it instead of the dead officer's belongings. The grave is now knee deep and we stand in it bent, very much bent, and make our shovels fly.

Smack! A grunt as the breath leaves his body with a jump and Farmer is knocked eight or ten feet before he falls. We rush to him as the officer eases him round. 'Blast him! He's got me,' Farmer tells us in an off-hand, uninterested sort of way.

'Where, Farm, where?' we say anxiously.

'Here in me arm.' And he clutches his left shoulder fiercely, screws his eyes shut tight and curls his lip up like a pup with a dry fox-tail up his nose. We ease the now blood-stained hand away from the wounded arm and see the bullet has gone through the colour patch on his arm. As we bend over Farmer, the sniper has another go at us. We turn and snarl and swear in his direction.

'He's getting close. Get this man into the trench and we'll finish later,' says the officer, and whilst he grabs my helmet, Dark and I help Farmer up and hurry him on towards the trench as the rest of the men streak for its safety. Snow, the one bloke a sniper couldn't hunt, wins the race easily.

×

Farmer is steadied down into the trench and we examine his wound. The bullet has entered his arm just below the shoulder and hasn't come out. We get our field dressings out, dab iodine around the wound and get sworn at as the good strong iodine works into the raw wound. Then we bandage the wound up carefully. Farmer tells us, 'The worst pain is here.' And he rubs the small of his back. Snow pulls Farmer's shirt up and we see a swelling low down near his spine. We know what it is. The bullet has somehow followed the spine down and lodged in the small of his back.

Word has passed for the stretcher-bearers and they come up. We rake up about forty-odd francs amongst us and make Farmer take them, 'Because you might be stuck in hospital for weeks before you get a pay.'

Further up that bog-hole we work. On a bend we see a round white object in the trench wall. We go and have a look – it's the top of a man's head jutting out of the wall. The brushing of countless arms against the head has worn the hair and skin off, and the bones have become polished like a billiard ball. The wits have been at work on it. 'The Dome of St Paul's' is written on it in indelible pencil, and beneath is drawn a fine fat spider. The Prof is disgusted and can't see the point in drawing the spider there, until someone explains, 'It's to keep the flies away, you dope.'

For another forty yards we work on and just outside the trench see a dead Fritz. He is absolutely naked except for his oval-shaped identification disc.

'Nothing on but a dead meat ticket. That's strange.'

'Never seen it before, but Fritz reckon our flying-pig trench mortars will blow a man clean out of his clothes. If they are any worse than his *minenwerfers*, I don't doubt it at all.'

Across country we strike for Switch Trench along a snow-covered path. The tramping of hundreds of feet has crushed the snow into a hard, solid wedge of slippery ice like walking on raised glass, but it's better than trudging through the snow-covered mud. I did know the track before the snow fell, but it's a very different matter now as snow alters the aspect of everything. I lead the boys along in the dark. I guide by my ears now. At each step I listen to my foot contacting the firmly beaten snow lying an inch under the covering of the freshly fallen. If I get off the path I immediately detect a softer sound as my foot fails to meet the solidly crushed snow. Then I kick about till I find the path and lead on again.

Being almost frozen, we make back to our trench to find it empty as the men are all out on fatigues. The cooks have a dixie of hot stew waiting made of bully beef boiled up in water. Darky reckons it's like the beer they sell over in Blighty – 'All head and legs, no body in it' – but to us its great beauty lies in its warmth, so we have all we can get.

We're barely asleep when *Crash!* A great shell lands and the dugout shudders under the vibration of the burst. Great lumps of mud fall on us. *Whizz-bang! Bang! Bang!* and small shells are landing in dozens, whilst every now and again comes the awful crash and shock of a nine-two bursting nearby. In silence we sit up. Darky finds his tunic and pulls it on. 'Bloomin' cold, isn't it,' he says.

The shelling is getting heavier. Sitting huddled together in a tiny dugout that shivers and shakes to each shuddering shell burst, we feel our war-worn nerves beating a tattoo to those shattering shells searching for this very trench. We sit in silence. Every minute or so the place is lit with a dancing red or yellow glow as a shell lands beyond us.

Crash! and we fairly jump again as the trench gets a direct hit. The reeling, rocking earth seems to be toppling to its very doom, toppling over us and under us to the crashing of shells.

Men run past. 'Stretcher-bearers!' is shouted.

Above the crash of another shell comes an unearthly yell of pain and fear from a badly wounded man. It sounds like a man's last yell.

Crash! Crash! Crash! through the night, as more shells land in a glowing, slashing roar, and the sharp fumes of burnt explosives are everywhere.

'Shovels, quick!', 'Stretcher-bearers!', 'Men buried!' we hear from along the trench, and we rush out as men are charging along for those cries. Shells are whistling and wailing. Down again in the trench we crouch in awful suspense. *Bang! Bang!* and with a shuddering jump we're up and on again before the flame of the shell burst has quite gone.

'Dugout blown in!' We hear an awed whisper as we rush on and come to a party of men who have just torn the iron roof off a blown-in dugout.

'Ah, that's better. A man can see what's goin' on about him now. How long have I been locked up in here?' And the imprisoned man we thought was dead climbs out as cool as an iced lager.

An officer spins the chap round. 'How are you?' he anxiously enquires of the resurrected one.

'I'm fine, only me poor bloomin' home's gone west.' And he crawls back into it through where the roof was and pelts his gear out.

Crash! Bang! We get another salvo all along the trench and duck and dive to dodge the flying fragments.

'Come on, scatter out, don't bunch there!' And we move along looking for safety, or luck.

'Cripes, they're getting it down at Company headquarters.' And we see the shells are falling heavier on that end of the trench, though we are getting all we need here. Still the shells crash upon us, but by a miracle we seem to be just where they don't burst.

Suddenly one again lands fair in the trench and a great heavy duckboard is thrown yards out of the trench. 'Men hit!' comes the call from nearby, and Dark and I race up towards it. A man is crawling along through the mud, crawling on his stomach and dragging his shattered legs after him. He wears no strides, only underpants, sodden wet with blood. We make to lift him up. 'No,' he moans. 'Get Scotty. I'm right.' And he tries to crawl on. 'Find Scotty, Scoo, Sc . . .' and he sags and is out of it. Mate before self, as ever.

'Stretcher-bearers!' Dark yells, and turns to me, his cool face white and set. 'I'll fix him. Get after Scotty.' And I run on, getting my field dressing out as I go. Three or four men are helping two wounded men along the trench, and right where several shells have burst on the rim of the trench, I find a stretcher party attending to Scotty.

A tourniquet is being twisted on an arm, a mangled and shattered arm, but his face is terrible to look upon. Mouth and nose have been chopped horribly. His top lip is slit clean back from his teeth. Blood is pouring from his face and filling his gas respirator bag. Suddenly he shudders and chokes. A bearer bends his head and with a gurgled moan the blood pours from his mouth and great bubbles form and break at each breath. Through it all his eyes follow us. Eyes of pain and fear. We get his face fixed into a pad. He pulls it away with his good hand and 'Is Blue right?' comes in queer anxious tones. Afraid to ask and afraid of our answer too.

'Yes, got a Blighty. Couple of leg wounds,' I lie to him, and he settles down and is taken away on the stretcher.

The shelling is over. I find Dark just back from carrying Bluey to the doctor. 'The quack reckons he'll lose his left foot, but will pull through all right. They've got seven dead men down there and reckon twenty were wounded.'

Into our dugout we crawl. Soon our boots are off and we're down, curled up around the warm Yacob as we shiver ourselves to sleep once more.

SIX
Fallen Comrades

Morning breaks, freezing cold as usual. Our damp blankets are frozen stiff on top of our sleeping bodies. We threw our wet boots into a corner last night and now we can't get our feet into them as the leather has become frozen as hard as iron whilst we slept. Not a budge nor a bend can we get out of them. We search our pockets for letters and burn a couple inside each boot and it thaws out enough to be tugged on. We'll use our boots as pillows in future.

A daylight fatigue is to go out along a big valley, past a collection of deep dugouts known as the Chalk Pits, and then swing left behind some artillery positions, finally coming to the back part of Delville Wood. Our job is to work a corner of the wood, salvaging any war material we can find. And we get a lot: picks, shovels, rifles, machine-guns with ready-filled belts, boxes of ammunition, old shells, miles of barbed wire that has never been unrolled, and odds and ends of every kind. It's a rotten job wandering around amongst hundreds of dead men, whole and in pieces everywhere. And fat rats.

Just outside the wood we come to a well-constructed trench. In it there's a British soldier to every yard, killed on the parapet in trying to hop-off. Twenty yards in front, a row of dead British soldiers in perfect line as if on parade, N.C.O.s in position, and a half-dozen paces ahead, their platoon officer, a rusty revolver in one outstretched hand, his whistle still clasped in the other, mowed down by machine-guns.

Further on we see another perfect line that met the same fate, and almost on top of the trench they charged, yet another line of British bodies. The three waves of the advance that surged on to break forever against an invisible barrier of machine-gun bullets. We inspect the enemy trench these men charged and their mates took. Its floor is covered with the bodies of grey-uniformed Fritz, many killed by hand grenades which are scattered everywhere from boxes and boxes opened, but not used.

There amongst them are two dead Tommies with enemy bayonets still through them, a rifle hanging by its bayonet from each body. One man has his two shrunken hands clasped around the bayonet that he has been trying to pull out of his chest. Cold steel has been the order here, cruel cold steel. Near a dugout entrance, a tall Fritz soldier hangs head down, pinned to the wooden frame of his dugout by a British bayonet that has been sent clean through him to the hilt into the hardwood behind. It has been unclipped from its rifle and left there with him impaled on it.

'Get an eyeful of this,' someone calls, and we see two men, a Fritz and a Tommy dead within a yard of each other; the Fritz has a British bayonet through his throat whilst the Tommy lies doubled over a Fritz bayonet whose point protrudes from his back.

In a wide part of the trench we find a very big Tommy sergeant. Across him are sprawled two Fritz and their bayonets are driven through his body. No less than seven Fritz lie nearby with their necks horribly gashed, whilst one has been opened from his shoulder halfway down his chest. Between the sergeant and the side of the trench is an enemy officer whose steel helmet, head and face are cleft by a Fritz trench-spade, the blade of which is still in the opened head, whilst the broken handle lies near the British sergeant.

'What do you think of that? The Tommy sergeant, using a Fritz spade, chopped six Fritz necks nearly off, slit another's chest open, and then smashed the spade when he cleaned the officer up with it.'

'Yes, and two Fritz got him with their bayonets when the spade broke.'

'And his own men got the two who bayoneted him.'

'These Tommies will do me.'

We've seen enough here so go on to the next trench, which we find has been heavily shelled. A British burial party is at work filling in the trench of men, friend and foe, who fell in or near it. This party has to establish identification wherever possible, which means searching for identification discs on men who have been dead for months. They can have their job, so we move off elsewhere.

There's a little knob nearby. We recognise it as a natural stronghold and inspect it. Every inch of it has been shelled again and again. The signs are easily read. It has been held and lost by both sides many times. Its shell-ploughed mound has been saturated with the blood of Britain and Germany, of men who held it and of those who took it and retook it. The poor shattered bodies of British and Fritz are intermingled in their last long sleep that knows no waking. Bits of bodies and scraps of uniforms are to be seen in the scraggy, torn tree branches, blown there by shellfire. A heavy machine-gun hangs caught in the fork of a shell-rent tree, twenty feet above the churned-up ground, testimony to the lifting power of modern explosives.

Our job is done. We've made a good collection that may be turned to some further use in the scientific destruction of our fellow man, and reach the support lines. The men are getting ready to move out to more fatigues after dark.

Half an hour's slushing through the snow-capped mud and we're at our job. A long emergency trench is to be dug as precaution against an enemy advance. We're digging on the side of a steep, well-drained hill in frozen mud like iron. Bits of frozen earth continually strike us on the shins, raising bruises and blasphemy. We work on with little to show as progress is very slow.

Still working we hear the *chut-chut-chut-chut* of an enemy machine-gun firing from up near the front line. A few moments and there comes to our ears the soothing, humming whistle of a fleet of machine-gun bullets flying over our heads so we drop to the ground.

Again we dig. Again the sound of the enemy gun reaches us. Down again in the snow and again the bullets whistle overhead, The gun is a long way from us. Mostly a bullet is half a mile past before you hear the report of its discharge from rifle or machine-gun. All night we work on a recognisable trench. We prepare to go back to the support lines, but we're not yet finished. We have to gather up handfuls of snow to cover our soil and the floor of the trench, for it must not be observed by the enemy planes that reconnoitre all day.

At last we finish and a long line of us starts back. Our hands are frozen from gathering snow and we thankfully seize our sheepskin gloves. In silence we trudge on when someone drops a sharp spade blade onto the toes of the man behind us and an argument begins. Two men hop about in the snow beginning to fight. Soon we're in our support lines where rum is issued to each of us. The cooks have some watery soup after which we crawl into our dugouts and sleep.

Morning breaks cold and the day passes slowly. Some Australian mail comes up and we are wonderfully bucked up as letters and papers are gratefully seized upon and passed around, read and talked about. Parcels are opened and the eatables shared by the recipient and his mates.

Our dugout is lucky. I collect a whole heap of letters, and Dark gets some letters and a good parcel from one of his 'lonely soldier sheilas' as he calls them. We're happy and hunt up the rest of the mates who have scored too, and we discuss family affairs and general news from home.

Longun hands over a *Church News* of some sort from his sister in Brewarrina. 'May interest some of you coves. I'm sort of out of touch with that stuff now. Wish she'd send a *Referee* or a *Bulletin* instead.' And he's busy reading weather reports, three months old, in the Prof's *Sydney Morning Herald*. Dark seizes on the *Church News* and tells us with a laugh, 'Come in handy to thaw our boots out of a morning.' And we agree.

Longun is stirred up by something he sees in a Dubbo paper. He snorts hard. 'The lyin' cow! Here, take a look at this.' And he shows us a letter in the paper from a man over here. The letter is headed 'In a leaky little dugout, somewhere in France'.

'Well, what's wrong with that? What're you getting up on your hind legs about anyway?'

'Ah! The flamin' liar! In a leaky little dugout! A bloomin' clerk back at army headquarters, that's what he is. Livin' in a fine chateau somewhere. Why the devil doesn't he be honest and write home and tell 'em he's having the best time he's ever had, or is ever likely to have? These floppin' heroes get my goat.'

A commotion sets up outside. We look out and see about thirty strange men without battalion colours on. New reinforcements joining up. They are very sunburnt. Almost dark brown. More than one of us is struck by their colour for they are all so much darker than we are.

'Wonder if the people in Aussie are as black as that?'

'No. These coves get like that coming through the tropics.'

Out we climb to see if we know any of them. We don't.

'Where're you chaps from?'

'New South Wales.'

'Anyone from Tarcoon, or Milparinka way?' Longun wants to know.

'Don't think so.'

'Of course there isn't,' puts in Snow. 'These men are from Australia.' And the laugh's on Longun. We fire questions at them, dozens of questions. They do their best to answer us all, but get marched on before we're half through with them. Darky asks whether it's true that Tasmania has been torpedoed and sunk, but gets no answer.

An hour later the new men come back in ones and twos looking for dugouts. A young cove comes and asks if he can get in with us, and he says he's in '15 Platoon, wherever that is'. I tell him to crawl in and we'll see what we can do.

'Not much room, but hop in, mate, and don't drop any dead matches or cigarette ash on the carpet,' Dark welcomes him.

He tells us his name and says his mates all got put into 13 Platoon. He's a real newspaper, a whole newsagency in fact to us, and we spend the day asking all manner of questions. We enjoy having young Jacko with us. He's 'young Jacko' to us although he's two years older than I am and a year older than Snow. He provides a touch of home, a kind of connecting link between it and us. Our past life has become somewhat dimmed under the dark cloud of drill, mud, shellfire and soldiering, but young Jacko somehow leads us to look on to the days to be, to the future in which the memory of all this will have been blanched by the sunshine of our own land, our own Australia Fair.

Another night comes down, dark and cold as usual. We file out to work on the trench-digging fatigue once more. Now we have Jacko with us everything takes on a fresh interest. Jacko is shown the enemy flares and told about their tricks. He's told how a man must remain perfectly still whilst a flare is up, to close his eyes till the flare drops in order to be able to see better through the darkness when the flare has gone. For another ten minutes we trudge on. Jacko is being educated. The belching roar of our big guns is described to him. Next the savage bark of a battery of 18-pounders doing rapid fire comes under his notice.

Talk gets on to the sounds made by shells, and the *minenwerfers* that we can run from if our luck's in, and about the spiteful little *whizz-bang* that it's generally too late to run from when he's heard.

At last we reach the trench and commence to work when our friend opens up his machine-gun. Down into the half-dug trench we crouch, taking care that Jacko and the other new men are well down. A pause and we point out to them the sound of bullets flying overhead. More digging and the gun fires again. Jacko makes to get down, but has a nasty shock when he sees that none of us has even bobbed. We explain that we knew by the sound of the gun that it was not firing in our direction.

Shellfire is developing all along the front. The men are becoming silent. Jacko and his mates doing their first night in the forward area catch something of our tightening up and are more on pins and needles than they admit. It's their baptism of fire and they're nervous, but they're not squealers, so they say little and slog on. Still we work on, but we are listening with trained ears to the shellfire. 'Those shells falling back there are searching for our guns,' we hear someone remark.

Suddenly the earth shakes under a series of tremors as an ammunition dump of ours goes sky high half a mile back. Beyond the next rise we can just see the burst of the exploding shells licking the night sky with fiery red tongues of flame as the dump of shells explodes, splitting the night with deafening detonations.

'Fritz has scored a lucky hit there.'

Small shells are now bursting along the gully below us.

'Hear that dud? That's four duds in the last batch.'

'Another couple of duds, that lot,' as a battery drops a salvo of six or eight shells in a bunch.

Men are screwing their gas-masks about and listening for the sound of dud shells.

Jacko comes up to me. 'Hey, Nulla, why are they taking more notice of the shells that don't explode than the ones that burst? Duds are nothing to worry about, are they?'

I tell him, 'They're getting breezy that Fritz is putting gas over. Gas shells are sometimes hard to distinguish from duds. They land with a little *putt-tt* sort of sound. Just enough explosive in them to burst the case and release the gas without scattering it. Been shown how to adjust your respirator?'

'Yes, we went through all that at the Bull Ring.'

'Mightn't be anything, but keep near me for a while and I'll show you what to do.' And he comes and works next to me whilst I endeavour to put him wise to the shelling and mention some facts about gas that may some day mean a lot to him. We aren't doing much digging now, more listening. More of our guns are joining in, replying to the enemy strafe. Most of us are glad to hear them giving Fritz a bit of their own back, though some men would sooner our guns remained silent as they fear retaliatory firing will mean a general bombardment.

'Look out! What's this coming?' And from out of the gully behind we hear men running our way. They get closer and go through us at a run, laughing and joking. It's the divisional machine-gun crowd rushing their big, heavy machine-guns up to their forward positions to be in readiness if wanted.

The officer in charge of the fatigue party is now walking up and down the length of our line. He is undecided what to do, but doesn't have much longer to wait as a runner comes up looking for him.

'Colonel's message, Sir. Return to the support lines at the double and stand to. All parties are recalled.'

'Gather up your tools, pass it on.' And the order goes along the half-dug trench. The metallic ring of steel on steel tells of the order being obeyed.

'File along to the right.' And we head for our supports.

The officer makes to the rear of the file as the sergeant runs past to lead us off. He takes his place at the head of the file and calls 'double' and we break into a steady run following him. I spurt and catch up to Jacko. 'Keep behind me and do as I do,' I tell him, for I can see that we must pass through a shelled area. A quarter of a mile we jog and reach a gully into which Fritz is heavily shelling. We ease into a walk and keep close under the brow of the hill as we skirt the shelled gully.

Over our heads the shells are now wailing to explode with a crashing roar only a hundred yards away. Pieces of shell and great lumps of frozen ground are whistling through the air everywhere. *Crash!* A shell bursts and a large piece lands on the ground with a hollow thud ten feet short of our party. We stop a shower of snow and frozen earth and laugh as we hurry on. Another shell bursts close, but its burst is forward and so we're fairly safe. *Whizz! Crash!* And from the burst another great fragment, a piece large enough to chop a man in half, roars overhead as we duck.

A terrific rushing of air and the screaming whistle of a big shell, and flat on the ground we all drop and *Crash! Bang!* it bursts almost upon us! In silence we jump up and 'Anyone hit?' is anxiously called. No answer and on we go, running hard. Once again a shell wails and whistles overhead to burst dangerously close. Down, up and on again we race. Down in a little gully we hear a queer noise. Horses and mules giving trouble under shellfire. 'Listen to the flamin' mules squealin'. Shells put the breeze up them properly.'

'Yes, until they're hit, and then they just fall down and lie still until they peg out. Not a budge or a sound out of wounded mules.'

The colonel and officers are in a group with their equipment on. They have a dozen things to do, but carry on as coolly as if they had but one. Our officers are a pretty efficient crowd. As we pass the colonel, he tells us, 'Get your equipment on and stand to. We think he may be coming over in a big attack and we can't let him through here, men.'

'Let him come, blast him.' And we are buckling on our equipment and loading our rifles as we watch the line for signs of an attack. We'd ask nothing better than that Fritz comes over in daylight. It'd be a decent war then. The shelling continues, but it's not on this trench. Guns are roaring along the whole front and the horizon is a luminous circle of darting flame and bursting shells.

An officer comes along. 'Watch for our S.O.S. from the front line. Tonight it's three flares: red, green and red. Remember it's red over green over red. Report it immediately you see it go up.'

'Goodo, Sir.' And he wanders on to the next group.

With loaded rifles lying on the parapet in front, we stand waiting for what may come.

'Fritz won't shift us out of here.'

'Suppose he won't, but he's shifted us before and we've shifted him too. Fritz won't do it, but his flamin' shells might. What about Pozières and Mouquet Farm?'

'How'll we hold this if he breaks through Gueudecourt and works up the gullies to our left?'

Word comes for me to report for duty as a runner, so I go along to the battalion headquarters dugout where I am instructed to stand by in case I'm needed. Every few minutes a signaller sends through to brigade headquarters back in the Chalk Pits. This incessant sounding through is necessary for with so many shells falling, the wires may be cut at any minute, severing communication between the support lines and our brigade. We hear the wires have been broken five times already and that the brigade signallers are now out following the wires and fixing the breaks.

Towards morning, the shelling increases just as we expect, heralding the launching of the enemy attack. It eases off and gradually dies down, but we are still standing-to – not running any risks. We discuss the shelling and decide it was to avenge a defeat in some other sector or to celebrate the birthday of some big Fritz general.

Quietly the morning breaks and we stand down. Another attack scare is over. We reaped some good out of it in that we got out of a couple of hours of trench digging. Good on you, Fritz. The heavy shelling caught the artillery, though. We hear a few guns were put out of action and many casualties occurred amongst the gunners and drivers. Away back behind us we can make out dead horses and mules, overturned gun-limbers and G.S. wagons. Now and again a revolver shot as the drivers put some poor wounded horse out of his misery. The killing and wounding of horses is one of the most detestable phases of war and one we'll never get hardened to, tough though we are.

Out along the tracks and in amongst the nearest gun positions, we see stretcher parties at work, moving about, collecting the dead for hasty burial. Dead men are lying in rough rows in the snow near the big burial ground, lying waiting for all that's to come to them now. And for what do they wait? A few short prayers spoken by a strange padre and a grave in the Somme mud. The Somme mud may take your brave bodies from us, boys, but neither mud, time nor distance will efface the memory of your mateship. Yesterday, mates of men. Today, 'fallen comrades', but mates still in the minds of mates.

Midday finds the trench deserted. The men are curled up in the dugouts sleeping. Afternoon sees a few wandering, yarning, arguing or small parties playing poker or rummy. Others are letter writing; others sleep on, oblivious to all.

I see young Jacko and another lad from the new reinforcement wandering about between the support trenches, so I join them. Old Fritz bayonets, a few pounds of shrapnel pellets, nose-caps of shells, flattened Fritz copper-clad machine-gun bullets and all kinds of useless stuff which I tell them to pelt away.

'Hey, Nulla, there's a pair of pretty decent rubber knee boots over there. No one seems to own them,' Jacko tells me.

'Get hold of them then. They're worth seizing onto. Hard to get hold of too. Where are they?'

'Over here a bit. I'll show you.' And he hopefully leads us to where a pair of rubber boots are sticking up, upside down, in the snow.

'Just about my fit too.' And he grabs one, but it won't budge as it appears to be stuck in the snow. He gives another tug and then lets it go as if it were red hot and reels back, looking pretty sheepish, as the realisation breaks upon him that the boots are on a man – a dead man – buried under the snow and mud.

Back to the trench we watch a game of two-up in progress. The spinner stands over a blanket spread in the mud. The ringkeeper gets him set and the two pennies float up to turn, turn, turn and drop down onto the blanket. The game goes on. Men's heads go up and down, up and down, following the flight of the pennies like chickens into hot soup.

Night settles down once more and the men wander away on fatigues carrying picks and shovels for grave digging for our 'fallen comrades'.

I get sent back to brigade to guide up a padre who is to bury the men killed here last night. As I lead the padre on towards the cemetery, he yarns about all manner of things. He seems a pretty decent sort of bloke, though a little too jammy in speech to become over popular with our crowd. They will stand a lot of anything, but very little of anything that they look upon as affectation.

I land the padre at the cemetery where a long row of shallow graves are dug. Near each open grave lies the body of an Australian soldier. A few are sewn up in grey blankets. Others just lie there in their muddy uniforms, waiting to go to their muddy beds. Into each grave a body is lowered. The men nearby stand to attention. A few of them remove their steel helmets and the padre says a brief burial service and passes on to the next, whilst the wet mud is showered in upon the body of an Australian lad.

C'est la guerre!

Hard livers, hard doers – yet there's a tightening of jaws, a treading softly through the muddy lanes between the graves and a hushed seriousness over all tonight. A communing between man and Maker, unspoken, unproclaimed by lip, but our innermost hearts are furrowed by grief for mates gone west.

Still along the row of waiting graves we follow the chaplain's muffled dirge. Men stoop, rise and lower into a grave a gunner clad only in breeches and singlet.

'Cripes, mate, you'll sleep cold tonight,' a man remarks as he tenderly straightens the poor broken body in its grave of mud. There's nothing irreverent or callous or frivolous in the remark. It's just familiarity, the sorrowful, friendly familiarity of the sad side of soldiering.

The last man has been lowered by the hands of his countrymen into his last resting place, and the padre follows me back to the brigade. We two move in silence; how else could we go after the last couple of hours?

Over and over in my thoughts run the lines of the blind digger, Tom Skeyhill.

Halt! Thy tread is on heroes' graves,
Australian lads lie sleeping below;
Just rough wooden crosses at their heads

To let their comrades know.
They'd sleep no better for marble slabs,
Nor monuments so grand,
They lie content, now their day is done
In that far-off foreign land.

So sings the poet; please God, may he be right! Tonight alone we have forty fine Australian lads in rest in the mud of a far-off foreign land.

Soldier rest, thy warfare o'er
Dream of fighting fields no more,
Sleep the sleep that knows not breaking,
Morn of toil nor night of waking.

[Sir Walter Scott]

So long, Digs, So long!

SEVEN

Straightening the Line

Last night we moved up from the huts at Mametz and took over the support lines from the 14th Battalion. We effected the relief quite early and, except for a party that had to go back to Delville Wood to dig out a useless tank that had fallen through into an old Fritz dugout, we had a quiet night. No fatigue parties were sent out and we became suspicious that we were being given a rest, not out of kindness, but to have us fresh for some stunt when we get into the front line tonight.

Today was ushered in with the usual morning wake-up shelling from Fritz batteries searching for our artillery lines. We are lying in cold, cramped dugouts getting off letters, for some perhaps the last letters to their loved ones, and it is this depressive knowledge that makes us write so cheerfully. We kid ourselves that we won't be the poor beggars who'll be killed this trip. It's this ability to camouflage our fear from our innermost selves that saves our self-respect before our mates and saves many a man from the self-torture of a too lively and vivid imagination. If we could only be inoculated against thinking, how much more bearable this war would be!

The day is done and as the long, cold twilight fades into a colder night, the trench comes to life. Word comes for each man to fill his water bottle from the water cart. Then we get some lukewarm tea and a mess-tin lid of stew made from Maconochie rations that has been made some miles back and is greasy and almost cold, but we're used to little things like that. We collect our rations, stick them in our packs and sit around waiting for the move to the front line.

It gets darker. Out of the darkness behind us emerge our men moving off for the line, and as they pass, a muffled joke tells us we're all in for a stunt tonight but they don't know the details. An hour of fidgety suspense goes by and word is passed along, 'D Company, fall in.' We climb into our equipment and wait, which we're good at. Another message comes along, 'D Company runner report to company headquarters.' That's me so up I trudge off to where a waterproof sheet is stretched across the trench to serve as company headquarters.

The O.C. asks me if I know the way to Switch Trench.

'Yes, Sir.'

'Can you find your way from there to the dump near an old tank on the end of Bull Trench?'

'Yes, Sir.'

'And are you sure of the way from the dump to the sunken road near the big dugouts? It's a pretty dark night and easy to miss the sunken road and walk through into Fritz's lines, you know.'

I assure him I know the way as I was over it all many times when we were in three weeks ago. He seems satisfied, looks at the half-dozen officers and N.C.O.s standing around, then gets down to business and we listen carefully to the battle plan. He asks if the idea is quite clear. We tell him it is. 'Straightening the line', he calls it.

'Now, Nulla, you're to lead B and D companies from here across Switch Trench, then to the dump I just spoke of where Mills grenades will be picked up ready bagged and from there to Fritz's Folly, where the various sections will pick up their guides and the officers in charge of the operation. Further details will be explained by platoon commanders when you reach Fritz's Folly.'

He again asks if all is clear and wishes us 'good luck'. Then he turns the good luck on by fishing out half a demijohn of rum and telling us to wade in. Someone digs up a mess-tin lid and we all get a good issue and go off to our various jobs full of rum and determination.

I have to pass through my mates to find the B Company O.C. and I lead off on my journey with about four hundred men following. We cross Switch Trench, go on to the dump near Bull's Run, get our bombs and then cross a long shell-torn expanse of slushy country where dead men and dead horses lie in all manners of grotesque, mud-encased attitudes.

We slip and slide our swearing way through the mud. All is as black as an infantryman's future. I'm guiding by instinct inherited from my pioneer ancestors. The officer asks if I'm sure we're going in the right direction. I tell him we are going well. He's jumpy and wants to know if I recognise any landmarks so I tell him, 'Yes, plenty of them,' when I recognise none, for on this job it's madness to look for small landmarks that can't be found. I always guide by the distant horizon and when I can't see that, by sense of direction and luck. Sometimes I get off my track, but never admit it for if there's one thing a big mob of men can't stand, it is to be following a guide who they know or suspect is lost. A man's got to be a good liar to get on in our army.

Fritz flares seem to be on three sides of us. We are getting near the line now. It is very quiet. Just a few whizz-bangs spasmodically bursting where the main duckboard track leads back from the line. We go in absolute silence, self-enforced, but very necessary. The old soldiers know how to approach the line and our reinforcements on their first trip in aren't happy enough to kick up a noise. It's strange, but they never seem to march in singing about being on their way to Berlin, like we read about.

We slush on for another ten minutes, during which time I've assured the officer about ten times that we're not lost when, 'Ssh! Halt!' he whispers, grabs my arm and frightens the devil out of me.

'What's that?' he says, pointing through the gloom with one hand and drawing his revolver with the other.

'Four blokes with a stretcher,' I tell him.

'I thought so,' he lies, and seems relieved. I swallow a temptation to tell him I saw them when we were forty yards back.

We reach Fritz's Folly. About twenty guides and officers are running about and whispering for their sections and platoons. Party after party trail off into the black night towards the front line. I make my way up to the front line to find the D Company O.C. Hoping for a rum, all I get is a half-mile trip back to an artillery observation post to make sure their watches have been synchronised and stumble off through the darkness till I find the O.P. As I expected, their watches have been synchronised, as an important detail like this isn't overlooked when our division goes into action.

Back towards the lines I go, but knowing I'm not needed, crawl into an old dugout in the sunken road, have a smoke and get my wind before going up to the front line to find our chaps ready to go over. Each man has his battle-order equipment on, bayonet fixed. He has a sandbag of Mills bombs slung in front with the neck of the bag turned back to give ready access to the grenades. Each third or fourth man has a pair of wire cutters to cut the Fritz barbed wire that the shellfire has missed. Every second man has a spade shoved down his back and nearly all have half a dozen empty sandbags jammed through their equipment somewhere.

Time drags on slowly. Somewhere a Fritz machine-gun opens up, randomly firing into the night. Then one of our Lewis guns gives a few bursts and the silence is split with the hurried savagery of its *rat-tat-tat-tat*. It stops and the silence comes down blacker and more intense than ever. Away on the left a bombardment opens as flares go up in hundreds. Must be a raid or a false alarm for it soon dies down. A few shells are flying overhead to land miles behind the lines, searching for ammunition dumps or to crash onto important crossroads where continuous streams of traffic flow ever onward all night, every night.

Half an hour drags by. A stretcher-bearer comes along the trench with a bag of field dressings. 'Anyone want a spare field dressing?' he whispers. We all know that some of us will want one before long, but keep that to ourselves.

A wave of movement spreads along the trench. It's the stretcher-bearers getting into position behind the men who are to go over so soon. Someone wants to know why they always must parade their stretchers under our noses at moments like these, but most of us are relieved to know they will be following us. Many a time have we heard the desperate pleadings for 'stretcher-bearers!' when none was to be had, the agonised appeal cutting through the crash of the battle with the awful, compelling significance of its urgency. Stay with us this morning, you S.B.s, for very soon your mates will need you as they have never needed man or woman before.

It's very quiet, a quietness that almost unnerves one. Men glance at watches. Five minutes to go! More than one man is silently and earnestly making his peace with God.

The dawn has crept up on us unheralded. We can see dimly across no-man's-land. I glance around me. A man's bottom jaw is quivering. I see a mere boy sickly pale from apprehension. It's his first hop-over and he's living its horrors, just five minutes too soon. Faces are drawn and set as the men wait, inwardly flayed by the nervous tension of the waiting.

A whisper passes along the trench: 'Three minutes to go – get ready.' As the men take a grip on the parapet, those remaining behind place their hands under the attackers' feet in readiness to hoist them over when the word comes.

I move beside our O.C. I must keep near him and follow closely to take his messages or orders back to our battalion commander – or forward to the officers or men ahead should he collect his issue.

It's but seconds now. We stand tensely gripping the trench ready to spring over into no-man's-land. Officers glance right and left. The O.C. has one hand on the trench and his eyes are glued upon his watch.

Whish! Swish! A breathtaking rush of air from hundreds of shells flying overhead! *Bang! Crash!* And the Fritz trenches seem to fairly heave in an inferno of flame and deafening roar as they get the first awful crash of our barrage right upon them!

'Come on!' roars our O.C. and we fly across the parapet as the reverberating boom of our guns reaches us from behind. We run half doubled up across no-man's-land. We hear nothing but the explosions of the roaring crash of our barrage on the trench we are charging flat out for, yet we see men dropping every few yards, dropping to wriggle down into shell holes or to crumble up upon the ground and remain still forever, so we know we are charging through a stream of bullets. Still on we rush till we are within thirty yards of the line of bursting shells. The O.C. gives a wave and down we go flat on the ground. Each man gets a bomb, straightens the pin in his teeth and lies flat on his stomach in the mud or huddled up in a shell hole. The shells crash into the enemy trench only thirty yards ahead. On our right we hear a Fritz machine-gun firing savagely, then the ear-splitting bursts of our Mills grenades.

We know that Number 5 Platoon is meeting with opposition in the sap and fighting it with the bombs.

Another enemy machine-gun opens up from our left and its bullets smack and bite into the mud all around us as we clutch closer to the ground. A fearful crash right overhead and no-man's-land is swept with Fritz shrapnel. Pity help our wounded men now! The air is filled with the swishing drone of enemy machine-gun bullets spraying just behind us. A rush of air, a hair-raising screech of shells and a crashing, shuddering thud as the Fritz S.O.S. barrage comes down savagely upon no-man's-land and our own front line.

We lie in comparative safety as we are so close to the enemy trenches that his shells clear us. We look back at the trench we just left and heave sighs of relief that we aren't in there still. Instinctively we mutter, 'God help the poor beggars left there.'

We've been here only a minute, but it seems ages. Our work is still before us. 'Look out!' someone yells, and there right before us on the enemy trench in the midst of that exploding inferno is a big Fritz officer standing upright with his little automatic savagely spitting at us. A gargled yell comes from my left and four of us jab our rifles and let blaze. The enemy officer momentarily straightens, staggers and falls face down across the parapet he has given his brave life to defend.

I glance to my left. A man is kneeling straight up clutching his collar bone, his steel helmet gone. Blood oozes through his shaking fingers. Suddenly he seems to shudder and goes over backwards dead into a small shell hole, his knees still visible above the rim.

Suddenly our barrage lifts from the enemy trench. No command is given or needed. We fly to our feet and as each man rises, he flings a bomb into the trench then grasps his rifle and, coming to the On Guard position with his fixed bayonet, charges for the trench. We hear our own bombs burst just as we come to it. Down we jump. Several poor, nerve-shattered, trembling Fritz are crouching on the floor. As our shouts galvanise them into action they raise their arms in fear and tremblingly call, '*Kamerad! Kamerad!*' through ashen grey mud-bespattered lips that tremble upon chattering teeth.

We let them be, these poor victims of shellfire. We charge along looking for their dugouts and down each fling our bombs. The pleading cry '*Kamerad!*' comes up from the very bowels of the earth. We yell down the dugouts and up come nerve-shattered men, hands held high. They are afraid to come up, but more afraid to remain in their dugouts as they know that another Mills bomb is likely to come down at any minute. We fight hot and hard.

The enemy trench is smashed badly. It's full of sulphur fumes, and the smell of phosphorus everywhere mingles with the hot, sickly smell of torn and bleeding human flesh. The floor is covered with grey-clad wounded men, dead men and the remains of men. It's ghastly, but we can't do anything but make our shovels fly to build up some sort of protection against the shelling and perhaps the counter-attack we expect. Enemy shells are falling closer, searching for this trench.

Our Lewis gunners are setting up theirs guns in feverish haste lest the counter-attack develop before they are ready to stop it. Every few yards a man is on duty watching the enemy positions to see what is to happen. All spare men are shovelling and digging at breakneck speed to repair the trench. Sandbags are being filled and carried to Lewis gun positions or used to top off the rim of the trench.

'Walking wounded make for the sap on the right,' is the order passed along by word of mouth from man to man. We know that our men have captured the sap. Now we dig on! Mud and perspiration are flying as our shovels bite into that black Somme mud!

'Stretcher-bearers wanted on the left!' is passed along, then 'Stretcher-bearers wanted on the right!' comes the call from the other end. Then a tremendous shout comes high above the noise: 'Where the blazes have those bearers got to?' Seek where the wounded lie thickest and you won't seek in vain, old man! Just now most of our bearers are out in the open behind us, regardless of death and danger to themselves, picking up the men who fell during the advance.

Enemy prisoners collected by our mopping-up party are being shepherded along the trench towards the old sap. Some are wounded and have to be helped along by others. They lose no time and we don't blame them. They were here when our gunners shelled the trench and they have no wish to be still in it if their own guns open up.

The enemy shelling eases off. We see a big batch of prisoners going back across the open towards our second trench. From a dozen points of this trench and from no-man's-land we see our stretcher-bearers making off for the battalion aid post with the more seriously wounded.

'D Company runner wanted on the right,' is passed along. I grab my rifle and make haste along the trench till I find the O.C.

'Tell the colonel that our objective has been taken at very small loss and that hourly reports will be sent back during the morning,' he says.

I dump my rifle near him and tear back across the open, passing half a dozen stretcher parties with their little white rag flags held high for Fritz to see. As I fly past the first stretcher with its burden of suffering I'm told, 'Get to blazes away from us, you flamin' goat.' And I veer off to the left for I know I am a legitimate target for the enemy machine-gunners and snipers and of course have no wish to draw fire upon the stretcher parties.

On I go till a burst of machine-gun bullets goes *phut, phut, phut* into the mud around me. I jump high and dive for the safety of a nearby shell hole. I'm just in it when the gun lets go again, chops the rim of the shell hole, splashing mud on to my hands and face and putting the breeze right up me. I'm now sorry I became a runner, sorry I ever became a soldier at all. I can't stay in this shell hole all day, much as I'd like to. I know that the enemy gunner is on to me and I'm not game to think what might happen if I leave the hole, but I grab my fear hard for I know the colonel is waiting, and brigade and division are waiting for my message. With a bound I am out of the hole and fly to my left as I hear the gun open on me again. Into another shell hole, no pause, up and off to my right again and into another hole.

In my mad haste I have noticed a little sunken water course twenty yards ahead and make straight for it. *Swish! Swish! Swish!* I clench my teeth hard to keep my heart from jumping out and break for the water course. I reach it still unperforated and with a tremendous dive, land hard on my water bottle, nearly breaking my ribs. I roll over and have a drink out of it. I feel better and away I go, crawling for the sap on my elbows, my face just grazing the mud and dragging my legs after me. Even now I'm not too sure whether that Fritz gunner can see me or not.

I reach the sap and soon come to an overturned enemy machine-gun and the paraphernalia that shows this has been a strongly held position. Ten badly smashed Fritz are dead by the gun. Our mob has killed them with bombs. Their uniforms are full of frayed, tattered, uneven holes, just like a moth-eaten blanket.

On towards the trench passing eleven Australian dead. The first six or seven have been killed by enemy bombs as they rushed the gun position while the others have caught machine-gun bullets when charging across the broken part of the trench.

I arrive at our old hop-off trench, ask for the colonel and am told he's now back in the battalion signallers' position in the sunken road. The boys ask how things went with us. I say I don't know, but they have seen seventeen stretcher cases come back and about forty wounded are collected in the sap up behind me so they have heard. They also know that about eighty Fritz prisoners were captured, but their own trench has been badly smashed about and there are about twenty of my own company's men lying dead near the newly won position and I am to tell the colonel we took our objective with small loss. Heaven help an army's sense of proportion!

The shelling has eased down. I eventually reach the communication sap leading back to the sunken road. It's broad daylight now so I fish out a cigarette and light up as I trail down the sap to deliver my message. I find the colonel and give my message. He is surprised the message came through so soon after our capture of the position. 'You didn't lose any time getting down from the line.'

'Not much, Sir,' I grin, remembering that Fritz machine-gun.

'Wait here, runner.' He questions me and gets the brigadier on the phone.

'The stunt is over,' he says, and tells him everything he's just got out of me. The old colonel seems happy.

Over, is it? For some it's over as mortal life goes, poor beggars. Is it over for those who are writhing in the excruciating agony of shattered bones, of torn intestines, of punctured lungs, or shot-off limbs, of bruised and mangled flesh? Is it over for those who will never again walk upright as men, but pass what's left of their suffering lives as cripples – getting their country's sympathy but little else? Is it over for the women who wait and pray and are doomed to long, lonely years ahead with nothing but a memory to cherish and nothing but that memory to comfort them along the road they had so hoped to tread with their soldier boy? Is it over for the kiddies who'll face life handicapped in so many ways by the loss of their daddy? Colonel, you are mistaken! The stunt isn't over. It's barely begun for those upon whom it falls the heaviest.

The colonel leaves the phone. He calls the adjutant and they hold a consultation with a couple of other officers before the adjutant hands me a couple of pages of written instructions for my O.C. The colonel gives me some advice and tells me to be careful and not to go over the top, but to follow the sap. He doesn't want me to get killed. He places great value on my life when I'm carrying his precious messages. I go a few yards when the old man calls me back. 'Did you place the messages in your left breast pocket?'

'Yes, Sir.' I wheel to get away, but he's not done with me yet. Colonels are like that.

'Why aren't you wearing your red arm-band, your runner's badge?' he enquires.

That gets me into an awkward fix. The runner's badge, a nice four-inch red flannel armlet, was issued to me when we were coming into the line only three weeks ago, as the old man is aware. His memory is good, too flamin' good to be comfortable.

Sensing victory, the colonel doesn't give me time to reply, but gets indignant. 'Do you mean that your O.C. allowed you to come into an important engagement like this as his runner without your distinctive badge?' He snorts, just like the colonels I've read about.

He is working himself up needlessly and I'd so hate to see him become upset, with me especially. He mutters something that ends on a note of impatience: 'Utter negligence!' My company O.C. has got me out of more than one scrape and I'm not going to get him in the soup if I can help it, so I tell the colonel, 'I can swear that I was wearing my badge when we hopped over this morning, Sir.'

'Oh, well that's a different matter, lad,' he says. 'Must have worked loose during the engagement.' And he asks the adjutant to send a requisition for a fresh badge to be sent to D Company with the rations tonight. The colonel is sorry he was unjustly snappy and though he doesn't admit it, pats me on the shoulder and says, 'Well, so long, Nulla, get your message through, lad.'

We part the best of friends. I trudge on for the line wondering if he'd be so friendly if he knew that I'm still wearing my runner's badge where I wore it when we hopped over this morning – as a patch across the seat of my underpants.

By now it's a nice bright day and as Fritz snipers are good on clear days, I obey the colonel's instructions and follow the communication sap to our old hop-off trench and then the newly won sap to Hoop Trench.

I've been gone only an hour but our chaps have made a wonderful difference to the captured trench. The wounded men have all been returned to the rear. Those the stretcher-bearers couldn't handle were taken back slung in Fritz blankets, found in their dugouts and carried by four Fritz prisoners. A blanket makes a good stretcher until some coot drops his corner and spills the load in the mud.

The Fritz prisoners and wounded have gone back too. Their dead have been thrown back over the trench and earth shovelled on to them to help build up the parapet. It's not good burial but it's good warfare and that's our job just now. We're not undertakers.

Our men are still digging. Our machine-guns are set up along the trench. Fire steps are being made by each man while others dig narrow cuts into the trench wall to crawl into if the enemy guns open on us. We don't dig deep dugouts because although they give protection, they can so easily become deathtraps. And the false sense of security they give is no good as it saps our morale and interferes with our fighting efficiency.

I find the O.C. and deliver the messages. He reads them – 'Nothing to go back, yet' – so I wander along the trench. Every few yards a man is peeping out across no-man's-land, trying to look as much like the mud as he can. That's not difficult either. The men on the lookout plaster their helmets with mud and cautiously raise their heads until their eyes just peer over the rim of the trench. Some scratch little peep holes through the parapet. To see and not be seen is our watchword and safeguard.

I prowl along to find many men I knew well have been killed. Many more wounded. I can't make it out for I thought we reached the trench with much lighter loss. I know Fritz didn't put up a fight and his shelling was not very severe, and find that about thirty men on the left of the advance were hit as we neared the barbed wire. The men say that the machine-gun that got them is still out on the left somewhere. They have been trying all day to spot its position.

Away towards the left of the trench I find my own section. Yacob has collected a wound, a bullet through the skin, and has been taken away to the rear. Lucky cow! Painful wound, no doubt, but what's a bit of pain when it means a spell from the nerve-racking turmoil and the uncertainty of life here? A clean bed. Clean clothes. Decent tucker. No chats. Real sleep in a real bed and most likely a trip to England.

A message is passed along the trench that the O.C. wants me. Back I go.

'Find Lieutenant Breen, please.'

Along the trench I go till I come across Mr Breen. 'The O.C. would like to see you for a minute, Sir.'

'What the blazes is up with him now?' replies Breen, who is busy helping the signallers scratch out a hole in the wall of the trench for their field phone. I hope they get their phone in working order soon. It saves on runners.

Lieutenant Breen and I reach the O.C. who asks him to take charge of the line as he wants to go back and see the colonel. I go with the O.C. and we slush along knee deep in mud down the captured trench, passing dead Fritz in their old gun position.

'Tell the sergeant of 15 Platoon to have these Jerries tossed out of the sap when you get back.'

'Goodo,' I reply.

Down the slushy sap we trudge, reach Fritz's Folly and find the colonel and his battalion headquarters staff all in a great dugout some engineers have built. We sit down and have a cup of café au lait in little coffee tins, which we thoroughly enjoy.

The colonel and officers do a great deal of talking. Every now and again the phone rings and interrupts them. Mostly someone back on brigade or division wanting to know something. The officers get worked up. Maps and field notebooks come out. They get on to talking of picks and shovels and spare men and putting out strong covering parties. Something in the nature of another stunt is brewing so I curl up on a heap of old damp bags and go to sleep. I've had one night without any sleep and by the talk going on there will be more stoush than sleep tonight.

It wouldn't be such a bad war, so far as wars go, if we could only get more sleep. Sleep is Nature's way of providing rest and recuperation for overworked nerve cells and fatigued muscles. After the past twenty-four hours I feel that I am just a heap of unstrung, overworked muscles, held together by will-force and muddied skin.

I pull my steel helmet down over my tired eyes and a few weighty wet bags across my tired legs and let them win the war all on their own, as I succumb to sleep. Wonderful sleep, the soldier's restorative shield against the dangers to brain and body of our unnatural life.

EIGHT

A Night in the Line

I've had an hour's sleep when the O.C. drums his great wet boot along my ribs and I wake up. That's the worst of being touchy about the ribs.

'When you're ready, Nulla, we'll push along.' He smiles.

I'm not ready. In fact I am anything but ready, but we push along all the same. It's like that in the army.

As we slip and slither along the sap, he tells me of what's on tonight. It appears that the brilliant strategists back at army headquarters are not happy because Fritz didn't counter-attack in an endeavour to retake the trench we won this morning or even try to shell us out of the position, just out of hate or petulancy at losing the slushy sepulchre we now call Hoop Trench. They feel that an attack will be launched on us and as we are occupying a former Fritz position, they know he has its range to an inch and can blow us to smithereens whenever he decides to do so. Therefore it has been decided that we shall advance our whole line fifty yards by going out tonight and digging in on a new line across no-man's-land.

Everything is set. Fritz is back in trenches three hundred yards away. The present front line will be held by a skeleton force tonight whilst the rest of the battalion, helped by the Pioneers, will go out and dig in on the new line. Bombs, picks and shovels, Lewis gun magazines and barbed wire are to be picked up at the sunken road after dark.

We reach our trench. The O.C. finds a seat on an old Fritz machine-gun belt box. 'Nick along and ask the officers to come to me.'

I nick along as well as a man can nick when at every step he sinks over his boot tops. I find the officers and send them along. The briefing lasts quite a while and ends by two officers and three sergeants being sent back to battalion headquarters for coaching in the coming stunt.

The O.C. spends the afternoon wandering along the trench putting the men wise to the attack ahead. The Fritz machine-gun that fired on us during the advance this morning is still out there somewhere on our left front. It sends a burst along our parapet every now and again. It's got the O.C. worried and us too. He wants its position located, but somehow doesn't seem to have time to go out into no-man's-land to look for it himself.

I follow the O.C. along the trench. We reach 14 Platoon where my mates are holding a rifle post. Just four of them here: Longun, Dark, Snow and the Prof. Our little crowd is beginning to dwindle with Farmer and Yacob away wounded.

The O.C. talks to the men and tells us he'll give ten days' leave to England to the man who spots the position of that Fritz gun. As the O.C. gets his smelly old pipe alight, we wander back along the trench. The men are having their tea of bully beef and biscuits, stale bread and jam out of the inevitable cigarette tin. Here and there we spot a lump of cheese. Hard dry tucker, washed down with water. We come to one crowd eating some buttery-looking stuff out of little blue cardboard boxes, which they found in a Fritz dugout and say it's butter though it might be boot grease for all they know.

We reach the signallers. They give us some black wizened-up sausage they found hidden on the top of a Fritz gas-respirator tin. The sausage looks all right but doesn't taste too pure as the Fritz had carried some cigars in the respirator cavity along with the sausage.

The phone rings. A signaller pokes the headphones towards the O.C. who adjusts them and says 'yes' seven times into the mouthpiece, then to me, 'Better get some scran into you and report to the colonel.' As an afterthought he adds, 'See if you can get a revolver and some cartridges for me when you're back at H.Q.'

I leave him and clean up a tin of Maconochie rations I have in my pack, one I souvenired from the H.Q. cooks this morning.

Just on dark, I reach battalion H.Q. and tell the colonel I've been sent to report to him.

'Just wait around here and I'll call you when I am ready.' Then he asks if I have had anything to eat lately. 'Not much, Sir.' And I'm sent to the H.Q. cooks who fix me up with a good hot meal. They want to know if there's any chance of getting them a Fritz pistol or watch or a pair of field glasses. That's the worst of being left out of hop-overs. You don't get the chance to collect the things you want, but then again you don't run the risk of collecting a lot of things you don't want.

I spot the colonel mooching about and give him my O.C.'s request for a revolver and cartridges. He gets a big revolver and some cartridges from somewhere and gives them to me.

'Good revolver, that; you should carry one too.' He warms up. 'They're NSW Police Department issue. I'll see if I can get one for you. You mustn't get into that careless habit of going about unarmed.'

I don't want his police revolver. They're too hard to pull off. My mate Snow had one at Grease Trench and had it on a patrol when a big Fritz private bayonet charged him. Snow saw the Fritz but he fired about a yard over the Fritz's head and would have been skewered only for Longun's sudden rifle shot from the hip. After this, Longun announced he was fed up with being a lifesaver and that if any more of us wanted to carry those revolvers, we had better take a copper along with us to fire the dashed thing.

It's dark. An hour goes by and about fifty men are now collected under the rim of the sunken road and loaded up with coils of barbed wire and screw pickets. Another half hour and a Pioneer Battalion comes along loaded with picks and shovels, wearing battle order equipment and carrying rifles. It's not often that the Pioneers have the chance to get out in front of our lines, but they'll have it tonight all right. The Pioneers have two Lewis gun crews, supplied by battalions in reserve.

Word comes along, 'Runner Nulla wanted,' so I make down the steps of the big dugout to where the colonel is very busy completing arrangements for the operation. The major of our battalion is also here, having landed back today from leave in England. What a day to get back! He's in tailor-made riding strides and good humour.

'Righto, Nulla, you're my bird,' he says and we go and hunt up the officers in charge of the wiring party and the pioneers. Then, like a long black muddied snake, we wind our way up Eve Alley to the front line, though the going is difficult. We reach the front line and I lead them over the open till they are strung out behind our trench. Suddenly a Fritz machine-gun sends a long burst just over our trench and all drop down in the mud.

I leave the parties and guide the major along till we find the company O.C. A few minutes talking and the O.C. turns to me. 'I'd like you to attach yourself as runner to Lieutenant Breen. You'll find him with 6 Section, 14 Platoon.'

That's my own mob so along I go to hunt them up.

I find the boys and Mr Breen but I'm not so happy when Breen says, 'Come on, we've been waiting for you – we're going out after that enemy machine-gun.' And hands me a bag of bombs. 'Here, get a grip on some of these.' I ram as many as I can into my pockets and get a rifle from the next post, see it's fully loaded, take its bayonet off and we're ready.

A few instructions from Mr Breen and we crawl out into no-man's-land. We steer half left, crawling one behind the other. Mr Breen leads and I follow. Each time he stops I give his foot a firm, gentle push and feel Longun push on my boot. I know we are keeping contact so far.

On we crawl. It's slow, nervy work. Each man lies his flattest in the mud and slush, silently reaches forward to almost full arm's length and holding his rifle clear of the mud digs his elbow into the ground and silently draws his body up to his elbows. Every now and again a Fritz flare goes up. We hear it and prop still as statues as the flare reaches its highest point and bursts into a flood of light. The place is brilliantly lit up. We lie in a sea of light, half-expecting Fritz to spot us and open fire any minute. We don't move, not a twitch for we know that unless we make a movement, it isn't very likely they'll see us. The flare starts to burn out and begins to fall to the ground, gathering speed as it does so and great black shadows like the wings of death fly across the mud in all manner of shivering shapes. The flare goes out. It is now blacker than ever and on we go till the hissing of another ascending flare halts our progress.

On and on we go. Slowly, but in deadly earnest. We are looking for a death-dealing machine-gun and its four or five men. All we know is that it is somewhere ahead. In a shell hole we surmise: there are thousands of shell holes of which we only want one. If any of us are to get back again we must get close enough to heave our bombs upon the gun crew and charge them before they see us, or it's 'good night, Nurse' for us.

As we move over the ground, we're all peering through the darkness trying to locate that gun. We strain our ears hoping against hope for a sound to guide us. Each man has a bomb ready in his hand. The tension is terrific.

Still we crawl on, to death – our own or Fritz's. I have one eye on Mr Breen who has his eyes glued on his watch. Dead silence. From away in the distance we can hear the *chut-chut-chut* of a Fritz machine-gun firing from a mile or two behind his lines. Its sound stops and we hear the *swish, swish* of its bullets going high overhead. We know the gun is a long way off for its sound is beating the bullets to us.

A few more crawls and Mr Breen's foot turns sideways and just touches the ground twice. I pass the signal on to Longun, he on to Dark, to Snow, to the Prof. How we flatten out now! How our eyes peer through the gloom in every direction! We're watching and waiting. Every nerve, every sense on the *qui vive*. Then it comes – *rat-a-tat-tat-tat* – our Lewis gun firing over our heads in an endeavour to kid our quarry to retaliate, thereby exposing its position. Nothing happens. Then we hear a metallic click and a muffled guttural voice just to our right front. That sound is registered on every fibre of our keyed-up bodies!

Again our gun fires. A longer burst. We know from its sound that it is sweeping the length of the enemy trench.

A twitch, a suppressed shudder, and we feel our blood fairly scorch the underlayer of our cold, clammy skins as *Crack! Crack! Crack!* bursts in our very eardrums as the Fritz gun lets go, barely thirty yards ahead to our right. We relax. We're not in his line of fire or vision. The gods have been kind to us tonight. We have crossed his line of fire and are in a good position to get behind him when we might so easily have crawled right up to his cruel muzzle. We're thirty yards from him when we expected to be eighty.

No more reflecting. All is forgotten in our determination to get that gun crew. Fritz fires again and we crawl away to get behind him. The firing stops and so do we. We've made another ten yards. Still as death we lie, but watching, ever watching in the direction from where we saw the streaming flow of flashes as Fritz fired their gun.

Lieutenant Breen beckons. I slide silently up to him. A faint whisper, 'No bombs. We'll rush them. Tell the others.' I see Breen silently cock his revolver. I crawl back to each man and give the order. Each is grim as he bends the pin in his grenade and places it quietly back in his pocket. I hold my cocked rifle under each man's face and each nods and sees to his rifle. I crawl back to Mr Breen.

We worm our way on for another six or seven yards. A flare goes up. Our eyes burn into the enemy gunners. We are lying flat on the ground and can just make out our four Fritz calmly sitting there with their backs towards us.

Again Mr Breen beckons. I crawl up and Longun slides up on his right. He just goes to wave Dark and Snow when a Fritz gives a humorous grunt and drops down behind the gun. The other three Fritz sink lower into the mud as the gun blazes into action with a hard *Crack! Crack! Crack!* We know the chance may never come again and as Fritz fires, the three of us leap to our feet and charge, our rifles pointing straight for those three backs just a dozen yards or so ahead. As we bound forward we hear Snow's excited, 'At 'em!' as he and Dark put in their rush followed by the Prof.

Our noise is drowned by the gun's own firing and we are almost on to the gunners before they hear us. The first gets Longun's rifle jabbed into his back just as hard as Longun can jab it. Flat out he goes with his back almost broken and Longun lands hard upon the small of the fellow's back with his two great feet burying the Fritz into the mud, whilst down comes the muzzle of Longun's rifle upon the Fritz's neck.

I just about reach my man when he spins, seeing me and Breen almost on him. Quick as lightning and with the fear of death hard upon him, his hands fly above his head and '*Kamerad!*' jumps from his mouth. He's just in time, too, for I've already taken the pressure upon the trigger and my rifle is barely a foot from his side. I hear an hysterical scream – '*Kamerad!*' – on my right and know the lieutenant too has made a capture, and as I swing my barrel to miss my man I see the gunner low down in the hole beside his gun make a dive to his left for something.

I'm the nearest to him and with a bound I land in the shell hole beside him. He's already half up. I realise he means to fight and with my utmost speed sweep my rifle for him and press the trigger. *Bang!* And the flame strikes him across the arm and shoulder. My shot seems to lift his body a foot into the air. '*Mein Gott!*' he gasps and sags to his knees. There's no time to reload, and my bayonet isn't fixed, so I sweep my barrel hard at his head and it catches him across the neck and he goes over backwards, whilst Darky, fighting mad, lands amongst us and jabs his rifle into the man's side.

We've got them. I hurriedly work my bolt to eject the spent cartridge and reload. *Clat-clat-clip-click!* goes the bolt and to us it seems as if the noise can be heard in Berlin.

'Steady!' whispers Breen. 'Get 'em up and search 'em.'

Longun motions with his rifle and the fellow he knocked rises shivering like a leaf and Snow smacks at the man's belt and pockets looking for pistols or bombs. He doesn't carry a pistol, but raises his leg towards Snow who fishes out a long, murderous trench dagger from the fellow's boot top. The Prof gets busy on the two Fritz who surrendered when we made our rush. They have nothing much, but the Prof grabs a bag of egg bombs that one fellow had slung round his back.

The man I shot lies moaning. Darky bends towards him and the man raises his left arm, and rubs and squeezes his arm below the shoulder. I feel sorry for the poor wretch as I realise I have probably shattered his arm. Dark and I prop him up. He looks at me and a faint smile shows for a fleeting moment in the light of a flare as he points under his legs. I rake around under him with my boot and find a big automatic pistol. I grab it and know by its weight that it is fully loaded. I feel along it. The safety catch is off. I realise what a narrow squeak I've had and no longer feel anyway upset about getting in first.

Flares are now going up in dozens. Fritz have heard my shot and are becoming anxious. We all crouch low expecting a shower of Fritz bullets at any moment. A fierce clatter and our own Lewis guns, three of them, are splitting the night as they pour burst after burst into the parapet of the enemy trench. We are relieved for we know that will keep a few inquisitive heads down till we make our escape. We know our gunners have heard my shot and are doing all they can to stand by us and thrill to the comradeship of our mates on the Lewis guns. It seems an age, but we have been in this machine-gun nest barely two minutes.

'We'll make a break. That firing'll hide our noise,' says Breen.

I sling my rifle over my shoulder and poke my Mauser pistol in my belt after ensuring the safety catch is on. I'd hate to shoot myself just now.

Mr Breen has been fooling about with the enemy gun. He's pretty good on machine-guns. 'We'll take the gun,' says he. 'Someone guard those men, the rest come here.' I whip out my Mauser and stand over the four prisoners who are quite inoffensively crouched on the edge of the hole. A few curt directions from Mr Breen, and Snow and the Prof climb out of the hole carrying the heavy machine-gun while Breen has the gun's tripod draped over his neck. The Prof still has the bag of egg bombs slung over his shoulder.

A pause till two flares die down. 'Lead on,' Mr Breen tells me and, Mauser in hand and doubled in half, I strike out for our trench. I go half left, half a dozen steps, when *Bang! Hiss . . . Sss!* A flare goes up. *Phut!* And it bursts into light. We all prop still until it drops into a muddy shell hole and then go on running, heads bent, like lost geese through long grass. Another flare and we prop again. 'All there?' I whisper back. From behind I hear the creak of the prisoners' equipment and the water rattling in the cooling chamber of their gun, and above the muffled moan of the wounded Fritz comes Mr Breen's 'All set. Keep on going.'

The flare drops and we're off again. I keep straining my eyes and ears, trying to locate our trench. Suddenly I see the stabbing jets of flame as one of our Lewis guns lets go. Goodo, if I work a little to the left we'll be on a direct line for our trench. A few more short runs between flares. Fritz isn't firing near us as he doesn't yet know we've lifted his gun and gunners.

Another flare. I glance back. Snow and Prof are behind me carrying the gun. A Fritz comes next with the gun's tripod round his neck and carries a box of machine-gun-bullet belts. Longun has another ammunition box. Then come two Fritz supporting their wounded comrade.

Dark, rifle in hand, is on one side and Mr Breen with his revolver as the prisoners brings up the rear.

As we near our trench we stop running and walk quietly. We all know of occasions when patrols have been fired on by their own men and we're not running any risks. We get within about sixty yards of our trench when Mr Breen calls me, so I slip back to him. 'You'd better go ahead and let them know we are coming in.'

'Yes, Sir.' And I head off for our trench. I know what's on his mind. Thinks some windy coot may hear us and open fire. Likely, too, as the men have been warned to expect a counter-attack tonight. Of course, it is better that only one man be exposed to that risk than the whole patrol. Be far better still if I wasn't that one man, but that can't be helped so on I go. Twenty yards and I get down and crawl very quietly towards our trench. I can hear voices. They come clearly across the ground to me. I hate approaching our trenches from no-man's-land at night almost as much as I hate leaving them. It's dangerous too. I lie still. The hum of whispered talk increases. I give a low whistle. The talking stops abruptly. Heads show above the rim of the parapet. I hear rifles sliding through the mud. I give another low whistle. 'Who's that?' comes from the trench.

'It's me,' I answer back. That's not correct parade-ground answering, I know. The Prof would say it's not correct English, either, but it's near enough English for our mob to know it's not Fritz.

'Come on,' someone calls.

Up I jump and walk onto the parapet.

'Patrol and prisoners coming in. Pass it on,' I say, and to left and right I hear the message being passed. I sit on the parapet, trying to locate the rest of the patrol. Hurried footsteps through the slush of the trench, and the O.C. and the major rush up.

'Who's that? Nulla, is it?'

'Yes, Sir.'

'You've got some prisoners. Who'd you get? The gun crew? We heard a shot. Anyone hurt?'

'Yes, Sir. Got four men and the gun too. We winged a Fritz. None of us hurt.'

'Great work, great work,' says the major.

'Here they come,' a man calls, and the patrol enters the trench. The O.C. congratulates us on what they reckon is fine work. The officers are particularly glad we landed some live prisoners as they say information is badly needed.

The captain tells us, 'You men remain on your post tonight. You're relieved from all other duties. Be sure to tell the C.S.M. if he details you for wiring or other fatigues tonight.' He can rest assured that we won't be backward in telling the C.S.M. that.

The major turns to Mr Breen. 'Be as well if you went down now and made your report to the colonel. Take the runner with you and you could take the Fritz along. We're going out in front in an hour's time. If you hurry, you might be back in time for the fun.'

'Blast the fun. We've had all the fun we want for one night,' Mr Breen tells him.

Then he beckons the four Fritz and the six of us to make for the sunken road, which is not far so we hurry along and soon reach it. The prisoners seem quite resigned to their fate and hurry on with us though the wounded man is becoming weak.

'Mind these coves here for a minute.' And Mr Breen, poking his revolver in its muddy holster, clambers down the slippery steps of the big dugout as a crowd gathers round the prisoners.

'Where'd you get 'em? Out of a tin of bully beef?' puts in one chap, an A.M.C. sergeant. I'm an infantry private and fed up with it, so I rejoin, 'No. Found them under a bed in a base hospital, forty miles behind the line.' It's an uncalled for reply, but these night patrols aren't soothing powders for frayed tempers.

The sergeant goes to market properly and another war is brewing, but Mr Breen's 'Righto, Nulla, bring 'em down' stops hostilities and I shoo the Fritz down the dugout steps ahead of me where all eyes are upon them.

'Fifty francs for the automatic,' says the adjutant. I grin and shove it in my top pocket as I see everyone eyeing it off.

'Let me have a look at it,' requests the colonel, and I hand it over, telling him, 'She's loaded, Sir.'

Four or five officers swoop down upon it. They all would like it. The signal officer looks at the adjutant and me. 'I'll raise you fifty,' he laughs. The medical officer, busy cutting away the scorched sleeve from the Fritz's wounded arm looks up. 'For the first and second, third and last time, going, going –'

'Gone!' laughs the colonel as he passes it back to me. Mr Breen explains how I got it and how close I went to sampling its contents.

'No wonder the boy doesn't feel like parting with it,' remarks the colonel, when we are interrupted by a sergeant coming in. He has been sent for and can speak Fritz fairly well. The sergeant examines the numbers on the prisoners' uniforms and tells the colonel what regiment they are from as the adjutant writes it down. The doctor gives the Fritz a cigarette each from the adjutant's tin of smokes and strikes a match for them to light up. He again adjusts the bandage on the wounded man and gives him an anti-tetanus injection and a drink of water.

'Pass my tin of cigarettes back,' says the adjutant to the signal officer, 'before he does any more healing with them. I'm not buying smokes for the Fritz army as well as for all you bods.'

The sergeant begins to make funny noises at the Fritz and they all seem to get on well, having a great yarn. A clatter on the steps, the blankets that hang down across the entrance part and a Pioneer officer and two corporals come in. They carry three or four rolls of nice white tape, and the officer tells the colonel that he has been sent up to assist in laying the tapes for the new trench and asks for directions.

They get busy for a few minutes over a map then the colonel calls, 'Nulla, I have a run for you.'

'Yes, Sir.'

'This runner will guide you to the major up in the front line.'

'Thank you, Sir. Good-night.'

'Good-night, and good luck,' floats after us as we climb up the steps, setting out for the front line.

It is too boggy in the sap so we go straight across country for our trench. It's as black as pitch. It's generally like that. The moon seems to shine only when we don't want it.

'Where'd those Fritz prisoners come from?' a corporal wants to know and I tell him about our patrol. The officer reckons he's glad he's not in the infantry if that's the sort of stunts we come at.

'You were in the infantry once, were you, Sir?'

'Yes, I was in the 13th Battalion, but got put into the Pioneers. You see I was in my last year of Engineering at Sydney University so they evidently thought I'd be an expert on a pick and shovel.'

We reach the trench, chock full of men: the Pioneers, the wiring party, all jammed together. What a terrible carnage there would be if the enemy shelled the trench now! Nearly every man in it realises this and is anxious to be out. The four of us wander along the top of the trench till we find the major.

'Glad you're here. We're waiting for those tapes and we'll get them down as soon as you are ready,' he greets the Pioneer officer. It's now getting on for midnight and very cold and quiet. The major and others with a load of little wire pegs, make out into no-man's-land and silently fade into the night.

Twenty minutes drag by. The machine-gun sergeant comes back and a few orders are whispered along the trench. Some shoving and bumping and eight Lewis gun crews climb over the top of the parapet. The O.C. is going with them so I go too.

We wander about sixty yards out where a little white tape is zig-zagging across the mud. Black moving lumps show up here and there – our men. The O.C. and I wander along till we find the major and the Pioneer officer. The machine-gun sergeant collects three crews and we follow the tape along till we come to some men of the 47th Battalion, holding the line on our right. 'We go from here about fifty yards and join up onto our own trench,' they tell us. 'The men are already digging the end of the trench of our section. We have some listening posts and three guns out in front.'

The O.C. tells the gunner sergeant, 'Place your right-hand gun forty yards out. Your guns will be at intervals of sixty yards. Your men all know the recall signal – three short bursts followed by a long one from the gun in Hoop Trench?'

'Yes, Sir. They know it.' He turns to a gun crew. 'Step forty yards dead ahead and get your gun set up. Our next gun will be sixty yards on your left, and in line with you. No patrols are out so any movement in front will be the enemy. Remember, no firing unless you have a definite target. The enemy line will be over a hundred and fifty yards ahead of you. If Fritz hears the digging, they'll send patrols out but you mustn't let them through. Listening posts will be established between each gun. If all's clear, you can push out.'

A gun team goes ahead into the night to protect the digging party from an enemy raid. The gunner sergeant ties some tape to a little peg and sticks it in the ground a few yards ahead of the tape line and tells the O.C. he is marking the position of each gun in that way.

'You go with Sergeant Case, Nulla, and report to me immediately all guns are out. I'll be somewhere on the tape line.'

'Very well, Sir.' And I follow the gunner sergeant as he steps sixty yards along the tape. He pauses and sends his second team out. On he goes, as methodical as if on parade. That's discipline, the discipline that really counts. Eventually the sergeant gets all eight guns out and I hurry back and find the O.C. With him is a bunch of men carrying rifles. He asks me if I know where the guns are set up.

'Sergeant Case put each gun forty yards out from the pegs,' I tell him.

'Think you can place a listening post midway between each gun?'

'I'll have a go.'

'That's the idea. We should be digging now. Be as quick as you can. Get these men out and report to me in Hoop Trench.' He turns to the men, 'Remember to establish contact with the gun on either side of you as soon as you can. Don't get ahead of the guns, and let no one through. Send one man back immediately you hear anything suspicious out in front.'

The men follow me to the sergeant's first peg. I step thirty yards along the peg, stop and ask, 'Who's first?' Three chaps come over. 'We're Number 1 Post,' they say, and I tell them, 'Step forty yards out, and no further.'

'That's easy enough,' a man replies, 'but what about this getting in touch with the guns? How do we find them out there in the dark?'

'The guns will be only thirty yards on each side of you and won't be hard to find.'

Number 1 Post goes out. On we travel till I find the sergeant's second peg. Then I step my thirty yards. 'Number 2 Post?' And up come three men from the little mob following me. 'All set?'

'Sure.' And out they go.

On I go till all seven listening posts are out, then strike across for Hoop Trench. I wander along till I find the O.C. and report all posts are out.

'Good. Quick work. Here, have a sip.' And he offers me his water bottle. I have a sip all right. I have several sips all rolled into one and it's not water, either, but good old S.R.D. rum. I begin to feel it's not such a bad war after all.

'This way,' he calls and we wander along and find a group of officers. The Pioneer officer, Lieutenants Brew and Breen and two strange officers, who I guess are in charge of the wiring party.

The O.C. turns to Mr Breen. 'Take over this position, Ern.'

'Goodo,' replies Mr Breen.

'Get your men into it, gentlemen,' he tells the other officers. 'With me, Nulla.' And I trail after him to the tape line where a number of men are scattered about. He speaks to the 47th Battalion men and we silently make our way straight ahead into no-man's-land.

All is very quiet and eerie. The O.C. draws his revolver, shows it to me and I fish out my big Mauser and shove the safety catch off. Side by side we move forward. Just to our left I spot one of our tin hats and we sneak up. The gunners have heard our approach and are watching us. We drop down into the shell hole with them. The O.C. yarns for a while and asks where Number 5 listening post is. A gunner points into the utter darkness and tells us, 'Over that way, somewhere.'

We leave the gunners and veer a little to our left to avoid approaching the post from the front and soon find it. Down drops the O.C. for another few words and on again, from listening post to machine-gun post, until we reach the last gun then back along our outpost line. Behind we hear the faint sound of digging. Now and again there comes a metallic click as two shovels meet. 'Blasted careless fools,' growls the O.C.

An odd flare goes up from the enemy lines. Desultory firing by the artillery is going on all along the front. 'Firing on map reference positions,' comes the O.C.'s whisper.

We reach Number 1 gun and tack along the lonely line we patrol. The way is familiar to us now and the men lying and listening there in the cold, freezing mud seem to welcome our little visits. For two more hours we patrol the outposts. 'Wonder how they are getting on?' I venture, thinking of our new trench and wishing I was in it.

'This is great. Another hour and the men should be done,' comes the O.C.'s happy whisper. 'Never hoped for such luck as this.'

Such luck as this! This is great! Nothing very great or lucky in having to do three hours' continuous trudging up and down this line of posts. Nevertheless the battalion has been lucky tonight in its work. Fritz must surely be asleep.

Five more minutes of quietly slinking along from post to post and *Crack! Crack! Crack!* We feel we're hit by the savage sound of the gun very close. We drop flat as bullets whistle overhead. I hug the ground as does the O.C., but he chuckles and across the mud comes his whisper, 'Too late to duck when you hear the bullets from a gun that close. Bullets are half a mile on before the sound reaches you.'

The gun stops and we move on again, but more cautiously. Again the gun opens and then silence. Its shots are just skimming the ground. Every few minutes it fires so we get down and crawl on hands and knees from one post to another whilst ever it is firing. Those Fritz aren't going to stop our patrolling unless he stops one of us. Our backs are up, even if the wind's up too, and on and on we move, now walking, now crawling, but moving along all the time.

'Wonder if he smells a rat?' I whisper.

'Wish I could give him a smell of this.' And the captain shakes his revolver as Fritz lets go another burst and we hear a very distinct *pinggg* as a bullet ricochets off a spade or something at the new trench.

Another burst and a sharply cut-off yell of pain from our digging party.

'Blast him! He's got someone!' The Fritz hears the yell and opens up an extra long burst.

The O.C. grabs my arm hard. 'There! Not fifty yards away! I saw the men behind the flash of the gun. Get Corporal Taylor here with his gun as fast as you can.'

Taylor's our crack shot. Up I jump and run to the third post behind me and tell Taylor, 'Quick! Fetch your gun! We can see where he's firing from.'

Taylor's crew grab their gun and follow me. The gun opens again. The bullets stream by our legs and we step high, afraid of stopping one and not game to drop for fear we may collect one in the body. It's a rotten experience this stepping through a shower of bullets, but our luck's in again and somehow no one gets hit.

We reach the captain, and drop down in the mud with him to listen and look for Fritz's gun.

'He heard that yell,' whispers the O.C. 'He'll fire in that direction all night. His shots aren't crossing here. Get your gun steady and sight it on his flashes.'

They mount the gun and the O.C. aims it in the direction of the enemy gun. Then he makes way for Taylor who squats down in the mud behind the Lewis. Another burst during which Taylor is busy sighting at the fiery dancing glow out there in the dark.

'I'm right on to him, Sir.'

'Let him have it next time he fires.' And we sit waiting and watching through the darkness, too keyed up to breathe comfortably. Snowy Taylor is down behind his gun and his crew in position. If Taylor misses, we can expect dozens of enemy bullets fair amongst us here.

'Blast you, Fritz! Open up!' whispers a man, and as if in answer straight away comes *Crack! Crack! Crack!* We are looking at the enemy gun! Behind its jumping glow we can make out three or four men. Isn't Taylor ever going to fire? Fritz will stop and the chance will be gone perhaps forever! Why doesn't he fire? *Bang! Rat-ata-tat-tat* and Taylor's little gun is quivering and jumping and we can actually hear its bullets fairly rattling on the Fritz gun out there in the blackness. Two separate yells – startled, frightened yells of pain – come across above the rattle of Taylor's firing. He pours a whole magazine of bullets in – burst after burst – and stops, and his men change magazines like lightning, but it's all over. Snowy has got that gun fair and square. We're relieved and flushed with excitement.

'Get!' from the O.C., and he and I go on towards Number 1 Post whilst Taylor's crew make back to their post.

As we pass each post, the O.C. warns them to watch out for trench mortars. Flares go up in dozens. Fritz is awake with a vengeance now. Three enemy machine-guns rake no-man's-land. We crouch, huddled in the bottom of a shell hole. 'The trench should be deep enough by now to afford protection,' says the O.C., thinking of the big digging party out there in the open.

Crash! Crash! And two flashes of livid flame erupt forty yards ahead in no-man's-land. 'His trench mortars. Just what I expected. Won't hurt us if he pelts a hundred out there.' And we hear the droning roar of more *minenwerfers* coming over. We can track them by their sparks. The ground thuds and shivers under the fearful explosion of a dozen or so great 'minnies' and all is quiet again. Then a fresh burst from a Fritz gun in their front line. Several rifle shots snap out savagely and we hug the bottom of our big shell hole till Fritz cools down once more.

He takes a long time to quieten down as every few minutes a gun opens and we have a lively time on our next two or three trips between the outposts. Gradually all is quiet again and we can hear the soft, faint, regular sound of the men steadily digging on behind us.

We hear steps. I crouch, waiting, revolver ready to fire. The steps are coming from our posts and a man hurries up. He is from Number 2 gun post and reports, 'We can hear the Jerries moving about out where that gun was. Will we have a go at them?'

'No, too risky with so many men out in the open. Don't stir him up any more. We mightn't be so lucky next time. Probably a patrol investigating what's happened to their forward gun. Don't shoot unless they walk right into our lines.' And a disappointed gunner fades back to his mates. As we go along to the posts, the O.C. warns the men about the enemy moving in front and about no firing at random. We make the length of the outpost line once more.

'Well I must slip back and see how the trench is coming along.' And we go back and find the major, who escorts the O.C. along its whole length. It's been great work. A nice narrow trench properly laid out in bays has been dug to a depth of four feet. Tomorrow night and every night for a week its occupants will deepen it.

The officers discuss the situation and the major asks me to 'slip across to Hoop Trench and tell Mr Breen to have the men ready to move in and man this trench in ten minutes' time'.

I deliver my message and make back, passing the Pioneers. They have left the new trench and are stringing out between it and Hoop

Trench, getting ready to dig a communication sap between the two. I reach the new trench. The men of the wiring party have been taken off digging and are standing ready to go out and commence putting up their wire in front of the trench.

The men of my battalion are manning the nearly dug trench, scratching little shelter possies for themselves. It's the new hands who are so energetic. The older ones are wiser for they know they will be moved a dozen times before each platoon gets its permanent position, and they aren't digging possies for someone else to use.

I reach the officers. 'Ah, here he is,' they say as if I'd been away for a week or two, and I'm told to go along the outpost line and tell the listening posts to fall back and rejoin their sections in the new trench. 'And warn the gun posts that the listening posts are being withdrawn and to be doubly vigilant,' adds the major.

'Yes, Sir.' And away into no-man's-land I go for a nice quiet walk in the beautiful night air! Forty yards out and then a good quarter mile along the outposts all on my own, except for the creeps.

I find Number 1 Post of the gunners, deliver my warning, duly saying my piece about being doubly vigilant, and get told to go and bring an interpreter with me if I have any more foreign orders to put over again. On I go to the Number 1 listening post and tell them to get back and rejoin their sections. Up they go and make off. No one asks me if I'll be lonely or offers to come with me for a walk.

On again and I'm in a shell hole as machine-gun bullets whizz and *whit, whit, whit* just over me, the crackle of the gun sounding horribly close. Another burst and I keep down, but hear a distant *plonk* from the direction of our trench. I go cold. I know that sound. It's not the first time I've heard a man get a bullet in the stomach. Poor beggar, your chances aren't much!

The last listening post has been sent in and I go on and warn our left-hand gun that there's now nothing but sixty yards of mud, unless it be some Fritz patrol between them and the next gun. I'm now almost to it and bump a long line of men busy screwing iron pickets in the ground ready for the wire. Some coot hisses 'Halt!' And a rifle barrel points at my stomach. I am annoyed and tell him, 'It's all right. I'm a runner on duty, you officious cow,' for the fellow has given me an unexpected start.

'It might be if you know the password.'

'Desert Gold, you mad goat,' I whisper.

'Righto, come on.' And the rifle is lowered and I pass through the men and reach the new trench.

Our men are holding it in force. When I enquire of the O.C.'s whereabouts someone replies, 'Up in Annie's room.' Along the top of the trench I go looking for him. A great clod of mud lands near me and I hear a snigger and find my mates. They want to know where the devil I've been since our patrol. Darky adds, 'Longun collected your rum issue for you.'

'Where is it, Longun?' I ask, but he reckons he's too busy winning the war to remember just now where he put it.

'The jar is in the signallers' possie. Go and have a decent nip. Plenty there, only you and the gun crews to come and we have plenty left.'

I find the jar of S.R.D. and have a nip, a decent man-sized nip. There's too much in the jar for the D Company gun crews so I souvenir half a water bottle of it for my mates and know I've done my good deed for the day. Another water bottle lies nearby, so I half-fill that too, and slip back along the trench to my mates. I give one bottle to Dark telling him, 'Here, get this inside you and keep quiet about it.'

I report back to the captain just as Mr Brew comes in to say he can do with all the men he can get out on the wire now. A few minutes and a Lewis gun back in Hoop Trench fires over our heads, giving three short bursts followed by a long one – the 'come in' call to our gunners. The O.C. tells another man, 'Run out to the wiring party and pass the word along outposts coming in.' And makes off.

In ten minutes he is back. 'Those guns are a long while getting in,' I remark to him.

'They're remaining out near the wire whilst the working party is there. Never do for Fritz to rush the wiring party.' And again he's off somewhere else.

Someone's blanket is on a firestep, so I settle down on it. A noise sets up along the trench. Men are climbing out over the top. Our C.S.M. comes up to me. 'You'll do. Hop out and help with the wire.'

'Nothing doing, Serg. I'm on duty. Runner.' And I poke my face out from under the blanket.

'Oh, it's you, Nulla? Goodo.' And he sends out the next man who reckons he wishes he was a 'bloomin' runner, gettin' out of everything'.

'You'd jolly soon wish you weren't, wouldn't he, Nulla?' And the C.S.M. has gone on, detailing men to go out and rip and tear their uniforms and hands and arms on the wire we so like to see in front of us, so long as someone else puts it there.

Again I curl up on the muddy blanket, but the signal corporal comes along and tells me to hop into their dugout if I feel like a doze. I feel like a doze all right, like a whole night of them, so I fold myself up in their little dugout and am almost asleep when the O.C. comes in and uses the phone.

He spots me and says, 'Be as well if you make this your headquarters. I'm getting a bit of a possie fixed up round the next bay.' And off he goes.

My headquarters! Not bad. First time I ever knew a runner had headquarters – never before suspected he had a head.

I get to sleep, or almost, when the O.C. pokes his head in. 'Nulla here, Corporal?'

'Yes, Sir. Asleep, I fancy.'

'Oh well, it doesn't matter. I'll get someone else. He's had a pretty rough night.' And up he goes in my estimation as an O.C. so much so that I feel like going after him to ask if I can be of any help, but I easily, very easily, restrain myself, shout myself and the two signallers a good rum each from my water bottle and drop off to sleep.

An hour's cold, cramped sleep during which I am oblivious to everything about the war except that I'm cold, freezing cold. There's two things I'll never be able to forget – cold and chats.

A signaller shakes me and I crawl out and take a rifle for a walk along the trench to stretch my cramped legs. It's half an hour before daylight. The men are standing-to in readiness for Fritz should he decide to come over, but nothing is doing. The Pioneers, the wiring party and all spare parts have gone back to the support lines and we are now holding the front line on our own, and as it becomes brighter, our Lewis gunners get busy selecting positions allowing the greatest field of fire across no-man's-land. I peep over the top. The new wire looks good. They got a lot of it up last night. The trench, too, is pretty good, but shallow so you have to walk bent in two.

Tucker comes up and I hunt up my mates to get our share. A corporal and two men come along carrying two greasy black dixies. We get two cold boiled spuds each and a lump of cold, boiled bacon, mostly fat and rind. The corporal hands a loaf of bread to Longun.

'How many here?' asks the corporal.

'Five.'

'It's seven to a loaf.' And he gets his jack-knife out and hacks from our loaf what he estimates is two men's share.

'Here's a tin of jam. Four men to a tin. Collect a jam ration from Snowy Taylor's post. Want any cheese?'

Of course we want it. We want all we can get and a lot we can't so he gives us a fair lump of it. We get a mess tin half full of tea to each man, which is almost cold as it has been brought from two miles back. It is in petrol tins and petrol floats on the tea, but we drink it all the same. The corporal brings out some cigarettes and matches, and hands over three packets of fags – two packets to every four men.

'That's as near as I can get to it.' Some matches come to hand. 'A box of Lucifers a man.' And we get five boxes of matches and the corporal makes to move on, but he doesn't get away till we have wrangled another lump of bacon out of him and swapped the tin of plum jam for a tin of quince.

We get a box of matches each and share out the smokes. The Prof doesn't smoke cigarettes so that gives us a couple extra for each man. Snow takes an empty cigarette tin and goes off to Snow Taylor after our jam ration, whilst Longun takes a packet of fags along to the next post. He tosses the fellows there to see if he'll give them a full packet or none and loses the toss, so we're going to be a bit shorter than usual for smokes today and have to redistribute what we have left.

I make back to the signallers. The two sigs are very decent and have collected rations for me so I'm set in two places for tucker and smokes. These two sigs got more tucker than the five of us as theirs came up in what we call the H.Q. issue, so I have no hesitation in taking a second breakfast with them in their little dugout. They give me two packets of cigarettes and I put one packet in my cigarette case and keep the other to hand over to the boys.

The sigs are going to toss me to see which one does the first stretch on the phone, but they get a shock, a pleasant shock, when I offer to do the first couple of hours on the phone for them. 'But you can't take any messages. All messages from battalion come up in Morse.'

I tell them I hold two Signal School passes as a first-class signaller and they are satisfied to drop off to sleep whilst I adjust the headphones and sound through to see that the wires are okay.

For two hours I sit at the phone. All is quiet. Every quarter of an hour battalion sounds through to make sure a break hasn't occurred in the wires. I yarn a bit to the sig back in battalion H.Q. but it's a lop-sided yarn as he won't speak, and answers in Morse all the time. He tells me he can't speak as all the officers and men in the H.Q. dugout are asleep.

'What's that horrible noise coming through? Something wrong with your phone?' I ask him and he sends back: '-.-./---/.-../---/-./. /.-../ . . . /-./---/.-. /.. / -. /--. /' ('colonel snoring') and I laugh as I read his buzzing through.

The two hours are up so I wake a signaller and curl up under the blanket he has just left. Pushing close in against the sleeping corporal sig for a bit of warmth, I drop off to catch up on some of the sleep I missed last night.

NINE

The Carrying Party

We're living, or rather existing in the dirty damp billets of the shell-torn, rat-infested shambles that once was the French town of Dernancourt. This place has changed hands more than once in the fluctuating fortunes of war and is little more than a spot on a map, but what wealth of blood has been spilt here in its various fights! And how we hate this hole, its dirty dilapidated dwellings, remains of sheds and damp, foul-smelling cellars which house our battalion. We're as mud-stained, wet and weary as the place itself.

What a wretched time we've had cooped up here for eight days so Fritz planes and observation balloons can't spot us. We've not been cooped up at night though – the heads have seen to that. Every night we have been out on fatigues somewhere. Some parties repairing the corduroy roads that the enemy shells and our own overladen wagons and gun limbers nightly tear to pieces again. Others out on bridge repair work. Some more shiver and freeze on a bleak hillside where they have been spending the past few nights digging row upon row of graves in the rapidly growing cemetery that has been established here to serve as a last resting place for the dead. Men, horses and mules are killed every night up to ten miles behind the line. That's almost being killed in cold blood.

It's the end of the 1916 winter and the conditions are almost unbelievable. We live in a world of Somme mud. We sleep in it, work in it, fight in it, wade in it and many of us die in it. We see it, feel it, eat it and curse it, but we can't escape it, not even by dying.

We go out every night and work on various fatigues. Jobs anywhere within five or six miles of Dernancourt. All night we work. During the day we potter around on jobs close to the village so that we may slink off, like rats, to our holes as soon as the enemy observation balloon tops the muddy rim of the distant horizon, or when the hum of an enemy plane is heard. We mustn't be observed here or the place will surely be shelled. The enemy doesn't know we're here. He gives us credit for having more sense and we'd hate to disillusion him for we know just what it would mean to him, and to us.

We settle down. It rains as a mob of Fritz prisoners who have been scraping mud off the roads are taken back to the P.O.W. cages some miles away, and we, a fighting battalion, go out in the rain to finish the muck scraping. It is too wet to keep the Fritz prisoners on the job, but not too wet to send out an Australian battalion that is going into the front line tonight. We get through our job and land back in the billets about sunset. You don't see it rise and you don't see it during the day, either, when the real Somme weather is upon the menu.

Night comes down cold. We fall in and march off towards Delville Wood, fighting and pushing our way through a continuous stream of horses, mules and wagons, guns, limbers and ambulances, then branch off the road and enter the miles of duckboards leading towards the line. On through Delville Wood, once a large forest, but now just a mass of jagged, torn stumps upon which the blood of friend and foe has intermingled. Not a whole tree is left standing as shellfire has reaped the lot. The wood is crisscrossed by lines of trenches, taken and retaken. Report says that eight thousand South Africans have been killed here and thousands of British and Fritz too, no doubt. Even now, dead men can be seen every few yards. Devil's Wood indeed!

We leave Devil's Wood and follow along the duckboard track towards our support lines. A few field guns fire now and again, which makes us jumpy. What if the Fritz guns retaliates in an endeavour to quieten ours? His shells mightn't find our guns, but they are pretty sure to find us, out in the open, so we abuse our gunners and quicken our pace along the duckboards. One behind the other we file on through the cold drizzling rain in a pitch black night. Ahead we hear a mumble,

'Wire under foot.' As each man comes to the phone wire he steps over it and 'Wire under foot' calls to the man behind him.

Another hundred yards and we see the men ahead get off the duckboards and stand in the mud to make way for a stretcher coming back. As we meet the stretcher we in turn make way for one in worse plight than ourselves, though we thought that tonight we had a monopoly on the miseries of war.

On we go. 'Break in the boards' is passed back as each man comes to where a shell has made a direct hit and torn up three yards of duckboard. That means slushing knee deep through the mud. Just when we get back on the board, we see a couple of rifles and three heaps of equipment; the shell caught at least three men. The bodies aren't here so we suppose the men weren't killed outright.

Past our support line, we can just make out an old disabled tank on our right. We've often seen it. Some of our names are scratched upon its useless iron sides. A sudden burst of speed and we're passing more broken duckboards and there in the mud lie four huddled heaps awaiting the scanty burial that is all the army or the world holds for them now.

In tired silence we go on. Up to our left, shells are bursting in what was once Gueudecourt village. Fritz is always shelling it as the common belief is that he left a large dump of shells there and is trying to explode them before they fall into our hands.

At last we reach the embankment of the sunken road we call Fritz's Folly and follow it along. We're just in time too, as the enemy has begun to shell along the duckboard track. We keep close under the embankment as we go along for some whizz-bangs are just clearing its edge to burst sixty yards away. No one gets hit as the bursting power of the shells is greatly diminished by the mud into which they sink deep before exploding. Good old Somme mud! Sticking to us! Round a bend and we're at a cluster of dugouts we know as Headquarters. The guides from the front line are awaiting us.

'Lead on, B Company,' comes the low-toned command. We lead on a few yards and hear 13, 15 and 16 Platoons make off with their guides for the front line. Our 14 Platoon hasn't yet been called so we just hang around and wait on in the rain.

Half an hour drags by and nothing happens. Another half hour's standing in the rain and our sergeant appears from somewhere, a guide with him. 'Righto, 14, follow on.' Out of Fritz's Folly we climb and hit across towards the line, passing the last of the 3rd Battalion men making back. One of our officers is with them and he tells us that the relief has been successfully carried out.

A wide sap opens before us and the guide points out a few dugouts. We don't know where we are. This is not Eve Alley. Must be a new sap or part of a line that has been captured since we were here last. It's got the look of an old front line about it, but runs the wrong way, so we decide it's an old communication sap recently taken. The sergeant tells us, 'There's eight or ten dugouts here.' So we scatter ourselves out amongst the few miserable dugouts to dodge the rain and await events.

Longun, Dark and I get into the same rat of a dugout. We get our equipment off, load our rifles – 'Just in case,' as Longun says – and the three of us squat down on the muddy floor and huddle together for warmth. It's very quiet all along the front and we're almost asleep when Snow pokes his head in – 'Anyone here?' – and tells us the sergeant wants us. He informs us that we're in Grease Trench – last week's front line.

'Righto, we have to go back to Switch Trench for food for the line. We're the carrying party this trip in.'

The sergeant leads off and we follow, trudging across the black mud to Switch Trench where we find our cookers set up in a trench wall. The cooks are friendly. We get some good hot stew into us and some bread, jam and cheese and have several tins of tea – good strong cook's tea with milk and sugar in it. We feel much better and Jacko reckons, 'This carrying party business will do me.'

We climb into the straps that fasten a great heavy container of boiling stew upon our backs and stagger forth well loaded up. The sergeant and a few more carry dixies of tea between them with bags of bread and tins of jam, which crack them on the shins every false step.

The sergeant-cook dismisses us with 'Good luck and see you don't forget to have those dixies and containers back here before daylight.' And we're off with the food supply for the men in the front line. On across the mud. These great awkward containers get heavier and heavier and their straps cut into our shoulders. We get our hands back under the bottom to ease the weight on our shoulders and on we go, humped like camels.

Fritz starts shelling so we jog. The stew starts to rattle. Every now and then we stumble and boiling-hot stew splashes across the back of our necks. Boiling stew and icy-cold rain together trickle down our spines. We're very far from happy. Jacko admits, 'This carrying isn't all it's cracked up to be.' But we struggle on.

There's a clatter, a thud, a splashy oozy sound and real stark profanity as Longun lands upside down in a shell hole of water, getting well scalded with the red hot stew spilt all over him.

It does us good. We laugh, but Longun doesn't share our mirth. He well and truly abuses each and every one of us and everything he can think of. Real stark-naked bullock-driver abuse it is. He pulls the empty container off, boots it hard, hurts his toes and swears some more. Then he tries to stand upside-down to empty the stew out of his tunic pockets and empties his paybook out into the mud. That annoys him a lot more. He tips a lot of stew out of his respirator bag. Then he undoes his belt, shakes his shirt tails out all around and gets rid of more beautiful stew from around the ribs. He shoves the sopping-wet shirt back inside his breeches swearing some more horrible oaths as the wet shirt makes contact with his cold skin. A couple of gallons of stew has worked down each leg and lodged about his knees and he can't shift it without taking his puttees off and unlacing his riding strides. Longun's in a fix all right. For the first time Jacko seems to be enjoying the war and Snow chiacks Longun to 'Take your strides off and shake 'em', getting roared at for his pains.

Prof says something we can't catch, but Longun catches it and wants to fight him then and there. The sergeant tells Longun, 'Get some bloomin' sense,' and Longun wants to fight him too. 'And any more of you flash cows who seem so floppin' well amused,' he adds, when there comes a high-piercing scream of an approaching shell. In deadly silence and tremendous haste we drop on our knees and try to get as low as we can without spilling the stew over ourselves. With a soul-freezing scream the shell comes straight for us, and flat on the mud we go regardless of containers of stew, but impelled by the law of self-preservation. We flatten out in the mud as the shell lands with an awful explosion right amongst us.

Bang! Crash! And the very earth seems to rise and fall beneath us! Our heads are fit to burst from the buzzing in our ears and we shake from the vibration and shock. Here, flat out we shudder as pieces of flying shell *whir, whistle* and *burr* through the air all around. The flying fragments sing and meow away through the night. Down upon us, from the very sky it seems, drops a great shower of mud that was belched upwards when the shell exploded.

'Anyone hit?' calls the sergeant as we scramble to our feet trying to get the great heavy containers back where they should be and becoming aware for the first time that hot stew has leaked all over us. We're on the edge of a big barrage. Shells are landing in a continuous shower between us and Fritz's Folly. We'll never get through now.

'Make for the old gun pits over there!' roars the sergeant, and we take a few hurried steps when 'Wait!' is called in agony behind us, and we wheel and dimly see Prof, who has half-risen, collapse in the mud.

Four shells burst close as we rush to our hurt mate. He seems badly hit, but we have no time to examine him as we must get away from here, for the shellfire is increasing. Longun grabs the Prof under the arms. I grip his legs, Snow supporting the middle, and with Dark holding the weight of the stew container off his back, we go as fast as we can for the meagre shelter of the old blown-in gun pits.

We reach them and lower Prof down, taking the container off him and trying to make him comfortable. Longun knows his own hands are covered in warm blood. 'Where'd it get you, old mate?' he asks.

'My side, my shoulder.' The Prof seems very weak as we try to get his tunic off.

With a smack, Darky's container lands on the ground. 'I'm off for the stretcher-bearers,' he whispers and is gone out into the night and the shellfire to bring skilled aid for our mate. We get Prof's tunic off and the sergeant's jack-knife slits the shirt and singlet away. The right shoulder has a great gash in it and the side is a mangled mess, bleeding profusely.

Two field dressings come to light. Jacko and someone else press pads to the side wound whilst Snow bandages up the shoulder wound. I'm supporting Prof's head and can see he is only semi-conscious though he appears much easier.

The well known *squelch, squelch* of boots in the mud comes to our ears and Dark leads a stretcher party down. The bearers examine Prof who tells them he's 'not too bad'. They put fresh bandages, bigger ones, on him and they get him onto their stretcher. An old army blanket is placed over him and a waterproof sheet guards his head against the rain. The bearers shoulder the stretcher to carry back to the dressing station two miles away. We call cheery messages after them and Prof's hand rises and falls in weak acknowledgement as he is borne away into the black night. We realise it might have been worse, but are downhearted nevertheless. Three of our little band gone now. The odds are that some of the rest must follow soon.

'She's eased down a bit,' we hear someone say and look out to see the shelling is much lighter.

Longun shoulders Prof's stew container and we get the rest of the food gathered up and make on for the line. One of the boys has Longun's empty container full of tins of jam, which, as he walks, rattle more than we like. 'See you stop that flamin' rattling before we get near the line or Fritz'll machine-gun us,' the sergeant tells him, and the man runs back to the gun pit and gets the sandbag he threw away, jamming it down amongst his tins and on we go.

At last we reach the front line. The men are glad to see us and their stew. Half an hour's rest comes our way whilst the section corporals are distributing the food. They don't know we lost a whole container of stew and we don't tell them either. They're complaining enough as it is and blame the cooks for the shortage. Cooks come in handy at times.

The empty containers and dixies are gathered up and we make back to Switch Trench and hand them over to the cooks and get another drink of tea. The transport officer is here who tells us that we're to get bags of Mills grenades to take up to the front line. In all we make three trips with bombs without any mishap, finally getting back to our dugouts when a runner comes along and tells us to report for more carrying to the front line.

We arrive to be told by the O.C. that the enemy is holding the left flank of this trench, which he calls Stormy Trench. He says the battalion will attack beyond the block in the trench and that we'll be carriers for the attacking parties. As he speaks, we see the attackers crawling out into shell holes and worming their way along from hole to hole. The men's bayonets are fixed and they all carry bags of bombs. Amongst them is a party of rifle grenadiers with the grenade cups on their rifles.

We grab a couple of bags of bombs each and file along the trench to where we find Lieutenant Brew waiting for us. He is in charge of the carrying party and tells us we are to take our bombs into the captured portion of the trench as soon as it is taken and then come back for shovels and sandbags and anything else that is wanted.

We're all ready and waiting. There's not going to be any artillery barrage on the enemy, but our machine-guns and the Stokes mortars will fire on the trench whilst the men are making for it.

A wait of a few minutes and we hear our little trench mortar guns *cough, cough, coughing* and then we hear the Stokes bombs flying over in a stream. *Bang! Bang! Bang!* and they're bursting on the Fritz end of the trench. *Rat-a-tat, rat-a-tat, rat-a-tat-tat-tat,* and the machine-guns are into it too, pouring a stream of lead along the top of the enemy trench.

'That'll keep their heads down.'

'The Jerry who looks over now will deserve an Iron Cross, all right.'

'Yeah! And get a wooden one instead.'

'Come on, carriers,' shouts Mr Brew, and grabbing our bag of bombs we file along the trench.

The Stokes mortars and the machine-guns stop and fifty shouts split the morning. Our heads pop over and we can just see the attacking party charging the Fritz position. Half a dozen rifle shots ring out. 'That's Fritz,' says Mr Brew. A couple of enemy flares go up. *Whang! Whang! Whang!* We hear the Mills exploding and know our men are bombing the trench and hasten on hard to get to them with fresh bombs.

Enemy rifles are still firing. *Whang! Whang! Whang!* go our bombs, further away now. An enemy gun bursts into action with a savage *tut-tut-tut-tut* and above the noise of its firing there floats a shout, high and scared. Twenty more hoarse, angry yells blend with the savage *Whang! Whang!* of our Mills grenades and the gun is silent.

'Give it to the bastards!' yells an excited barracker fifty yards behind.

'Some bloke gettin' a bit excited over something,' drawls Darky, and we laugh and hasten on. We climb over the old block and are into the enemy's part of the trench which is wide, broken and half full of muddy water, and sink up to our waists.

'We'll go over the top. Come on carriers!' yells Mr Brew as over he climbs with four of us hard on his heels. For forty yards we race along when *pit, pit, pit, pit* fly the enemy bullets all around us as the gun's savage *tut-tut-tut-tut* strikes venomously in our ears.

'Back into the trench!' roars Brew, but before the words are out of his mouth, down he crashes in the mud, beside me. I drop a bag of bombs and grab him under the arm, heave and he's up and hanging on to me hard. Hopping on one leg and dragging the other, we race for the trench and leap for the muddy protection it offers.

The other carriers are all back in the trench when we drop into it.

'Where'd it get you, Sir?'

'In me shin, but go on, get the bombs up, don't stop here all day, I'm right.' And he angrily waves us as he sinks in pain into the muddy trench wall.

Someone yells 'Stretcher-bearers!' as we rush along.

'Pass the word they're not wanted,' from Mr Brew, but no one passes that message and we're away along the trench, hard as we can go through the mud.

We reach a great squashy patch of churned up mud. There ahead of us we see Mr Breen beckoning us on whilst we hear our attackers shouting desperately for bombs. Our two leading carriers go down to their waists in the mud and are bogged. Mr Breen jumps across and pulls them out and on they go. Another fellow gets bogged whilst 'Bombs! Pass the word for bombs!' is being roared out from on ahead where the fighting is hottest.

Another carrier is stuck in the bog-hole and as Mr Breen pulls at him, two more carriers jump to get over the top into no-man's-land. One man goes unscathed through a hail of bullets and delivers his bags to the bombing party thirty yards ahead. The second is only half out of the trench when *Smack!* We hear a bullet bite into him and back head over heels into the trench he reels. We take just one glance at him. From the top of his nose to the crown of his head he's split as clean as an axe could split him. We see his brain twitching and pulsating and then a film of blood covers all as the man gives a twitching shudder and goes over on his poor smashed face in the mud.

'Bombs! Bombs!' come the urgent shouts from ahead, where men fight and where all but the luckiest die.

'Bombs! Bombs! Hurry the bombs!'

'Keep to the trench! Don't go over!' orders Mr Breen.

'Quick, hold me back someone, I'm goin' over,' jokes Longun. Jokes amidst falling men and flying lead and our spirits rise as we push and pull to get through the bog-hole for we must reach those shouts and meet that desperate call.

'Bombs! Bombs! Shake it up!'

Another man is hauled through the bog-hole and as he races on, another chap with the initiative of a born soldier goes down on his hands and knees across the bog-hole, tearing along to deliver those so badly needed bombs. Each step buries the man deeper in the slush and Mr Breen has his work cut out to keep the man's face from sinking into the slush.

Now we're well along the enemy's trench. We rush past the men of our mopping-up party who are busy collecting prisoners from the dugouts. The moppers-up rush to a dugout. 'Come on! Up you come!' they roar into its black depths, and '*Kamerad! Kamerad!*' come the frightened yells from below, and scared-looking Fritz rush up with hands held high. Our men motion with bombs or bayonet and the prisoners climb out into the open with hands high, racing for our trench. 'Any more down there?' yells one man. No answer from the dugout. 'Well, catch this! Take this if you won't come up!' And two bombs rattle down the steps and explode with muffled reports deep down in the bowels of the earth. The attackers are at the next dugout shouting down into its black mouth. No answer comes from below.

'Empty,' says a man.

'Better make sure. Here, split this up amongst you, Fritz.' And two more bombs go down, and burst hard.

On past the attackers we race. Many dead and wounded Fritz are here. The wounded are trying to make towards our position to surrender. Hands fly up as we rush past. '*Kamerad*' we hear as we tear past them in a mighty hurry. We come to an overturned machine-gun and behind it are four terribly lacerated dead or dying gunners. One of our wounded men comes limping along using his rifle as a crutch. Another goes by with blood flowing from a bullet hole in each cheek.

'They get you, Harry?' He can't speak, but waves his bayonet gleefully, a bayonet red with blood. He's given more than he's taken. Three of our men are dead on the floor of the trench. Most of our casualties are out in the shell holes, hit before they reached the trench. Round a big bend we come to Lieutenant Walsh having a badly smashed hand bandaged up.

'Run back and ask Mr Breen to come up as I'm hit,' he tells Snow. Snow leaves his bombs and races back as we hurry along and deliver the bombs to our attacking party. A sergeant is in charge here. The attack is over and the men are hard at it building a sandbag block in the trench. Two big bomb-throwers are keeping up a barrage of bombs into the trench ahead in case any Fritz are crawling up to rush the position the men are so feverishly consolidating.

Our bags are grabbed from us and the bombs shared out and placed handy to the throwers.

'How many more bags are coming?' the sergeant wants to know.

'Couple dozen or so,' Dark tells him.

'Seen the officers about?'

'Yes, Walsh's wounded and Breen's back getting the bombs up. Brew's wounded too. You'll soon be a flamin' field marshal, Serg.'

'Yes, I know all about that, Dark, but you fellows get back as hard as you can go and tell the O.C. we want all the shovels and bags he can find, and want 'em quickly too, and ask Mr Breen to come up here.'

'Tell 'em to send up more Lewis gun magazines, loaded ones,' the gunner calls to us. 'We're getting short here.' And he blazes half a mag away along the top of the Fritz trench.

'Blast this carryin' anyway. Sooner stay here with the boys. Fritz'll come over any minute now,' growls Longun, and *Woof!* A *minenwerfer* explodes with a tremendous thud twenty yards behind us and Longun becomes very keen to get away after those shovels. Ahead of us we see about forty prisoners running across the top of our trenches. Behind them is another bunch moving slowly – the wounded ones of whom half are being carried or helped along.

Mr Breen runs past going flat out to take over Mr Walsh's command. 'Shake it up and get back,' he calls as he runs by, but we're shaking it up all we know how.

Soon we reach the bog-hole. The trench wall has been shovelled away and a path cut round the hole. A few of our wounded men are just ahead of us making back. They are laughing and joking, but seem a bit unstrung. We bump the O.C. and he gives Jacko and me two bags of bombs each to take back to the newly won position.

With a heavy load of bombs in each hand we make off and are soon at the old Fritz part of the trench. Passing some dugouts, a blanket, which hangs down over the mouth of one, moves. 'One of our coves down after souvenirs,' I venture, and follow on after Jacko.

We get within six or seven feet of the dugout when the blanket is flung violently aside and a big Fritz springs out of the mouth of the dugout and with fixed bayonet charges madly straight for young Jacko, bellowing as he comes.

Fear freezes my steps as there comes to me the awful realisation that we're both unarmed. I yell to Jacko to run, but before he can turn, the big Fritz is almost on him. The bayonet shimmers and shines in the early dawn and, with the slithery savagery of a striking snake, that quivering carrier of a stabbing, tearing death flashes straight for Jacko's throat.

I swallow hard and fling a bag of bombs right at the fellow's face as I somehow realise that Jacko has not time for anything unless it be to die. The bag flies crooked, but the man has to swing his head sideways to dodge it. That motion brings Jacko out of his frozen stance and snaps the partial paralysis of his approaching death; he ducks and with the desperation of death hard upon him, dives for the attacker's legs. As he flies through the air I see the bayonet's point rip off his left shoulder-strap, but with a thud young Jacko has him, carrying the man's legs clean from him as they hit the floor of the trench with a splash and a grunt.

With a bound I have kicked the man's hands off the rifle and grab it, twisting it round ready to stab, but before I can do anything Jacko's boot lands with a mighty crash fair into the fellow's face. The Fritz is desperately working his knees to get Jacko, but the boy is grimly hanging on to the fellow's legs, and driven by desperation and the urge of self-preservation, his boot, with every ounce he can put behind it, again kicks the man hard in the face. A third time the boot with a sickening thud lands in that face.

Jacko is no longer an Australian schoolboy. He's gone back fifty thousand years. No joy, aim or ambition in life but to smash that face into a gory pulp. Another crash and Jacko's boot catches his man fair in the throat and with a shiver the Fritz goes limp. I know the fellow has gone out to it and Jacko hopes he's killed him, but he doesn't kick again. Civilisation regains control; the caveman's paroxysm of bloodlust gives way to the sportsman's code that won't kick a man when he's out to it.

Jacko, savage but no way scared, jumps to his feet. He is trembling from excitement and exertion and is plastered in mud from his struggle. The Fritz is practically all in. He lies covered in mud, his face puffed and swollen. Blood flows from his smashed nose and from great gashes along one jaw; his chin is half-buried in a puddle of blood and mud. His chest heaves with the laboured breathing of a body desperately fighting for life. At each gasped intake of breath his throat screws to the side and we see the veins rise in knots.

He is coming round. His hand comes up and I instinctively tense my grip on the rifle as I'm not taking any chances. But we need fear that hand little now and a spasm of remorse goes through me as we see the poor crippled creature feebly making an effort to make a sign of the cross. A fellow Christian, but of what a fellowship! His eyes flicker open and the pupils dilate with fear as his pain-muddled brain slowly takes in the significance of a khaki uniform behind the ready bayonet.

He becomes agitated as consciousness returns, grasps his injured throat and tries to say '*Kamerad*'. He has surrendered. He cannot speak, but the pained animal pleading of blue, frightened Saxon eyes cannot be misread.

'What'll we do with him?' asks Jacko.

I know what some of our chaps would do with him, but how can you bayonet a fellow lying hurt at your feet? Two of our men come along going back. 'Here, take this Fritz along.' And I motion with the bayonet. The Fritz understands and gets up on wobbly legs.

'Cripes, you've clubbed him with a rifle, have you?' a man laughs.

'Jacko gave him a bit of a crack. Don't run any risks with him. We haven't searched him, he may have a gun.' Our man whips out a pistol and his mate searches the Fritz whilst Jacko and I gather up our bags of bombs.

'Come on, Fritz; Loos, Loos; *Allez tout de suite; Imshi Allah,*' the men tell him, and he takes a few staggering steps, turns agitatedly, and says something that we can't understand.

'Wants to kiss you good-bye,' a fellow jokes, being far nearer the truth than he guesses, and we turn our backs on the Fritz as the men hurry him off.

'Better see if there's any more down this dugout, Jacko, or we might stop one in the back.' And we stand well aside of the entrance and shout, but no answer comes up, so we throw a Mills grenade. *Bang!* But no other sound is heard, so we drop another just to be sure and make on to deliver our bombs.

'Glad you didn't tell those chaps what I did. You won't, will you?'

'Of course I won't.' Jacko's too clean for this game. 'What the devil else could you have done?'

As we go along we can see our stretcher-bearers carrying our wounded back. They plod slowly on, sinking to their ankles at each step. It is now broad daylight and the fight is over. We reach the newly won position and deliver our bombs. The men are hard at work making the place fit to withstand a counter-attack.

Our job is done so we make back to find the men breakfasting on bully beef and bread. Our food is in our packs back in Grease Trench so Jacko and I find the equipment left behind by a wounded man and help ourselves to the rations in it. Things are quiet now. We stand in the mud and talk. Souvenirs are shown. Watches, iron crosses, field glasses and a few pistols and trench daggers have been souvenired from captured Fritz.

'Look at the Fritzie stretcher-bearers,' calls someone and we cautiously peep over and see four big Fritz carrying an empty stretcher from some back trench towards our lines. The Fritz bearers wander about a bit.

'Lookin' for wounded,' a man says. They are about two hundred and fifty yards from us. They stop, open their stretcher and climb into a big shell hole with it. Their heads and shoulders can still be seen and they appear to be doing a lot of moving about, bobbing up and down. We plainly see one man shake a brown blanket out in the wind. A few minutes go by and the party climbs out of the hole with the stretcher on their shoulders. A blanket-clad form lies upon it.

'Dimmer! Corporal Dimmer!' And an officer comes rushing along the trench to where Jack Dimmer's Lewis gun is set up.

Dimmer hops round all alert. 'Yes, Sir.'

'Here, fire on that stretcher party! Come on! Shake it up! They'll be out of sight in a minute!'

'What? Fire on stretcher-bearers! I'm not shootin' bearers for anyone.' And he glares indignation at the officer.

'You'll do as you're told! It's my orders! They haven't got a man on that stretcher. They've got a gun! Or a trench mortar! I saw them wrap a blanket round it.' And he waves a pair of field glasses at Jack. 'Come on! Stir it up!'

Jack stirs it up all right. He fairly jumps to his gun. 'Do me,' he calls as *rat-a-tat-tat-tat-tat* barks his machine-gun.

The aim is wild and the first burst clean misses the stretcher party. They break into a fast run, heads bent low. *Rat-a-tat-tat-tat-tat* the gun quivers another burst. One man flops into a sitting position and slowly rolls over dead. A second reels sideways for a few staggering uneven steps before his legs give out and he topples into the mud. He crawls a few yards and is lost to sight; into a shell hole probably. The remaining two, still somehow holding on to the stretcher, rush on a few yards and men, stretcher and all, dive sideways and disappear into a depression of some sort.

Angry shouts from our men arise along the trench. This firing on stretcher-bearers gets under their skin. It's one of the things we won't come at.

'Cease firing that gun!' And our O.C. races up livid with rage. 'Who fired on that party?'

'My orders, Sir,' the lieutenant tells him, and goes on to explain what he saw through the glasses.

'Aha! Is that their stunt? Pity you didn't get the lot, Corporal.' And the two officers make off.

We settle down and discuss and argue about the turnout. It's new even to our oldest soldiers and interesting to all of us. The general opinion is that Fritz got what they were looking for anyway.

We settle down for a spell and hunt up what food we can and eventually doze off. An hour drags by. We sleep soundly. A big drop of water falls *plonk* in my ear. I give a startled jump, which of course wakes the other two. 'If you've got to jump about like that, get outside and do it. We want a bit of sleep, if you don't.'

Well into the afternoon we sleep. Fritz shells land close, waking us, and we just lie listening as the shellfire increases. Shells land closer and each explosion sets up a vibration we clearly feel, which seems to run in waves under the ground. Closer now fall the shells. *Zonk! Bang!* lands one, too close to be comfortable. The ground shakes and great lumps of mud fall on our faces. We spit out mud and sit up, so cold and cramped that any movement is painful.

We hear the screeching, shrieking, wailing whistle of a shell coming straight for us and we cower and crouch to make ourselves as small as we can; *Zonk! Bang!* and the dugout seems to heave again under the vibrating shock of that bursting shell.

The shell has landed a few yards away and from the roof, great cakes of mud fall all over us. The acrid fumes irritate our nostrils and throats. My head is fairly spinning; I'm dizzy, and my neck feels as if it's broken. Straight out of the dugout I crawl and Longun comes after me, asking what's wrong. I reel about the trench, holding my neck and fighting hard to keep on my feet. Spots and great black patches float before me. The pain in the back of my head and my neck is agonising. I'm quite sure my neck is broken.

Longun catches up to me as I'm circling down the trench. He grabs me. 'Here, what's wrong?'

I bend my head down as far as it will go. 'My neck's broken, I think,' I tell him and he grabs my chin and, cupping his other hand on the back of my neck, works my head about which hurts a lot.

'Your neck broken, is it? Is that all? Thought there was something up with you.'

Darky pokes his head out. 'What's gone wrong with him? What's he runnin' about at anyway?'

'Nothin' serious,' Longun tells him with a grin. 'Only broken his neck and lookin' for a nice quiet place to die.' And I begin to feel that I mightn't quite die after all.

Cr–up! from a big black shrapnel overhead. Its pellets whine through the air. Down against the side of the trench we crouch and hear the pellets go *zip zap* into the ground nearby. More shells rush and burst around the position as Longun and I slip along, hugging the trench wall and collecting our equipment and rifles. A Fritz attack may be coming, though it's not very likely as he doesn't specialise in these daylight stunts – neither do we for that matter.

The shellfire is getting heavier. It's on the front line as well as on the sap. Our men are out of their dugouts now, looking anxious and worried. Longun steps up to our little dugout. 'Hey, where're you, Dark?'

'Here. What's up?' replies Dark from the dugout.

'Let us know when it's all over and I'll come out,' he chuckles in a cracking-hardy sort of mirth.

Whizz! Bang! and a small shell explodes just behind the trench and we hurriedly duck. As we do, we see Dark coming out of the dugout backwards and in a mighty hurry. Two disreputable-looking feet followed by a great muddy dome and Darky's out fixing a tin hat on top of a badly scared face.

More shrapnel and high-explosive strikes about the trench and we duck and dive seeking safety.

'Man buried!' a beseeching cry comes from up the trench. We forget shrapnel and whizz-bangs and our own safety as we race for that cry. A little dugout has been blown in. Half a dozen men reef and tear and claw at the heap of mud covering the dugout entrance. We join in and shift a lot of mud. The sergeant rushes up with a spade and does the work of three men. Madly we work to rescue the entombed man. One foot comes to light and now we know where he lies. *Bang! Crash! Bang!* fall the shells. On we work, oblivious to all but the necessity of rescuing the man before he smothers.

Cr–up! bursts a shrapnel. Over bowls one of the men. Another jumps into his place and feverishly claws and scoops at the mud. Shrapnel pellets flap and whistle all around us and the whirring nose cap of a shell smashes into the mud just behind. The hit man writhes in agony on the floor of the trench. Someone pulls him over against the wall of the trench, but the men never pause in their frantic tearing at the mud. As last the weight of mud is removed and we haul the man out – a dead, mangled mess. He has been chopped clean in half, blown in two across the chest. His gory, plastered flesh is quivering.

Back we reel, sickened. 'There's another chap behind him! And we lean across the dead man and pull out a dazed fellow, a young boy; one of Jacko's reinforcement. He throws his arms about and fights for air. Someone undoes his tunic collar and Jacko fans his face with a steel helmet and his breathing becomes easier. His face is black from the smoke of the explosion. He comes round, but begins to shiver and lapses into a coma.

'Let's have a look at him.' And two stretcher-bearers are with us. Two more are seeing to the wounded man on the floor of the trench. A shrapnel pellet has smashed into his hip. The bearers bandage him up and leave him against the wall of the trench till he can be carried out. His mates are with him. The bearers get busy with the boy from the blown-in dugout. They lay him on the stretcher and start off. He sits straight up and laughs hysterically; louder and louder he laughs as he is borne away.

'Lucky if he doesn't end up a gibbering idiot,' says Dark, as we see the bearers trying to force him down on the stretcher again, and he passes from us.

The sergeant pulls the dead man's body up against the trench wall. Then he gropes in the dugout and grasps a hand and pulls out the top half of the man and drops it on the body. Very drawn and white-looking, the sergeant says, 'Get his paybook and things.' And someone undoes his blood-sodden pocket and takes out a paybook and a bundle of blood-stained letters. The sergeant shrinks from taking them.

'Put them back. It's better that way,' says the sergeant.

'I'll get his particulars from someone who knows him.' And back in the blood-filled pocket go all his poor belongings to be buried with him. A mate solemnly covers the body with a blanket and says, 'We'll bury him tonight,' as another mate gives the dead man's name and regimental number to the sergeant to enter up in his notebook. Another name to be handed in to battalion headquarters, another name for the casualty lists, another Australian body to find its final repose in the Somme mud.

The shelling has stopped. We're all subdued and smoking hard. Two men crouch near the man with the wounded hip, trying to cheer him up for he needs it. The stretcher party that carried out the boy from the dugout returns and we enquire after him.

'The quack gave him a needle and he's gone back, asleep. He'll be okay.' We sincerely hope so, but doubt it.

The bearers are getting the stretcher under the wounded man when 'Look out!' is shouted as a man, a stretcher-bearer, races flat out along the trench going his hardest for the battalion dressing station and its doctor back in Fritz's Folly. The running man is grasping his neck, and as he passes wild-eyed and frightened, we see the blood jetting out from a wound in the side of his neck. He leaves a thin trail of blood spots as he goes.

'Best thing he could do. Follow him, Tim,' says a bearer, and another bearer jumps up and races along with the bleeding man. The other bearers get Longun to help with the stretcher as far as Fritz's Folly.

Longun comes back and says the wounded bearer reached the doctor and had his torn artery tied. His presence of mind saved his life. Half a dozen wounded men are carried along the sap. They are from the front line. Some are dying already. Others seem cheerful and ask, 'Got any messages for Blighty?' as they pass by and Dark rejoins, 'Have a few pints for me when you get to the Strand.'

The O.C. comes down from the front line. He asks how we fared here and we're told, 'Get out of these dugouts if he shells again.' We'll do that all right.

Six days go by. Six cold, quiet days with nothing to do and six miserable nights of ration carrying. Tonight the 58th Battalion is to relieve us. The O.C. visits the sap and directs our sergeant, 'Move your party straight back to Mametz Camp as soon as it gets dark. No need to wait for relief for this position.' And on he goes leaving a glow of gladness by his news.

It needs an hour or so till dark, so with our gear gathered up in readiness to push off, we sit about.

'We can get a move on any time now,' says the sergeant.

'I'll get a party to bury those two men who were killed this morning.' And off he goes to detail a burying party.

We wait on whilst the dead men are buried. A shallow grave marked by a rifle stuck up in the mud is all that can be done. It gives some satisfaction to do that, although we are well aware that the men so buried will be thrown up and reburied by shellfire time after time until the fighting shifts on from here. Some day they may have real graves. What a lot to look forward to! It's as well their people can't fully realise what finding a soldier's grave really means.

Darkness comes and we file down the sap. At the sunken road we are stopped by the adjutant who orders, 'Go to the Mametz Camp and report to the battalion's billeting officer, who'll allot you your huts.'

'Very well, Sir.' And on we go into the gathering night, heading for the duckboard track along which we came in only last week, though it seems an age.

'Something new to be relieved after only one week in the line.'

'Yes, but that's because we did that stunt along Stormy Trench, or whatever it's called.'

We meet a party of our own stretcher-bearers making back towards the line. They've been right back to the A.M.C. Advanced Dressing Station with a wounded stretcher-bearer. They tell us he got a bullet through the side of his head when a Fritz gun opened up on some C Company bearers who were carrying a wounded man. It appears that two stretcher parties that had attempted to go across the open this morning were fired on, bearers being wounded on each occasion. And it's a week since Dimmer began the rot.

To our knowledge this is the first occasion of Fritz deliberately gunning our bearers, but we started it by shooting his bearers that morning. Of course, if they were illegally using a stretcher, under international law they merited death. Whoever's in the right and whoever's in the wrong, the fact remains that every stretcher party of ours that now ventures to show in the open is fired upon. As a consequence, the wounded suffer and the bearers have to trudge knee deep along the saps when carrying men out.

We reach Delville Wood and pass several battalions moving up to take over the front line and the supports. They ask what sort of a time we've had and what the line's like. We tell them and pass on to meet another battalion. These incoming battalions are of the 15th Brigade and are nice and clean and smart looking, so different in appearance from us. But then we're returning from the line whilst they're going in. A night or two in the line will remove that parade-ground smartness. Though on appearances no one would think it, we went into Dernancourt only a fortnight ago with the mark of much spit and polish upon us. We go in the line a spick and span soldierly looking lot and come out a nondescript mob, all mud and whiskers.

Half an hour's tramp and we are at a little Salvation Army canteen at the edge of Delville Wood where we get hot coffee and a few biscuits. A few spare smokes are on tap for those who are without. Here, almost at the front line, we can get our letters posted and get writing material if we wish to write home. Here, day and night, hot drinks are offered to all, to the men going in, to the men coming out. Many a wounded man has here been given the drink that has provided him with sufficient strength to hang on long enough to reach the main dressing station alive. All creeds and classes are welcomed. The enemy prisoner on his way back to the P.O.W. cages is just as sure of that little touch of humanity that is supposed to make the whole world kin as is the ribbon-bedecked general of a British Army Corps. Officers and privates, all religions and no religion, friend and foe, will here find a helpful welcome from that splendid organisation whose sincerity carries it above and beyond the petty borders of class, creed and country.

We're in no hurry so decide on a spell.

The discussion falls on the various organisations that carry comforts to the men in the field. Darky strikes the general opinion when he affirms, 'These Salvation Army joints will do me. The Salvos are the best of the lot. Out on their own, easy.'

'Poor old Prof. Wonder if he pulled through all right?' And we become sober again, gather up our gear and tramp off through the night to find those Mametz huts. For hours we seem to wade and push through a stream of horses and mules and mud and men and motor-lorries and mud and more mud till at last we reach Mametz.

'D Company's huts are in the third row. Platoon numbers are chalked on the doors.' And we go and find our hut and dump our rifles and equipment with a rattle on the floor.

A corporal comes along and tells us where we can get blankets, so we go and get two blankets a man, getting our name taken so that we can't double up. There's a tin brazier in the hut but no fuel; we need a fire badly so rip a few lining boards from the wall of the hut and soon have a fire going. We make our beds near the fire and sleep in twos. That way we have one blanket under and three over us. We fold our tunics for pillows. The floor is hard but so are our hips.

Dark and Snow dig up a few francs and go out to bribe the Tommy engine-drivers to give them a bag or two of coal. The rest of us wait, and watch young Jacko toasting dodger on the end of his bayonet, whilst we dry our wet feet before the little fire, or do any jobs we can close to it.

Snow and Dark return. They have no coal but have quite a lot to say about 'miserable stingy cows frightened of losing their good jobs'.

'Here, Nulla, we'll give it a go.' And Longun and I go out with a bag each to try our luck. We meet a man coming back from the coal dump with a bucket – an empty one. We ask him, 'What's it like for getting some coal down here?' He heaps abuse upon the coal dump guard and tells us to go back to get some sleep.

We're determined to give it a go so keep on. An engine is just shunting up the water tanks, its tender full of coal, so we devise a plan of campaign. Longun creeps up as close as he can to where the engine will stop. He keeps in the darkest patches as he makes off, whilst I go a hundred and fifty yards down the line to where the train now is.

The train shunts on to the water tanks and stops. Steam hisses from it. I wait till the hissing dies down and then as loudly as I can I roar, 'Man run over! Pass word to hold the train!' And duck away. Men run out from the huts nearby and race towards where I shouted from. More men and some officers tear up in the dark. 'Who called?' 'Where'd it happen?' No one seems to know, and it's pitch-black night so we can't see anything. Men are rushing everywhere. 'Can anyone bring a light?' 'The call seemed to come from down the line,' says someone and we move down fifty yards or so. The Tommy engine-driver and his fireman race up. 'Oi, chooms, where be the man?' asks the driver excitedly. No one can tell him.

'Search further down the line,' an officer directs and again we all move along the rails for another fifty yards. After another fruitless search someone says, 'Some cow's gone mad and seein' accidents in his sleep.' And we begin to break up, but an officer takes the engine-driver's name and unit and the number of the train and quite spoils the night for the poor Tommies.

The men drift back to their huts no wiser but a lot colder, and the Tommies go back to their engine. I wander over to our hut and get Snow and Jacko to bring a couple of blankets and come with me. They growl a bit, but do as I ask.

We make for the water tanks. The train is still there so we sit down behind the empty hut and wait. Presently the train moves on, gathering speed, so we slip down and go just across the rails to find Longun bagging up some lumps of coal he has thrown off the tender whilst the train crew were away. 'Lookin' for the bloke they ran over,' he chuckles.

A great supply is gathered up. I have a waterproof bread bag full of it. Longun has a sandbag full and Snow and Jacko each have a blanket of coal slung over their shoulders.

We reach the hut and with it make a roaring fire. We're not risking losing any so we pull up three flooring boards and dump our supply under the floor and replace the boards. All we keep out is a bag for immediate use. Now we have enough coal to outlast our stay here, so we're set for once.

Crowding around the glowing brazier we all get warm and, after placing our wet boots and socks to dry, we curl up in our blankets near the fire. Soon we doze off. Whistles blow. 'Lights out!' shout the men on guard who have caught the hum of an approaching enemy bombing plane. The camp goes black. Soon there comes another signal on the whistle – the 'all clear' – but our candle stays out as we're almost asleep.

Towards morning, we are awakened by men moving past the huts. It's our chaps from the front line just marching in. Questions and orders are flying everywhere as the platoons search out their allotted huts. Our door opens. A sudden blast of freezing wind rattles the rough hut. 'What platoon's in here?' a voice calls.

'Shut the door!' 'Get out.' 'Put the bit of wood in the hole!' 'Shut the door, you goat!'

'Fourteen, of course; can't you read?'

'Right!' the fellow yells, and gives the door a tremendous bang and is gone.

The door swings back open. Ugh! How the icy wind howls through the hut! No one ventures out to close the door. We're all hoping someone else will get up and close it.

No one moves. We lie still, still hoping hard. We can't sleep with that wind howling over us and we can't somehow bring ourselves to get up and close the door, not whilst there's a chance of someone else doing it.

'Eh! Jacko, what about making a hero of yourself and shuttin' the flamin' door?' No answer.

'You awake, Nulla?' No answer again, and not likely to be.

'By cripes! You blokes are tough all right.' Longun crawls out and shuts the door with a bang that wakes everyone within a hundred yards. Then back under his blankets he shivers and swears himself to sleep as the grey dawn breaks over the big camp of wearied and worn-out men just back from the line.

TEN

Mixing it at Messines

We've been on the move pretty constantly since our last innings at Stormy Trench. We got three weeks at Mametz of hard training on the hard frozen ground; three weeks of charging and gallantly capturing Fritz trenches from which they'd been hunted miles away nine months or so before.

Then we did a march, or rather a fight through mud and traffic to a camp at Shelter Wood, near Fricourt, where we scored a hot bath and clean underclothing and had our uniforms steamed and the inside seams of our pants ironed in an effort to kill the chats.

They gave us a few days at Shelter Wood and then we marched on to some tents at Le Barque near the infamous Butte de Warlencourt, before marching into Bapaume to do salvage work.

Things were moving towards the big Bullecourt stunt and on the 11th April, we took over the old front line at Noreuil from where we spent two busy days helping to carry in dozens and dozens of wounded men of the 13th and 16th Battalions who said they got knocked hopping in for their cut to help the 46th and 48th men who bumped a snag.

It was up at Noreuil that Longun met a chap he knew, a man of the 13th who was walking out wounded. Longun went to shake hands, but the cove didn't offer his hand; he kept it, and the other one too, across his abdomen, up under his singlet. Longun wanted to know why and said so.

'What the devil's the matter with you?'

The man just grinned and said, 'Sorry I can't shake hands, but if I take my hand away my guts'll fall in the dirt.' And the men looked and found the fellow's belly had been slit clean across by a bullet and he had his fingers clasped over his protruding bowels to keep them in. That man wouldn't be carried out, but walked out and told us that if we had any stretchers to spare to keep them for the badly wounded men as he was quite okay.

Then we came across an old man in a broken-down trench who had a bullet through each knee and a big hole in his hand from a Fritz bomb. He was nursing a spade and crying like a spoilt kid. We told him, 'You're set now, mate. We'll soon get you back,' but the old beggar kept on crying and repeating, 'There were seven of 'em, and three ran away.' And every time he'd say 'and three ran away' he'd fairly howl from temper. He wouldn't get on the stretcher as he reckoned his mate was round the trench with a bayonet still in his leg and wanted us to get him first.

So we went to where he pointed and sure enough his mate was there with a Fritz bayonet stuck through his leg, but another bayonet through his back and as dead as a man could be along with half a dozen Fritz. Then we went into a wide, broken bay of the trench and found four Fritz dead with faces gashed horribly and now knew how the old man had wielded that spade he still clutched. We didn't blame the three Fritz who ran away, though they did upset the old man badly by not waiting till he chopped them up along with their comrades. Our men carried the old fellow out, but he was pretty far gone and we lost track of him.

We also found a young lad of seventeen who had his knee slit clean open by a piece of shell. He was quite hysterical and couldn't stop laughing as he'd tell us.

'They came at us in a big bunch. We didn't have time to pull the pins out of the bombs so we flung the bombs in their faces. Flung 'em hard at their foreheads when they were only a rifle length from us, and bolted, and they never got any of us.' And then he'd laugh, quite unstrung.

The day of the Bullecourt hop-over, we saw a strange thing. A big Fritz was lying badly wounded alongside his machine-gun. Our bearers had bandaged up seven separate wounds on the man, but he was left there alongside his gun. The boys couldn't carry him out for he was chained to his great heavy gun by a strong chain and two padlocks. The chain was tightly padlocked round an ankle and the other end was padlocked to the gun. When our fellows came across him the story spread that Fritz were chaining their gunners to their guns, but we couldn't believe that for we knew of many Fritz who had died working their gun to the last. Some of the bravest men we've ever bumped have been Fritz gunners; we know that to our sorrow.

This Fritz rallied and could speak English and told us where he'd thrown the key of the padlocks, but it couldn't be found as the place had been tramped over by hundreds of feet during the fight. Towards night someone brought a big file back from the rear and released him and carried him out.

Of course he was eagerly questioned and told them he had chained himself to the gun and thrown the key beyond reach. He said they'd been warned to expect another Pozières and that he was afraid his nerves might break. He seemed to have had a dread of deserting his post. The man spoke of his unit, some special house or bodyguards of the Prussian army, and said that in the two hundred years since its formation, no member of it had ever deserted before an enemy.

On the 13th April we were relieved and marched into Bapaume then on, via Albert, to Shelter Wood before a month's spell in Bresle. From here, Snow and I slipped off to Franvillers one day and jumped a ride in a Tommy motor lorry to Rivery and visited Amiens, sampled its cognac and had several helpings of chipped spuds, eggs and watercress and wandered about buying pretty silk postcards.

Then we got dry again and found a nice quiet little estaminet and just began enjoying ourselves when four useless great military policemen dropped in and asked if we happened to have a leave pass. We didn't so they landed us into a clink and notified our battalion. Late that night a sergeant and three men came down from the battalion and we all had to tramp about twelve miles back to Bresle where Snow and I spent the night in the battalion clink.

Darky discovered us early next morning, then after breakfast, Jacko turned up with our shaving gear and half a mess tin of warm tea that he had saved for shaving water for us. We had a shave, polished our boots nicely and when we were paraded before the colonel we were clean and respectable. The colonel looked us up and down and seemed quite taken with us.

'Well, at least I'm glad to know you didn't get drunk, dirty and disgrace your battalion, so in consideration of your fine record, I will take a lenient view of your A.W.L. this once.' And he fined us seven days' pay each and told us we were 'confined to barracks' for seven days, and were to report to the transport officer for duty today and tomorrow. After handing our pay books over for the red-ink entry, we about turned, clicked our heels and marched out – honorary soldiers for a week.

We made off to the transport lines where we found the drivers all very busy scraping mud off the bellies of the mules, painting horses' hooves black, and cleaning waggons and field cookers for some competition or other. The transport officer was very glad to see us and we spent a whole day cleaning trace chains and polishing each separate link with spit and sand and blasphemy.

We stayed at Bresle till the 12th May when we marched to Bouzincourt and were put into a train for Bailleul. We had a decent train trip for cattle truck tourists and reached Bailleul where we were billeted and the next day marched into some tents in a very nice little camp near Neuve-Église. Here we spent a couple of weeks digging gun pits for British batteries and unloading thousands of shells from ammunition trains and were dead lucky too. For one night, Fritz put a shell through the roof of a truck of shells and blew a man's finger off. Just as that shell burst a man in the truck dropped the 60-pounder for which I was reaching fair onto my arm and dislocated my shoulder. Had the shell entered the truck roof just two feet lower, the whole load – twenty trucks of them, would have gone up sky high and the angels would have been sweeping little scraps of Australian bodies off the floor of Heaven for a week or more.

We had a look at Wulvergem dump, which had been blown up. The place was utter chaos. Shells, whole and in bits, boards and boxes and scraps of ironmongery were scattered for hundreds of yards. Pieces of men and fragments of uniforms were draped across tree limbs everywhere, hung up on view by the window-dressing efforts of the god of war.

Another day we had a wonderful example of absolute utter stupidity. A party of us was being taken away on work by a British artillery officer and as we went along a road, Fritz began shelling ahead of us. The officer never slackened, but marched us on straight into the shelled patch of road. Perhaps he thought we were a party of armour-plated heroes, or perhaps he wasn't capable of thinking, or maybe was afraid to show fear before a bunch of Australians. To us it appeared as mad stiff-necked pride of neither sense nor use. It would have been different if Fritz could have seen us, but no, it was put on, as far as we could see, out of pure cussedness. Through the shells we marched, all but four men who were wounded and ran off the road into safety. We showed that Tommy officer that we'd go anywhere he was game to lead.

Just beyond the shelled area he halted us at his battery line and told the six men in the rear to escort the wounded back to our A.M.C. And then we opened up on him. He heard more about himself and his parentage in five minutes from our mob than the Genealogical Society could have told him in a year. We told him what we really thought of him and of his job too, and explained explicitly just what he could do with his job. Then we turned, left him standing on the road in full view and bearing of his own battery crowd, gathered up our wounded and went back to camp. We heard no more of the insubordination proceedings he threatened.

At Neuve-Église was an old French woman and her daughter running an estaminet and making their fortunes. Whenever Fritz began shelling the village, they would yell at us 'fin, Monsieur' and bustle us out and close-up shop. Then the old woman would grab the money box, race out into the yard and collar her cow by the horn and lead it down into their big cellar. The fat daughter would run screaming into the yard and drive their two big fat white pigs down into the cellar also. The girl would generally take whatever particular New Zealander she was doing well with at the time down into the safety of that bottle-laden cellar too.

One day when Fritz had hunted them all into the cellar, some New Zealanders and some of our crowd got into the estaminet and had the time of their lives. They didn't care if Fritz shelled all day so long as the liquor held out. Before they had properly quenched their thirst, the Fritz shelling eased up, so a bloke raced away and collected a box of Mills grenades. Every time they heard the old madam's sabots begin to clip-clop up the cellar steps, they'd burst a Mills in the backyard and she'd get down under cover for another ten minutes. The bombs ran out before the grog did and the old Madame landed up amongst them. Then they got called every kind of 'brigand' and 'no bon' that Madame knew and she quite spoilt the happy party.

On our last days at Neuve-Église, we had our bayonets sharpened and knew that something was sure to be doing pretty soon. Then we were marched away and shown a large relief model of Messines Ridge and the ground beyond that we were to attack. We knew we were in for another whopper stunt then, though the great concentration of guns and the tremendous preparations going on were read by us as soon as we landed at the Kortypyp Lines, Neuve-Église.

Now we are all out in the gathering dusk watching an enemy aeroplane flying towards five of our observation balloons that ride suspended in the distant sky. The plane makes for one of our balloons; two black dots drop like stones from the balloon and fall quickly. Suddenly a parachute opens above each black speck and slowly they float downwards, two men leaving their balloon by parachute. The plane nears the balloon; a puff of black smoke jumps from it and a smoke ball spreads and glows and the balloon, afire from stem to stern, is falling rapidly to the ground. The enemy plane turns to our second balloon; two more men drop from it and that balloon bursts into smoke and flame. Towards the third balloon we see the enemy plane fly but three of our own air machines swoop for it. The enemy machine out-manoeuvres ours and, with the three of them sitting on his tail, charges on and our third balloon is just a falling ball of smoke. Without a pause the Fritz machine has our fourth balloon down, but our planes have closed on him and he makes for home with three planes streaming after him.

We discuss his bravery and ability as our planes chase him home. Suddenly someone shouts, 'They're getting out of that last sausage too!' And sure enough the balloon men are dropping from it. 'There he is!

Look, comin' out of that cloud!' And there's the enemy plane emerging from a cloud just above that last balloon. Straight for it he flies and against the dark cloud we see his incendiary bullets jutting through the sky straight for the balloon.

'She's a goner!' And up in smoke goes our Number 5, as our three planes come from out of the cloud still after the Fritz machine. Our planes force him down lower and lower till he appears to be barely skimming the distant tree tops as he flattens out for home and gets clean away from our pursuing planes.

We try to sleep but we are continually being wakened by the gas guard and warnings. Snow comes in and says, 'The mines are to go up soon,' so I get up to see if I can see the explosion. Snow and I get into our boots and we go out and join some men and officers. We tramp off a good mile and climb a big hill where we settle down to watch. An officer tells us that zero hour has been fixed at 3.10 a.m. and that it is nearly three o'clock now.

We talk on. A few guns are firing, but the firing is not nearly so heavy as it has been for the past week. Enemy shells are falling on various spots not far away. Away in the distance half a dozen beams of light pierce the sky as our searchlights try to locate enemy aeroplanes coming over on bombing raids. Almost zero hour and we are quiet and expectant. We look at a watch. It is nine minutes past three.

'The cat's about to jump,' laughs someone.

Hardly are the words out of his mouth when, like the slamming of the door of Doom, a terrific roar goes up as hundreds of great guns let go right along our front. A dancing glow lights the whole countryside and on every side for miles we see darting pin pricks of flame as our guns roar into action. Our heavies are into it hard and solid.

'Look!' And there to the north on the crown of the great black dome we know is Messines Hill, we see a movement as of an enormous black tin hat slowly rising out of the hill. Suddenly the great rising mass is shattered into a black cloud of whirling dust as a huge rosette of flame bursts from it and great flames lick, dancing and flickering. High up in the sky above the explosion we see a bank of dark clouds turn red from the reflection of the terrible burst below. A minute or so later, we get the appalling roar, drowning even our guns' firing, as the sound of nineteen great mines going up bursts upon our ears. The ground rumbles, shivers and vibrates under us. The vibration passes on and months of mining and tunnelling work has reached its object. The mines have been fired!

We set off back for Kortypyp. Our guns belch and roar. Away up on the side of the Messines Ridge, shells can be seen bursting and above them, a roofing of bursting, flashing dots that we know is our shrapnel.

'That woke a few Fritz.'

'And sent a few to sleep too.'

'One of those mines would blow a battalion of men up.'

'There's the machine-guns!' And under the roaring of our huge artillery barrage we catch the crackling of our machine-gun barrage coming into action.

'They're going over up there now.' And we hear that our 3rd Divvy goes over the top in front of Ploegsteert Wood and attacks towards Warneton. The New Zealanders are to take Messines Ridge and village and the British 25th Division is on their left, whilst further to the left still the 9th Army Corps is to go through Wijtschate. It's a tremendous stunt.

Enemy shells are seen bursting all about the back areas now, so we hurry on for our huts. Fritz shells are falling thicker now, searching for our hidden guns. Luckily no shells land near us, but we hurry on nevertheless for Fritz shells are likely to jump our way any old time.

'Wonder how the attack is going?'

'This part of the attack will go off all right, but it might be a different tale when our turn comes. Fritz will have ten hours to get over this shock and be ready for us when we go over.'

'Too right. I know when I'd sooner go over.' And we'd change places with the N.Z.s now.

We reach camp. Our men are sleeping except for a few restless spirits, so we too turn in. Reveille goes early and as we turn out, a few Fritz shrapnel shells burst over the camp, ripping and tearing through the roof and walls of huts, so we get sent some distance away till things quieten down.

Breakfast is ready when we get back, but we have to fall in on parade, which we do in full battle equipment before we get that breakfast. We fall in, get lined up and receive final instructions about today's stunt then take our gear off and each man dumps his where he stands, gets his mess tin and goes after the hot stew that is ready.

The green stew has a queer taste: sharp, sour and bitter. There's something wrong with it. Soon we know. The stew has gas in it! The enemy gas of last night has been drawn up out of the grass by the morning mist that rose with the sun. We throw it away. Men are vomiting everywhere. Vomiting the gas-tainted stew; vomiting from nervousness as they realise they have swallowed gas along with what stew they've already eaten. There's nothing for it now but tinned meat so we get some bully beef and have that. We'll feel the need of that hot breakfast before the day is out. A good meal prior to the heavy exertion of a big battle is a great standby.

We get our equipment on and platoon after platoon moves off for Stinking Farm around to the north of Hill 63. We pass a horrible sight here. Three gunners are dead near some little gas shell holes. The gunners have been dead a day or two; killed by the cases or gas of the shells that fell amongst them. Their poor bodies are swollen dreadfully and their faces are green. We look away sickened and hurry past those bloated gas-filled bodies about to burst.

X

It's now eleven o'clock and we are at what was our front line last night. We are stopped and ordered to get our respirators on. We do and half-smothering in them, file along some old trenches and into a low valley in which gas still hangs. It's a red-hot day and we are stifling in the clammy respirators. Across the old front-line trenches we climb and are now out in what last night was no-man's-land.

We thankfully get our respirators off and see Fritz barbed wire everywhere. As we stand here waiting about in the glaring heat, we notice some tanks collecting nearby and a battery of 18-pounder guns galloping up. The horses halt in a cloud of dust, the guns are swung round, horses unhitched and galloped back. A few curt orders are given and the guns roar into action doing rapid fire. We watch the gunlayer on the nearest gun. He sits on his job laying his gun just as fast as the men can feed and fire it. His body jerks to the kicking recall. Blood is streaming from his nose and ears but he never lets up – bleeding from concussion.

Half past eleven comes and the great tanks move towards the big Messines Ridge. In artillery formation we move off to climb that great dusty, smoking hill. We go in little groups of six or eight, one man behind the other. Dozens of those little groups are climbing the hill, the tanks just ahead of us all the way. Suddenly the hillside above us kicks up in fifty places as the Fritz barrage of screeching, roaring, bursting shells comes down and through which we must somehow walk.

Following on through the dust and smoke of bursting shells, we see the tanks crawling ever upwards and ahead, a little Tank Corps man walking thirty yards ahead of each to guide it along. As we climb on we watch our other sections and the tanks. Great sprays of smoky black dust rise everywhere as the big 9.2 inch shells fall amongst us, searching for the tanks. A tank stops a direct hit, roars up and spins clean round and out of action.

Shells wail straight for us. Down on the ground we fling ourselves in an agony of suspense. *Crash! Bang!* and we're up and rushing on through the dust and smoke. We see a section of men get a shell clean amongst them and get tossed like ninepins everywhere. One lone man rises and moves on where eight moved only a minute before.

Dust and smoke cover everything. We can barely see the sections on either hand yet somehow they seem still to climb on and so do we. Eyes stinging from gas, dust and smoke, our dry throats burning from the biting fumes of the shells, coated with sweat and dirt, we climb through this terrible barrage, walking on the crumbling edge of a roaring, flashing volcano.

Fifty times we're up and down as shells nearly get us. Mad with thirst we move ever on. The leading two men of our little section go down hit. We step by them and climb on as orders are that no man is to fall out to attend the wounded. Now I'm in the lead and am desperately peering through the smoke and dust to keep my distance from the sections on either hand. Ahead I watch for the enemy as we are now very close to the brow of the Ridge.

Through the crashing shells I feel a thump on my back and hear Darky's roar, 'Snow's hit!' Another thump. 'Go on, don't stop, he's right.' And again I lead on and we are out of the barrage, through it, and on top of Messines Ridge. On either side, our men still advance in perfect formation. Not as many men have been hit as we expected, yet we've climbed through the fires of Hell.

Over dozens of broken, smashed trenches. Dead Fritz are here in their hundreds. We come to a mine crater. A huge hole a hundred yards in diameter and thirty yards deep. The enemy trenches for nearly a hundred and fifty yards on either side are blotted out, completely filled in. Under the explosion they have collapsed, smothering the men garrisoning them.

Dozens and dozens must be buried here to be reported 'missing, believed killed'.

Forward across more trenches and smashed dugouts. We've yet to cross the trenches that the main body of New Zealanders were to take this morning. That is the Black Line and out ahead somewhere is the Dotted Line, which the Auckland Regiment should now be holding by a series of outposts. Somewhere between those two lines, our own battalion scouts are laying the jumping-off tape for our big attack, which we are to launch at ten past one. It is now well past twelve so we hurry on.

Through the crumbled rubble heap of Messines we move. Steel helmets show below us, men cheer and we are up to the New Zealanders. Across the trench we jump. We've topped the Ridge and see below a sweep of beautiful country stretching for miles away into the distance.

Down the slope we move, as Fritz guns open and we're under another barrage. An odd machine-gun barks at us from down the gully in front, but a terrific barrage of machine-gun bullets enfilades us from half right. The bullets are coming from the direction of Warneton in front of the 3rd Division's position. Thicker and thicker fly the bullets. Men are dropping everywhere and we can almost feel them as they whistle past in a never-ending stream of death.

A flurried rush and we're at our jumping-off tape line, thankfully dropping down to seek what little cover we can find and grabbing for our water bottles. We carry two each and have orders that no water is to be touched until we are on our objective, but objective or no objective, orders or no orders, we must ease the maddening thirst of the past hour or so.

We're on a long line of white tape. It's the jumping-off tape of our battalion. Little flags showing our battalion colours are stuck into the ground and nearby are the mangled bodies of on officer and a corporal, two of the three men who so gallantly laid this tape under heavy shellfire.

Hugging what little cover the ground affords, we lie here as hundreds of machine-gun bullets fly overhead or smack into the ground nearby; every bullet searching for us. Back behind us, the track we so lately trod is dotted with khaki heaps. Our own mates, dead or dying. We see men ever moving amongst the fallen and know the New Zealanders are trying to get our wounded men under cover, but many back there are beyond the need for cover.

Shells are still falling on the other side of the ridge where poor Snow and dozens of others are lying wounded, but we can't go to their help as we jump-off in twenty minutes on our attack of half a mile against three strongly held positions. We can't spare a man to go back to the wounded. We're thinned out as it is.

An officer crawls along the position telling us that our attack has been postponed for two hours. We're to advance at 3.10 p.m. at which time the Tommies will attack on the left of Wijtschate. 'Blast the Tommies!' we tell him and sink lower into the ground to lie out in the open in full view of Fritz for over two hours. Machine-gunned and sniped at from the front, enfiladed by machine-guns from the right – how many of us will be alive when those two hours are up? But we can do nothing but cower down and wait for a bullet to smack into us or a shell to come and blow us sky high. Criminal mismanagement somewhere, but what can we do?

Our platoon is ordered back to the New Zealand position and with a rush we're in it, losing some more men in the movement. Suddenly we see a big Fritz attack out on our left. Battalions of grey-clad Fritz are lumbering forward. We line the parapet of the trench and side by side with the New Zealanders fire at those advancing men. A few minutes' rapid fire and the enemy attack falters, fails and the survivors are racing back for their trench; the counter-attack has been beaten off.

Another hour goes by. Twenty minutes to three now and word comes to prepare to advance. 'Come on, 14.' And following a wounded officer we're out of the N.Z. trench and racing once more for the tape line. Machine-guns are at us again as we charge towards the tape, jumping or side-stepping our dead mates. *Flop!* And we're down near the tape, wriggling into shell holes.

Another wait under machine-gun fire. It's now a red-hot day and our water is long gone. We hug the ground and wait. Shells are falling all around and the air above our heads is thick with the swish of enemy bullets. Thirsty, worn out, utterly exhausted, our men are falling asleep in the blazing sun as we wait for zero hour and the launching of our attack.

Jacko and I are together in a shell hole watching some Fritz 9.2 mm shells bursting close by. We hear the awful screaming of the shell and watch. There, about thirty feet above the ground, we see something like a little black pill fall from the sky and down we crouch as with a deafening roar and a trembling of the ground a huge funnel of black earth and smoke flies skywards.

Suddenly we shudder and shrink into our little shell hole as an enemy barrage is down upon us. *Crash! Bang! Thud!* and shells are bursting all about us. Dirt showers upon us. Fumes burn our throats and bring tears to our eyes. *Orr–up! Rr–up! Rr–up!* and shrapnel is bursting overhead. The pellets patter upon the ground ten yards behind us. We roll on our sides and are digging into the side of the shell hole to scoop out a cover for our heads; cover from that shrapnel in the open!

Heavier comes the barrage, by the greatest of good fortune falling just short of our line. The shells are missing us by a matter of yards. Noise is everywhere. We lie on the shuddering ground, rocking to the vibrations, under a shower of solid noise we feel we could reach out and touch. The shells come, burst and are gone, but that invisible noise keeps on – now near, now far, now near, now far again. Flat, unceasing noise.

A man jumps into our shell hole. 'Prepare to advance!' he roars as he drops down on top of us. I crawl out above the hole and wriggle on a few yards to where three men are lying behind a dead Fritz and roar the message. A man crawls away to his left to carry the message on and I flop into his place.

'Soon be at 'em now, Nulla,' one of the men shouts.

'Won't be any worse than this,' I yell back and wait on behind the dead Fritz, watching the yellowish green face of the boy on my left who is dry-vomiting desperately.

'Come on!'

Fifty men echo the shout as we rise to our feet and rush through the barrage.

'Come on! Come on!'

And we fly across that white road as enemy bullets in dozens bounce off it. Men scream, yell and roar, and we are down ten yards beyond it. Up, another rush, and our now thinning line is down again. I dive for cover behind a grave mound. The little wooden cross still carries its weather-stained lettering: '*Hier ruht in Gott*'. The grave of a fallen enemy shelters me. *Smack! Crack!* And the little wooden cross goes flying, hit by a bullet.

Up again and on once more. A rip, a tear and the respirator on my chest gives a tug sideways as a bullet flips through it. A narrow squeak. Three inches, a mere fraction of a second, half a step and . . . but no time for thinking as after my mates I madly career, my shining bayonet flashing in the sun for the enemy gunners to range on.

We are walking steadier now and advancing under deadly fire, which is taking a heavy toll. On our right we see Fritz prisoners making back towards the N.Z. line and behind them we see our men in an enemy trench. That's Oxygen Trench, we know, and the men are some of our A and B companies who have just captured it.

A big trench looms up before us; our first objective, Owl Trench. From this trench right in front of us a terrific machine-gun fire opens. We can't advance into that. Over on our right we see the A and B Company men veer off to their right. They too can't advance into this murderous fire. With a rush we are swinging to our left, down and worming our way onwards. Enemy heads show in the position. They're firing at us from forty yards away. Enemy bombs are flying through the air towards us. *Crack! Crack! Crack!* and our rifles are blazing away at the enemy as we charge on fair for that trench and the men in it.

'They're off!' And we stand and fire point blank at some Fritz who are racing from the trench. Our rifles crack and with a rush we dive into Owl Trench and it's ours. The strong-point from which the heavy firing came is in this trench and just along to the right a little. We get our bombs ready and work along the trench for that strongpoint, a concrete pill-box half hidden by broken earth. Straight for it we charge with the bayonet.

'*Kamerad! Kamerad!*' And a small bunch of Fritz rush out of the pill-box as we near it.

'*Kamerad* this amongst yourselves!' And *Whang!* one of our men has thrown a bomb at them. Terrified, they fly out of the trench. *Crack! Crack! Crack!* blaze our rifles and not an enemy is on his feet. They've gone the way most machine-gunners go who leave their surrender too late. War is war.

Shouts are heard along the trench further to the right and A and B companies are into it too. The whole length of Owl Trench is ours. From amongst the rubbish behind the pill-box, a big Fritz rises, a long machine-gun belt in his hand. He looks towards the noise A and B are kicking up, ducks round the pill-box, charges on and jumps into the trench right amongst our leading men. With a savage snarl, one of them is at him. A thud, a scream, and a bayonet is through him and he's on the ground dying.

'Come on!' And we climb out and make for our final objective, Owl Support, which we are told was 250 yards further on.

'C Company remain here!' an order is shouted from Owl Trench behind us.

'Come on, D!' is called from the front, and we see that C and D companies are all boxed up somehow. C was supposed to take Owl Trench and D was to leap-frog them and go on to take Owl Support, but somehow we all landed in Owl Trench together, probably due to the strong-point holding C up for a while.

Straight on for Owl Support makes D Company with a few of C Company racing along with us. Terrific fire is coming from Owl Support still 200 yards ahead. One of the tanks that has been co-operating with us makes for it and fires upon the trench and Fritz is quiet. The tank turns to make back, but as we charge on, the fire from the trench increases. We yell and wave to the tank, but it takes no notice and moves away, leaving a handful of us to charge that strongly held position. We are without officers to direct us, without N.C.O.s except one lone corporal as far as I can see. We work onwards still. No longer charging, but just a few of us worming our way from shell hole to shell hole with men falling every metre or so.

'Where's that flamin' tank?' But the tank is gone.

'Pass the word for the wounded to get back.' And we crouch in the shell holes, a mere handful of worn-out men, just a little isolated mob out of touch with the men on either side, facing an impossible task in front and the almost equally impossible task of getting back to Owl Trench alive.

For ten minutes we hold on here to give our wounded a chance to work back – if they can. Then someone shouts 'Make a break!' And we turn our backs on Owl Support, the trench we are unable to take, and desperately dive from shell hole to shell hole in the forlorn hope of getting back to the C Company men in Owl Trench.

Crack! Crack! Crack! and the enemy rifles are firing at our fleeing backs. It's now every man for himself. The wounded must get back as best they can or lie here to be collected by enemy patrols after dark. A mad rush, eyes searching for the next bit of cover, a flying dive into a shell hole, a pause, up, and the desperate race goes on, and still somehow the stinging crash of a bullet in the back has not yet come.

Yet another rush. 'Help me in!' And I'm into a big shell hole alongside a wounded man.

'They got me in the ankle going over, and I've got another one in the other leg, high up. Got it coming back.'

'Got any water on you?' Of course I haven't.

'Come on then, we'll give her a go.' And with our arms around each other I reef and tug him along somehow as he drags one leg and hops on the other wounded one.

'Keep going. Don't stop!' he implores. And we put in a mad rush and land in Owl Trench as men reach to help us in.

Men are still coming in. The remnants of old D Company. I see Longun, Dark and two other chaps charging back. A clatter, and they've made the trench too. We get together, the three of us, and hear Dark's opinion of the tanks. He's got less faith in them now than he had at Bullecourt.

A small crowd of C and D Company men are holding this trench. Our officers and N.C.O.s are gone. All we can do is hang on. Our dead dot the ground on every side. Here and there we see wounded men crawling in. We are out of touch with A and B companies on our right and can't see any of the 13th Brigade chaps on our left.

We intend to hold what we've got. A group of men, all wounded, are making in. A big fat man with a white handkerchief held high on a stick leads them. Suddenly the little group is knocked left and right as a burst of bullets gets them. A few crawl on – just a few. The rest lie there beside their leader, dead; the leader is the big jovial man, who but a few days ago was chewing our ears.

A man in the trench falls dead, shot through the head from behind. We wonder if someone in the New Zealand trench is firing on us. *Smack!* And another gets a bullet through the face. Someone is shooting us from behind! The men are yelling for rifle grenadiers. Darky and I have grenade cups on our rifles so make along to a group of men who say there's a sniper in the tree behind. We fire Mills grenades at the tree; they burst amongst its branches. Still another shot crashes into the trench and a man thirty yards down yells at us to burst our grenades in a heap of rubbish further to the right. We send grenade after grenade for that rubbish heap. With our rifle butts on the ground we fire as the men along the trench shout directions to us as they observe where our grenades are falling.

'They've got him! Here he comes!' And we look over the trench and see a big Fritz racing out of the rubbish. With hands held high he takes half a dozen steps. *Crack! Crack! Crack!* a dozen rifles fire, and the sniper falls riddled, dead before he hits the ground. It's short shrift for snipers who fire into men's backs.

For a while longer we hang on. It is getting dark and our wounded have begun to make as best we can to the N.Z. line. A long, cruel journey, for many will never make it.

'Fritz is coming! Stand to! Stand to!' And as far as we can see to left and right we see the enemy advancing. We line the trench and fire and fire and fire. Still the attackers come on! Still we fire in a desperate attempt to stop them. Nearer and nearer they come! They're thinning, but still closing in on us! They're faltering and we are stopping the attack.

'They're getting in behind us!' the alarmed shout goes up and out on our left, out where we thought the 13th Brigade was to be, is a long, struggling stream of Fritz – hundreds of them. They are working in behind us and we'll be cut off and taken prisoners! They've worked in whilst we were repelling the attack from the front. Closer and closer, Fritz are closing in on us, getting behind us in the gathering gloom! Hundreds of them. The attack from the front has been renewed too.

'We're goners,' a man laughs amidst the cracking of the rifles as we desperately fire into both attacks.

'You wounded men get back like blazes!' comes a roar from someone, and Dark asks Longun if he has his ticket for Berlin. Longun makes no reply, but empties his rifle at those moving patches.

'What about it, you chaps? We can't hold them off and it's nearly dark now. They'll surround us in the dark.'

'Come on, clear out. Let 'em have the stinkin' place.' And with a glance at our dead whom we must leave behind, we are scrambling out over the back of the trench.

We make back towards the N.Z. line of trenches. The men walk. Somehow they won't run. They'll retire, but they won't run. We gather up what wounded we can and our progress is slow. The gathering gloom favours our retirement and we reach the New Zealanders and climb down into their trench.

There aren't many of us now. Just the remnants of two fine companies that have suffered terribly. Not an officer or sergeant remains. We don't know what to do so remain with the N.Z.s in a little position near the tape line. We hear that things have gone better on the right where A and B companies have taken Owl Trench and Owl Support on their frontage and are holding them still.

Suddenly an avalanche of shells sweeps over us and our artillery is putting down a terrific barrage right along in front of our tape line. The men go nearly mad with rage as they realise the awful fact that our own artillery is firing upon them, especially A and B companies which are still holding the right-hand sections of Owl Trench and Owl Support. Frantic messages are sent, but communication is either not established or badly disorganised, for the barrage keeps up. Soon we see men staggering through the shellfire back towards us. A and B companies too are back, and the whole length of Owl Trench and Owl Support has been abandoned.

The A and B men are furious. They had repelled attack after attack against their front and on the flank until our barrage got to them from the rear. Shelled out of two dearly bought positions and by our own guns killing or wounding again our wounded mates out there in the shell holes! Our own guns have done what the enemy counter-attack couldn't do. Everything in front is now back in enemy hands. The gallant work of a hard-fought day, the deaths of dozens of men and the wounds of hundreds more have all gone for nothing.

'Blast our barrage!' is on every man's tongue.

We stand in the New Zealanders' trench for some time. Our few remaining officers come along, endeavouring to reorganise what's left of our battalion, and we move into some old enemy trenches. We're barely in them when an enemy barrage is down upon us. It's pitch dark as we wander around the maze of old Fritz trenches, vainly seeking cover from the exploding shells.

The shelling eases off and stops. Eventually we get sorted out into companies. We have no food and no water. All we do is stand about in the dark and talk. The men are incensed about the two-hour postponement of our attack this afternoon. They know how much easier our job would have been had we gone over when Fritz was disorganised from the mines, the barrage and the N.Z. attack. That two-hours delay gave the enemy time to reorganise and rush his reserves up.

Above all, the men can't forgive the dreadful shelling from our own guns. We suppose that the retirement of C and D companies on the left was taken to mean that A and B had retired also. All night long the ridge behind us is subjected to fierce enemy bombardment. Food can't be brought up through it. The wounded can't be taken back. The phone wires are smashed away, severing communication. Officers, runners and signallers trying to work through that fierce shelling are wounded or killed.

Morning dawns and we find that during the night, a communication sap has been dug right up to the N.Z. line of trenches through that heavy shelling. Men have fiercely worked under that barrage all night and these men are the Maoris of New Zealand. You Maoris'll do us!

It's daylight now. Eleven of us are in an old Fritz trench going through our packs, searching for food for we're starving, but they yield nothing so we crawl about searching for equipment left behind by wounded men. An officer comes up and tells us that the battalion, helped by two companies of the 40th Battalion, is again to hop-over and retake Owl Trench and Owl Support. He wants some of us to find a supply of enemy bombs as our grenades are running short.

Longun and I get a couple of bags each and wander around the Fritz trench to find some bombs. We crawl down his old broken dugouts, strike matches and gingerly step over torn dead Fritz everywhere.

'Come on, out of this. We'll find enough up on top. This rattin' is no good to me,' Longun complains, so we get up in the open again, just as an enemy barrage comes down hard and solid. We can't get back to our mates and have a rotten ten minutes crouched in a little trench till the barrage is over.

We go back, hand over our bombs and then hurry along to see if any food has been left for us. Just as we round a bend of the trench, we find one of the men we left, his two legs absolutely shattered. Desperate from fear, he lies on his side frantically clawing away at the trench wall to get cover. The sight of this poor unstrung, dying fellow is terrible. We marvel that any man so mangled can live, even for a minute.

Round the bend we hurry, afraid to speak, afraid of what we expect to find. Three men are dead where we left them sitting as we went off for bombs. Another man lies tossed across the side of the trench. There's no sign of Dark or the other three men we left, but smashed rifles, torn and frayed equipment and little spots of blood that tell us a shell landed fair amongst the party. We go on to the next bay where the men there tell us that Dark escaped lightest with only a leg wound and the other three were taken out also. We ask why the man with shot-off legs wasn't taken out too and we're told that the stretcher-bearers gave him no hope. Back we go to get a stretcher for him, but the bearers knew best. The poor wretch is dead.

'We advance in five minutes,' is passed along, and Longun and I rush around to find a rifle each and equipment as ours are all smashed up from the shell burst.

It's 8.30 a.m. as we hop-over again to retake the positions we lost last night. Our guns are keeping a heavy barrage on the enemy trench. We move on, passing our dead who fell yesterday. We are nearing Owl Trench now and see a few of our wounded who have been out all night. The poor wretches roll over and feebly wave to us, hoping to be saved.

On we go through rifle and machine-gun fire. Owl Trench is just ahead. Our barrage lifts from it and we see the men of our first wave throwing their bombs into it and then jumping in with the bayonets going. Enemy prisoners climb out and begin to make their way back.

With a rush we are passing them and trying to make them understand to take our wounded back as they go.

Owl Trench is under us. We cross it and race on towards where our shells are bombarding Owl Support. Closer and closer to the bursting shells we crawl. The barrage lifts and with a mad charge we're into the trench yelling. I see Fritz climbing out with hands held high. Others kneel in the trench and hold their arms up or cover their eyes in fear. The position is ours.

'Men wanted on the left!' is roared by someone and I rush along to where a bomb fight is going on. The din is terrific. Our shouts mingle with the calls of Fritz. Egg bombs and stick bombs fly at us. Men are falling everywhere, but still our men are throwing their Mills grenades. I rush up and throw the two bombs I have left. Someone yells at me from on top of the trench and I jump up there and lie beside young Jacko and fire at the Fritz helmets bobbing about down along the trench where those Fritz bombs are coming from. The Fritz give way and our men are steadily advancing along the trench. We can't see any more enemy heads to fire at so we jump down, pull the spades out from under our equipment and get to work throwing earth up on our parapet.

A sergeant rushes by. 'Pass all bombs to the left.' And a few are passed along. An officer comes along inspecting the position and encouraging us to dig on. Word comes to load all rifles to the full and we pause our digging and get our rifle magazines full. A young officer staggers along the trench, his head swathed in blood-stained bandages. His face is white and nervous-looking. As he passes by, led along by a stretcher-bearer, he keeps on repeating, 'We can still say the old 45th has never lost a position, boys.'

We continue working on. It's now well into the afternoon. An enemy bombardment opens upon us. We expect it to stop any moment and to have Fritz counter-attack but the bombardment keeps on. Every now and again a shell gets the trench as stretcher-bearers race up and down. We expect Fritz to come over and men's heads bob up above the trench, take a hurried glance and pop down again. Still no sign of Fritz counter-attack and still the shells fall upon us.

It's almost dark now. The shelling stops abruptly and a massed formation of Fritz is coming for us, bayonets streaking silver in the fading light. 'Come on, into them!' And we line the parapet and empty our rifles at them. They are mowed down, but more take their places. For a few more minutes we fire and the counter-attack scatters as the men break and run. Into their fleeing backs we fire until they are out of sight. Our rifles are hot. We're flushed and excited. *Bang! Crash!* And down we get under the trench wall as the barrage is on to us again.

For over three hours we get shelled then all is quiet. The quietness seems strange, unnatural. Our bearers are getting the wounded out. Those of us who are still left line the trench watching, listening and waiting for the next counter-attack. Jacko and I, nervous, unstrung, and hungry, sit against the trench wall almost asleep, worn out and despondent.

Towards morning some tea tasting of petrol is passed round and we drink and drink all we can get and bags of dates also; the first food to reach our post since we came in from Kortypyp early yesterday morning. Longun, Jacko and I eat dates till we are almost sick. No shortage of them, as a supply sufficient for the whole battalion came up and the far greater part of the old 45th is now lying dead or on its way to hospital.

It's just breaking day and the three of us get in some sniping at lost Fritz poking about down a gully. We reckon we got fourteen of them between us. The last of our stretcher parties come in. They have been out behind us all night searching for wounded.

Morning drags on. Shells are falling spasmodically on our trench. One lands fair above us and we dive sideways. I feel a red-hot pain in my left wrist as a piece of shell gets me. My watch falls and I grab my wrist, which is bleeding freely. The pain is severe and the whole arm is numb, but I know the wound isn't deep. Jacko rescues my watch and I slip it into my pocket. We examine the wound. The shell fragment has cut the leather band of the watch strap and made a long, deep flesh wound. Longun bandages it and tells me to make out whilst it's a bit quiet, but I can't do that as many a man in the trench has wounds ten times as bad and is carrying on with the job.

Another hour goes by. Longun and Jacko are away somewhere digging. My arm is sore and very swollen already so I have been left on 'look out' duty.

'Nulla!' I hear Longun frantically call. He walks up to me in a dazed sort of way. 'Come here.' His voice breaks. He's out of his calmness for the first time since I've known him. Without a word he turns and slouches away, head bent between sagging shoulders. I follow and see him stop along the trench and hear a forced cheerfulness from him as he softly says, 'How's it now, old chap? Here's Nulla.' And there lying against the back of the trench is poor little Jacko dying.

Big, terrified eyes flickering above a strangely blue-tinged frightened face. A man is supporting him against the trench. His right thigh is a great, black, blood-edged hole of mangled flesh from which protrude pieces of reddish bone. His thin little girlish lips are twitching. I can't speak. I want to cheer him up, to make him believe he'll be all right, but I can't speak. Jacko seems to be receding into the trench wall. Two frail little boyish hands paw towards me. I grab them and Longun's great hands close over ours and I feel Longun's hands trembling above mine as I hold Jacko's two.

'You fellows been . . . been good . . . to me. Ole man . . . ole . . .' And he shudders, his brave little shoulders droop. 'Tell Daddy I found it, Mummy. Ole man, ole man, ole . . .' And we grab him as he falls and lower him down, dead.

'A dud got him through the leg. A floppin' dud,' a man says disgustedly.

'God help him,' Longun says reverently from the very depths of his heart. 'And God help the next flamin' Fritz I get near!' he adds with all the hatred, the pent-up emotion and the savagery of a strong soul in the depths of despair.

I wasn't able to speak to our little mate and can't speak now. I look at Longun and realise I've seen murder in a man's face. Furrows line his cheeks, and his eyes are all pupils and filled with tears. One more look at the dead boy's face as I cover it with his helmet and turn away. My jaws feel that they will lock and snap, they are tightening, so I rush back to my post, take a look over the top and hide my face in my arms there across the parapet as the tears blind me to all. I see Jacko as I've seen him the last few minutes, see a dark night in the snow of the Somme and hear a young boy doing his first night in the forward area ask me, 'Duds are nothing to worry about, are they, Nulla?'

Poor little Jacko, you know the answer! God help you, little pal!

It's now early afternoon and we file along to our left to hunt some Fritz who are in the left of the trench in a part we didn't take yesterday. A snappy bombardment on the enemy trench and our bombers are rushing along, bombing as they go. Our bayonet men are with the bombers. Longun and I and a few more follow along to mop-up or to take the places of the bayonet men who fall. We race on, following the shouts and bursting bombs. Past dead and dying men of our crowd, into the enemy trench we jump.

'Here's one! Under these coats,' a man shouts, and I can see two feet showing under a couple of Fritz greatcoats as a Fritz hides in a little depression of the trench wall. 'There's a gun or something under them too,' the man calls as he props before the hiding Fritz.

'Go on, root him out! Let him have it!' orders the sergeant, motioning to the man to bayonet the enemy who won't come out.

'Go on, use your bayonet.'

'Oh, I couldn't have it on my conscience.'

The sergeant drops the Lewis gun panniers he was carrying, and reaches to take the man's rifle.

'Blast your conscience. This is the one place where your conscience doesn't count. Your conscience is back in your pack, stored at the transport lines.'

Bang! And Fritz fires a pistol from his hiding place and the man who wouldn't bayonet him reels back with a bullet through his shoulder.

A wild beast snarl and Longun jumps straight for the hidden man. *Stab, stab, stab*, and three times his bayonet has sunk deep into those coats. With a jump, Longun reefs at the coats and down at our feet clatters a machine-gun, whilst a man rolls down across the gun grabbing his legs and screaming in terror. Three patches of blood stain his grey trouser leg where the bayonet has gone home. The sergeant stoops, secures the fallen pistol and detaches a man – 'Stay and see this joker doesn't try to work that gun.' And on we race to catch up with the attack.

A Fritz officer in spotless uniform, and three dirty, ragged Fritz stand with hands up near a dugout. The sergeant yells down the dugout.

'None man,' says the officer as the sergeant again calls into the dugout. *Whong! Whong!* A man bursts two bombs in it to make sure, and laughs.

'Take these men back,' the sergeant tells me.

I wave my bayonet and the three Fritz move towards me, but the officer remains stationary. He looks at us haughtily.

'Officer surrender to officer. Bring officer.'

Longun jumps up behind him and laughs gleefully.

'Want an officer, do you? Here's an officer. Captain bayonet.'

And with a savage jab his ready bayonet is through the seat of the officer's pants. The officer doesn't wait any longer, but screams as he jumps about four feet in the air and runs towards his three men yelling like a pup with a broken tail. I hurry the prisoners along and as I make off, Longun's laughter floats after me.

'Just prod him a bit if he jibs on you.'

The officer doesn't wait to be prodded, but hurries on holding his hands across his injured part, and I see the blood working through his shaking fingers. I halt them near the gunner Longun wounded and motion to the three Fritz to carry him.

I get them back to our old position and tell an officer how our men are going. I tell him the Fritz officer speaks English. He questions him, but the man won't answer his questions. The Fritz officer goes off a packet about what Longun did, but somehow fails to take in our officer's meaning when he politely assures him that he is jolly lucky. The flash joker rubs his injured part very gingerly and is taken away wondering where his luck comes in.

I am given two bags of bombs and race back along the trench to deliver them where they are so badly needed. I pass more prisoners, nearly all wounded, making back.

One of our badly wounded is sagging against the trench.

'Get down. He's sniping through this gap,' the man warns me.

I get down and crawl past a gap that a shell has blown in the trench wall. I crawl past a dead officer and two dead men, noticing that the men have been shot through the head and the young officer through the throat and know a sniper's rifle is trained on the gap. A badly wounded man still somehow slogging on has certainly saved my life. I'm nearing the fight now. Our wounded men are staggering dazedly back, bleeding from unbandaged wounds. I come to Longun and the bayonet men crouched against the trench waiting. They spot my bombs.

'Quick, get 'em up!' someone shouts as I race up to the bomb throwers and spill the bombs out for them. An officer excitedly tells me, 'Your blood's worth bottling, lad,' as he grabs a pocket full of bombs.

Enemy bombs are falling and bursting everywhere. We reef the pins out of our grenades and throw them towards the Fritz. *Whang! Whang! Whang!* They explode ahead and we are still advancing along the sap, hunting the Fritz before us.

Bang! A Fritz egg bomb bursts on the trench above my head. My mouth and eyes are filled with dust, my head spins, my ears are ringing, but I'm not killed yet and tear along still bombing. *Bang!* And an enemy potato-masher bursts fair in the trench. An awful crack on the shin and I grab my leg, thinking it is chopped in two, and there at my feet is the wooden handle of that stick bomb. The handle has caught me fair across the shin.

'Bayonet men!' And a dozen men led by a tearing mad Longun race up to us.

'Wait for the burst and into 'em!' the officer calls, and as the bayonet men pause there comes a 'Now bombers, altogether – get ready – throw!' And we each throw a bomb into a wide part of the trench from where Fritz is making a stand. *Whang! Whang! Whang! Whang!*

'Into 'em!'

'At 'em!'

'Come on!' And our bayonet men are past and racing straight for the batch of Fritzes. Yells, curses, shouts, screams and roars are intermingled with the frenzied calls of '*Kamerad!*' And we land into the mix-up on the heels of our bayonet men. Across seven or eight dead and dying Fritz soldiers we rush. These men were caught by our Mills grenades.

On we charge past half a dozen bayoneted Fritz who are on the ground twitching, rolling and kicking in agony. Past them we tear to get into the dirty work ourselves.

Ahead we see Longun and two others leading the rush. We can see the enemy are running before the heat of our charge. Suddenly a huge Fritz officer lands dead in front of our leading men. *Crack! Crack!* His pistol spits twice and two men on Longun's right are down and Longun is charging straight on to that little black pistol, recklessly charging right on to it. He's between us and the Fritz officer. We can do nothing but rush on with a help we know will be too late. We see the officer jerking at his pistol, but it doesn't fire – it's empty or jammed.

Longun is at him. 'Get 'em up!' he roars in his animal madness, but the Fritz officer jumps back out of reach and has grabbed a rifle and charges with the bayonet at Longun. Their bayonets meet with a ringing clank and as the Fritz parries Longun's thrust to one side, we see him spit fair at Longun's face.

Back the man jumps and with all the overbearing arrogance of centuries of militarism behind him, again spits as they meet man to man in that narrow trench. They're mad, both of them, mad in the recklessness of their blood lust and fury.

Clank! Clank! Clank! meet the bayonets, and still we can't get past Longun. *Ping!* And that enemy bayonet flies up the side of Longun's face and sends his head sideways with a terrible jerk as his steel helmet flies clean out of the trench. In a flash we see the butt of Longun's rifle shoot back as he sways sideways, but like lightning he straightens up, lunges onwards and with a terrified scream of agony, the Fritz officer goes over backwards and Longun, a great raw gash on his cheek to the top of his head, is trembling and laughing as he wipes his blood-smeared bayonet against the wall of the trench.

We leave him there dazed and rush on, but run into a shower of enemy bombs. The floor, sides and top of the trench ahead are just a mass of dancing dust as the enemy bombs rain down. Several enemy machine-guns, firing from two concrete pill-boxes ahead, are chopping and cutting the rim of the trench away. Our advance is absolutely checked. We can't go on without help from the artillery now.

Like mad we work on with our shovels, trying to throw earth up to make a block in the trench. Two Lewis gun crews rush up and take up temporary positions to cover us from attack whilst we make the block. Like demons we drive our shovels, digging madly on. Enemy bullets crash about us. Some bombs burst near and we know Fritz is crawling up to bomb us out before we can construct the block. One of our Lewis guns puts a burst in and the other gun rattles into action too and no more bombs are thrown at us. Still we work on, working like madmen. *Crack!* comes a sniper's shot, and our officer goes down dead, shot through the head as he walked past a break in the top of the trench. Two sandbags are filled and thrown across the gap, blocking it, and the desperate shovelling goes on.

The sergeant grabs my spade. 'Race back and report the position. Tell the major we'll have to have artillery support if we're to take those two pill-boxes.'

I hurry back and catch up to a stream of wounded who are making back towards the rear. A few wounded Fritz are with them. I run past, waving to Longun as I go. He just nods, very sick looking. I deliver the sergeant's message and the only available officer goes up to inspect the captured length of trench. Back here the wounded are being collected and bandaged. Longun has a horrible gash up his face and head and reckons, 'This'll cruel me pitch with the sheilas now,' but soon gets serious and tells me, 'I got three of them Fritz with me old skewer before I fixed that flamin' spittin' machine of an officer of theirs. Between what I did and what you did with the bombs you fellows pelted into them, I reckon we're sort of gettin' square for little Jacko.'

Then he tells me to 'Write to Jacko's old people and tell 'em he got a bullet through the head and be sure and say he never felt a thing. And tell 'em how popular he was.'

After instructions about how I'm to try to locate Snow and Dark, we shake hands and he goes to the rear and I'm left on my own, the last of our little crowd.

I'm back in the captured part of the trench now. We've taken about two hundred yards of it. Evening draws on. Fritz counter-attacks twice and each time they go back badly thinned out. Shells and snipers are getting our men all evening. Still thinning us out.

Night, our third night, comes down and we are all set to work digging a sap towards the Fritz lines. We dig on, desperately weary, falling asleep as we dig. Three days and nights of continuous fighting. We're like men in a dream, a bad nightmare. Twice through the night we go out on bombing attacks and gain a little ground, losing more men each time. Nightmare fights in the dark over unknown ground.

Daylight dawns. Our fourth day drags slowly by. We just hold on, just the few of us who are left. Fritz is now leaving us alone except for a red bull-nosed aeroplane that flies along over our trench every now and again with its machine-gun rattling at us. We duck and dive round bays to dodge him and as he passes we empty our rifles at him, only to hear the bullets pinging harmlessly off his armour plating. Our curses follow him as he flies away.

The night of the 10th June, our fourth night, comes down. A man moans out in front. The moan shapes into unintelligible calls. We don't go out to him as our bearers say that they have thoroughly combed the ground out there, leaving none but dead men. The calls become more pleading so a stretcher party decides to go out, but two riflemen crawl out carefully ahead of them as we fear a trap. A few minutes go by and they are all in again with a man in the stretcher, a man who has been in a shell hole for three days and three nights. A man shot through the lungs, a man our bearers have dozens of times passed by as dead.

The bearers carry the man back and later return to tell us the doctor says he should pull through. Leaving him unconscious out in that shell hole has saved his life. Had he been moved three days ago he would most surely have died. Just a man's luck!

Word has just come that we are to be relieved at midnight after four days and four nights of attacks, repelling enemy attacks, advancing and retiring, digging or crawling around in the black night of a strange, ill-defined no-man's-land of dead men and mystery. The news of relief awakes no enthusiasm and very little hope. We're past caring and almost past hope. So many of our mates have gone west and we find it hard to realise that we are somehow to be saved where so many have fallen.

Our gear is collected and we are ready to move out as more shells fall and there are a few more men for whom the relief will be too late. The shells land all along our trench, but don't get many of us. There aren't many of us to get. Each man must be holding twenty yards of trench on his own.

A chap comes past and tells me, 'Paddy's gone. A shell got him. Took half his face off as clean as a whistle. Didn't you hear him scream?'

No, I didn't hear him scream. We don't any longer notice screams. We're used to them. Paddy had gone to find his brother Jim, for whom he's spent the past three nights searching – crawling around in no-man's-land turning dead men over in a vain search for the brother who fell on that first day. Three nights exposed to rifle and machine-gun fire and from us. In memory still we can hear that low, pleading call, 'Jim, Jimmy, Jimmo,' amid the rattle of the enemy guns and rifles at him. Then silence as we wonder if they got him. Silence for ten minutes or so and again there would come from some other direction the pleading call. The call of brother, for brother laid low days before.

Still we can see the agony in his face as he wandered the trench all day seeking news of Jim. Half a dozen men assured him that they saw Jim fall with a blue dot in his forehead, but he wasn't convinced. He must find Jim. He has found him! For days we have been telling each other that brothers should not be allowed to serve together; one pair, at least, of brothers will no longer serve in our battalion.

Ten o'clock! A sergeant comes down the trench and counts.

'How many, Serg?'

'Sixty-one,' he quietly says.

Sixty-one left of a whole battalion and many of them wounded, but hanging on.

We think we'll soon be out of it but our officer comes along detailing forty-five of us to come with him in a last attack on those two pill-boxes that blocked us yesterday afternoon. We pity ourselves but can't say much to the officer. We have heard the break in the voice as he told us of the attack. It's not his doing. Already he has led three separate bombing attacks and been out on patrols every night. His responsibility has been heavy. We know how he regrets the order that must send many of the few survivors to their deaths, but he is powerless to do other than lead us to the slaughter.

We get our rifles and bombs and, led by the officer and a sergeant, we crawl desperately out towards the concrete pill-boxes like men going to their doom. Suddenly a few of our trench mortar shells begin exploding ahead. Enemy flares go up in dozens. We lie under a jumping sheet of light as enemy machine-guns rake no-man's-land. Hundreds of bullets are flying over us, amongst us, and into us. So close are we to the enemy guns that their long rattling *crack, crack, crack* seems to be bursting in our very ear drums. Huddled in the shell holes, we feel the dust being showered upon us by the sheet of bullets, a sheet of death above us.

Suddenly a whistle shrills out and we are on our feet charging for the pill-boxes. Dozens of flares go up. We see Fritz firing at us from all sides of the pill-boxes. From four or five points we see the flash of machine-guns. Our men are falling on every side. Enemy bombs are among us. We reach some barbed wire. Men are getting through a gap in it. We see our brave officer clutch both hands to his eye and fall into some strands of wire. For a moment he hangs suspended and is lost to sight. We somehow know he is dead.

Twenty yards from the enemy now. We are throwing our grenades as we run. A Fritz right in front of me flings a bomb straight at me. I hear it thud near my feet. *Bang!* And I dive sideways to miss the burst. Too late. *Smack, smack, smack,* I feel the pieces of red-hot iron driving into my back as I fall on the edge of a shell hole. A wriggle and I roll into a hole in agony. Dust flies into my face as bullets chop the rim of the hole away from in front of me. A call as from afar floats over to me: 'Get back! Get back!' *Crack! Crack! Crack!* Surely these machine-guns are bursting inside my head.

I realise my mates are running back, what is left of them. Fritz still holds the pill-boxes and still fires from them and I'm only twenty yards from him. Flares go up. I can't move, I can't get out. Then the enemy fire is easing a little and the flares die down. I feel my back will snap if I move again, but enemy patrols will be out to collect the wounded, I know. I wait till a machine-gun eases down and wriggle on again. In the light of the distant flare I can see two men running for our trench. Somehow I must follow them. Must get back to our trench, if I can.

On I go crawling. A groan nearby and I slip into a shell hole alongside a wounded man. He is moaning in pain and has a bullet in each hip. He strikes at my rifle. 'Throw that away. If Fritz catches us with a rifle he'll bayonet us.' But somehow I can't part with it.

For ten minutes more we lie there. The pain in my back is even worse. Blood is streaming down my back, I know. I'm dizzy, weak and dazed.

'We'll have to go. Fritz'll be out any minute,' I whisper. We peep about. It is silent and dark. Somehow I get the man propped up and he falls across my shoulders and I rise with him and stagger on, suffering agony from his added weight. Twenty yards we go when a shell bursts almost under us and we are flung sideways. I roll into a shell hole and hear the man I was carrying, crying in delirium and crawling away as he cries.

I'm losing my grip, going out to it. I seem to feel my own head moving away from my body, moving on towards our trench, and out there behind me I hear that moaning man still moving away from me, but somehow I know that in his delirium he is desperately moving on, moving on straight back towards the enemy! Poor demented wretch!

I must reach our trench. I begin to crawl up the side of the shell hole I'm in. The side of the hole keeps moving upwards. Struggle as I may I can't get out, can't climb that moving bank. I begin to slip back, back, back into the hole and the bottom has dropped out of it. I can't climb, can't cling to the moving sides of this bottomless hole, and begin to drop, drop, drop into swaying utter blackness.

ELEVEN

A Quiet Innings

I'm back in a big Casualty Clearing Station near Steenwerck, having some of Fritz's ironmongery removed from my back. It's decent here where we sleep between sheets and get about in pyjamas all day, have our wounds dressed and play poker and two-up. We're the leisured class of the fighting army. Of course we know of plenty of leisured gents in other branches of the army having the time of their lives even though their letters do come addressed 'On Active Service', but it would be a poor sort of war that didn't have a few leisured gentlemen in it.

Of my night in the shell hole at Messines I remember nothing. I do recall dawn the next day when I saw four Fritz some distance off tramping slowly along under heavy loads and remember looking for my rifle to have a pot at them. The rifle was gone and soon I discovered it stuck in the ground by its bayonet and knew a stretcher party had come across me in the night thus marking my position. Everything seemed slewed round. I kept pretty low, wondering how far I had got from those pill-boxes last night. All was very quiet and I wondered if I could somehow work back in during the day.

Shots, revolver shots, suddenly came to me from in front so I got well down in that big shell hole. More revolver shots and men laughing. Surely the laughs of our men, not Fritz, for somehow I couldn't associate laughter with Fritz. I began to think that I must have crawled very close to our trenches the previous night and then raised my head for a hurried peep, but instead of looking at our trench, I found myself looking at the two great Fritz pill-boxes, with a digger calmly standing on the roof of one and firing a revolver at empty jam tins on the roof of the other. More diggers walking round just as if they owned the place or didn't give a cuss who did.

That was good enough for me, so I up-ended myself and made in to them, feeling pretty crook too. The men looked at me and began to laugh. I sat down and asked what the joke was and found out that my face was quite black. Then I knew how close that shell had been last night and wondered where the poor wounded wretch had got to after the shell had separated us.

The men round the pill-boxes were fellows of the 48th Battalion who said that our attack on those pill-boxes last night had been unsuccessful, but I knew that. An officer was interested and gave me some rum from his water bottle then said that a Fritz, captured during the night, gave information that they were ordered to vacate their pill-boxes and to be in a new line of trenches three-quarters of a mile to the rear by 1.30 that night. And we had attacked and suffered so, just three hours before that retirement! What ill luck to top off four luckless days!

Some 48th bearers bound up my wounds and put the breeze up me by saying they didn't like the look of them. I told them I could walk out, and after the officer had told me my battalion was at the La Plus Douve Farm lines, I set out to find them, wondering just how far I'd get before the gangrene and tetanus would set in and fix me.

Back over the great Messines Ridge I climbed. Dead men turning green were dotted everywhere, but they weren't of my battalion as I was half a mile from where we had climbed the Ridge and glad of it too.

About dinnertime I found a dressing station attached to the artillery and went in and asked the Tommy doctor to give me an injection. He had a look at my back, spilt plenty of iodine on it and gave me an injection in the chest, a blooming good one, too, that made me sorry I'd ever gone near him. Then he laughed and said, 'I think you need something in the other end. Just a minute and I'll get it for you.' I got the breeze up some more and was just about to nick away and lose my luckless great self when the quack returned with a big dish of red-hot stew and saved my life again.

I wandered about till dark and couldn't find that La Plus joint or anyone who'd ever heard of it so I was pretty fed up with everything. I asked some Scotty gunners if I could camp in their battery lines for the night. The Jocks were just fixing me up nicely when a young Scottish officer blew along and said I'd be more comfortable in his dugout, so along I went with him. He sent his batman for a tin hat of warm water and they bathed my back wounds and gave me several decent nips of whisky. I felt much better after the hot fomentations and the whisky. They did me the world of good, especially the whisky, and I got in a good night's sleep, waking up next day feeling pretty set, except for my sore back.

I stayed with the Jocks till dinnertime, but Fritz began shelling pretty heavily so I decided my place was with the old battalion and wandered about till I found the La Plus Douve Farm trenches. I landed there just as the men were having tea, preparatory to marching off somewhere. I reported myself and the company sergeant looked at his roll and said I'd been reported 'missing, believed killed', so I borrowed a few francs and sent a cable to my people telling them I was quite okay on the 12th June as I knew they would receive an official advice that I had been reported 'missing, believed killed on 10th June, 1917'.

After dark that night we marched back to La Crèche to have our first wash and shave in a week. On the march we discussed the Messines stunt and I learnt that the battalion had gone into the stunt as the strongest in the brigade and had come out the weakest. We had lost sixteen officers and five hundred and fifty odd men. Every C Company officer who went in had been killed and every D Company officer either killed or wounded. It was a sore and sorry battalion that marched towards La Crèche that night. Our mates back on Messines Ridge were ever on our minds.

Lonely and worn out we trudged along, yet as we went into La Crèche, a little crowd began to sing and it caught on, and we marched in, all in step, heads up, braving it out and doing our best to show we were not downhearted as we let it go.

Take me back to dear old Aussie,
Put me on a boat for Woolloomooloo;

Take me over there, drop me anywhere,
Sydney, Melbourne, Adelaide, well I don't care;
I just want to see my best girl,
Cuddling up again we soon shall be;
Oh! France it is a failure,
Take me back to Australia,
Aussie is the place for me.

Next morning I went on sick parade, got sent off to the Casualty Clearing Station and finished up in hospital where the quacks probed about into my seven wounds looking for bomb fragments. They took four pieces of iron out and left three in. The quack reckoned those three pieces would not cause me any worry unless I happened to scratch my back with a magnet.

Last night a few of the boys came over to see me and we fought Messines over again. They told me that the stunt is in the French and English papers as a great success for the British army and I know they feel a bit sore that the British army should get the credit for a stunt carried out by the 2nd Anzac Corps. It is generally like that though. Any decent thing we pull off goes before the public as a British victory, yet if a couple of our blokes helped by a dozen Tommies smash up a boozer, the papers jolly soon pin that on to 'a group of Australian soldiers'.

The boys also spoke of that last stunt of ours against the pill-boxes and told me that of the forty-five who went out only twenty-two returned – and in a tearing hurry too.

My hospital period at Steenwerck is over. I was discharged as physically fit yesterday morning after eleven days in hospital, given two days' dry rations and told to report to my unit at Renescure – discharged physically fit with seven open wounds covered with adhesive tape.

After leaving Steenwerck I tramped to Bailleul and jumped rides in several motor lorries till I landed at Renescure to find that the battalion had that very day gone to Le Doulieu by motor bus. Back to Le Doulieu, just three miles from Steenwerck and I had travelled over twenty miles from Steenwerck to find the battalion. The old luck let me down.

I stayed at Renescure last night. Struck up a yarn with an old French farmer couple where I bought a meal and they gave me a bed in a real bedroom. I enjoyed myself and I sat up till after midnight listening to the old boy speaking of when he was boxing on against the *Boche*.

They were very taken with me because I could speak to them in French and reckoned I was '*un homme très amiable*', so I had to live up to it. On parting this morning, I gave the old boy my jack-knife and the old madame a pair of Fritz field glasses. As I made off, the old couple were sitting together on a white-washed stone seeing what they could see through those Fritz glasses, but they'll never, never see their three fine sons again. Georges, the one '*si jovial*', or Alfred of whom the old father spoke as '*plus reservé*' or the '*très franche*' Paul, the *mitrailleur*, who died across his smoking gun out in the Champagne in 1914.

Poor lonely old couple! Three sons dead '*pour la patrie*'. What is ahead for them now? It was with a sad appreciation of what war means to French families that I climbed the dusty tail-board of a passing motor lorry with that brave old man's '*bonne chance*' and the old madame's motherly '*prenez garde*, Nulla', floating after me. 'Good luck.' Thanks, Monsieur, for I can do with it. 'Take care, Nulla.' Yes, Madame, I'll do my best in that direction too.

I reached Doulieu this afternoon and rejoined the old platoon in good billets in a farm. The battalion is to send a party of men in to Bailleul tomorrow to some big showy parade before the Duke of Connaught, a cobber of the king. Only the big men are being chosen. 'The big strappin' Anzacs' we jokingly call them. We hope the Duke likes them, but if he ever happens to inspect us when we're in the line, he'll find many a man-sized job being done by little men as well as big.

⨯

A few more days have gone by and we are back at old Kortypyp Camp from where we marched to Messines three weeks ago. After one night, we marched up to the Catacombs, a huge series of tunnels dug into Hill 63 where we are now living. These Catacombs hold hundreds of men and are fitted up with bunks arranged one above the other. The tunnels all connect up with each other and are called streets, bearing the name plates like real streets, and are lit by electricity and have gas-proof doors. The boys found some jackets of armour here and have been acting Ned Kelly in them.

Nearby is Hyde Park corner, all shell holes, dead mules and overturned wagons, little lonely graves and big cemeteries. Some men of our company are here. Fellows rejoining from hospital and a few new reinforcement jokers.

'Well, strike me pink! I thought the daisies'd be a foot high on your grave by now!' And here's Longun back with us again. He looks well, but carries a livid, tender-looking scar right along one side of his face. We remark on the scar and he tells us, 'Yes, that Fritz left his flamin' trade-mark on the old dial, but he only got into the meat a bit, no damage much.'

Longun goes away, digs up his gear, humps it along and finds a bunk near mine. We settle down together and yarn about our hospital experiences. Talk gets round to our mates now dotted far and wide. We recall how we came together in the camps back in Aussie in a mateship that has held together and stood the test. Seven of us there were at first, but now just we two are left together.

We were a pretty mixed crowd. There was Longun here, the longest and deadliest of the lot. Six feet two of long leisurely bullock-driver from the black soil of the outback. He has always been our leader and our hope. A cove who fears neither man nor beast – officers and N.C.O.s least of all. Left school the day he was long enough to balance a bullock whip. A great and serious reader and easily the best-educated man amongst us if education be judged upon how it keeps a man along life's rugged road.

Then Darky. Wiry, wild and witty. As hard-boiled as you make 'em. A fellow who'd been everywhere and done everything and perhaps everyone worth doing.

Yacob, a fat Russian Jew who used to swap his bacon with us for a few cigarettes. Had just deserted a ship to enlist when he first joined our crowd. Good-hearted poor beggar, as strong as a mule, he served as our handy man. Poor old Yacob, always becoming hot and bothered. How he used to run to oil and Russian lingo when excited.

And young Snow whose chief asset was a fond mother and plenty of sisters who were always sending along great hampers of decent tucker and more knitted socks and scarves than Snow had feet or neck for. We wouldn't have lost Snow for anything when we were down on the Somme, for we'd have hated to go back to army-issue socks.

Farmer was another in our crowd. We kept him chiefly for digging our dugouts or repairing them after some coot had fallen through the roof. He could do anything with a dugout except stop the leaks. A slow podgy old cove but very useful.

Number 6, the Prof. A man always prompt on parade, clean and methodical. Would have made a real good soldier if there hadn't been a war on. Prof was a high school teacher in civvy life. In some ways he was very learned, book wise, but in other ways he was a dope. A nice polite dope, but a full-blown dope nevertheless. To that we owe our 'educated fools'.

I made the seventh. My uses were a good sense of direction and the ability to speak to the Froggies in their own language or the *patois* of Flanders. My first asset so often helped to see us in safely from patrols in no-man's-land, or to guide us back to billets along the by-ways when the French gendarmes or our own military police were waiting to greet us along the highways.

Then my *parlez vousing* was a great help in making life better behind the lines. How often have I visited a Froggie family and kept them all safely indoors entertaining me whilst Longun and Dark cleaned up their eggs and butter, and Farmer and Yacob bandicooted an army pack of spuds and turnips for the Prof and Snow to peel and cook. We used to practise division of labour in our little lot.

We used to laugh often and joke about a speech the Prof made the night young Snow got a bad attack of conscience after eating too much roast sucking pig down at Plesselles. Longun and Dark had landed back in the billet with a nicely dressed young pig they had found hanging up in a farmhouse barn somewhere or other. Then I had to tramp about six miles with Longun and the pig to parley to an old madame to cook it for us, hang about for hours and hours till she had it nicely done, and then cart it back to Plesselles all wrapped up in paper and greatcoats.

Anyway, the Frogs got paid about three times its value for their pig. A French liaison officer saw to that. But we didn't pay. It was paid for by a Yorkshire battalion after the thing's greasy bones were found on the roof of one of their billets, the roof of that shed where Darky had so carefully placed them as we were returning from our little banquet.

Where's our little crowd now? Farmer collected a sniper's bullet in the arm whilst burying a dead officer near Fritz's Folly down on the Somme and is over in England at Dartford Hospital. Yacob stopped a bullet in the shin during a hop-over in front of Gueudecourt one cold frosty morning and we have no idea where he is, because being unable to write in English, we've had no word from him. The Prof got it whilst carrying food up to the men in the front line on the Somme too, and his front-line war service is over. He's at 12th Brigade Training Battalion at Codford in England as a clerk, and good luck to him, the decent old cove.

Messines fixed the rest of us. Snow went first with shell wounds as we were climbing the Ridge that first morning. We don't rightly know what he collected in the way of wounds. All we know is that he got safely back to the Casualty Clearing Station. We expect a letter any day, though of course he doesn't know where any of us are. Darky lasted till the second morning of Messines and escaped with a leg wound, a slight one, so no doubt he will be back soon. Longun got in the way of a bayonet in our third afternoon of that same stunt, but is back with the battalion again. I'm also back. But Messines got poor little Jacko for keeps. It was on our third day that the little chap shut his knife forever. Ever since he had joined up, down on the Somme, we had looked upon him as one of the crowd.

It's night again and we are marching up through Ploegsteert Wood to work on fatigues just behind the reserve lines. We pass empty shell cases hung up everywhere in readiness for beating should gas be sent over. Evidently gas warfare has been very active about the lines around St Yvon and Ploegsteert Wood.

'Come on, double!' And we are running full tilt along the road. *Crash! Bang! Bang! Crash!* And shells are all around us. We realise Fritz has seen us and rush off the road into small holes nearby. As the shelling keeps up, we duck and dive along the edge of the road for two hundred yards till we reach some old trenches, which we follow along till we can safely come out, and then form up and march back to the Catacombs.

Early afternoon comes round and a large party of armed men make off to comb Ploegsteert Wood for snipers who are supposed to be in it. They don't get any snipers, but get some information about a big cellar over near St Yvon somewhere, which Longun decides to look into. He is always very keen on those French cellars so the pair of us wander away to investigate and eventually find the cellar.

'You wait here and keep your eyes skinned in case anyone is poking about. I'll slip down and see what's in here.' And he disappears down the cellar.

Soon he's up again. 'Well, get any champagne?' I ask hopefully.

'Champagne, no! Flamin' joint is full of stinking gas fumes.' So we wander back.

Near the Catacombs we meet a bloke we call 'Pom'. He's been out all day lying near the road where we were shelled this morning. Got into a shell hole when the first salvo of shells came over and was too frightened to budge all day for fear Fritz would shell him. The war must be terrible to these poor windy buggers. Their worst enemy isn't Fritz shells, but their own vivid imagination.

We leave the Lumm Farm reserve line to take over the front line near Wambeke. Early afternoon finds us ready to move off for the line after dark. The O.C. asks if I'd like to go on battalion headquarters as a battalion runner. I tell him I'll give it a go, get my gear together and poke off and join the H.Q. crowd.

It's dark and we move off into the night. We tramp along unknown roads and sloppy little tracks, wind through small dark woods until we meet the 48th Battalion guides and see our A and C companies fade off into the murk to take over the front line from the 48th Battalion. Then B and D men lead off to go into the second line of trenches.

After our four companies have gone on into their positions, the H.Q. staff follows a guide who takes us to where several concrete pillboxes are dotted about on the edge of the wood where we eventually begin to get sorted out.

No one knows anything about the place, but I fall for the first trip to the line to learn the general whereabouts of our positions and where the various company headquarters happen to have lost themselves.

We wander off into the night and a 46th Battalion runner shows me around, impressing on me every landmark we happen to pass and having a good look round myself. I shall run very little risk of becoming lost after he has taken me over the ground. We find my D Company in a big concrete pill-box and in some trenches around it. On we go and soon find B Company. A long, duckboarded sap, the sides capped in many places with sandbags, leads on towards the line but eventually loses itself in mud and a few sloppy trenches that some of our boys are holding.

Over the top I follow the runner and we find half a dozen men in a ten-foot length of trench which is part of the front line. Then we come to a big hole with the C Company O.C. and a few men in it; this is the headquarters of the companies holding the front line. We walk the length of this haphazard front line. No trench is here, just a rough line of big holes and short trenches held by our men. It's one of those front lines that a man can so easily miss and walk across into Fritz.

Our tour of the line completed, we make back to the sap. We are passing a much-damaged pill-box.

'See that? Fritz landed a big shell on it a week ago when there were twenty-eight men in it, and one man came out alive. The rest were killed by the shell or by concussion. A lot of them bled to death as blood vessels in their heads burst.'

I'm to live in one of these for the next week or so. Nice thought that.

'I'll show you a short cut from here to Cabin Hill.'

'Where's Cabin Hill anyway?' I ask.

'That's the joint where your battalion H.Q. is.'

So I follow him along, learning the short cut. He winds about a lot and soon I am following him along the edge of a wood.

Misty rain is falling and we can hardly see. The man is on a little slippery path. He slips a good deal and comes down twice. Then I'm down with an awful flop into the mud. What I take to be a little gutter runs parallel with the path so I decide to walk in it thinking it won't be quite as slippery as the muddy path. I step straight into the water when down, down, down I sink until even my head has gone down under that freezing water. With a splash and a struggle I'm up, scrambling out as fast as I can. I have walked into a drainage channel, no more than two-feet wide, but a good six-feet deep, as I know to my sorrow.

'What! Did you walk into that channel? Didn't you see it?'

'Of course I saw it. No, I didn't walk into it. D'you think a man's mad? I flamin' well slipped in.' And I stand saturated through and through.

We make on and soon reach Cabin Hill. The 48th runner grabs his gear and goes. The colonel would like to be taken round the battalion's front and I'm the only one here who knows where the companies are and where the front line is, so sopping wet and far from home I fall for the job of escorting the colonel. As I have no ambition to do all the runs that are to be done, I suggest that it would be a good idea if some of the other runners come along to learn their way about. Four of them join the party and we set off.

I take them on a full tour of the whole battalion and after an hour's trudging and slushing about, we land back at Cabin Hill. Everything I wear is still sopping wet, but if all goes well I shall not fall for any more runs tonight. I get into our big concrete pill-box and get out of every stitch I'm wearing, carry them outside and wring them out several times. Then I cart the wet soggy mass inside and spread them on the cement floor, throw a blanket over them and quite naked drop down upon the blanket, pull another one over me and drop off to sleep.

Morning now and I awaken to find that my clothes have practically dried while I slept on them during the night, so I get dressed again.

It is very quiet here and we inspect the pill-boxes. They have been well built and should withstand anything but a direct hit from a big shell. The walls are written over. Names and addresses of dozens of Fritz are everywhere. Here and there we see what we reckon is poetry. A few pencil drawings, too, and some very fine caricatures of Fritz soldiers done in charcoal. The men remark on the fact that caricatures of Fritz officers are not shown, whereas amongst our crowd, it is generally the officers who form the subjects of our billet and dugout artists.

Night again. I do an early run to the line. All is quiet though some shells caught a few of our men just about dusk. After a quiet trip up and back, I settle down with the men and we pass the night in various ways.

Nearly morning now and five Fritz prisoners come down from the line. These are some men who tried to raid one of our posts and came a gutser.

I fall for the job of taking the prisoners back to brigade. On my way back, I see a big working party of Tommies burying a great heap of shells because someone has fallen down on his job and failed to make arrangements for their removal and storage elsewhere. These buried shells will most likely be forgotten. A wilful, criminal waste of shells we have so often longed for and may perhaps live to long for again. Maybe a man will die because these very shells are being buried in the ground instead of being fed into the breech of a British gun. More muddling organisation.

×

Night finds me making my way up the sap again. A party of men are out in the open carrying sheets of new corrugated iron. It's easy to see the men are jumpy and don't fancy their job. The iron shines in the moonlight. Fritz must see it – he can't miss it.

Suddenly an enemy machine-gun is blazing a stream of bullets at the carrying party. In an instant the men are flat on the ground or hidden in shell holes. All but one man who props his great sheet of iron straight up and gets down behind it. *Rrrrip!* And a stream of bullets is rattling across that iron as its carrier with a yell of fright drops it and races for the trench, followed by the laughs of his mates, lying down there under the bullets. Men all along the trench are laughing. It's about the most stupid act they've ever seen and the poor coot who brought it off is none other than poor windy old Pom.

Almost morning and I'm leaving the front line to return to Cabin Hill when an enemy barrage comes down upon the sap. There's no need for me to go through this shelling so I wait till it eases down and then set off.

The sap has been knocked about a fair bit. Luckily there were few men in it. Further down the sap I go. Some stretcher-bearers are here with a man who is shaking whilst his shuddering moans rend the still morning air. His tunic and shirt are torn away from his back. The frayed shirt and singlet are blood-stained. I glance at his wound. One glance is enough. His shoulder blade has been shot away and two ribs laid back, and in the wound the pink lung can be seen. I can do nothing, so hurry on.

Fifty yards on I meet a man being led down the sap. In the distance he looks like a masked man. The forehead and upper part of his face is covered by a red mask of his own blood.

We're moving out tonight. The guides of the Wiltshire Regiment are already here with us. We've taken them around the positions and are almost ready to shove off. The men are being relieved up in the line now. Soon word will be here that the Wiltshires have taken over and then we'll be off.

We've been in here eight days now and have had an exceptionally quiet innings, but quiet and all as it has been, we have had five or six men killed and thirty-odd wounded. Even the quietest parts of the line take their toll. Even in a quiet innings the wickets fall and players get their despatch to the pavilion, their innings ended.

'Follow on, H.Q.' And just as daylight begins to creep over the long, swampy countryside, we push out from Wambeke on the first stage of our day's march to Dranouter.

Another tour of the line is over; a few more men of the battalion have gone west and a few more to the hospitals, but the old battalion has done its job in its accustomed way.

TWELVE

Passing it on at Passchendaele

We've been on the move pretty constantly since we came out of Wambeke. We had a week at Dranouter of pretty rough drill where our corps commander, General Plumer, poked along and wiggled his little white moustache at us for a while and made off elsewhere. Then our new divisional commander, Sinclair-Maclagan, also had a look at us, but we stood it pretty well.

From Dranouter we did a long, tiring march to the Forêt de Nieppe, had the night there and because it was teeming rain the next day, were put on the road again. Through that pouring rain we slogged along mile after mile until we reached a little joint called Wallon-Cappel near Staple where we went into billets.

We had about three days there. More drill and another inspection, this time from Birdwood. A big draft of new men joined up and some old hands rejoined from hospitals, base camps and a few from furlough. Three inspections, plenty of reinforcements and an overdose of drill told us we were in for another stunt. A few inspections from the heads and it's a case of 'into the line' again. We know it only too well. It's not the first time we've seen the cooks inspecting the geese.

We scored a ride in motor-buses from Wallon-Cappel to Cuhem where we were billeted for a fortnight. There, more solid drill, broken by a couple of unauthorised trips that Longun and I made to St Omer, and one to Hazebrouck; two decent towns, but over-populated by staff officers and military police.

More motor lorries took us from Cuhem to Maison Blanche, near Nieppe. A few days' rest in peaceful rural surroundings came our way at the farm and we were really enjoying ourselves for once. There word came that our 1st and 2nd Divisions had been in a big stunt at the Menin Road and that we were to go in near Passchendaele. When word came about the move, some of the men very decidedly voiced their opinions that the army heads had broken faith with our division, the Fighting Fourth, as we call ourselves. We know that since Bullecourt and the Hindenburg Line stunts, the 1st, 2nd and 5th Divisions have been out for nearly five months' spell. We thought that we'd also go out for a rest after Noreuil, but that rest has not yet come. The Fourth has been in the line constantly, including Messines and two other front-line stunts, and now we're to go into Passchendaele along with the rest.

It can't be wondered at that a few of the men are growling, but the fact that more aren't grumbling is a wonderful indication of the fine spirit of the men. What grousing there is is born not of an aversion to tackling Passchendaele, but rather of the suspicion that the heads have broken faith with us.

Our three days at Maison Blanche come to an end and we march to Steenvoorde. The next day we are moved by motor-buses to Dominion Camp near Poperinge then march to Belgian Chateau, not far from Ypres. One night there and we go in the reserve line at Westhoek Ridge whilst some of our division and the Fifth are in the Polygon Wood attack.

We won't forget in a hurry that march from Belgian Chateau to Westhoek Ridge through stark desolation. We come through Ypres, once a fine city now smashed and burned to a crumbling shell. We see all that is left of the Ypres Cathedral and the famous Cloth Hall, a few shell-riddled broken walls precariously balanced around a heap of rubble that was once the architectural glory of Ypres. On we march through the town, hushed by the ghost of a fallen city's calamity. Out through the Menin Gate – just two great shattered walls converging on a torn and broken road that we know is the Menin Road.

Along it, we pass the dreaded Hell Fire Corner of such ill-repute. On again and we are at a busy intersection known as Birr Crossroads. Branching off at three crossroads, we follow along a corduroy road till we come to some rising shell-torn ground of Bellewaerde Ridge. The track from Bellewaerde to Westhoek Ridge is hell, just a narrow strip of corduroy laid down across miles of unending mud, pock-marked by thousands of watery shell holes. The whole road is bordered by dead mules and mud-splattered horses, smashed wagons and limbers and freshly killed men who have been tossed off the track to leave the corduroy open for the never-ending stream of traffic.

For six days and six nights we work under shellfire most of the time, in and around the reserve lines doing repair work on the road leading to Zonnebeke. Our casualties never cease to mount up, but the work goes on for the lines of communication must ever be kept open.

On the last night in September, the 2nd Battalion men come and relieve us and we somehow get back to Hell Fire Corner. Our period in the reserve lines is over, but we've left twenty men on Westhoek Ridge and have had another fifty wounded.

An officer is here now. 'We're in for it, men. The 2nd Division has made a couple of attacks and have been badly cut up. We're to take over the front line tonight.'

We're to be thrown into the front line just when we least expected it!

'Where is the front line?'

'No one knows just where the line is, but they've been fighting on Broodseinde Ridge all day. That's all we can gather.'

We move off. All night we force march along narrow corduroy roads getting five minutes' spell in each hour. The place is a stream of traffic. Wounded are coming back in hundreds – pale, quiet, drawn-looking men from the big attacks.

Every little while a shell lands on the corduroy and a traffic jam occurs whilst the dead or injured horses and mules are tossed off the road and the broken wagons tipped after them. Drivers run by, bleeding from freshly made wounds, but seeking to escape this constant shelling. They won't even wait to be bandaged, but rush headlong back.

We're now well past the traffic and very close to the front line. Enemy flares go up and machine-guns sound very close. Every fifty yards we are halted. Officers make off into the pitch blackness, seeking information as to where the 5th Brigade is, for we are to take over from them and it is now dangerously close to daylight.

Still we move on, passing our dead and certain we'll attack today. Machine-gun bullets are flying around. Now and again we see one of our men going back wounded. Several stretcher cases come by as we move on towards the flares.

Now we are passing dead Fritz in dozens so know we are on territory recently taken from the enemy. Again we halt. The guides from the line have met us, so at last the uncertainty is lifting.

'No talking. Pass the word.' And platoon after platoon follows on after the guide. Quietly we move on into the mud and slush of a black night over freshly shelled ground. An enemy flare goes up not a hundred yards off and we see our guide bend very low and creep along under a big bank. We do likewise.

Chut-chut-chut-chut! And an enemy gun is tearing bullets into the bank above our heads!

'Down!' hoarsely whispers our guide, and we are on hands and knees moving nervously along under those bullets that seem to be barely clearing us. The guide is up and walking and we rise and follow on across an absolute quagmire, on into unknown darkness.

Our platoon officer holds up a hand and we halt as he and the guide disappear into the darkness ahead. Muffled whispers are heard. Movement just ahead. Men are moving. Sounds of boots in the mud come to us from a big black path ahead. The black patch moves, takes form and men are hurrying back past us. They whisper 'good luck' and are gone.

'Lead on, 14.' And we go twenty yards forward and are in a roughly dug hole.

'This is our post.' And we load our rifles, get our bayonets fixed and place our bombs handy. The officer takes Longun and they crawl away to the right to find the next post. The sergeant and I crawl to the left to establish contact with the post on that side. We crawl a few yards and can hear Fritz cough now and again. Their flares go up, now near, now far, so we're unable to judge their line from them. A sound comes across the mud from our left and we edge in that way, a Mills grenade held ready to throw should we crawl into a Fritz post instead of one of our own. The sounds are clearer now, men moving about in one spot. Another few yards and the sounds stop. We lie here and wait, then move cautiously on.

Hiss! And we prop.

'What's up? Who's that?' An anxious whisper floats over to us and we have located the post. The sergeant whispers back in reply and we rise and walk in. The men here have a few yards of trench dug near a railway bank. Lying across the little trench is a great length of railway line – flung there by shellfire during the day.

The company O.C. tells us that no one knows just where the lines are or the location and disposition of the enemy and our own line is no more than a series of outposts. All we can do is to hang on and hope that daylight gets to us before Fritz launches an attack.

The sergeant and I crawl away and reach our post just as the eastern sky is beginning to brighten. Our platoon officer is back and asks me to come with him to find the battalion H.Q. We hurriedly make back and find the H.Q. staff in an old, shattered pill-box just on our side of Broodseinde. Men are at work dragging dead Fritz away from around the pill-box while Australian dead are lying in a row awaiting burial.

Our battalion is holding the newly captured line just on the south side of the Ypres–Roulers railway line. The major tells us that the battalion suffered twenty casualties in the relief of the line. No word is through as to whether we are to do an attack or just hold on. It is almost daylight so we hurry back to our post and get in just as the enemy gunners and snipers are getting busy.

The day goes by slowly. Every now and again we are shelled, but the enemy is uncertain as to our location and keeps jumping his shells all over the place searching for us.

Night is closing in and we now have a better idea where we are. We are to keep up constant patrolling tonight and are ready to go out when it is dark enough.

Time passes. Our first patrol is out and back again. We know another patrol is out. Suddenly rifles crash in front. An enemy machine-gun is spluttering savagely out in the darkness. We grab our rifles and stand to anxiously. Gradually the racket quietens down. Word comes along that our patrol almost walked into an enemy post and were fired upon. The patrol had to run for it and got back in, but every man was wounded.

Our turn to go out. Six of us sneak out and move cautiously into the sloppy stretch of black mud that separates us from the enemy. Quietly forward, carefully placing each foot to the ground to avoid any sound. Fifty, sixty, seventy yards when we come to a few strands of barbed wire. Very slowly we move along it. It is intact. No gaps, so we know the enemy hasn't yet opened it for a counter-attack. We follow the wire to the railway embankment and move back towards our line, hugging the big broken bank. We crouch against it and wait as the sergeant moves in towards our outpost line. An odd flare goes up. Whispered talk comes from the direction of our line. Someone is moving towards us. Our rifles turn towards the sound as it approaches and soon the sergeant is up to us. We make into one of our posts, then along to our own post and slip down into its muddy cover. Our patrol is over. The sergeant goes away to report that we have patrolled the enemy wire from opposite our post to the railway embankment and found it intact.

Night drags slowly on. We hear that a patrol has captured three Fritz. An hour or so later word comes through that another patrol has landed two more prisoners. The boys are doing good work tonight.

Day dawns wet and miserable. All day we stand in the cold drizzle as the enemy continues shelling heavily and a steady stream of walking wounded and stretcher cases files back along the duckboard tracks. The miserable day fades into night and Longun and others are taken away for work on carrying parties while the rest of us man our posts and wait. Our company O.C. comes along.

'Has Nulla gone back on the carrying parties?'

'No, Sir. I'm here.'

'Feel like doing some running for the rest of the stunt?'

I feel like doing some running all right, ten miles of it – straight back, non-stop, but I can't tell him that, so just say, 'Oh, yes, I'll give her a go again.'

'Goodo, well take this report back to H.Q. and see if there's anything there for me.'

Away I go, deliver the O.C.'s written report and am told, 'Just hang on a minute, there'll be messages to go back to the line.' I make out of the crowded pill-box and do my 'hanging on' sitting on a heap of old smashed planks watching the enemy shells bursting about and hoping I am well away when those Fritz gunners remember the pill-box they left behind.

Two big carrying parties come by and stand around waiting for instructions. I mooch across to them and ask Longun what he reckons he's supposed to be up to anyway.

'We're just waiting for the officer. He's gone over to get instructions so he'll know where to go and get lost.'

Then he tells me that a big attack is to be launched tonight by the 3rd Division and the 47th and 48th Battalions and that these two carrying parties are to cart bombs and ammunition, wire, picks and shovels up to our front line somewhere.

'Establishing forward dumps for the attack,' a sergeant calls it, and says the stuff has to be dumped as far forward as they can get it in order to be readily accessible to the consolidating parties when the attack has reached its objective.

The carriers fade away to do their work towards the success of the coming advance, one that is not sought after by any of us, that carries no limelight, but only hard, thankless toil and grave danger.

'D Company runner?' comes from within the pill-box.

'Here, Sir.' I go over and collect a note from the O.C. and am just making off when 'Runner' is called so back I go.

'Where's your rifle?'

'Up at 14 Platoon post, Sir.'

'Well get it when you go up, and ask your company C.O. to issue instructions that no man is to move out of his post unarmed.'

'Very well, Sir.' And away I go. Lumping a heavy rifle is a nuisance when doing runs.

I reach the line after a lot of ducking and diving, trying to dodge Fritz machine-guns that seem to be continually sweeping the track that I must follow.

I am kept on the job doing runs all night. About two hours before dawn I reach the H.Q. pill-box and find about a hundred men from our second line here. They carry shovels and tell me they are to dig a communication sap from our present line to the first objective as soon as it is captured. They can have their job on their own.

A group of strange officers is at the pill-box and a dozen or so men from our front-line posts are here to act as guides. Soon the guides make off back towards the rear and after a while they come past leading the attacking battalion up to our posts.

The major tells me, 'Slip on ahead and warn your O.C. that the first wave of the attack is moving into position.'

On I go passing platoon after platoon of the men who are to go over soon. The men are very quiet as they file on. Their job is a tough one. They are to advance over a thick, muddy, shell-torn stretch of country that is unknown to them, against a foe of whose strength or whereabouts they have but a very hazy idea and to take an objective which is merely a map position.

Ahead of the leading files, I reach the O.C., deliver the message and get sent along the length of our line to warn all men to 'stand to'. Hundreds of men are quietly lying in the mud just behind our outpost line and waiting to launch themselves through to the attack. There's a keyed-up feeling amongst us all. Men waiting for the blow to fall, expecting it to fall on them.

The O.C. shoves a note into my hand, written standing in the dark. I hurry back with it. About halfway, I pass through a battalion strung out in open order as far as I can see on either side. These men are the second wave of the attack and are to take the second objective wherever that is. I am given another written message at battalion H.Q. and reach the O.C. with it. He crawls down on the floor of a little trench and, covering his head and shoulders with a man's greatcoat, he flashes a torch on the note and reads it.

Whish! Whish! Whist! Whizz! Whizz! Whizz! and *Crash! Crash! Crash! Bang! Bang! Crash! Crash!* Our barrage is just clearing our heads and bursting on the enemy wire and on his forward positions and back areas. Out in front of us, shells are landing in a jumping, flashing, glowing roar of vivid lightning. The very night is afire.

Edward Lynch around the time of his second birthday. *Courtesy of family archive*

Private Lynch (right) with Private J. Cotterill, a friend from the 45th Battalion, taken while on leave in Weymouth, England, 17 October 1917.
Courtesy of family archive

Lynch is seated on the left with soldiers from his unit – probably his platoon – in 1917. The inscription on the rear of the photograph reads: 'What do you think of this for roughness? As usual I had more than a fair issue of the sun on my face.'
Courtesy of family archive

This photograph of Lynch was probably taken after a stint in hospital in England in 1917. *Courtesy of family archive*

Lynch, seated. On his lower right sleeve are length of service stripes and on his upper sleeve his colour patch. The Rising Sun insignia can be seen on his collar. *Courtesy of family archive*

Australians near Petit Pont, Belgium, study a large relief model of the Messines battlefield in June 1917.
Australian War Memorial negative no. E00632

Private John Hines, the 'souvenir king', in Polygon Wood, Belgium, September 1917.
Australian War Memorial negative no. E00822

Water carriers of the 45th Battalion near the Helles pill-box, Ypres Salient, September 1917.
Australian War Memorial negative no. E00770

45th Battalion medical detail at Anzac Ridge, Ypres Sector, September 1917.
Australian War Memorial negative no. E00839

45th Battalion men wearing gas regulators at Garter Point, Ypres Sector, September 1917.
Australian War Memorial negative no. E00825

The heavily damaged corduroy road near Westhoek in October 1917.
Australian War Memorial negative no. E01318

A dummy tree photographed in December 1917, which was used as an observation post on Hill 63 during the Battle of Messines. *Australian War Memorial negative no. E03861*

An Australian burial party surveys the bodies of German prisoners killed by a German shell the previous morning while being escorted to a prisoner-of-war cage. Villers-Bretonneux, April 1918.
Australian War Memorial negative no. E04768

Australian soldiers in May 1918 resting at the ferry landing on the bank of the Somme, Vaux-sur-Somme.
Australian War Memorial negative no. E04795

The chateau at Villers-Bretonneux in August 1918. *Australian War Memorial negative no. E03910*

An 'Albion' motor lorry, a common form of troop transport, in the damaged Villers-Bretonneux village. *Australian War Memorial negative no. E05412*

Troops of the 45th Battalion at Ascension Farm, sniping retreating Germans on the far hillside. The man kneeling on the far left is believed to be the author in September 1918. *Australian War Memorial negative no. E03260*

Back in civilian clothes in 1921, Lynch looks much older than in the photos taken of him in 1917. *Courtesy of family archive*

Lynch with his fiancée, Yvonne, at the home of her parents on the day of their engagement. *Courtesy of family archive*

Lynch with his youngest son, Greg, in the 1940s. By this stage Lynch was a captain in the army and had five children. *Courtesy of family archive*

Edward Lynch with his eldest son, Ned, off to the horseraces in December 1946. *Courtesy of family archive*

Enemy flares are going up everywhere. Fritz machine-guns are barking savagely. *Whonk! Bang!* And the enemy barrage is down upon us as we crouch in our little post knowing that one direct hit will fix us all. We glance behind – the enemy shells are everywhere. Blinding flashes of bursting fireballs.

Slush, slush, slush, the men of the first wave are jumping our post and steadily and slowly advancing towards where our shells are bursting. The enemy shells are falling everywhere, but their machine-guns are quiet. The advancing men are well ahead and cannot now be seen.

Suddenly our barrage lifts and we can now hear the slushing patter of running men as the first wave charge for the enemy. Flares go up in dozens, the machine-guns are fairly spluttering again out in front, shouts float back from ahead where we can see the first streaks of daylight creeping over the eternal mud.

Enemy shells are crashing everywhere and through the flashing flames of their roaring bursts, we can see the second wave of the advance coming through at the run. We give a yell of encouragement as they jump our trench and they are gone on towards the more distant point where our shells are now tearing into Fritz.

The first batches of the wounded are coming back. Walking, staggering, lurching, limping back. Men with blood-stained bandages and men with none. Men carrying smashed arms, others painfully limping on shattered legs. Laughing men and shivering men. Men with calm, quiet faces and fellows with jumping blood-shot eyes above strangely lined pain-racked and tortured faces. Men walking back as if there's nothing left to harm them and others who flinch and jump and throw themselves into shell holes at every shell burst and at each whistle of a passing bullet. Wounded men who have done their job.

Man after man slides down into our little post and we get their field dressings out, bandage their bleeding wounds and they pass on to the rear, joking or suffering silently. Our teeth and lips are brown with iodine stains from biting through the tops of iodine bottles. Longun lands back amongst us from the carrying party and tells us who of the carriers have been hit and how their job went off.

It is broad daylight now. The barrage is still well ahead. Word comes back that the first objective has been taken.

'Take the word for the digging party!' the O.C. roars at me above the dreadful din, and I climb out and race like mad. Shells crash nearby and bullets whistle and hiss past as I race for the shelter of the railway embankment and run along under it, head bent, going my hardest. I see dead and wounded men everywhere and know they are men of the two waves who have been caught by enemy shells and bullets before the advance really began. Our big digging party is strung out along the embankment. I deliver the message and they go forward on the run, rifles slung over their backs, spades in hand.

I turn and race back passing the stream of wounded men. Stretcher cases are coming in now and Fritz prisoners are helping our wounded men. Back at our post, I find it full of wounded men who can go no further, but must wait for the stretcher-bearers. A runner unstrung and excited jumps over our trench shouting, 'We've taken the second objective.' And is gone, tearing back with the message.

A wounded man is wandering about out in front. A man goes out and leads him in and we bandage his shoulder where a piece of shell hit him. He says he's not going out just yet and sits down on the floor and tells us about how the first objective was taken.

'Saw a terrible thing up there. A few of us rushed a Fritz post, but as we were right on top of it, a Fritz fired a flare gun at us and the flare went into a man's stomach. God! He screamed and screamed! He was running round and round trying to tear that burning flare out of his inside and all the time we could smell his flesh burning, just like grilled meat. He gave an awful scream and fell dead, but that horrible smell of burning flesh kept on. I can smell it still.' And he shudders and shakes at the memory of it all.

'Did you get the Fritz?'

'Too true we got him. Seven or eight bayonets got him, the flamin' mongrel!' And the man gets up and goes away, vomiting.

A big, happy boy comes by riding on the back of a powerful Fritz prisoner. The lad's two legs are bloodstained.

'What do you think of me hack?' he calls.

'Needs a bit of the gut worked off him.'

'Looks a bit broken-winded.' And they pass on.

Four Fritz are coming back. They are blood-stained and plastered in mud and have the terrified appearance of men at the end of their tether. One of them sees our trench and runs straight into it, whining as he comes.

Longun jumps in front of him.

'Get to blazes out of this! Keep goin'!' but the Fritz seems to misunderstand Longun and throws his arms about and pokes his face up as he tries to kiss him. Longun's great fists snap out; *crack, crack*, on the Fritz's face and *thud!* he is over on his back then up and running after the other three, whimpering like a frightened child.

The O.C. comes along to the position.

'Want you.' He beckons and I follow him. Each post is full of wounded men. Dozens and dozens are walking back. More prisoners are coming in. The stretcher-bearers are out everywhere carrying in wounded men. The ground as far ahead as we can see is dotted with men who will never again need the stretcher-bearers or anyone else. Their fighting is done. They've dug in on their final objective, poor beggars.

I follow the O.C. along the length of the position and back again on his tour of inspection. We see a big party of our own battalion hard at work digging a communication sap out to the first objective, which is now our second line. For hours they will dig on. An enemy plane comes over looking for someone to fire on or to lay a few big bombs. The digging party gets down in the mud until the plane goes off to worry someone else, then they're up and into it again.

It is night now – we're to be relieved before morning and glad of it. We've been in here for three days and although we haven't done any hop-overs, we have had nearly two hundred casualties. Fritz has been shelling our posts and working parties heavily, but our artillery has been pelting everything they have at Fritz and they must be as badly shaken as we are.

The night is very dark. Enemy fire is intense and our casualties are mounting up. I have had a hard, gruelling day running messages mostly under snipers' rifles, but they haven't got me yet. The runners are now working in pairs to ensure the messages get through. I am running with a man we call 'Turk' who's a stranger to me. We've been together all day and now are at the first objective taken in the big attack and have been told to wait for another message to go back.

Suddenly an enemy barrage is down around us. *Crash! Crash!* as the shells explode, sending spouts of mud skywards at each burst. A clatter and a smack and a runner from the second objective line out ahead is amongst us, scared after a mad headlong career through the shells.

'Where's the O.C. on this line?' he calls, his almost breathless voice ringing with urgency.

The O.C., busy writing his reply for us to take back, looks up.

'Here, what's wrong?' And the man rushes up and hands him a note.

'For you,' he gasps, and the O.C. crouches and flashes a torch on it, signs his name on the message and tells me, 'Get this to the battalion commander with all speed.'

Turk and I make to climb out.

'No, don't go through that. Go along and follow the new sap back, it's safer.' And we run along the trench till we reach the sap and begin rushing down it. I have the message in my pocket and Turk is on my heels. We're a quarter of the way down the sap and all hell breaks loose. Enemy shells are crashing and killing and wounding men every few yards. None can escape as the enemy barrage has caught the sap absolutely full of men from a big working and carrying party.

'Stretcher-bearers! Pass the word for bearers! Men hit!'

'Bearers wanted!' The urgent calls are being shouted from end to end of the sap.

Turk and I are shoving and fighting our way over dead and wounded men. We can't wait to help anyone. Our message must go through.

We're now halfway down the sap. Here it is full of men carrying duckboards, 'A' frames and sheets of corrugated iron. *Bang! Bang!* And the shells are crashing in an unending stream of flames and whistling roars all about us, as we forge ahead ducking and diving and shoving our way along. The scene is terrible. Men are lying in agony everywhere. Some reach out to us to be helped along. We brush them off and struggle and climb over 'A' frames and up-ended duckboards for a few more yards.

Crash! And just behind us another shell lands fair into the trench. We know what now lies where it burst, and shove along, but *Crash! Crash!* and two more land a few yards ahead. The flame lights up everything. A rush of air and another phosphorus-laden blast is in our faces. It's only a minute and we must catch a shell. We can't last. We're barely making a metre a minute so dense is the jam of men and material along the trench.

Bang! Crash! Bang! We're fair in the centre of a terrific shelling. I turn to Turk and roar, 'Give it a go over the top?'

He nods and in a far-away, hopeless, despairing voice his shout comes back, 'Can't be any worse.'

We grab the trench wall, waiting. Three shells land together almost on us. 'Now!' I roar, and we are out of the trench and racing madly along its side. Turk leads. I see his racing figure flinch, duck and jump from side to side as the shells burst close. I'm gaining on him, we're racing side by side, step for step, I'm drawing ahead as on we dash.

'Wait! Don't leave me! Wait! Wait!' His frenzied calls are following me, but I've seen a black patch ahead where shells aren't bursting and know we're getting beyond the barrage. I'll wait for him there, not here, and fly madly on.

Above the shouts of Turk, above the roar of the shell bursts, my terrified ears catch the wailing shriek of a shell coming fair for me! I screw and twist in my stride, trying to fling myself down. *Whizz! Crash!* The ground under my feet is heaving upwards. I'm surrounded by a shower of mud and blue, vicious flame. My feet are rising, rising, my head is going down, down, I'm falling, falling, falling through a solid cloud of roaring sound. *Smack!* And I am on my back, winded. My head and back have had an awful thud. I'm dazed.

Clatter, clatter, clatter, someone is coming to me, someone running on wood. A man's boot lands hard on my chest.

'Wait! Wait!' comes from above the boot. *Clatter, clat, clat*, the sounds are going from me now.

'Wait! Wait!' drifts back to me from away ahead. Pain, gnawing pain, shoots through me. My hip, my knee, my leg, my foot. I come to my senses and, getting my breath back, realise that Turk has stamped on me, over me, and gone tearing on ahead in a frenzy of fear. I look about and am lying on my back in a deep trench, lying on hard wooden duckboards. I realise that a shell has burst under me and tossed me into the trench. I know my leg is smashed, it's numb, and now a shooting mass of jumping pain. I must examine it, must bandage it, must stop the bleeding, but somehow all I can do is to roll and roll on that leg, pressing it harder and harder into the boards.

Hands are pressing my shoulders, hands are forcing me to my back.

'Steady, steady, where're you hit?' And two or three men are holding me.

'Here, have a drink!' I am held up, a man's water bottle is being held to my mouth and I am greedily drinking cold water. I'm better now and clearly realise where I am and just lie still, suffering agony from my foot as the numbness gives way to pain. I can feel my boot is full of blood. A man straightens my leg, hands touch my foot. A groan escapes against my will as the boot is moved and a voice says, 'Better leave it till we get the bearers.'

I sit up. My whole leg is numb, but my foot is paining terribly. I glance at it. The boot is cut in two through the sole. The toe is pointing back towards the heel.

Someone says, 'We thought you were a goner. A shell burst right under you and you seemed to rise up out of the flame and go sailing through the air like a spread-eagled frog.'

'Two shells got under him. The first was a dud, that's what hit you, for you were falling when the second burst and threw you back up,' says a second man.

'She's easing off, Bill.'

I can hear that the barrage is only light now.

'Here's some stretcher-bearers.' And four 46th Battalion bearers are with us. They get busy on my boot. One bearer can't undo the lace.

'Cut it,' his mate tells him and passes a razor across. The first bearer steadies the boot and cuts at the lace. It seems tough and they are hurting me. Through at last.

'Blast it all! Look at me razor, all gapped! What the blazes have you got for laces?' And I remember that it's insulated telephone wire.

The boot is off. They slit the sock off with scissors and examine the foot. 'You've got a nice Blighty, son. You'll never see any more stoush. Your foot's broken clean back and cut right along the side and underneath too.' And they are bandaging it up. Soon it is swathed in bandages.

The bearers begin opening the stretcher.

'No, we don't want that. Can't carry it in this sap and it's too risky to go over the top. The shelling might open again any minute,' a bearer tells his mates.

'Here, stick him on me back, he's only a little codger,' a big bearer laughs, and I am hoisted up piggy-back fashion and the man sets off down the trench with me on his back. The shellfire begins again though not quite so heavily. Shells are again landing all along the sap. I'm very uncomfortable, very unhappy. My bandaged foot is continually bumping someone or something, or brushing against the side of the trench wall. Hanging down is painful. *Whizz! Bang!* Shells skim the trench and I can't duck. My head and shoulders are well above the top of the trench as the big man carrying me strides steadily on.

At last we reach the old outpost line. The bearers put me on the stretcher and, hoisting it shoulder high, strike out across the open for the rear. It's my first ride on a stretcher. I never want another. Every few steps a bearer's foot slips and I feel I'm being tipped off and there's nothing to grab to save myself. I hear shells whistling through the air. Now and again I catch the soft, deathly hum of enemy bullets. From my airy perch I see on either side the dancing death-fires of bursting shells. I'm helpless. Held sky-high so it seems, I'm moved on, unable even to duck my head. I've often yelled for stretchers for other blokes, but I'll guarantee I'll never yell for one for myself if I ever get off this alive.

Once we're back into comparative safety I realise my fears have been my worst worry. It's not too bad on a stretcher after all when you get used to it and when the bullets aren't humming around your lofty pig-rooting bed.

I've been watching and enquiring for Turk. No one knows just where he is. No one seems to know him and the few who do haven't seen him. He should have kept in touch with me. Should have taken our message on when I got hit, but he's not here and that important message is still in my pocket and must be delivered somehow.

The bearers lower me down. Many other bearers are here. It is a changeover station for the relays of bearers. I recognise it as only a couple of hundred yards from where my message must be delivered. I sit up on the stretcher and begin to twist round in search of someone to carry my message on.

Hands are forcing me down and an officer with soft white hands is gently easing me back on the stretcher. An elderly delicate white face shows above the polished Sam Browne. The officer speaks, 'Take it easy, lad. Let me make you more comfortable.' He kneels beside me.

'I'm a minister of God. Is there anything I can do for you?'

'Yes, Sir.' And I'm gleefully ripping open my pocket.

'Would you please deliver this message to that pill-box over there? It's a message from the front line and important.'

The padre has the message. 'Maybe a call from the boys in the front line for succour.'

'More likely a call for rum.' A bearer laughs.

'You men will have your joke.' And the old padre is hurrying off straight for the pill-box, happy to be rendering active service in the field.

'Hey, you've got a bloomin' cheek sendin' a message by a chaplain. Don't you know they're non-combatants?'

Another bearer is into the argument. 'If you'd seen some of the places that 12th Brigade padre, Father Devine, took himself into at Pozières and Mouquet Farm, you wouldn't reckon they were non-combatants.' My stretcher is shouldered and I'm being carried still further back.

The bearers follow along duckboard tracks that have been laid down over the mud. It would be impossible even to walk, much less carry stretcher cases out, were it not for these duckboards.

An enemy plane is coming low over us. 'Stop!' a bearer warns in alarm and the men stand. In the pale moonlight I can see a great black bat-like shape moving directly overhead. It appears to be directly over my stretcher. Its engine is droning steadily.

Whoosh! Zonk! Bang! A huge bomb lands thirty yards behind us. *Whoosh! Whoosh! Whoosh!* More aerial bombs are falling straight for us.

'Come on! Get!'

And the front of the stretcher bumps on the duckboards and I'm on my feet and racing with the four bearers for the shelter of a dark wood thirty yards ahead as the awful thudding bang of three big bombs lends speed to our flying feet. More bombs are whistling and crashing back on the duckboard track as we dive for the butts of the trees.

The plane passes on and we move together. A bearer laughs, 'Hey, you told him his foot was smashed? Flamin' near cleaned the lot of us up! Wouldn't like to have to run him down if he's feelin' real good.'

They laugh and carry me back to the duckboard track.

I'm on the stretcher again. My bandages are black with mud and nearly off. I tell the bearers that I'm right. I don't want to be on this track when the bomber returns. The fixing of the bandages can wait.

On through the night the bearers carry me. We are at some busy place now. My stretcher is placed on a trolley and is being pushed along. There are four stretchers on it, but no sound comes from the other three men. When I see their three quiet forms, I realise that I'm lucky in my wound.

We are at some road. Motor engines are running nearby. I am being lifted into a dark motor ambulance. Four stretcher cases are inside and I'm in the top bunk on one side. Gears are slipped, the engine revs and we are moving, jolting terribly over the rough, broken roads. At every jolt the man in the bed below groans. The lorry is gaining speed; the man's groans become one continuous, awful noise. The man opposite whispers that the poor wretch has stomach wounds, that it would be far kinder to put him out to die quietly on the roadside than to torture him to death like this. I quite agree.

The ambulance is fairly racing now. Above its roaring engine we catch the occasional burst of a shell.

'The road's being shelled!' a man calls from a bottom bunk and we lie in the bucking, lurching ambulance unable to do anything but think, grip our wounds to ease the jarring and hope for the best. We've seen ambulances tipped over before.

The shell bursts can no longer be heard. We are moving very slowly. We stop, on a few yards, stop again, crawl on again. We hear the grating of iron wheels on stone, the rattle of a passing motor lorry. The thick, heavy smell of burnt oil hangs everywhere, the friendly, hot smell of sweating horses drifts in. We know we are in a stream of traffic.

We are moving steadily onward. Must be a quiet road somewhere. We stop. Doors are opened from outside. Lamps are being carried about. An A.M.C. orderly enters the ambulance and shines a bright light on us.

'How are you, right?'

'Think the flamin' ride has fixed one chap,' says the man opposite to the orderly, and they hurry away the man who was moaning, but who for the past hour has been so silent. The rest of us wait on in the ambulance. The orderlies return and I hear someone ask after the case they've just carried away.

I don't catch the orderly's reply, but the man who enquired says, 'Reckoned as much. Knew for the last hour I was ridin' in a flamin' hearse, not an ambulance.'

My stretcher passes into a long tent of dazzling lights. I am at a big Casualty Clearing Station. The orderlies place my stretcher on some trestles near the entrance. I have a look round the large marquee and see row upon row of beds, clean beds. Just the sight of a bed with snowy sheets seems to fly one into another world, a world removed from mud and slush, from bursting shells and tangled wire, from belching guns and circling flares.

Leisurely looking doctors and busy, efficient little nurses are everywhere. Orderlies are continually carrying stretcher cases about.

'Hullo! Another Aussie.' And a spotlessly clean little Australian army sister is speaking. I wish she wouldn't stand so close for somehow it seems wrong that such starched cleanliness should hover so close to the mud and filth that is me. She laughs and jokes and says it would never do for my best girl to see me now, and all the time she is writing my particulars on a little card.

'Where are you from?' she says, undoing my mud-plastered bandages.

'Up Bathurst way, New South.'

'No, I don't mean that. Where were you when you were wounded?' She laughs.

'Up near Passchendaele.'

'Passchendaele, Ypres, Menin Road, Westhoek, Broodseinde, Polygon Wood. For six weeks we've heard nothing else. And are you still passing it on with the enemy at Passchendaele?'

'Yes, Sister, and Fritz is passing a lot of it back too.'

She goes to tie the little card to a button hole, but I take it and fasten it for her. Somehow I can't let her touch the dirty black mud with which I am encased.

The sister has gone away. A happy-go-lucky doctor gives me a needle, writes something on my card and is gone.

'Get your pockets emptied into that.' And an A.A.M.C. digger gives me a little calico bag with a running string through the top. I put my pay-book, wallet and smokes in the bag, then the orderly helps me out of my muddy uniform and into a clean singlet and pyjamas. I am carried away to the operating theatre.

The doctors examine my wound and clean it out very carefully; then a sister bandages it up and I am being carried out. That theatre puts the breezes up me, for the first thing I saw was a bucket of arms and hands and feet being carried out.

Now I'm in a real bed, sitting up drinking hot soup. I am quite comfortable, but the pain of my wound prevents me from getting the sleep I have been craving ever since I saw these beds.

Morning comes in wet and miserable. The marquee is all bustle, for the word has come through that an ambulance train leaves this morning. Doctors are visiting the beds deciding who will be sent away in the train. Two doctors approach my bed. They don't examine me, but examine my card and tell me I shall be sent back to the base hospital.

Orderlies place me on a stretcher and I am carried into a long hospital train. I get a top bunk so can see very little of the surrounding country as we steam slowly southward.

For two days our train moves slowly on, but just on dusk on the second day, we pull into Rouen station and the patients are taken into a large General Hospital.

All wounds are undone, examined and treated. I score a hot bath, but I don't want another. This lying in bed on a cold, wet waterproof sheet and being rubbed down with a bit of wet rag doesn't appeal to me much. I'd almost as soon remain warm and dirty.

It is now three days since my hospital train reached Rouen. I have already been twice under anaesthetic to have my foot straightened and set. Little rubber tubes are in the wound to drain it and the whole foot is done up in plaster of Paris. Most of the pain has gone and I get some much-needed sleep.

I am to leave Rouen with a big batch for England. The men with slighter wounds went yesterday to some other French town. By tonight the hospital will be almost empty and I reckon a fresh stunt must be brewing. It certainly looks as if preparations are being made for a big influx.

Streams of motor ambulances have been going all day, removing their patients. Orderlies are at my bed and I'm being lifted onto a stretcher rigged out with blankets and pillows. The stretcher is placed in a motor ambulance. Girls in khaki uniforms are skilfully driving these ambulances and with much consideration for their freight of pain.

A short drive and we are placed in a great white hospital train; dinner is brought round and our cards are checked. We learn we are to sail from Le Havre for Southampton tomorrow morning.

The train moves on. Nearly all the men are happy at the prospect of seeing Blighty. The Tommies are wonderfully cheered up and so they should be, for to them Blighty means home and their own people. It means much to us too, but not the chance of seeing our own people. The Tommies have it over us this time.

Our train journeys on through the evening, pulling into Le Havre at dusk. We are to sleep in the train tonight so make the best of it. Nurses are moving about all night, replacing bandages and splints or doing whatever they can to ease the suffering. Several men are taken bad and removed from the train during the night.

The night has passed. We are having breakfast on the train. Soon we'll be aboard ship for England! Orderlies are moving about; the first cases are being carried out – more and more go.

'Come on, Australia.' And four elderly Tommies are carrying me out. Across several dockyards and I see our ship – a great red cross painted across the whole side. The men carry me in. Its decks are crowded with walking wounded, mostly arm and hand wounds with a few head and face wounds. I am placed in a bed and a R.A.M.C. sergeant comes and asks if I'm comfortable, then tying a lifebelt around me, makes sure I won't be comfortable any longer.

Soon we move off from Le Havre and head for the Channel. We have a very quiet crossing, but even so, dozens of wounded men are violently seasick. Seriously wounded men to whom every movement is torture fall victims to *mal-de-mer* and to them the voyage must be a nightmare of nauseating pain.

A buzzing of voices from the decks tells us we are nearing our destination. Cheers float across from passing boats. Launches toot. We can hear motor cars passing the wharf, but we can see nothing as we are down below deck.

We feel the ship grating and bumping against the wharf. Soon she steadies. We hear the walking wounded making off, then we hear cheers and calls from the wharf and their laughing answers floating back.

Men in uniforms with white bands on cap and arms are moving amongst us, carrying out the stretcher cases. These men are the conscientious objectors whose religious beliefs save them from actively fighting for their country. They are perhaps doing their bit on home service, but nevertheless we somehow despise them. Able-bodied men lurking at home when hundreds of army nurses and other women's units are often under shellfire across the Channel.

The objector jokers get me on a stretcher and carry me out of the hospital ship. With skilful hands they ease me down the gangway and lower me down to the wharf.

I've landed safely in England again – my second landing, but what a river of turmoil has passed since that other landing in England just over a year ago. What a scattering of mates this year has seen. I wonder what the future holds. That is in the lap of the gods. My only worry is to get well so that I can see as much as possible of this quiet haven into which I've been tossed and enjoy the serene friendliness of old Blighty.

THIRTEEN

Digging in at Dernancourt

Back with the old battalion again after half a year in English hospitals and various base depots and feeling good. Longun, Dark and Snow are with the battalion still, and four of us are together again in the old platoon.

We're at Méteren near Bailleul. The boys have been in the line around Armentières and Ypres lately and now are in reserve.

Excitement is in the air and rumours are flying everywhere. Four days ago, Fritz launched a tremendous attack from Arras to St Quentin. We have heard that the British Third Army is holding the enemy on the left of the attack, but that the enemy is routing and rolling back our Fifth Army down on the Somme. The battalion is ready to move to the south to meet the big Fritz advance somewhere and all spare gear is in storage at Méteren school. We are ready to move out at an hour's notice.

Longun lands in the billet. 'We're off. Just saw the order. We're to embus at ten o'clock on 25th March, that's tomorrow. Goin' in motor buses. That means goin' a long way. Must be off down Amiens way because they reckon Fritz'll have that in a few days' time.'

Darky rolls over. 'Hooray, we'll soon be dead.' And for some time we discuss the breakthrough until Snow lands along to tell us that Fritz has taken all the old joints we fought over from November 1916 to April 1917.

'An' he's flamin' welcome to 'em,' comes fervently from Dark whose mind has probably flashed back to that 1916 winter down there. Memories of Switch and Gap Trenches, of Bull's Run and Pilgrim's Way, of Grease Trench, of Stormy Trench and Fritz's Folly. Memories of mud! Of Pozières and Mouquet Farm, of Flers and Gueudecourt, of Bapaume and Bullecourt – of blood!

Far into the night we talk of the big Fritz attack and the hundreds of spare battalions Fritz must have now that Russia is no longer hammering at his eastern frontier. Of the open warfare we'll perhaps experience and what we'll do to any mass Fritz formation attacks.

The men are in great spirits. Up till now we have been the ones rushing enemy trenches packed with rifles, but now it'll be reversed. The enemy will do the charging and we'll do the shooting, and straight and solid shooting it's going to be. We'll be getting a bit of our own back with a vengeance, or we'll know the reason why.

'Fritz has half a dozen divisions to throw against every one of ours. We'll meet some big battalions down there,' the know-all of our platoon warns us.

'Let 'em come!' Snow tells him. 'The bigger they come the harder they'll fall.'

We're in a long stream of buses moving away from Méteren; miles of transport, all leading south. Away on the horizon, clouds of dust. We know that the roads are jammed with traffic as all available modes of transport are rushing men, guns, shells and food south.

Village after village flits by as our cloud of dust rolls over them and we are gone. Through big St Pol we go. Dusk closes in and the sun goes down through a haze of dust. Night is upon us and still the buses move on. We are squatting on the floor and dozing, but we wake and look out at each village as thousands of French civilians are fleeing and carrying their few belongings with them. The poor driven wretches wave and call to us, hoping against all hope that we'll stop the great advance from overtaking them in their flight.

The buses have stopped again. We're in a village somewhere and get sorted out into billets. It is now after midnight so we try for some sleep. We've been ordered to be ready to move out at a moment's notice, but that doesn't stop us from looking for sleep. Darky and Snow get detailed to go away to do picket duty on the roads. We are told Fritz might be anywhere so pickets are to be posted around the village while we sleep.

Dawn gets to us before we wanted it. We poke about and learn that we are at Bailleulmont, a joint on the main road from Arras to Doullens. We watch the stream of French civilians still trailing back.

Word comes that fleets of Fritz armoured cars have broken through and will soon be upon us so we wait near the billets where our rifles are. Longun and I get marched away to help guard one of the roads entering the town, watching every cloud of dust in case it's a Fritz armoured car.

We see our scouts and some officers make off to a line of high ground and soon word comes that we are to dig in on a ridge between Bellacourt and Berles-au-Bois and all pickets are to report back to the battalion in the village. Soon we hear that the armoured car yarn was just another furphy and that our battalion is to march out as the advance guard for the 12th Brigade. We also hear that our transport and field cookers have reached the village and that a hot meal is nearly ready. We're really interested in that as it's a day and a half since we had a hot meal; a day and a half of semi-starvation on inadequate dry rations secured for us by our Quarter Master under great difficulties.

Our midday hot meal over, we fall in wearing battle-order equipment and march off towards the advancing enemy to a place called Hannescamps to hold Fritz there until the rest of the brigade can come into action. We sit around watching the never-ending flight of the French population, pale and nervous, but relieved when they see hundreds of our men lolling about apparently unconcerned and happy. The refugees move on, but much of the flight has gone from their movements and the poor wretches feel assured. An old madame tells me that we've come too late to save her home, but she knows now that she is safe. It's wonderful the tremendous faith these simple villagers have in just one Australian battalion.

Dozens of high-sided French carts come through the village lumbering on towards the rear, piled high with all manner of household effects and grandmothers or grandfathers jammed amongst the load. Hundreds of overladen wheelbarrows trundle through the village with poor, lonely old men and broken-hearted women shoving all their earthly possessions before them. There's not an able bodied man amongst the lot. The war has drained the country of its manhood. And poor lost little kids seeking protection. Pinned inside one boy's pocket is a crumpled piece of paper bearing the pencilled address of a woman in Abbeville.

Night. Still in Bailleulmont and ready to move forward at any minute. Lying in our billets, we listen to the crunching wheels and the uneven hurrying of tired, frightened feet on the village roads.

'Fall in, 14 Platoon.' And we climb into our equipment and line up. We move past the village, join other platoons and soon we are marching into the black night, never knowing if we will march into the advancing Fritz army at any moment.

All is darkness and indescribable confusion ahead except for the steady, measured *tramp, tramp, tramp* of marching feet. We know that an advance guard of our battalion is ahead and that guarding parties are out on our flank and we are marching parallel to the ever-changing front line. Away on the horizon we see the gun flashes and here and there, the steady glow of a burning village.

Quietly we discuss the mighty Fritz breakthrough on a wide front and their advance of five miles a day. It took us nearly six months to advance five miles in our last big stunt, the so-called great Passchendaele offensive but Fritz, pushing through to Paris, will have something pretty solid to chew on if we can get our five divisions across their path.

Hour after hour, mile after mile is put behind us. Nearer, ever nearer through the darkness are we drawing towards the Fritz juggernaut.

Still into the night. Now we are resting by the roadside. Five minutes, sometimes ten, in each hour, then up and on again. Refugees still going by. Still the wild hysteria of the night, the wailing sobs of little children, too worn out or too frightened to cry properly, the unstrung, hysterical talk, the carts, the wheelbarrows and the prams, snowed under by an avalanche of beds and bedding, mattresses and blankets trailing over the sides, chairs, tables and saucepans surmounting all. The clatter of saucepan on saucepan, the cackling of hens, the grunting of caged pigs and talk, talk, talk.

Daybreak and we've marched over twenty miles since ten o'clock last night until we come to the little white-washed village of Senlis-le-Sec where the battalion halts. We've reached our destination, boots come off and blistered feet are rubbed. Men are on guard watching for the first sight of the enemy, but what will it be – cavalry, armoured cars or just the massed grey battalions of the infantry divisions.

Breakfast when word comes along to prepare to move off. This, after marching all night! Not even time to eat breakfast in comfort. Falling in again and on the march with men drinking and eating as they go.

Our company commander says we've been ordered to Millencourt where the 12th Brigade will concentrate. We have no definite word of things in front, but we do know the retreating army is fighting rear-guard actions as it moves back and that the enemy has captured Albert, five miles away, a few hours ago. But we also know that our men are aggressive and determined and no one doubts that the battalion will give a good account of itself when we come to grips with the enemy.

From Millencourt, we march towards Albert and spread out to take up positions to wait for Fritz. The 47th and 48th Battalions have gone ahead towards Albert to take over the front line from some regiments of the British 9th Division and are holding a big railway embankment which we remember from the 1916–17 winter.

Our battalion is digging in to be a support line from Dernancourt up to Albert and all day we've worked hard digging, but haven't seen any Fritz yet. They'd have to get through our battalions to reach us in the support line. Enemy shells have been landing haphazardly and Fritz planes are flying very low. We know that the 47th and 48th are having a rough spin as Fritz artillery has been shelling the railway embankment all day.

Night and we wonder if they'll attack during the darkness. For hour upon hour we work away doing what we can to improve the support trenches for we may need them at any minute.

Some Tommies are coming back through us. Men who've fought for seven days and nights, these poor red-eyed, whiskered, unstrung wretches are just a remnant of the British 9th Division. Just a few scattered men of Gough's Fifth Army who've fought from north of Roisel, opposite Bellicourt, have fallen back fighting and stood to fight again. Time and again they've rallied and held on for a few vital hours, only to have to retire again. For a week, for twenty-five miles, they've carried the honour of their race on their sagging shoulders. They did not run away!

Word is just through that B Company of our battalion has gone into the front line at Dernancourt to reinforce the 47th Battalion which has suffered heavily since taking over this morning from the British. The rest of us, keyed up, are still holding the Millencourt support trenches. It is just after midnight when a wave of movement extends along the trench. Men climb out and move forward, going silently ahead into the fog-thickened darkness, stringing out on a long hill which slopes towards Dernancourt. Officers are moving our line into position by taking compass bearings in the pitch darkness.

Some moving about, altering of the line and now we're in position, digging in as fast as we can. It's about two o'clock and we must be dug-in before daylight for when day breaks the position will be in full view of Fritz. Hard at it we go. Very little talking, but each desperately working his hardest. With loaded rifles lying close at hand we work on, digging our trench in the white chalk of the hillside.

Dawn and we can dimly see along the line. Below us lies the Ancre River and old Dernancourt enveloped in a great cloud of fog. Will the next few minutes see the great enemy attack come rolling towards us from under that cloud? Into the brightening day we work on, digging in in front of Dernancourt.

Daylight and Fritz hasn't recommenced his great thrust towards Amiens and Paris. Surely it cannot be long delayed now. Suddenly down below us from along the railway embankment near Dernancourt rattles the steady clatter of our machine-guns and the unevenly spaced cracking of our rifles.

'Stand to! He's coming!'

Now our turn has come! We line our trench, waiting and watching for the enemy. Our introduction to the 'big push'!

'He's attacking the embankment!' Yes, the enemy has launched an attack against the embankment held by the 47th and 48th Battalions and our B Company men. We're being warned that our men from the embankment may be falling back on this trench any minute and we know that means Fritz will be on their heels. It's going to be awkward. We won't be able to shoot through our men, but we don't want to miss the chance of shooting a Fritz.

Stray shells and bullets are landing amongst us. The man in the next trench bay spins and falls. I rush to his aid. There's a neat hole in his forehead and an ounce of burning copper-clad lead in his brain. Our first casualty. Probably many will soon follow.

'They're charging the embankment!' And we watch, but there's no sign of our men leaving it.

'Fritz is at the embankment!' Still there's no backward movement away from it. 'You're bumping a tough mob, Fritz!'

'Fritz has struck a snag, all right!'

'The attack's breaking! It's beaten off!' And we're keyed up with joy. 'He couldn't shift our coves!'

'The Jerries are running away!' And our rifles and machine-guns are spluttering at top speed, giving them some hurry up.

The firing has died down. The attack is over. Not an inch has been given. Enemy prisoners are coming back. Our men have made a few catches.

It's quiet now. Below us we see Dernancourt. Away on the rising ground beyond it we see the lines of old 1916 trenches, gleaming chalky white under the morning sun.

'We're to take Dernancourt this evening,' the word comes back. The three companies in this trench are to attack, but as preparations are being made another Fritz attack is launched. It soon fades out.

'You're up against it, Fritz!' we laugh.

The morning drifts slowly by. Fritz makes several attacks, but his luck is clean out and each attempted attack meets with disaster.

Afternoon. Though the enemy shelling is becoming heavier, we are prepared to launch our attack against Dernancourt, getting in some sniping at moving parties of the enemy. He must mean to attack tonight for we see party after party of Fritz moving up towards their front line. Careless in their cock-sureness, they march straight in and our guns open. *Rat-a-tat-tat-tat-tat*; then the rifles crash all along our trench and another enemy party has been smashed.

Word is through that we are not to make our attack on Dernancourt after all, so we again settle down to improve our trench and wait. If he cares to call our way in the night, he'll find us at home. The shelling is getting heavier and our casualties are mounting all the time. Our guns are retaliating steadily, firing from any old position they can get, many just firing from the open.

Slowly the night rolls by, but the enemy attack is not renewed, probably waiting for spare divisions to come up. They know the opposition has strengthened, for yesterday we repelled no less than ten attacks, not one of which reached our front line: the railway embankment below us. We've been getting in some decent shooting from here, but the boys manning the embankment have been having a rare time. Ten attacks on their line in daytime. Fritz must have men to waste. The dead are lying thick out in front of the embankment and they'll be thicker still, poor wretches. The Grim Reaper has gathered a bumper harvest today. Human lives snuffed out by the crook of a finger on a rifle trigger.

Daytime. Our third here. Tonight we go into the front line. We've been that close to it for the past three days that we have that front line feeling, but when we go down onto that embankment we'll know what to expect for surely the big attack must be renewed soon.

Night. We're relieving the 47th Battalion. Our line is running north from Dernancourt and we spend the night working hard to improve our position. Patrols have been out all night, watching and listening for signs of the enemy, but he is quiet. We won't take any chances.

Night has gone and it's well into the day. All quiet. Just some odd shelling as the enemy guns range on us, catching our men while now and again a rifle cracks somewhere along the trench. The men are sniping at Fritz moving about in Dernancourt only three hundred yards ahead, near the tumble-down billet we occupied eighteen months ago.

We've been here for three days now and still the Fritz attack hasn't been launched. Every night we've been patrolling out in front while the men continue sniping and we know that at least twenty of the enemy have been shot.

The night of 1st April comes down. Our last night here before we're relieved tomorrow night. We are sniping very heavily and Fritz is sniping from the houses in the village. Some of our men have been waving to two women in Dernancourt and they have been waving back and pointing to a house that some Fritz are in. Our chaps have been trying to get the women to come across to our lines, but of course they couldn't do that under the eyes of a Fritz-occupied village.

I have just had a very queer experience. A big Fritz stood up and slowly walked along a broken bank less than two hundred yards from us. It was such an easy shot. The boys left him to me as I am supposed to be something of a shot and haven't had an outright failure in my four days' sniping. I aimed and was just on the point of pressing the trigger when it flashed on me that I might have an empty cartridge in my rifle. So I quickly worked my rifle bolt to examine the cartridge. The cartridge shell came out leaving the bullet jammed in the barrel and leaving me with a useless rifle and an enemy less than two hundred yards away. Before anyone else realised what was wrong, the Fritz had disappeared.

Night again. We have just been relieved and are moving back to a reserve position somewhere near Laviéville, our seven days around Dernancourt are over. As we move back, we see that our artillery has come up in strength during the week. All is feverish activity back here as everyone expects a fresh attack as Fritz is now so near Amiens and well on the road to Paris and victory.

We've now had two days in the Laviéville reserve trenches where things are quiet. We're cleaning up and reorganising, for during our week in front of Dernancourt, we had twenty men killed and over sixty wounded.

Talk. Men moving. Orders. The creak of equipment and we half wake and wonder what it's all about.

'Come on, you fellows! Are you going to stay there all night?' And an officer is standing over us.

He means business and means it in a hurry, so we get up on our feet and half asleep ask, 'What's gone wrong with the lot of you anyway?'

They soon tell us the news, and we wonder if it's correct as we bump about in the dark finding our gear and climbing into it. Word has come through that the enemy is to make his big attack at Dernancourt tomorrow.

'How do they know anyway?'

'Some Fritz were captured by a patrol tonight and one of them spilt the beans and told that the attack is to be put over tomorrow.'

We're moving off into the night towards the front line we left only the night before last to take up a support position a mile to the left of Dernancourt. Fog is everywhere thickened by the smoke of bursting shells from a severe enemy shelling. On, on we move through our nightmare march as high explosive shells fall amongst us, slipping down through the foggy darkness to crash with shuddering spouts of flame all around. The fires of hell flicker and lick the darkness with vicious tongues of roaring flame on every side and clods of dirt are flung high. The acrid fumes of the smoke thicken the fog that now enshrouds us. Through the fog we now and then see our men. A wailing shriek, a crash and against the flash of the shell we see great ungainly figures in the fog. They can't be men, yet they must be, for they duck and dive, yell and curse, and ever move on in line with us through the fog and shells.

We're at our destination. A hill slopes down into the fog towards the Ancre River and so down towards the enemy. We spread out and commence digging ourselves in, as we did just eight nights ago. The shelling is missing us as Fritz doesn't know we're here, but when morning comes he'll find a new trench along this hill with us in it.

Still digging in, the night fades away as the foggy morning is upon us, but we've beaten the daylight and are now dug in. As the fog lifts from the valley, we can see the tops of the trees along the Ancre River, and beyond Dernancourt, the chalky trenches. Out of the fog looms the village church tower, now smashed by shellfire and the railway embankment our men are still holding.

All is very quiet, no different to what it was two days ago. We wonder if that Fritz prisoner gave correct information when he named today as the day for the renewal of the attack. If so, the quiet-looking village must even now house thousands of fixed bayonets waiting to be launched against us. We look at the railway embankment just below and can see some of our men wandering about this side of it. Every few yards along that high embankment we can pick out men lying very still and know our boys are watching for the first sign of movement.

'Listen!' From afar we catch the sounds of band music, the faint, unmistakable, measured beat of marching music.

'Look!' And there, a mile or more beyond old Dernancourt, we catch the flash of band instruments in the rays of the early sun.

'Get an eyeful of that!' And strung out behind that band we see a battalion of Fritz. Some officers on horses, company after company of marching men, a stream of horse-drawn transport, all slowly moving along under a little cloud of whitish dust.

'Must think they own the flamin' joint.' And then our rifles and machine-guns are at them. *Crack! Crack! Crack! Rat-a-ta-tat-tat-tat* and our trench is crackling from end to end under the savage rattle of rifle and machine-gun fire; a mile ahead there's a scattering of dust, horses are galloping their carts back and little bunches of men are rushing in all directions to disappear from view. The Fritz battalion has gone to earth and can no longer be seen. Something bright lies shining on the road – band instruments. Groups of men rush on a short way and fade into the ground. It's the battalion making towards Dernancourt as best they can under our fire. The precision and dignity of their entry has been swept aside by the hail of bullets from far away. We must have hit many men, but the dust hides them from our view.

Whee! Whist! Whit! Zonk! Crash! Crash! Crash! And smoke and chalky dust are blinding us and choking us as the very trench seems to pitch and toss under the crashing vibrations of a terrific bombardment. Already the call is going forth: 'Stretcher-bearers!' Then 'Stand to!' is yelled along.

Three or four shells burst almost on our little group. We scatter along the trench a little as we feel the heat of the explosions on our faces as if the lid's off hell, as shells crash and bang in an unceasing roar.

We crouch against the walls of the trench, holding our rifles. No longer do they rest on the parapet. We must guard them, shield them for soon now we'll need them. No need to tell us this bombardment is heralding the big attack that we must stop, if any of us are left to stop it. The shelling keeps on and on. Gas shells are being mixed in now. We are testing our gas helmets.

'Stand to! Keep watching ahead!' And an officer staggers along the trench, white-faced and scared, but doing his job.

The four of us here are taking it in turns to look over the top. I watch Dark. He lies with his head on the parapet, face pressed in the chalky earth, his eyes searching ever ahead through the dust and smoke. He lies there statue like, keeping his head above the trench by sheer willpower. One knee is twitch, twitch, twitching. Men are doing the same job everywhere. Every few yards a man's head is exposed to this awful inferno – the bursting of high explosive shells.

'Your go!' And Darky's voice trembles from the nervous relief as he drops back into the trench and waves at me.

My head is lying on the parapet now. I feel my body shake to each crushing shell. Dust and clods rain down everywhere. In front, a sea of mad, flaring shell bursts. I watch the railway embankment. A perfect rain of shells is on to it. A black length of railway line leaves the embankment and comes turning and screwing towards us, tossed by the shells. I can hear it humming through the air before it falls fifty yards ahead.

I'm watching the village. Our shells are crashing into it. It's a mass of dust and collapsing walls. I catch a fleeting glance of forms running from a burning, tottering house. Still no sign of the enemy attack.

Now I am watching the railway embankment again. Some men are carrying stretchers about. Clouds and clouds of black dust and smoke leap skywards at each shell burst. Two shells land together. Two black funnels of earth and smoke viciously kick upwards. There's nothing more solid in the mountain of dust. Something spinning and turning in the dust cloud. Something like a thick catapult fork. A man – with neither head nor arms, flying high above the embankment.

A tugging on my feet. I glance down into the trench. Snow gives my legs a hard pull and I slip into the trench as he scrambles up to take my place.

Our O.C. is here. 'Can't last much longer. Been on for an hour and a half now. Many hit around here?' And he goes crouching past us to inspect the line.

Still the barrage keeps on. Still the air is vibrant with the paralysing roar of the crashing detonations of exploding shells.

The unbelievable is happening not two feet above our cowering heads. One of our officers is walking upright along the top of our parapet amongst this dreadful barrage. He keeps looking into the trench as he goes along. 'Can't hurt you unless they hit you,' he keeps calling to the men as he walks the tight-rope to hell.

Where have I heard that before? Yes, I remember; this is the officer who had us on the burying party and who kept us out in the open until the sniper got Farmer. 'Can't hurt you unless he hits you.' Now I remember it well. Then I thought this officer was an absolute fool. Now I know him for an out and out hero, a hero if ever there was one.

Up and down the line he goes.

'Fatalism?' Snow asks.

The three of us shake our heads. It's not fatalism. The officer is practising fear control. He is setting a wonderful example to us all, for if a man can walk out there and live, so can we, and we begin to feel we're in comparative safety here in the trench. His brave example does us good. We feel better. Men begin to shout to each other along the trench. The tension is breaking.

It's after nine o'clock. Over two hours since the barrage began, and no sign of slackening yet. Our brains can't house this awful swelling sound much longer. Surely our heads will explode! The *buzz, buzzing* within our brain must find a way out. Heads weren't made to hold this noise!

Still we hang on, taking turns to look over the parapet with not a straight nerve in our bodies. Shattered and shaking, but grimly holding on through it all. The shelling has been on for two and a half hours, and seems like keeping on forever as Fritz mean to smash us up properly before launching his infantry.

The O.C. comes along and above the roaring shells shouts, 'Run your hardest to the major and tell him the enemy is massing. Warn every man as you go along.' And away along the trench I run. As I pass each man or group of men I yell, 'He's about to come over! Get ready!'

I find the major to give him the message, but the report of movement in the village has already reached him from other observers.

I make back. The nice trench we dug last night is shattered and smashed beyond recognition. Wounded men are everywhere waiting for the shelling to ease before they can get out. Dead men, many of them half buried, are everywhere along the trench. Many of our dead have bandages on, telling that they had already been wounded before getting their final issue.

Many men are huddled against the wall of the trench. White faces stained whiter still by the flying chalk dust. Some men have the appearance of dead men except for their jerky breathing.

Suddenly the shelling is off us. The men are flying, rifles in hand, to line the parapet. From out in front I catch the rattle of machine-guns and rifles.

'They're coming!'

'Stand to!'

'Give it to 'em!'

'Stand to' is being yelled everywhere as I race back to my post.

I see dazed, hopeless, despondent poor beggars rising from the floor of the trench like dead men from the grave, warmed back to life by the thought of getting some of their own back. I reach the post. Longun, Dark, Snow and the O.C. are together on the parapet pouring clip after clip of bullets towards Dernancourt.

'Any message from the major?' shouts the O.C.

'No, Sir. He knew.'

'Come on, your king and country need you!'

I hear Longun laugh and I'm up with them and doing rapid fire at those advancing men down below.

Thousands of Fritz are rushing the railway embankment from everywhere. We're bowling them over, but nearer to the embankment they draw. The ground behind is carpeted with grey forms that lie still, that twitch and kick, lashing the ground in agony, but hundreds and hundreds of other grey forms are leaping from shell hole to shell hole and ever drawing nearer to the few men left on the embankment.

Desperately we aim and fire to stem that closing grey wave. Many fall, but others rise in their places. Fritz is jumping through hell, but never slackens in that deadly advance. Sheer weight of numbers is carrying them towards our men.

'My God! I never thought it was in 'em!' Snow exclaims, unable to hide his admiration for the men who advance in the face of what we're giving them.

Wounded men are now seen running back from the embankment as Fritz gets there. Men stand and throw bombs at them, but still they close in on our chaps. We see two platoons leave our trench and race down to reinforce the 47th men on the embankment. Two more platoons race ahead and take up positions a little way behind the embankment.

In a couple of places, Fritz is now on the embankment as our men come back, then they finally take the embankment. Slowly our men are dropping back, firing as they come. Dragging or carrying their wounded with them. With a rush they're into some trenches behind the embankment. The enemy, now lining the embankment, is firing at them and at us. The rifle duelling is ear-splitting. Still we keep on firing and firing. Men in this trench are stopping Fritz lead now, but we've got a score of Fritz for every one of us who gets hit.

Fritz is now advancing from the embankment, but falters as our two platoons down there pour in deadly rifle and machine-gun fire. He's racing back for the shelter of the embankment! We've stopped him, though he's taken the embankment. Then Fritz is coming again in front of us. More terrific firing and more bomb work below, the overwhelming odds are telling and the remnants of our front line are falling back and jumping into support trenches.

Fritz is well up the ridge now and above Dernancourt. They've made a fair advance, but every yard of it is marked by a fallen man. He's bought his gain at tremendous cost! He still has to shift us if he wants all the ridge, as he undoubtedly does.

Time goes by. All is still, except for movement as wounded men try to crawl in. We expect the attack to be renewed any minute against a mere handful of men in those old support trenches between us and the enemy. Our turn next and we know it. Can we hope for better luck than the 47th? It's not possible that any men can fight harder or braver than they did, but the terrific odds outbalanced them.

Our officers are coming along the trench. 'Prepare to advance. We're going forward to reinforce the front line.' And we get set to hop-over.

'Come on!' And with a rush we're into the old support line, now our front line with the 47th and our C Company. We've lost a few men in the rush, but it was so rapid that we were into the trench before Fritz was awake to us.

We spread out along the trench where the sorely tried men welcome us. Ready for anything, we stand and wait, yarning about things seen and done today, brave deeds, passed unnoticed and unrewarded, taken as part of the day's work, though that part meant facing death, for mateship, or pride of battalion, fear of showing fear, or just pure cussedness.

For another hour we stand manning the trench. The officers come along and warn us that the battalion is to make a counter-attack at half past two to retake the high ground won by Fritz after he advanced from the railway embankment.

All preparations are made. We're ready. The 47th is to go over on our left and the 49th of the 13th Brigade on our right. An alteration. Some delay in getting the 49th up in time to go over so the attack is put back till just after five. We get busy on what food we can find. We're all hungry. Hardly any water is left. The dreadful shelling this morning used most of it up in washing the dust and smoke out of us.

Darky, busy cleaning up a tin of pork and beans he's pinched somewhere, warns us not to overeat – 'A bayonet in a full tucker box is dangerous.' But we notice he doesn't leave too much of those beans.

Time to hop-over comes round. We're all ready and know just what we're called upon to face. The men are quiet with a quietness born of nervous apprehension. What'll happen when we do go over? The tension of the waiting is terrific and a surge of relief goes up as we scramble out of the trench into the open. Now we'll meet it, but at least we won't be left any longer to think about it. These hop-overs are bad enough, but thinking makes them far worse.

Across the open and strung out, our platoons keep perfect parade-ground formation. Enemy machine-guns and rifles start up and men start dropping everywhere. Still we advance. Still that perfect parade-ground formation is kept despite flying bullets and falling mates, kept when each man knows any step may be his last, kept without an order or a direction given. Yet they say the Australians lack discipline – the biggest lie of jealous lying criticism.

We're nearing Fritz. We can see the steel helmets above the rifle-lined trench. On we go. The man next to me spins and gives a soft surprised gasp. The poor wretch staggers in front of me. I go cold and sick as I see the shuddering convulsion of his death shiver. He's down. I'm stepping over him like a man in a dream.

Another few yards. My foot strikes on something soft. I stumble over a man just fallen. He rolls over dead and I recognise him as the men begin to yell and shout. I'm running on with the rest, doing a desperate bayonet charge over the last hundred yards. The enemy are leaving the trench! They won't face our bayonets! They won't stand and fight it out! They're off! Running!

A tremendous rush and with a roar we're into the trench. We're all calling, shouting, roaring, laughing from the reaction and excitement. Across a long, open patch we've charged, charged with nerves tensed to meet the blow of biting lead, and now we're safe – inside the walls of a dirty, broken trench.

Along the trench we charge. Others line it and shoot down the flying enemy who are vainly trying to get away.

Still along the trench we race. Darky is ahead, Snow beside me. Three Fritz come at Darky with their bayonets. My rifle, held in the 'charge' position, cracks out as I run to catch up to Dark, and only two enemy bayonet-men are coming at us. *Crack!* Snow's rifle rings out almost in my ear, and only one Fritz faces us. Dark trips over a dead man and I'm in the lead. The Fritz still comes on. *Smack!* Our bayonets have met and locked. I've spun the Fritz bayonet clear of my body and am desperately shoving to keep it down.

'*Kamerad!*' he screams and drops his rifle and I stumble right on to his hot sweaty body. Snow grabs the fellow's rifle and throws it out of the trench and the Fritz is shepherded over the trench by Darky. The man runs and joins several other captured Fritz who are running back for our trench. We watch the unbalanced run of these men, running with hands held high.

The trench is ours. We've hunted the enemy! Some machine-guns have been captured and many prisoners taken. Desperately we work, consolidating the position. Wounded, shell-torn Fritz are crawling about. Many dead are in the trench. Our barrage caught parts of the trench properly.

A Fritz boy is holding two blood-red hands across his eyes and crying piteously. Darky pulls his hands down. His two eyes and the bridge of his nose have been slashed by a bullet. His eyes shot out, he's blind and mad from pain. We hail our bearers who put a pad across the horrible wound and leave him till our own wounded are bandaged up.

Another Fritz, an officer, staggers up past us. The poor wretch has no top lip. A shell fragment has cut it clean off. He, too, is a sickening sight. His blood-stained teeth show in a perpetual smile of misery. He passes on along the trench and we're glad to see him go. Poor beggar!

Fritz is well below us now, digging in. We snipe at him whenever we get a view of any movement. We are still working in this captured trench wondering if they'll come again, though somehow we feel they won't and their gallop to Amiens is at an end. They have had a terrible defeat today and it has ended with our bayonet charge, which has hunted him back from the high ground he won so dearly a few hours ago.

Night. And we're ready to move out. Dark forms, men of the 46th Battalion slip into the trench. We explain the lay of the land and quietly get out to move back a few hundred yards to our reserve trench we dug last night where we suffered such shelling this morning and from which we launched the first stage of our attack this afternoon.

All night we go out in parties gathering up our dead who fell in the hop-over and from the morning's shelling. We carry them back for burial. We can't spare men from our position to bury the dead so someone else will have to do that later.

Day dawns. 6th April. We are to be relieved tonight. The 2nd Division just down from the north will relieve us and we can do with a spell, too, after thirteen days in the line. The day passes quietly. Some odd shelling is down on us. Three men are killed and another twenty wounded. Ever the same; men fall on the last day as well as on the first, coming in and going out. Just the luck of the game!

Pitch dark. Out of the darkness comes Snow with our relief party of 22nd Battalion men. After we tell them what we know, the relief is effected.

'Right, 14, follow on.' And we climb out and make back over the brow of the hill. Through the night we trudge to the little village of

Baizieux, dropping to sleep in the first corner of the billets that we stumble into.

Our fortnight at Dernancourt is over. We have helped stop the great push, and Amiens and Paris are still safe. Despite his great advantage in both infantry and artillery, the only gain Fritz made in the past fortnight is that railway embankment. He can have the embankment, but we'll keep the high ground overlooking it and we'll keep Amiens and Paris.

We're properly worn out but we'll recover. The fortnight in front of Dernancourt has chopped the old 45th about; eight officers and ninety men have been killed, whilst another eight officers and a hundred and fifty men have gone out wounded. The battalion's strength is now weakened by two hundred and fifty. Our job at Dernancourt has been done, but in the doing of it . . . !

Awake again. Our few hours' sleep at Baizieux is over. A hot breakfast is served. Now we're on the road, marching off again. Tired and weary, we trudge along, hour after hour, mile after mile. Not a man but would like to fall out, but not a man does. We're grimly sticking it out. Seeing the job through.

Still on, heads down, shoulders dropping from weariness and the weight of rifle and equipment. Suddenly a band strikes up ahead and 'Colonel Bogey', our battalion march, rings out. The battalion's band has met us and is playing us into Bussy-lès-Daours.

Heads go up. Shoulders are squared. We're all in step and march into the village as if Dernancourt and the past fortnight were a year and not a day behind us. Into the billets.

'Soon have a decent sleep now.'

'It's a decent feed I want.'

'You can have all your sleep, all your feeds, so long as I get those boots off. I've had 'em off one night in the last fortnight.' And Snow drops down in the billet, pulls his boots off, and sends each boot hard against the ceiling. *Smack! Smack!* And rolls over, happy at last.

'Steady up, you goat. Do you want the flamin' great things to knock a man's brains out?' And Longun is busy dodging the falling boots.

Snow laughs. 'Dear friends have to part.' And flings his boots again hard into the ceiling as we grab our dirty mess tins and charge out after a hot meal, our only one in peace and comfort for a fortnight.

The meal is over; men are dropping to sleep everywhere. More and more join the sleeping battalion and soon we're all asleep, the first safe sleep that has come our way for a fortnight.

Good old sleep! You'll do us!

FOURTEEN

Around Villers-Bret

We have just marched into Cardonnette from Bussy-lès-Daours where we had two days after coming out of Dernancourt. Things weren't too bad at Bussy. We had good billets and a decent rest which we could do with. Bussy had been vacated by civilians a couple of weeks before we arrived. We could have stocked up a furniture emporium with the stuff they left behind, but we didn't happen to have an emporium about us anywhere at the time. And as our haversacks weren't of much use, we had to content ourselves with a supply of fresh cutlery and a few little knick-knacks.

Longun and Snow found three stray hens somewhere. The chooks seemed lonely and hungry and as we'd so often been lonely and hungry ourselves, we took pity on the poor lost hens and ate them. Anyway, they weren't lonely any longer and we weren't hungry either.

Our first day in Cardonnette and we are at a joint where hot baths are rigged up. They haven't got the great round wooden tubs like we had at Fricourt or some of those early bath joints. They have showers here, hot showers. We file along, dump our uniforms in one room, pelt our dirty underclothing and shirts into a big bin, wander along and wait for our turn under the shower. Ten of us get under together and they are turned on for a few minutes to thoroughly dampen the dried mud on us. Then the shower is turned off and we have a few minutes soaping and rubbing. The shower comes on again and we get half the soap away when the water is turned off and we remove the rest of the soap and mud by a good rub down. Move along a little further, get clean underclothing, then put our dirty old uniforms on again and bath night is over.

We've had two nights and a day at Cardonnette and now we are on the march for Fréchencourt, moving back towards the line and into some good billets. Things are becoming more settled around here. Every day it is becoming more difficult for Fritz to successfully renew his advance. On the march again after one night at Fréchencourt to Lahoussoye, an old tumble-down sort of a joint that Fritz has shelled and knocked about.

A week has gone by and tomorrow we are to march into Querrieu as reserves for the line and have been warned that we are to hold ourselves ready to move off at thirty minutes' notice.

We've left Querrieu and are marching up in platoons for the front line. We are to go in at Villers-Bretonneux. Today is the 27th April and we know that our 13th and 15th Brigades took the village back from Fritz on the 25th, just two days ago. We've been told that Amiens can be seen from Villers-Bretonneux and therefore Fritz will be sure to have a go to retake it, so we expect fireworks when we get into the line.

Near the village now and can see it and several thick woods nearby. We are halted near a crossroad. A large crucifix stands here bearing a life-size metal figure of Christ, all shot about by shrapnel. Within a radius of thirty yards we count eleven dead men of some British regiment and four dead Aussies. These crossroads have been a death-trap. Men have bled and died here. Christians killed by Christians and over their poor bodies, the gigantic cross of Christ! A shrapnel-torn, bullet-marked symbol of the cross upon which Christ died for men. We look at the cross and those fifteen bodies lying so still around it and wonder, thinking queer, half-logical reasonings we can't well express.

Darkness is here and we are moving across the open for the front-line trenches. An odd enemy gun sends a burst of bullets over and we get down until the gun stops and then move on again. We are going in across open ground that is dotted with the bodies of the men who fell in the attack two days ago.

Snow touches my arm and nods towards the ground. A young Australian boy lies dead at our feet. Still clasped in his two hands is a letter he had been reading as his life ebbed away on this open field. Opening and reading a letter with death approaching to dim his eyes forever. Poor little chap! His dying thoughts were centred on his letter and its beloved writer back in Australia. It's a harrowing sight to us. I take the letter, tear it into fifty pieces and scatter them in the breeze of the night.

We are skirting Villers-Bretonneux as it is evidently unsafe to move through the deserted village. Even now we can see the shell flashes as odd shells land in it. Nearly every shell burst is followed by the rumble of falling masonry. It is said that the village is full of gas fumes too. Shells, gas and dead men.

A party of men come by with stretchers, collecting the dead for burial. Forward again. Some 50th Battalion guides are here and we get led off in little groups to our respective posts. Our platoon reaches the front line and we jump into the trench, a nice new one, but we can see plenty of digging ahead.

A 50th Battalion bloke explains the situation, about gas attacks day and night and that working parties are continually under machine-gun fire.

'And we think a big Fritz attack is working up to overrun Villers-Bret again. If that is so, Fritz artillery will blow these trenches sky high because his attacking waves will have to pass over them,' a 50th sergeant further informs us.

'Oh, is that all?' Dark laughs.

'So long' and 'good luck' and the 50th clear out leaving us holding the line in front of Villers-Bretonneux. We settle down and do some quiet thinking about things in general, Fritz intentions in particular, and our own bad luck in being here just now. An hour or so passes. An officer comes along.

'If you hear a bit of strange yabber along to the right, you don't want to go opening your guns up. The French are holding the line a few yards along from us. We're now the right-hand battalion of the whole British Army.' He seems proud of it.

Every now and then machine-gun bullets knock sparks out of the stones just above our heads. A gas alarm goes some miles away to the left. Over to the right, artillery, machine-guns and rifles go mad.

Flares are going up in hundreds. An enemy raid or local attack most likely.

'Stand to' is passed along. An officer races along the trench. 'If he comes over here, we'll hop out and meet him with the bayonets as soon as he gets through our wire, if he does happen to get through.' And he's gone on to warn the next post.

A noise on our immediate right. A man is running towards us. He stops at the next post. We hear an excited crackle of French and one of our men telling him '*no comprez*'.

'Better slip along there, Nulla,' the sergeant tells me, but there's no need as the French soldier is racing up to us. He jumps down amongst us. Two arms wave, two hands flicker in our faces. Two anxious, excited eyes jump at us. A little black goatee beard is bobbing up and down under our noses. A hole opens in the beard and '*Aux Armes! Aux armes! L'ennemi!*' the man excitedly gasps, and his imploring eyes burn into each face of the post as he asks if we understand him. I answer in my best French that I understand him. He jumps at me and calls me 'comrade' half a dozen times and I tell him we are on guard already. Then he dives at me with his bristly beard and before I know what's what, the excited beggar is kissing me for all he's worth. I jump back, getting rid of that mouthful of beard and hear the boys roaring and rocking in mirth.

An officer lands amongst us.

'What's up? What's he saying? Get quiet! Have more sense!'

'He says to stand to,' I tell him.

The French soldier is in no hurry to go back to his post so he remains with us and points to the right where his brave comrades have repulsed the Fritz who were attacking just now. We get several speeches about brave Australian soldiers, but our officer lands back before the speeches are half through and gives the Frenchman half a dozen packets of our issue cigarettes and a whopper great dose of rum – our rum.

The man gets the rum into him and when he's done getting his breath back and smacking his whiskery lips, he makes another speech that I can't follow too well, but it ends all about the Entente Cordiale.

Snow laughs. 'Tell him it's not cordial, but flamin' good overproof rum,' and the man shakes hands all round, reckons I'm a clever boy and that we're all brave soldiers. Then he tells our officer that Paul Dupont salutes him and his brave Australian soldiers, and chucks the officer a far better salute than he's had from his brave Australian soldiers for many a day. Then the friendly soul climbs out of our trench. '*Je vous quitte. Au revoir. Au revoir.*' And he is gone.

Slowly the night passes. Our patrols have been out all night towards Monument Wood over on our left front and hear that one lone Fritz has been captured.

Day now and quiet, so except for the one man on watch, the rest of us have been sleeping.

We're now into our second night. Machine-guns have been busy since dusk spraying all around us. An officer has just visited our post, and Longun and I are to join his working party in half an hour's time, we're both very sorry to say.

Time goes by. The officer and a dozen men come by so Longun and I join in. We move back and go through Villers-Bret, which is not nearly so knocked about as we expected. We hurriedly make through the village. Too many fresh shell holes and overturned houses for our liking. The streets are splashed by great shadows. The moon lights up dead men every twenty yards, giving us the creeps.

'The city of the dead,' a man whispers as we hurry past a gruesome corner where Fritz has made a stand and paid for it.

Beyond the village, we follow a little path through a thick wood. More dead Fritz in the moonlight and in the black patches too. The place gets on our nerves. It's too ghost-like with its thick scrub, great black shadows and streaks of moonlight falling on fallen men, scattered gear and old blown-up guns.

This wood marks the limit of the enemy advance. It overlooked Amiens and was only retaken after a hard fight. Fritz put up a solid stand here and took some dislodging. We move on. The ground is absolutely littered with the bodies of the men of an English regiment, nearly all mere boys, lads of nineteen or twenty. They lie huddled in bunches everywhere. The story of their attack is easily read. We've seen it before. The old tale. Inexperienced troops thrown against machine-guns and the consequent bunching in mobs as they charged. Mad tactics! Mob psychology gone mad! We know that our open order method of attack is the better way. It requires more initiative, less of the machine and more of the man, but it saves precious lives and gets there.

We've passed the field of unburied dead and reach our destination where we get loaded up with coils of barbed wire and iron pickets. Fritz is now heavily shelling Villers-Bret. Our luck's in as we've missed that strafe by a quarter of an hour or less.

'We'll skirt the village going back,' our officer says, so he leads off along the way we went in last night. Several houses are burning in the village. Above the crashing shells we catch the hurried beat of galloping horses and the rumble of racing wheels on the cobbled streets.

Flaming madness sending transport up so close to the line, but it's none of our business so we move along. But we pity the men compelled to drive along these lanes of destruction.

The men are halting in front. 'We'll go in twos from here. Keep twenty-five-yard intervals.' And we set off. Pair after pair move off into the moonlight towards our trench. If a Fritz gun gets busy now we'll be caught in the open. On we hurry in absolute quietness expecting a sweeping sheet of bullets at any minute, but none comes and we deliver our wire to the front line without a casualty and spend the remainder of the night trench digging.

Nearly daylight and we're with twenty others on our way back to Villers-Bret, which doesn't look half so bad by daylight.

'Now listen,' the officer says. 'We're staying here all day. Gather up any military stuff you can, but leave the civilian property alone. We're to keep out of cellars. Supposed to be gas in them, though I'll bet there is more booze than gas.'

We mooch off in small parties to see what we can find. A lot of stuff is gathered up and dumped in a little blind street. We're getting quite a lot of it about here when *Smackety! Smack! Smack!* Machine-gun bullets are knocking brick dust and plaster off a dozen houses nearby so we decide to work the other end of the town for a change.

We gather up material for roofing some dugouts we are to make in the line, collect discarded rifles and equipment in dozens and hundreds of odds and ends. A whole town is ours for the taking, but what can we do beyond a few little souvenirs?

Longun and Dark have a bag of wine bottles. We go with them to a cellar and spend a lot of time sampling what's on the shelves. A bloke who doesn't drink has been left up on top to warn wanderers away from the dangers of the cellar. We don't want too many butting in for as Dark says, 'We can ride this donkey.'

Our officer tells Snow to 'slip up somewhere and find a couple of strong bags'. Snow buzzes off and soon lands back with two big bags, which the officer hands to us. 'Fill these up. We'll take a load back to the boys in the line. If anything's said about this wine when we get back, remember, I know nothing about it. You get me?'

'Too right, Sir. We'll keep our gate closed.'

Some more wandering around and we enter a great clothing factory. Now we're set. Shelves and shelves of socks and singlets, cardigans and jerseys here. Thousands of good knitted scarves too. The jerseys and scarves are of no use to us. It's too hot for them now, but oh! How we'd have stormed this place in that 1916–17 winter on the Somme!

We get loaded up with the stuff. I load up with socks and singlets for the boys and even the officer has a bag of it. Fritz has lifted hundreds of pounds' worth and they have made two attempts to set fire to the place.

It's dusk now and we're making back to the line loaded with bags of socks and singlets, wine, timber, corrugated iron, heavy planks and iron rails.

'If Fritz spots us he'll reckon the Camel Corps is coming into action.' The officer laughs at the queer unsoldierly spectacle we make lumping our stuff along.

We're back in the front line. The dugout material is dumped in a little sap then the men make back to their respective posts laden with singlets and socks, *vin rouge* and *vin blanc*.

The night passes off very well. New socks are on our feet and we have plenty of liquid refreshment. Half a dozen bottles have been sent along to the Frenchmen with compliments from the Australians and a bottle or two has been dropped at each of our other posts. Tonight things are more like what we reckon a war ought to be, except that we've been worked too hard digging this communication sap.

Daylight, and we've just got out of our gas-masks after Fritz gave us a gas barrage before daybreak, which we were prepared for.

30th April. We've had a very quiet day. Some men have been into Villers and found eight Fritz hiding down a cellar since the 25th, the night the Australians captured it.

Night finds us working along to the right to take over some of the French line.

Forward posts have been established well out in front of our position and the four of us are ready to go out to take over one of them. A man is coming in from the front. 'Ah, here you are. Ready?' And we follow him into the night.

'The post's about eighty yards out,' he tells us.

Straight ahead he makes, as we four trail after him.

'Must be pretty close to it now,' we whisper, but the man keeps making ahead.

'No, fair way to go yet.'

'Flamin' long eighty yards then,' Dark says, as the bloke still leads on.

'*Hist!*' And the very blackness seems to echo the sharp vibrant hiss that comes from we know not where. We prop, ready for anything, all our senses in tune. We peer ahead and to the sides, but there's nothing but darkness there.

'Hey!' an impelling whisper comes from behind. We turn and see a man sneaking towards us. One of our men. We can just see that. We meet him.

'You on patrol?' the man whispers.

'No. Goin' to an outpost.'

'Goin' to Fritz! That's where you're goin'! Come on!'

And he leads us back thirty yards to his post. We crawl into the shell hole alongside a Lewis gun crew and learn that we were heading straight for Fritz. The guard had taken us well beyond the outpost line. We're lucky all right. We get our bearings and the guide leads us on into the night once more and we find the post and take over. The men we're relieving make back towards the trench and the four of us are here in a big lump of a shell hole.

For hours we just sit in the hole looking and listening towards the enemy line, but not a sound comes from it except the crack of an odd flare gun, or the sharp cracking of a machine-gun firing into the night. Fritz is very quiet around here now.

Snow shoves his little luminous dialled watch at us and we see it is the time for our relief.

'Who's goin' for the relief?' he asks, and I tramp off back, for I know full well that it is a custom of ours that I do these guiding jobs. It's a simple matter of making back in and I hurry along taking stock of my bearings as I go.

The next four men for the post are ready so I return with them. A few directions to them and we're ready to move back to the trench. Longun leads off. 'Come on, follow me and you won't go far right,' he whispers as we trail after him back to the trench.

We're back in the trench, just standing around waiting for daylight so we can get down on the floor and sleep. An officer comes along, a demijohn of rum under his arm.

'What about a drop of S.R.D., men?'

'Too right! A big drop if you've got it, Sir.'

We get our mess-tin lids and the officer pours a couple of spoonfuls of rum into each and we get it into us. The officer gives the demijohn a shake, the rum rattles in it. He twists it round and gives it another shake. 'Getting a bit light on. Better have my nip before she's all gone. Lend me a lid,' he asks, has his nip and passes on.

He's at the next post now. We hear the friendly *glug, glug* as the rum is poured into each man's vessel. Then we hear again, 'Getting a bit light on. Better have my nip before she's all gone. Lend me a lid.'

'Cripes! He's tough, isn't he.' But we wish him the best for this officer is the joker who walked the parapet at Dernancourt whilst we shook and shivered in the trench. The man who did more to help us through than his weight in rum could have done that day. Go on, get it into you, man!

It's now the morning of 3rd May. We're all expecting fireworks soon as the 48th Battalion is to take Monument Wood on our left. We won't be in the fight, but no doubt we'll get shelled good and solid. Something to look forward to all right.

'Hey, Nulla.' And a runner is here.

'What's wrong, Joe?'

'Report to the O.C. now.' And he makes back.

I follow down the trench and come to the O.C. who says he wants me to get my gear and go back to Blangy-Tronville with Lieutenant Nett to arrange billets as we are to move out tomorrow night. I hasten back to the post and get my rifle and equipment, tell the boys I've clicked for a good job with the billeting officer and that I'll be seeing them again, and make off followed by instructions to get a good billet for them.

Mr Nett and I slip along an old sap and get into Villers-Bretonneux without being fired on. As we go through the village we see a most distressing sight. A party of men with axes and lumps of iron are at work smashing up all the wine that hasn't been gathered up for handing over to the French Mission. It might be wise, but what an awful waste. Bonzer wine, too.

We reach Blangy-Tronville and spend the day seeing what can be done about accommodating the battalion in the village. Eventually we have the village mapped out into billets and after getting a meal from some of our cooks who are here, we make off to have the sleep we can so well do with. Mr Nett has a good billet and so have I, so we enjoy a real night's rest at least.

⨯

It's dusk of 4th May. Mr Nett and I have been for a quiet little trip into Amiens. We found the city almost deserted with whole streets of shops shut and nailed up. French gendarmes everywhere, guarding the town and guiding returning refugees on their way. The few estaminets that were open were doing a roaring trade, serving meals and drinks all day and night. Traces of recent shelling were everywhere. We visited the cathedral and found its windows and altars covered with bags of sand to afford protection against the shelling. The big railway station was very battered, too, by shells and aeroplane bombs.

We arrived back in Blangy-Tronville just before dark, had our tea at the cookhouse where preparations are going ahead to serve a hot meal when the battalion marches in about midnight, and then wait on the outskirts of the village to guide the platoons to their billets. Traffic is rumbling past all night. Away in front of us we see the reflections of the batteries as they fire. The dull sound of bursting shells is faintly heard.

Still into the night we sit and yarn. The first batch of the battalion arrives. More and more of the battalion are coming in and we're kept on the move getting them to their billets. At last they are billeted and our job is over. It's been a very pleasant ending to a quiet time in the line.

We've been constantly moving since we came out of Villers-Bret on 4th May and then went into the reserve line at Tronville Switch before moving into the support lines at Aubigny which we held for five days; five days of hard, solid digging during which we made real trenches where mere scratches and little holes were before.

It's 20th May and our second innings of front-line duty near Villers-Bret.

Fritz is more active than when we were in here last time and as a consequence, our casualties are mounting up.

It's an hour till dusk and a party of us is making back along a sap from the front line. We follow the map till it runs out and then work through some old orchards and into Villers-Bret to a great chateau where our battalion headquarters is situated in the cellar because of the continual shelling.

Now we're off to the end of the village and out to a little wood where we find new barbed wire. We load up with the coils and set off to a little wood where we halt. It is not quite dark yet so we go forward in ones or twos as an enemy gun fires across the open ground that we must now cross to reach our front line.

Longun and Snow are the first two to make off, carrying a bundle of pickets each for fixing the barbed wire to. Two other men then set off and reach the trench in safety after Longun and Snow, then Dark and a couple more get across too and no sound from the gun. We decide it is too dark for the gunners to see us.

Our turn now and Joe Benns and I set off with a coil of new barbed wire. It is very heavy so we have a short stick through it and carry it between us. We move on, talking, laughing and joking as we walk waist high through a crop of standing wheat. Suddenly a *ping* and a spark darts from the coil of wire as a bullet hits it. *Swish! Swish! Swish!* fly a stream of bullets and we drop down into the wheat as the savage *chut-chut-chut-chut* of the gun cracks in our ears.

'Reckon he's spotted us, Joe,' I call to him as we lie full length in the wheat.

'Seems like it. Too straight for chance shooting, don't you think?'

We remain hidden in the wheat for another five minutes.

'Will we give it a go again, Joe?'

'Yes, just as well. We'll charge over for the sap. Remember what I told you about that jeweller in Bathurst, if he gets me.'

'He won't get you. Just as likely to get me, isn't he?'

'No, I don't think so, but if he does get me, remember there's fifty francs in my wallet. You take it and tell the jeweller about it.'

We crawl together through the wheat, find our coil of wire, take a grip on the stick and get ready to rise with the coil.

'Are you set?'

'Yes.'

'Well, come on! Over to our right!' And we're racing for the sap only thirty yards away, but *Swish! Swish! Swish! Chut-chut-chut-chut!* That gun is fair at us again. Bullets are skimming the wheat. We see the heads of the wheat flickering under the impact as the bullets tear through the crop.

'Down! Get down!' I yell as I realise we'll never make the sap, and as I do so Joe's head goes up and his mouth opens in a surprised sort of look and he's dropping into the wheat, but I've heard a muffled sound and know at once he has been hit in the stomach. I've heard that sound too often to be mistaken.

I wriggle through the wheat to him. He lies on his side, bending in agony. I lie alongside him and over our heads, just a few inches, the bullets are still chopping through the wheat.

'Where'd he get you, Joe?' I ask, but he just screws his face and clenches his hands open and shut, open and shut. Helpless in his agony.

'Known for a week this'd be my last stunt,' he says quite resigned and he seems almost relieved it's come at last.

'I knew it, Nulla.'

'Let me see where it got you, Joe.' I undo his belt and there's a little bruised puncture nearly in the centre of the abdomen. There's very little bleeding but he lets me put a pad on the wound and I bandage him firmly and he seems easier.

Again and again the machine-gun fires. We hear the bullets ripping through the wheat. A burst of bullets drives into the ground not ten feet away. The dust rises in a little scurrying cloud that floats over us. The next burst may be right on us. I'll have to get Joe into the sap, for his wound must have immediate attention.

I kneel beside him and get him across my shoulder. A stagger or two and I'm on my feet and carrying him, trying to run for the sap. Above his moaning I catch the *Swish! Swish!* of flying bullets, hear the gun reports coming loud and clear as in terror I rush on for the sap. Joe's weight steadies the pace I'd like to make. I seem to be staggering with him through bullets, bullets, bullets.

'Run! Run!' the poor wretch is moaning as on I go, staggering for the trench, struggling under fear and weight and bullets, fighting for Joe's life and mine.

The earth of the sap rises underfoot. I seem to be climbing from a mountain of loose earth into the very mouth of that loudly cracking gun. My feet are slipping, earthen walls are around us. We're in the sap. Safe.

I lower Joe down. He's unconscious. A minute and he comes round. He's getting up on his feet. I am holding him as I yell for stretcher-bearers. I'm dazed, can't see, I'm down on my back.

I realise that Joe has sent me flying. His fist has crashed into my face and 'Where are you, Nulla?' 'Can't anyone find Nulla?' I hear Joe call, and there he is climbing out of the sap, hurriedly climbing back into the open.

With a rush I am out too. The poor pain-mad fellow is tottering for the wheat again, calling for me. I have grabbed him and am somehow carrying a struggling, kicking man back to the sap. *Chut-chut-chut-chut!* The gun is at us again. Will he ever stop struggling? He's getting away from me! I can't hold him! I'll never get him in; I seem to be going mad. Shells seem to be falling all about. Queer shells that don't seem to crash and roar. A gong is ringing in my ears. 'Gas! Gas!' is being yelled furiously, and still the bullets whistle past. Still I struggle into them.

'Stick it to him, son!' And hands reach out and Joe and I are pulled into the sap, into the arms of some stretcher-bearers.

'Gas! Your helmet!' a bearer shouts at me. Through a haze I see the bearers getting into their respirators. Joe is lying on his back on the floor of the trench, and a bearer is putting a gas respirator on him. I'm done for breath. My chest and throat are heaving. I can't get my breath.

Someone is pulling at my chest. Pulling my respirator out. I hear gas shells landing everywhere now. Blood is pouring from my nose. I remember that Joe punched me. My steel helmet has been knocked off. Hands are forcing my respirator on. My breath is coming back, now I'm adjusting my respirator. I'm leaning against the trench, doing my best to breathe quietly into my respirator, but my chest still heaves from the exertion of the past few minutes. The clip of the respirator is hurting my sore nose.

The glass of the respirator is fogged. I wipe it clear and look about. The four bearers have Joe lying on a stretcher and are placing a fresh bandage round his body. A scuffle and Joe has shoved the bearers aside, given one bound and is up and clearing the seven-foot trench in a vault. He's in the open again. Now a bearer is out there holding Joe who struggles hard. The gun no longer fires. It is too dark now.

'Bring the stretcher!' And through the dimmed respirator glass I see the bearers get him on the stretcher and readjust his respirator. I help them get the stretcher back into the trench. Joe appears to be dead, so faintly is he breathing now. The bearers have had to remove his respirator as he is too weak to breathe through it.

'All clear,' is being called. The wind has blown the gas past us. We pull off our respirators.

'You can still smell it here. Hangs in these trenches. We'll get him back.' And the four bearers carry Joe away towards Villers-Bret. Walking in a dream, I make back into the wheat and kick about in the gathering gloom till I find the coil of barbed wire and carry it on to the front line.

I tell the boys about Joe. They are very down in the dumps, for poor old Joe was very popular and we know he has little chance of pulling through. Snow slowly pours water from a water bottle over my face and I get the blood off as slowly the night drifts by.

'Is there a cove named Nulla here?' And an A Company stretcher-bearer comes along.

'Yes, what's up?'

'A wounded man named Benns, back in the dressing station at Villers-Bret, wants you.' So Joe is alive. We're pleased beyond measure and a dozen questions are asked, but the bearer knows nothing beyond the message he was asked to deliver to me at D Company.

Longun and I slip along and get permission to visit the dressing station so we hurry away and soon reach it. Dozens of wounded men are lying on stretchers and tables. Two doctors are moving about, treating men by the light of two big lamps.

We find an A.M.C. sergeant and enquire where we'll find Joe.

'Benns? What kind of wound did he have?'

We tell him.

'Died twenty minutes ago, old man. No hope from the start. If you find that new chaplain they've sent up, he can tell you more than I can as he was with the man for some time. Forty men have died here since dark.'

We find the chaplain who tells us that Joe was never really conscious from when he reached the dressing station, and that he called 'Kitty, Kitty' for hours, but rallied later and asked for me, so a doctor sent the message by some bearers returning to the line.

A young doctor comes by. The chaplain tells him, 'Here's the man Private Benns asked for.' The doctor is a very fine sort and we learn much from him about Joe's death and he shows us where we can find the body when I mention Joe's request that I square up with the jeweller for him.

Longun and I find sixty bodies in a big courtyard and soon we discover Joe. He has had a couple of blankets thrown across him, the blankets he'll be sewn up in prior to burial, poor old chap.

We kneel beside him to get his wallet as he asked, but it's gone. Stolen from his body before it was cold. We're mad, clean mad, and here in this yard of death Longun's bitter imprecations ring out against the callousness of the low thievery of the vultures who prey on the pockets of dead men.

The chaplain rushes up and says, 'Tut! Tut! Man.' And has a lot to say about 'God's will being done'. And assures us that 'I shall bury your fallen mate in the morning. As a Christian soldier he'll receive proper burial.'

'Yes,' Longun tells him. 'And if we have to reach a higher civilisation by climbing your slippery ladder of blood and guts, the sooner we get back to savagery the better, if this is your flamin' civilisation.' And he waves at the yard of dead men and marches off.

As I catch up to Longun he tells me in a voice loud enough for all Villers-Bret to hear, 'These psalm-singin' cows get my goat.' And we trudge off through the early dawn, back to the front line where we're better understood than amongst the champions of the boosted higher civilisation.

FIFTEEN

Hammering at Hamel

Our second innings at Villers-Bretonneux is now just a recent memory. We had a quiet time there, but the battalion still had thirteen men killed and fifty-odd wounded which is light for eight days in the front line. Just the rats of war forever gnawing precious lives away.

We're now at Hospice St Victor at Rivery, and enjoying ourselves. The 47th Battalion has been disbanded owing to lack of reinforcements, and many men of that unit have joined us so we are up to full strength again. As we're close to Amiens the men have been visiting it a lot, but this is made difficult with the Fritz shelling and aerial bombardment and the fact that the French gendarmes have chased the civilians from the city.

Most of us enjoy our sightseeing around the little deserted farms along the Somme, walking between Villers-Bretonneux and Corbie, especially when we strike an orchard of ripe fruit. Our period in the supports is over and we're off for the front-line trenches near Vaire-sous-Corbie. In the gathering dusk we file along the tow-path of the Somme, moving in platoons, our long shadows shivering and shaking in the clear water. Great trees are on either side of the river. All is very still, yet out ahead toward the line can be heard the sharp staccato of bursting shells. Quietly we follow the Somme where a few boats are being rowed about. A big barge loaded with some engineers glides by and we exchange jokes.

For half an hour we move along. It is quite dark. A sound rustles through the treetops and a few leaves float down from stray enemy machine-gun bullets chopping their way through the leaves. The platoon halts as we collect a guide and move on for the front line again.

'Pass the word, "No talking" and "No smoking".' On we go in silence for fifty yards when suddenly, fifty of our guns let go right in our very ears, firing from just beyond a row of trees. We jump from the sudden shock. A bloke named Butcher gives a tremendous jump and lands *plonk* in the water. We're cheered up again and laugh as somebody helps him out, but Butcher doesn't laugh. He only looks around for someone to fight.

Our men are angry. It is madness for those batteries to fire as we are passing, for Fritz is sure to put over some counter-battery fire and catch us.

'Double!' And we are running along the bank of the Somme under the glare of our guns. We know we'll catch it any minute. Suddenly a spout of water leaps at us from the river and we just detect a rumble from the bed of the river as the shell bursts deep underneath, missing us by a few yards. Still running, we hear more shells exploding. The roaring of our guns is drowning the crash of the enemy shells. White splashes leap out of the black water ahead as more shells land in the river and spouts of flame leap from along the river bank. Longun hits me and points into the water.

'Where's your fryin' pan? Fish.' And dozens of little white things are drifting by; the upturned bellies of fish that have been killed by the shells that have landed in the water.

A few more yards and we cross a little swaying pontoon bridge. A man lies dead on the bank while four wounded men are crouched under some bushes waiting until it is safe to move back. We get halted by them. They tell us the one shell got the lot; five casualties where we could so easily have had fifty. Just the luck of the game.

The guide is leaving the river and leading along a little valley. We halt under a bank where the O.C. tells us to move forward in small parties as we are under direct fire from the machine-guns in the Fritz trench. In threes and fours the men move on and are soon swallowed in the darkness.

'Signallers?' And I join two signallers as I'm going in as a sig this stunt.

'Lead on. Straight ahead, you can't miss our trench.' And gathering up our gear, we walk forward into the black night. Fifty yards and we find the signallers' position. After the 39th Battalion signallers disconnect their phone, we connect up ours and ring through to battalion headquarters. Our part of the relief is over.

We spend a quiet night with an odd message to send through. We buzz through every fifteen minutes to make sure the line is okay and the signaller on the other end isn't asleep.

We have struck a very quiet sector. The men have been having some fun stirring up two dead mules that are in no-man's-land between us and Fritz. Every time the breeze comes towards us, Fritz machine-gunners pour bursts into the dead mule and as soon as the wind changes to blow towards them, our gunners rip them about for their benefit.

Wheeoo! Cronk! A big shrapnel shell bursts overhead and we crouch low in the trench. Pellets whistle over from behind us and smack into no-man's-land.

'Pass word the artillery's droppin' 'em short!' And an officer charges down to the phone to ring battalion H.Q. that we're being shelled by our own shrapnel, whilst the men curse our artillery to the full. Shrapnel explodes behind us as we crouch for cover.

'Look out! Stand to!' rings out and we hear muttering and shouts from no-man's-land as we spring to line the parapet. A big uneven shape looms towards us from out of the darkness of no-man's-land and one of our men staggers in, carrying in his arms a wounded man who is moaning piteously. Men help them into the trench.

'Our own stinkin' shrapnel got Frank! Landed all around us, two bursts of it! Got him in the side!' And the men examine Frank. A hole as big as a closed fist in his groin and the blood is flowing freely. Frank is quite unconscious.

Stretcher-bearers bandage him up. As regularly as clockwork, shrapnel bursts over us every two minutes. The men are mad with rage. Two fellows rush in from no-man's-land. They were on the next listening post to Frank and his mate. These men have been lying in a shell hole in front, lying there absolutely unprotected from our shrapnel whilst half a dozen shells have burst, flinging their pellets all around them. They've left their post and run back into the trench and no one blames them. Anyone would become demoralised in such circumstances. One of our shells falling short is more demoralising than a dozen coming from the enemy gunners.

Frank is carried out, but he'll be dead long before he reaches the aid post while the men have returned to the listening posts. The shrapnel is no longer falling short and a very upsetting few minutes have passed.

Night is down on us again. A patrol has been out and had a slap at an enemy patrol which they routed, capturing a prisoner. I'm having a sleep in a little recess of the trench when 'Nulla' is called. I wake and poke my head into the little dugout where the signaller on duty calls me.

'What's up?'

'The line's dead. Fritz has been dropping some heavy stuff and must have got the wires.'

I climb out and, holding the wire in my hand, walk back to find the break. On I go, the wire running through my hand. The wire drops. I kick around in the dark until I find it and discover that it has ended, snapped clean in two. I drop my steel helmet to mark this end of the wire, then search for the other end. For twenty minutes I kick and crawl about in the dark looking for the other end and finally find it blown thirty yards away by a shell. I tug the ends together, get my jack-knife and scrape the insulation off and join the wires. My pliers are lost. I have no means of clamping the join together so bite hard on the knot to close the join. Suddenly my head flies back, my teeth smack open and shut, red hot needles are in my tongue, black spots jump before me and I realise I've had an electric shock. Someone has been testing through just as I bit on the wires.

I'm okay. I bind some insulating tape round the join and make back to tell the sig how he nearly electrocuted me. We laugh and joke and another little experience is stored up as a memory.

The four days in support are over and my company is to go back into the line tonight. I'm not going in with them as I am to go to battalion H.Q. to relieve a signaller there.

The H.Q. is occupying a fine chateau, complete with piano and billiard table. Our phone is rigged up in a big, well-furnished cellar under the chateau with fine tables and lounge chairs and several comfortable couches. We'd hold this Vaire-sous-Corbie front for the duration. Out in the garden, the officers have a cow, while the signallers have a goat which they milk whenever someone else hasn't got in before them. The engineers had two goats, but they went into venison for the infantry so our men are keeping a close watch on our goat, for, if it has to be eaten, we're just the jokers to do it.

The signallers have a well-furnished cellar in the village, the walls adorned with great brass candlesticks. We also have chairs and tables and real beds with feather mattresses.

Midnight. The signal corporal and I, our period of duty over, have just left the battalion H.Q. cellar and are going back through the village to our sleeping quarters and our feather mattresses. All is quiet. We can faintly catch the sound of the ration boats being rowed up the Somme. We notice the village of Vaire is badly damaged with walls torn and broken, roofs gone, leaving only the ridge poles as gaunt reminders of what has been; skeleton houses of a dead town.

Suddenly shells scream and whistle round us. *Bang! Crash! Crash!* The place is a shuddering inferno as shells burst on the ground and against the walls and roofs of houses. *Crash! Crash! Crash!* screams out the awful din amidst the dreadful roar of crumbling houses.

Along a narrow street we race. An ear-splitting scream and we dive against a wall as a 9.2 inch lands in the next house. With a shudder the wall bulges, bends and falls with a dull roar in front of us. Another five yards and we'd have been squashed flat under that wall. Dust, smoke and fumes are blinding us. The house is beginning to blaze. *Crash! Crash! Crash!* Even more shells are bursting everywhere.

We charge up a little laneway into an open square enclosed by ruined houses. A shell hits the ridge pole of a smashed house and explodes ten yards above our heads. Red-hot sparks fly in all directions. The roof collapses into the courtyard. A little black hole is near me. I slip in and pull the corporal after me and we're in a stairway to the cellar. We move down into the blackness to seek shelter from the shell-bursts above.

'Got a match?'

'Got some somewhere.' And the corporal fishes in his pockets and a match flickers and is out. He tries several more, but they won't keep alight in the foul damp air of the cellar.

Above us the barrage is still crashing. Shells are exploding, walls and houses are toppling, but we're in comparative safety as the house will protect us from anything except a direct hit from a big shell. Another crash. The cellar shakes and a gust of wind rushes down to us. Earth and stones fall in the stairway. The fumes of a shell drift down.

'Say they blow the entrance in! We'd never get out. No one'd know we're here. Did you think of that?'

Too right I thought of it. I've been thinking of nothing else for the past five minutes.

Now above the crashing, we catch the far off sound of an empty shell case being struck again and again. The gonging we know and dread. The warning of gas! The gas gongs are going!

The corporal's voice comes queer and alarmed in my ear. 'Gas! We haven't our respirators!' Our respirators are back in the cellar where we slept, so we're in an awful fix. The corporal is sniffing hard.

'Believe I can smell it! It'll drift down these cellars!'

I too am well aware of that. Towards the stairway makes the corporal. 'Come on! We'll run for it. Sooner chance shells than gas. Keep together in case one of us gets hit. We'll stick her out together, Nulla. Keep close.'

And we run up the stairway. *Crash!* And a roaring flame savagely spits across the entrance and we're rushing back down into the cellar, legs overruling brains.

Gas alarms ringing out everywhere. With a rush I'm up the stairs again, the corporal at my heels. Flame is lighting the night above as we scramble up those steps.

We're now in the courtyard, shells crashing everywhere, houses collapsing. Death, riding on whistling shell fragments, reaching invisible tentacles out into the night to claim its victims. Recklessly we race on, determined to see each other through to our big cellar and respirators. A mad headlong rush and we arrive, push aside several blankets and are in. We find our respirators and get them ready.

The men adjust the blankets across the cellar opening and we sit still, listening to the barrage crashing above us, sniffing carefully for the first tainted whiff of gas, though we know that some gases cannot be detected by smell.

Half an hour and the barrage is over. A runner comes in from the chateau cellar and tells us Fritz gas-shelled the village and the front line.

We sit about and talk. I tell them of when I got an issue of mustard gas and never knew anything about it until the next day when I found I was skinned raw under the armpits and between my toes.

The corporal bends down to tie a bootlace. He remains bent and speaks with a tremor, 'Up near Polygon Wood I saw seven gassed men dying out behind a dressing station. They were in convulsions and black in the face and throat. Buckets of blood-specked foamy sort of jelly was coming from their mouths. The doctor and orderlies attending them wore gas-masks. The poor gassed beggars kept grabbing at things and I saw one man grab his own hand and smash his own fingers out of joint. One man tore his mouth nearly back to his ear trying to pull the gas out of his throat. And as each man died, they threw buckets of mud over their head and shoulders. Been far kinder to have smothered them before they died, not after.'

The corporal is stamping up the steps. 'If I ever get a dose of that stuff I'll swallow a flamin' Mills bomb with the pin out.' And he passes out as there drifts back to us the sounds of his desperate vomiting.

'Poor beggar, saw more than was good for him up at Polygon,' someone remarks, and I know now what put the abject terror into his voice when we two were back in that little cellar when the gas alarm went.

Morning comes. The giant of destruction has wielded a heavy axe on the village, slashing and battering all before him. We hear that three men were gassed, a dozen wounded and five killed during the night. The corporal is furiously tapping at the sending key. I know by the behaviour of the phone that our wire is down.

'She's dead, Nulla. Line's broken somewhere.' So I get my respirator fixed and get ready to go out to follow the wire to the front line to find where the disconnection has taken place.

The corporal speaks. 'The password tonight is "Black cat". You might get challenged up near the line. They're pretty keen on passwords lately.'

I set out to follow the wire. Last night I tracked it to the front line and back, only to find the break was on top of our dugout. A spade had chopped it in two. On I go. Through the village and along an orchard hedge, through a wheat crop and out in the open, finding the break a hundred yards behind our front trench. I pull the ends of the wire together and connect up the little phone I carry with me. I buzz our code call through and get both the chateau cellar and the front line, so know that there is only one break.

Today a party of us has been working near Vaire-sous-Corbie helping the engineers erect bridges over the Somme. We erect eight dummy bridges made of hessian and strips of canvas for Fritz to blow down, then we camouflage the real bridges to hide them from aerial observation. When the attack on Hamel is launched, we hope Fritz will expend hundreds of shells on the dummy bridges whilst our infantry cross the river in safety by the real bridges – the camouflaged ones.

We've finished our work and are back in the reserve trenches. In all we did a good day's work especially as four enemy planes flew over having a good look at those new dummy bridges.

The company O.C. has sent for me and I find him with a couple of other officers.

'You sent for me, Sir.'

'Yes. I want you to act as my runner again. The 42nd, who relieved us last night, are to hop-over at dawn in a big attack against Hamel and we are to go back in and take over the captured position on the night of the 5th. That's pretty sudden. Out of the line on the 2nd after sixteen days in and back in to take over a newly won position on the 5th.'

The O.C. is speaking again. 'You can come with me in the morning to have a look at the battle. We're going up to some high ground to see what can be seen. You might never have the chance again of seeing a battle from a gallery seat.'

Night comes quietly. Nothing unusual, just the ordinary shelling. We get in and sleep.

'Awake, Nulla?' I crawl out and join the little party then make off into the night for the O.C.'s gallery seat somewhere ahead.

We wander along, passing dozens of guns hidden everywhere. At each gun, its crew is waiting. We notice a few Yanks attached for experience.

'There's over two hundred guns and not one has fired a shot yet, so Fritz can't have any idea of their positions.'

What a shock for him when two hundred unsuspected guns open on his trenches and battery positions.

The enemy artillery has been remarkably quiet of late and we wonder whether they are short of artillery on this sector. Soon we reach the O.C.'s gallery seats and settle down to watch the attack on Hamel.

We learn that it is fixed for ten past three. It is almost three o'clock now and the officers are discussing the date of the attack: 4th July. They seem sure this was chosen as it is the Yanks' national day, and their army is to be up to its neck in it. During our sixteen days at Vaire-sous-Corbie, we had the Yanks with us to get front-line experience, but very soon they'll get more experience in sixteen seconds than in their sixteen days.

We sit on and wait. Very soon now the fireworks must begin. Hell's lid is working loose.

'Sounds like aeroplanes. Yes, it's planes all right.' And we hear many heavy planes flying up in the darkness.

The O.C. looks round. 'Bombing planes coming up. They're to fly up and down the Fritz trenches for eight minutes to drown the noise of our tanks as they approach the front line, the tanks which we've seen are hidden just eight minutes' journey from the line.'

The planes pass over and we hear the roar of their great engines as they circle round and round out there ahead of us and drop the odd bomb, but we know it is all for a purpose.

Bang! Bang! Bang! and our guns are firing. Away ahead we see little flashes jumping from the ground and see the shells bursting. *Rat-a-tat, rat-a-ta-ta-tat-tat,* and dozens of our machine-guns are into it.

'Eight minutes to go. Our M.G.s and planes are drowning the noise of the tanks' engines,' the officer yells into the din.

It is still dark. The roar of our planes drifts back to us in a droning buzz. The inconsistent rattling of our machine-gun barrage sounds far away. Our artillery is throwing a few shells over in an uninterested sort of way. We wonder how the tanks are getting on, but expect it'll be the same old tale, either ditched or smashed up before they can be of any use.

'The barrage should –' *Bang! Bang! Bang!* The voice is drowned under the terrific belching crash as hundreds of guns fire simultaneously. Hundreds of fiery tongues of red flame leap skyward into the night. A great sheet of glowing flame hangs above the gun positions, and *Boom! Boom! Boom!* The hundreds of guns give voice to an awful clattering, banging boom.

Away out there below us, the night is a dancing mass of shell bursts and on the right, we see the flaring glow from hundreds of bursting shells. From the centre of the shell bursts come ribbons of light that sweep up into the darkness above the explosions – Fritz flares.

'Look! Two red flares! Must be his S.O.S.'

'There it goes again, further to the right.' And two more scarlet-coloured flares go up into the darkness.

'Fritz S.O.S. on to our front line! How'd you like to be back there now?' someone yells, as we see the enemy shells landing out in front. Now, hundreds of explosions are spouting from the ground amongst the flashing guns of our artillery lines. The enemy retaliation is solid.

'Houses burning!' That's Hamel and we see against the flames, the gaunt ghostlike framework of several skeleton houses as another village goes up in smoke. A roar overhead and our big bombing planes are flying back to their hangars, their job done.

'The barrage is beginning to creep!' And we can see the flaming dots slowly drawing further away from us.

'She's to creep forward at a hundred yards every three minutes. The men are following it now. Should be into the first Fritz trench. Wonder if the tanks are still with them?'

The sky has brightened. The barrage is far from us now. Hamel can be seen and also several woods. Out where the fight is raging, we see just dust and smoke, but away to the left are great mountains of dirty clouds rising slowly from the ground.

'That's a smoke screen. It'll hide our attacking waves from exploding fire.'

Boom! Boom! Boom! Not for one second have our guns eased up. They're still hard at it, clearing the opposition from the path our infantry must take. The whole battle area is spouting dust and we know Fritz is heavily shelling the waves of infantry as they push on to objective after objective.

We see enemy planes in the sky above the dust. Some are flying high, ranging their artillery guns onto our attacking battalions, while others keep swooping down, gunning our men as they rush on across the open fields.

'We'll make back.' And we turn our backs on the scene and strike out for our trenches. Behind us is still the crashing of shells whilst on every side our guns are roaring.

We're back in the reserve lines at La Neuville. The noise of the battle has died down and the smoke and dust has drifted away. Now and again an odd battery lets go a few hundred rounds and we hear enemy shells fall just beyond the river. Then at times we catch the faint, clear rattling of some of our machine-guns or the more muffled tones of the big enemy machine-guns. Aeroplanes, our own and the enemy's, are still very busy over Hamel. Flights have been numerous all morning and we've seen half a dozen planes brought down.

The *chug-chug-chugging* of our tanks returning to their hiding places has ceased. We know that the opposing armies are sorting themselves out and settling down to make the best of things after the morning's melee of blood and dust. Daylight has stayed further activities.

Word is through that the stunt has been a model offensive and successful. The officers are very proud of the wonderful success of the Australian Army Corps in its first major operation under our Australian-born leader, General John Monash, and the co-ordination of infantry, tanks, artillery and aeroplanes in an irresistible attack.

The O.C. has just rounded up half a dozen of us and we're off for the hop-off trenches at Vaire-sous-Corbie. We cross the river and are at a place they've named 'Circular Quay'. On the old building is also printed 'S.S. Whizz-bang', along with plenty of other notices in charcoal.

Dozens of Fritz prisoners are coming back, shepherded along by our mopping-up party and by some very happy Yanks. The strained, unnatural faces of Fritz plainly tell what they have been through. We've seen that scared, nervously apprehensive look before, on Fritz faces and on our own. Men unstrung to the point of mental collapse. Somehow we can't keep our eyes off these poor devils for they aren't men but mere boys of no more than fifteen. Tear stains are on many of their boyish faces. Tears of fear. Boys thrown into what even hardened men can barely stand. We've often been inclined to laugh at prisoners, sometimes we've abused the poor down-hearted wretches, but now we're full of pity for these poor little lads called upon to do the job that men should not be asked to do.

The boys seem afraid of us because of what they have been told about the treatment of prisoners, probably malignant propaganda designed to make them afraid to surrender.

One of our men keeps asking the Fritz, 'You speak English?'

At last a little weedy man with big, round, silver-rimmed spectacles answers in a strangely piping voice.

'Yes, *Kamerad*, mine learn the English since four years.'

'Good! You tell these boys that we treat prisoners well. Send you all back to Fritzy after the war. No more war for you. All safe now. You understand me?'

'Yes, *Kamerad,* mine have comprehend,' and the boys are all talking at once as the English-speaking lad tells them what our man said.

'Perhaps,' snarls a Fritz officer in perfect English as he passes on, bringing up the rear.

An old runner is speaking: 'I've got three boys at home as old as those fellows. It should be absolutely illegal to put boys like that in the line. Enough to sicken anyone of the war.'

We come to a couple of wounded officers and the O.C. asks them how it went. They are both very enthusiastic about the tanks and the part they played in helping the infantry. Nevertheless, we'll have to see the tanks doing good work before we'll believe it as our experience with tanks has not been good.

'The tanks were great. They kept right on the barrage and each time a machine-gun nest held us up, we only had to signal to a tank and it just waded in and shot up the gun crew and all was serene again. We'll never go over without tanks again,' an officer enthuses as he eases an arm that carries two machine-gun bullets.

'Hear about the Yanks?'

The other wounded officer laughs.

'The Yanks in the first wave wanted to stop and either bayonet or rat every Fritz we overran. They were either racing fair into our barrage or getting lost and crowding in everywhere amongst our second wave.'

We hear that there is no front line, just a rough line consisting of narrow little disjointed trenches dug by the various platoons as they reached their objective. We also hear that enemy snipers are very active and that many casualties were caused by Fritz planes gunning our men as they dug. The wounded men are now moving back along the river and we are pushing on. Soon we're at our old trench.

How different it looks from what it was when we left it only the night before last. Fritz has peppered it properly and it's smashed and broken beyond recognition. Dead men, most of them badly mangled, are everywhere and burying parties are hard at work. I have a look at our old signallers' position and see two dead men in it, unmarked men whose faces are blue, killed by concussion and the bursting of blood vessels within their heads.

Dead men are scattered here and there. Some of the 42nd, a few Yanks and in the old trenches many dead Fritz. Now and again we come across a short length of trench that has been a machine-gun post. Practically all these posts are littered with Fritz dead, the tracks of the tanks around them, confirming their part in destroying these strong posts.

Our guide turns to the O.C. 'You've heard of a man being called a flat, haven't you, Sir?'

'Um, yes.'

'Well here's one.' And he leads us into a little patch of wheat squashed flat by the tank's great caterpillar tracks. The guide points and we see a Fritz uniform spread out on the ground. We look closer and see that a man is inside the uniform, squashed absolutely flat on the ground when a tank has gone over him. A terrible sight, and sickened, we turn away.

We pass through a couple of lines of rough support trenches, showing up very white in their chalky soil. The men here have been hard at work all day. Another hundred yards we go when several enemy machine-guns open and put us on the ground in a mighty hurry. We're lying in an open patch and a burst of bullets kicks the white dust over us, so we're off as hard as we can go, crawling on our bellies for a patch of crop thirty yards ahead.

Into the crop and we lie still for a few minutes. *Crash! Crash! Whizz! Bang! Bang! Bang!* And a Fritz barrage comes down around us. Our heads pop up above the crop, but there's nowhere to go so we just lie flat on the ground and hope for the best. We keep very still, listening to the shells. A few soft ones fall. Gas! The O.C. rolls over and tells me I have his permission to shoot him if ever he comes into the line again off his own bat.

'If these shells get any closer there'll be no need for anyone to shoot any of us.'

'You're pretty right there.' And the O.C. calls to the guide to ask how far we are from the front line.

'Coupla hundred yards, Sir.'

'Think we'll make a run for it, eh?'

I nod, too breezy to say much for we're under very heavy shellfire and there's gas coming over too and plenty of machine-gun bullets. We scramble to our feet knowing it's going to be a dangerous two hundred yards and we'd be safe back at La Neuville only for the keenness of the O.C. He's sorry now he left and so am I, real sorry.

A mad headlong rush, throwing ourselves down, hopping up only to go down again, up and on again and we're safe in a little post with some grinning men of the 42nd.

We get our breath back and have a look round at our future home. Just a narrow length of trench with some old wire netting stretched over it and upon the netting, some grass and a few white stones. Nice little home, especially as its three former occupiers are lying dead not three feet from it.

Out we jump and run to the next position, a little newly dug trench barely waist deep so we don't stop but keep running till we reach a dozen men who are holding a captured trench that looks better, and down into it we drop.

This has been an enemy reserve trench and boasts a few dirty little dugouts. The O.C. meets an officer here and they go off in the dusk to inspect the line, but I don't go with them, as I've seen all I want to see between here and La Neuville.

I yarn to the men and to three stray Yanks who wandered in early this morning. The Yanks don't know where they should be, nor where their unit is, but they're not worried. They've found the war at last so are quite content.

The sound of several of our aeroplanes is heard flying low and slowly. From a plane directly overhead something is falling, a parachute opens and two boxes of ammunition float slowly to the ground. A man runs out and in a few minutes is back dragging the bullets after him and stuffing a nice silk parachute inside his tunic.

'Make a silk blouse for the sheila.' He laughs.

We see ammunition being dropped all along the line and great bundles of picks and shovels are floating down, spinning and twirling as they come, swinging under big open parachutes. None of us has ever seen anything quite like this before.

I see the O.C. beckoning to me so climb out to join him, telling the men I'll see them tomorrow night. They tell me they'll be pleased to see me any time as they know I'm to guide their relief in. That's why they're so polite and pressing in their invitation to me to hurry up and get back. I'm awake to them.

'Think you can find the way back from here?' The O.C. laughs.

'Too bloomin' right I can.' And we set off in a hurry lest Fritz renew his barrage. We soon cross our old front line, then the reserve lines near Vaire and get across the river and reach the battalion at La Neuville.

The O.C. goes away to make a detailed report to the colonel and I slip off to find some food and some sleep for I'm exhausted. All night long we hear the shelling and can tell that every time our guns open up, Fritz replies as they're clearly nervous. We hope his nerves steady down a bit before tomorrow night, but that's a long way off so we roll the blankets over our heads to get some sleep.

The morning of 8th July. We are in the front line having taken over from the 42nd last night. All night we've been hard at work digging our trenches deeper and connecting them up, improving on our mates' work, so we'll soon have a real trench.

Early this morning I had a trip along the whole length of our battalion's position. Our right-hand post is on the left of Hamel and extends to the Somme Canal near the village of Bouzencourt. The canal runs straight out to Fritz so the boys reckon they'll be getting behind us in submarines if we don't lay some mines in the river.

An hour or so ago there was a nasty happening in D Company when one of the sergeants, while cleaning his rifle, accidentally killed a man in the post. This accident is the first of its kind and we are all very depressed. It's a cruel fate that strikes a man down by a comrade's bullet after he has dodged enemy bullets, shells and gas for two years.

×

A couple of days have gone by. We're in for some stunt, but have no idea how it will pan out. The Somme runs from our left, straight out towards Fritz. The 46th Battalion is on the opposite side of the river and tonight they are to advance their line. Whilst the enemy is busy trying to stop them, we are to move forward quietly and dig in on a new line some distance out ahead. This movement is possible because the enemy positions are hundreds of yards away.

We are not quite ready to move out. Equipment is tightened up: spades and picks are ready. Lewis guns are made ready for firing at any moment. The barrage is down beyond the river. Enemy guns are now replying. Machine-guns are getting into it. The flares are going up so we know the 46th men are attacking.

'Come on, D Company.' And we are moving out into the open, into the darkness. Silently we walk straight ahead. Will the enemy machine-guns begin to rattle? But not a sound comes as we advance. We reach a few of our men, officers and scouts who have been out choosing the site for the new trench. Quietly we move along amongst them until we are spread out on the new site.

'Get into it, men.' And we commence to dig for all we're worth. Out on our left we still hear the noise of the 46th Battalion stunt, but not a shot comes our way. Surely Fritz must hear us and open fire! On we dig;

still the death rattle on an enemy machine-gun does not come. Our luck's in.

Each man digs a narrow hole and as it deepens, he gets down in it and works to lengthen it towards the one the next man is digging. Slowly a hundred white mounds of chalky clay are rising across the ground, then lengthening into one continuous twisting white streak across the black night as the diggers link up hole after hole.

I get sent back with a message and return with another to the new line and find the O.C. who has just come in from patrolling along the Lewis gun and rifle posts.

'Message for you, Sir.' And I hand it over to him.

'How the devil am I to read it here?' He screws it under his nose in the dark trying to decipher the pencilled scrawl.

'It's to you and is signed in the Colonel's code name and says "All disturbed earth to be covered by screening of grass",' I tell him.

As the O.C. has no further use for me for a while, I follow him up and down our position, which consists of many short lengths of trench, really a series of outposts. Men come up carrying barbed wire and move out to erect it in no-man's-land. I score another of those quiet, dangerous jobs; following the O.C. out along the position where the men are putting up the wire and then out towards Fritz for another fifty yards until we find the covering parties.

Fritz is getting restless. An unusual number of flares is going up. A Lewis gun post out in front has reported hearing an enemy patrol moving about when suddenly we're under a savage artillery bombardment. Fritz has discovered what we're up to, but luckily for us, he isn't too certain as to our exact whereabouts. Shells are crashing everywhere. Feverishly our men keep digging in. The men doing the wiring out in front are getting it also and several wounded have come in already. Gas is coming over and work has been held up as the men can't exert themselves in gas respirators.

The barrage has eased down. We escaped very lightly under the enemy shelling as our casualties were one killed and a dozen or so wounded, of whom about half were gassed.

For the past hour we have been busily spreading grass over the white chalk we have thrown up by the digging to help hide the trench from observers in the enemy aeroplanes and from enemy machine-gunners and snipers.

Night again and a sergeant and I crawl out into no-man's-land on a wandering patrol. We've crawled through our barbed wire and lie very still, looking and listening into the night. Ahead of us somewhere a flare goes up every few minutes and we decide to get closer to see where they're coming from. On we crawl. Each flare rises from the same place and we plainly hear the flare-shooter eject each spent flare cartridge.

For a hundred yards we worm our way onwards to get around behind him. We are not more than thirty yards from him now. There's a bank of earth between us and him, when there's a tap on my arm.

'We'll take a peep over that mound. Might see him. If he's very far in front of their trench we'll have a go to get behind him and capture him.'

Quietly we crawl up to the mound. Another flare soars up so we hug the ground lying under the mound. The flare is out. Together we rise and look over the little mound and stare right into the faces of eight or nine Fritz no more than a metre from us! The shock drives the very breath from our bodies. The Fritz get a shock, too, that sends them diving and ducking to left and right!

An order is snapped out in Fritz! Metal clangs metal! A machine-gun belt bumps against the side of the gun! With a backwards dive we are racing in the darkness of no-man's-land as an excited babble of voices reaches us. *Crack!* A rifle fires from a dozen yards behind our flying heads. *Crack! Crack!* Two more shots ring out startling the night. Another savage *Crack! Phut!* A flare is going up!

'Down!' And we go headlong into a little depression where we lie under the flare listing to the talk and movement not thirty yards behind. *Chut-chut-chut-chut* and an enemy machine-gun is venomously spitting lead over us. Flares go up in dozens. The Fritz gun pours burst after burst and bullets thud into the ground just ahead. The fumes of burning cordite float across.

We're in a fix. If we move he'll see us, and the gun and rifles will riddle us. If we remain here much longer he must spot us and the result will be the same. One of our own Lewis guns is now firing, making matters worse. Its bullets must be going very close for undoubtedly it is shooting at the sound of this infernal ***bark, bark, barking*** right here on top of us. We'll never get out! The Lewis gun ruined what little hopes we had!

'Oh, Moses!' comes in a forlorn whisper of despair through the savage cracking of the Fritz gun. I don't say anything. I can't. The suspense of waiting to be torn and ripped to gory pieces is too great.

Suddenly hope rises high and through the ear-splitting clatter I whisper, 'Don't move. Keep still. They can't see us.' I realise that's the case or we'd have been riddled long ago, but we're not game to move a muscle to find out why it is they can't spot us.

The enemy gun stops. Our Lewis gun fires no more. 'Safe to stay here for a while till he settles down,' I whisper to the sergeant, but he whispers back, 'No, I can't. Must make a run for it now.' Still he doesn't move and for what seems an age we remain frozen to the ground.

'A bomb, quick! They're comin' out!' says the sergeant and slow reluctant steps are nearing us. Two little clicks and we've each pulled the pin from a bomb. The levers go up as we release them. Mechanically I count, 'One, two.' And rise to throw my bomb at those approaching feet. A rush of air and another, as our bombs fly through the night. *Whang! Whang!* they explode, and the enemy footsteps are now running, running from us, running back to their trench!

'Come on! Get!' And we are fairly racing across no-man's-land for our trench. Desperately we tear on and as we go the sergeant's panting voice hoarsely whispers, 'Not an ounce of guts among the lot of them, or they'd have got us.'

Sixty yards we make when their machine-gun is into it again. We jump into a little dry stream bed and are safe. The gun gives us ten minutes on and off and then all is silent so we find our wire and walk along until we reach a break in it, slip through and get down into a big shell hole.

The sergeant gives a whistle towards our trench. It is answered, so we get up and walk on to the parapet. *Phit! Phit! Phit!* Bullets are whipping into it, thudding into the chalky dust. I jump for cover and so does the sergeant, but he's too late for we all hear the hard smack as a bullet drives through his leg.

Now he lies on a stretcher, bandaged up. Our O.C. and two other officers are around him as he jokes and tells of our narrow escape out in front. We're the centre of attention, lucky devils, the pair of us.

'Give me half a dozen men and young Nulla to show us where their post is and I'll go out and fetch them in,' is the laughing offer being made to the O.C. by Lieutenant Fere. Now I wish the bottom would fall out of the trench and take him with it.

'We'll see about it.' And the O.C. wanders off with Mr Fere, and I join my mates and tell them what nearly happened to us. We yarn on. The sergeant is carried away as we discuss his luck in escaping from almost certain death to get a bullet just as he reaches our trench. Still he's lucky.

Another shock when Mr Fere asks me to lead six men to the enemy post.

'And you three can come too.' And with not a word, Longun, Dark and Snow are dipping into a bag of bombs and filling their pockets and soon we're ready to go out.

Silently I lead on for the enemy post again where the flare-shooter still guides me very well. Now we are forty yards from the mound and I point it out. We veer half right and crawl along until we are in line with it. Not a sound from anywhere. A flare is up and we sink into the ground. The flare is down and we crawl on a few more yards.

We're within ten yards of the mound. A flare goes up and we see a Fritz helmet move. The flare is down. Mr Fere's arm swings through the darkness just once. There's the dull thud of something hitting the ground. *Whang!* A little flash and the Mills bursts at the enemy post. 'At 'em!' And with a mad rush we're tearing for the post behind our straining bayonets.

The Fritz shout and, running like mad, leave the post. We're right at it! Three half-asleep Fritz cower in abject fear in the bottom of the trench. Bayonets are beckoning to them to get up, but they won't move. We hear shouts from some Fritz thirty yards further back towards where the men from this post bolted.

'Grab the bloke with the sandy moustache!' Mr Fere laughs, and a bayonet jabs the fellow with the little fair moustache in the ribs and he is up in a flash yelling '*Kamerad!*'

'Get with him!' And Longun and another man are racing the fear-stricken Fritz back into no-man's-land with two bayonets almost onto his back.

The men are trying to get the other two Fritz up, but they are too terrified to move. *Crack!* And a rifle fires from thirty yards off. Several men turn and fling bombs at the rifle's flash.

'Get back, men!' Mr Fere orders as he empties his revolver in the direction of the rifle shot.

'Split this up amongst you!' And Darky pelts two bombs down to the two Fritz still crouching below us. Snow sends another down as half a dozen of us pull the pins and fling a couple of bombs each towards the other enemy position just in the rear and then we're racing away into the darkness as the savage *Whang! Whang! Whang!* of our exploding bombs mingles with enemy shouts and a sickening scream as a man is blown asunder in the little post we've just left.

For twenty yards we rush straight ahead, then according to instructions thirty yards to our left, turn to the right and charge on for our trench. By doing so we hope the Fritz gunners will miss us. We're almost to our wire before an enemy gun opens. Mr Fere calls and we get down in little shell holes and for five minutes we wait as three enemy guns rake no-man's-land for us, but they fire in vain. The suddenness of our attack and departure has saved us.

The guns are silent. We get through our wire, close the gap we purposely left open and reach our trench.

Longun has our prisoner down with the O.C. where Mr Fere tells him how we mixed it with the enemy on the raid. Some rum comes to light and we get an issue each and someone says, 'What about Fritz?' And he too is given an issue, making short work of it.

Snow and another chap are told to hurry the Fritz prisoner back to battalion H.Q. and set out with him.

The O.C. is speaking: 'We're being relieved by the 33rd tomorrow night. How does that hit you?'

'Not too bad, Sir,' someone casually remarks as we break up and wander back to our posts.

To be relieved tomorrow night! That will be seven days in here this trip in which we've had forty casualties. Even if we'd had no casualties there would still have been music for us in the O.C.'s words 'to be relieved tomorrow night'.

SIXTEEN

Leap-frogging to Victory

We've been kept going for the past month. Relieved near Hamel on the 18th July, we marched back to our old reserve trenches at La Neuville where we slept away what was left of that night.

Next day the battalion marched back to Cardonnette where we went into billets. We had a much-needed shave, a hot bath and a general clean up of ourselves and equipment. Then we started solid training again; physical jerks, drill, skirmishing and route marches.

A week later, on the last day of July, the battalion marched to Cagny, near Amiens, where we slept in the open under the trees of an orchard in case Fritz planes came over, as secrecy was to be observed in mustering the troops up to the forward areas. After dark on 2nd August, we moved further up towards the line, not far from Daours. Here we took over billets from some French colonial troops where we got a new brand of chats – French colonial chats.

Two nights later, 4th August, we did another rotten night march to a place up on the left of Hamel. It took us six hours to march twelve miles as the roads were so congested with traffic. Every few yards we'd bump into the fellow in front and get sworn at or we'd turn round and roar at the joker behind who walked on our heels or jabbed his rifle into us. Motor traffic had the centre of the road whilst the slow-moving horses and mules kept to the outside edge of it. We were anywhere we could get, walking, running, dodging and shoving our swearing way in and out between motor wheels and horses' legs, abusing and being abused, swallowing dust, motor fumes and the smell of dirty mules. It was like the nightmare marches we used to do along the Mametz–Fricourt road only that the mud was missing.

We've been here near Hamel for three days now. It's the night of 7th August, my third birthday in the army. I've been wondering where I'll spend the next three.

Tomorrow, 8th August, a great offensive is to be launched on a scale unprecedented. To our Australian Corps is to fall the honour of forming the head of the great thrusting spear. The honour will be ours, but also the fighting and the dying. Up on our left, across the Somme, will be the divisions of the British Third Corps and on our right we'll have the Canadian Corps.

The Australians are to attack on a six-thousand-yard front from the Somme on our left, to Villers-Bretonneux on our right. Our 2nd, 3rd, 4th and 5th Divisions are to attack, whilst our 1st Division, which has recently been fighting up near Hazebrouck somewhere, is to be in reserve.

It is to be a 'leap-frog' advance. As one division reaches its objective, the next is to jump over it and continue till it reaches its objective. At 4.30 a.m. tomorrow our 2nd and 3rd Divisions are to hop-over and, helped by an artillery barrage and the tanks, are to advance 3000 yards to the first objective, known as the 'Green Line'. Then our division and the fifth are to leap-frog the Green Line and to advance through open warfare conditions to the 'Red Line', 4500 yards in advance. Some other brigades of the 4th and 5th Division will then leap-frog the Red Line and advance another 1000 or 1500 yards to the 'Blue Line'; the final objective of the attack.

In all, we are to advance about 9000 yards across country held by the enemy and give him a taste of what he gave our British Fifth Army during the massive Fritz offensive of March 1918.

It is well into the night and soon we'll be moving. The men are keen and confident of success and, after two years in France, our High Command is launching the kind of attack that every infantryman knows is the only kind that can pay. How often have we seen the utter futility of our small-brained, nibbling tactics and been decimated in capturing the enemy's forward trenches, and then had to sit down and dig in whilst he strengthened up another line for us to smash ourselves against in our next little advance?

I'm going in as a runner in this stunt. I've had several runs tonight and, back at Brigade H.Q., I heard that we've already suffered a serious loss in tanks when a Fritz shell landed amongst twenty-eight tanks near Villers-Bretonneux, hitting one that was full of tins of petrol, which exploded, and fifteen tanks went up in flames.

'Fall in, men.' And we are on the move for our big stunt. Silently we move forward calmly into the night. All is quiet except the usual shelling. No unusual sound reaches us though we know that moving with us through the night are thousands of men, battery upon battery of guns and miles of transport.

We are halted now, sitting on the ground waiting. It is just 4 a.m. and very dark, with a thick fog over all. Suddenly, with a resounding crash, our barrage opens. Thousands of guns roar in an unending bark that seems to shake the very earth to its foundations. Our men are laughing and shouting, glad in the knowledge of how much easier our task will be as the result of this terrific bombardment.

I turn to a new man in my section doing his first stunt. 'What do you think of her, Clem?'

Wild-eyed and scared he looks at me, but says nothing, as it's above him. He's never visualised anything like this. I see him shudder as he tries somehow to shrink into himself. He turns to me. 'Oh, this noise! If it would only let up for a minute!'

'You don't want to worry about a bit of noise. We're giving it to Fritz now. Wait till you're on the receiving end of a big barrage,' I joke with him.

'I'd die first shell, I'm sure.' He tries to laugh and I know the strain is working off. He is becoming more used to the unnatural noise. He's a very decent chap and I'll do what I can to help him through.

'The first wave's going over now,' the O.C. says as he looks at his watch, but we can hear nothing of the attack for we are in the midst of the bellowing guns.

An hour later and we are moving on for our second assembly position. Each platoon is in single file and advancing in artillery formation for we may come under enemy shelling at any minute. We head for the old front line from which the first assaulting wave jumped off at 4.30 a.m. on their 3000-yard advance into enemy territory. Visibility is very limited as a great bank of smoke-thickened fog hangs over the whole countryside.

Nearing Hamel we pass heaps of shells lying in the open, covered with straw, grass, bags and bushes. Planes are busy overhead, but we can barely see them so dense is the fog and the drifting smoke and dust. A man runs over to our platoon where the company O.C. is marching and yells above the roaring of the guns, 'There's an officer from a balloon hung up in a tree by his parachute just over there.'

The O.C. turns to us. 'Three men slip over and see what can be done.' And Snow, Clem and I run across to get the man down. The parachute is caught in the branches and the officer swings suspended a dozen feet above the ground. We rush up to him, but see that his head is sagging on his chest. His eyes are open but see nothing; he is dead. His two dangling boots are coated with dry blood, probably from body wounds. Riddled with bullets from a plane's machine-gun as he slowly floated down from the balloon he left too late.

'Imagine the helplessness of the poor beggar bleeding to death as he slowly drifted down to earth,' Snow remarks to Clem, who makes no reply for he is seeing his first dead man and is affected by the sight. We can do nothing to help now so leave the man hanging where he is and run along and catch up to our platoon.

We cross the old front-line and are in what was old no-man's-land a few hours ago. We pass through gaps in our wire and reach the enemy wire, which has been smashed and tossed about by our barrage. Several enemy bodies are lying about the wire, shattered and mutilated almost beyond recognition. Civilisation at war!

We're at the old enemy front-line trench now, blown and smashed to pieces. Dozens of dead everywhere and not a whole man amongst them. Limbless and headless they lie coated in chalk, torn and slashed by the shelling, slashed in life and again in death by our remorseless shelling. The old enemy trench is behind us and we are climbing a long sloping stretch of country with the dark edge of Accroche Wood to our right.

Passing it we see a broken machine-gun emplacement with five 3rd Division men lying dead just where they collapsed, bullet-riddled, as they gamely rushed the enemy gun. In several shell holes are rifles and equipment that have been left by the wounded men, so we know that the Fritz gun had reaped a heavy toll before it was silenced.

At the gun position we notice the broad tracks of a tank all about it. Two enemy gunners lie dead within a few yards of the gun while the gun itself is squashed flat, driven into the dust by the great weight of a tank that has driven over it. Flattened alongside the gun is a grey clothed heap of gory pulp, which but a few hours ago was the living body of a Fritz gunner.

On either hand are stretcher-bearers carrying out the wounded while others are walking back. An Australian mounted man comes riding behind a big batch of enemy prisoners. Through a break in the fog as we top a ridge, we see on every side prisoners, stretcher cases and walking wounded making back towards the rear. Their share of the stunt is over and we move on.

Field guns are firing ahead. We come up to them and find a row of howitzers lined up in the open, firing as fast as they can load. On past them we go and a dozen gun teams gallop back past us. Soon we reach the guns that those sweating horses have drawn up. Two batteries of Australian 18-pounder guns are doing rapid fire on ground that only an hour and a half ago was nearly two miles behind the Fritz front line. Good work is being done here this morning.

Still moving onwards. Odd shells falling about, bullets flying high overhead. Fritz is beginning to tighten the hooks on us now. Very soon we shall be into it good and solid.

Our dead and enemy dead are scattered far and wide. We pass several more Fritz machine-gun posts. The tale is the same. A sprinkling of Australian dead and the tossed-off gear of the wounded pave the way to each gun post. Then, the overturned gun, but no gunners as the enemy has not been fighting it out to the end. Scattered within fifty yards of the gun, Fritz bodies from a hidden gun reaping a heavy toll from our advancing men. Then the gunners, unable to stop that determined, resolute, onward sweeping line of Australian khaki, have abandoned their gun and made a frenzied, headlong rush towards their own lines, only to fall riddled as the men of our advancing wave dropped upon one knee and fired into their fleeing, terror-stricken backs.

Just ahead of us are dozens of horse- and mule-drawn G.S. wagons and gun limbers strung out under a long bank. More horses come galloping back and we know that they have been drawing field guns up to some forward position.

The fog is lifting. Behind us we see our battalion's transport following on. Smoke is issuing from the little chimneys of our field cookers. Our cooks are boiling the pot even as we advance into enemy territory.

We follow the battalion scouts just ahead and are soon strung out along our second assembly position, but we can see very little as the smoke and fog have become very dense again. The battalion halts and most of us get down on the ground for a rest. We've done a hot, tiring march, but our real work is still ahead for which we shall need all our energy and luck.

It is 7 a.m. so we have been an hour and a half on the march from our first assembly position.

'Ask the platoon commanders to rest the men. We may be here an hour or so,' the O.C. directs, and I make off to carry the order along the line.

I come to each of the other platoons of D Company and give the message. The men are tired, dusty and sweaty, but happy. Some are silent. These are the apprehensive men, the fellows who've been taking too much notice of the khaki forms in the grass for the past two miles. Doing too much thinking is bad in times like these.

I decide to walk along our battalion front as I'm interested in the Mark V tanks that are to go over with us when we advance. I feel very friendly towards these tanks, remembering those squashed machine-gun nests back there and the good work at Hamel a month ago.

Eight o'clock and we're ready to move forward on our stage of the attack. Last-minute instructions and warnings have been on issue and now we're moving for the Green Line, the objective of the first phase of the great attack. Little can be seen. Fog is rising from the ground in a great cloud and big banks of smoke are drifting overhead from the smoke barrage that our artillery laid down to hide the 3rd Division men as they went forwards four hours ago. Then we smell dust ahead and see men digging in so we know we are at the Green Line.

A few shouts, some jokes and we are moving through the ranks of the digging men, leap-frogging the first objective for the big attack, the Green Line, which also marks the end of the first phase and the capture of 3000 yards of enemy territory, dozens of enemy guns and hundreds of prisoners of war.

We are through the 3rd Division and setting out on our own advance of 4500 yards towards the Red Line. Ahead we can see smoke and fog through which is moving our six tanks and a screen of battalion scouts. Ahead, the enemy holds the 4500 yards of country from which we are to chase him. Ahead lies fighting and, we hope, victory. Straight on we move. Soon we'll know.

Our guns are firing from behind, but we won't have the intense artillery barrage that supported the first phase of the attack to the Green Line. We have been told to expect open warfare conditions and somehow we hope we shall get them. Out ahead of our tanks we can see our shells bursting about.

Bang! Whizz! Bang! Bang! and Fritz shells are falling around us as we steadily advance.

Chat-chut-chut-chut and a Fritz machine-gun is at us. Bullets whine and hum past and we quicken our pace, eyes peering through the fog to try to get the location of the gun. In grim silence we hurry on. Fingers are crooked on triggers, bayonets point steadily ahead.

'Get down!' And we drop to the ground behind a little mound of earth near which several of our scouts are lying. Bullets are raising little spouts of dust from the mound.

'Come on, you men,' the O.C. calls, and my section crawls up to him. He turns. 'The gun is in those bushes to the right of that smoke. We're going to rush it. Are you ready?' And the well-known hollow feeling sets up in our guts as we hear his words: '*Going to rush it!*'

The O.C. turns, gives a wave to the scouts. 'Come on!' he yells, and the seven of us are on our feet and following him. We leap the mound as a savage *crack, crack* rings out as the rest of the platoon and the scouts open up, doing rapid rifle fire at the hidden gun. Now we're level with the O.C. and on we race for that little clump of bushes. Just eight of us. Longun, Dark, Snow, the O.C., me and three new men, of whom one is Clem.

Chut-chut-chut-chut and Fritz has his gun on us! Its bullets flit and flip amongst us! The savage bark of the gun is right in our ears as we race for the bushes. Somehow we can hear our mates in the platoon desperately firing, but the gun keeps on. They can't silence it, but its aim is erratic now. Bullets fly over our heads, now they kick up the dust in a dozen places three yards ahead. Something shining, we've seen the gun and we're putting in a mad headlong rush and are down behind the mound of an old potato pit.

The O.C. crawls up to me. 'Take those three new men, rush to the edge of the bushes and open fire on the gun when you get there. The rest of us will work round to the left to get behind it.' Then he speaks to the men and gives them instructions. I listen, knowing that these three inexperienced men are to be thrown into the very mouth of the gun to draw its fire whilst the O.C., Longun, Dark and Snow, old stagers all, will independently work around behind whilst the gun is busy on us. It's our only hope, for our tank is away in the fog somewhere ahead having unknowingly passed the hidden gun. If we don't silence this gun it will wipe out half our company and already it has held up our advance.

The O.C. touches me. 'The platoon will do five rounds rapid and the moment they stop put your run in.'

'Yes, Sir.' And the O.C. wriggles away to the left.

'Ready?' I try to grin at my three men, but make a pretty poor fist of it. I'm sorry for these men and extra sorry for myself for having to lead them into what I know lies ahead.

The O.C. is signalling back to the scout officer, but fails to make himself understood so wriggles up to me again. 'Signal five rounds rapid,' he tells me.

'Yes, Sir.' And lying with my back on the old spud pit I wave my arms, semaphoring the message back. Over the mound, behind which is hidden the scout officer and the rest of the platoon, a rifle is raised. We watch that rifle. It sweeps about, signalling morse code to us.

'Dot, dash, dot; R,' I call.

Again the rifle is moving. Down to its right, a pause, back to the vertical and two short sweeps to the right and has disappeared in a cloud of dust as the enemy gun drills the mound.

'Get set,' he calls to my men, and *Crack! Crack! Crackety Crack! Crack!* Our men are doing their five rounds rapid fire.

Suddenly the rifles stop. My call of 'Come on!' mingles with the O.C.'s 'Go on!' And the four of us are over the pit in our mad thirty-yard charge for that gun. *Chut-chut-chut!* Right in our faces it comes! I feel the air rush by as bullets almost graze my head as I see Fritz move just twenty yards ahead there in the bushes! The lad beside me pitches headlong forward and I hear the soft sighing cough as the bullet-riddled body of the falling boy strikes the ground. Desperately I press my rifle trigger and *Bang!* I have sent a bullet fair for that movement in the bushes. An enemy rifle barks back and a man yells in a scream, 'Oh sufferin' cats! The floppin' stinkers've got me!' as he crumbles forward, grabbing at his leg.

Clem and I are left. Now we're at the edge of the bushes. A big Fritz is running through the stunted trees. Madly I work my bolt to reload, but Clem's flies to his shoulder. *Bang!* and the Fritz falls, head forward, to the ground.

We start to get down to fire at the gun, but Clem yells, 'They're leavin' the gun!'

'We'll get round 'em!' I shout excitedly, and we race to cut them off, but three Fritz gunners rush out of the bushes towards where the O.C. and my three mates should now be. Clem and I reach the enemy gun. We hear the water of its cooling chamber bubbling as it boils, so rapidly has the gun been fired. No Fritz are about. The scrub seems deserted.

To our left a rifle shot rings out, followed by the throaty bark of a heavy service revolver. We look towards the firing. The three Fritz who ran from the gun are no longer running; they're on the ground. The O.C. is pushing his revolver back into its holster, Snow is ejecting a spent cartridge from his rifle, and Dark and Longun are wiping their bayonets through the grass. Three grey forms are lying in the grass, no movement comes from them beyond a twitch of a stomach and a convulsive shudder or two. They're still forever, poor wretches. Determined, brave men who carried their determination just five minutes too long, who left their surrender just five minutes too late, caught and killed by the khaki wave they couldn't stop. Gone the way the brave gunners go!

The platoon has rushed up, the scouts are running out ahead. We see our stretcher-bearers take a glance at the boy who fell when so near to me in our rush of a few minutes ago. One glance, and the bearers leave him where he fell and are down beside the bloke who yelled 'Sufferin' cats' as he went down.

Through the little bushes we advance. Here's the Fritz that Clem dropped rolling on his side. He raises one hand in a call of '*Kamerad*', but we leave him and pass on. I see the blood-stains are high on his right shoulder. He's lucky for that isn't quite where Clem's excited shot was aimed.

Now we're beyond the little clump and running to catch up to the lines of tanks, for that hold-up by the enemy gun has thrown us out of line with the rest of the battalion. Enemy shells are bursting everywhere now. The air seems thick with the whistle and whine of enemy bullets. An odd man goes down here and there, but we advance steadily on.

On we go, sweltering under half a hundred-weight of bullets and gear. Perspiration of excitement and heat is pouring from us. Through a dense cloud of choking, smoking dust we move ever onward.

Every here and there, we see enemy men rise with hands held high calling '*Kamerad!*' We wave to the rear and they rush on, glad to be escaping it all. Here and there we pass enemy field guns abandoned by their crews. Every few minutes we see fleeing enemy soldiers who are rushing helter-skelter ahead of us on the ridges. We pause, fire at them and they disappear from sight, generally leaving a few dead and wounded to mark the way they went.

Still we advance, grilling in the heat of the August sun, stinging sweat in our eyes and smoke-born tears half blinding us. Our throats are parched from fumes and dust, yet ever we push on. No stopping now that at last we have Fritz on the run. We'll keep him at it, playing the tune and Fritz doing the dancing.

Behind galloping horses, an Australian 18-pounder battery races through us. Ahead of the racing guns, an artillery officer slides to a propping standstill and his hand goes up as he bellows, 'Halt!'

The gun-carriage horses are pulled hard back on steaming haunches, breeching-straps sinking deep into the sweat-lathered hind legs of the gallant animals.

'Action Front!' roars the officer. The guns are swung round, horses unharnessed and galloped back, and *Bang! Bang! Bang!* Six guns are pouring shells somewhere ahead. The artillery officer turns to us and in a laughing roar asks, 'Who's in the front line now, you infantry jokers?' And we pass through the guns and are gone on.

Over on our right we see a long troop carrier tank with twenty men walking behind it. The men were supposed to be carried by the tank, but they are walking behind it as they probably found it too fume-filled and stifling inside.

Our other companies are out ahead and we are to 'mop-up' the dugouts, gun positions and woods. We're having a great time racing about collecting frightened prisoners and heaving our bombs down dugouts.

We reach a disabled tank and lift a dead man out of it. Its officer tells us, 'An enemy gun firing over open sights from near the Amiens Road got me. I'll give him open sights too.' And he races off and climbs aboard another of our tanks which crawls away to the right to deal with the enemy field gun.

Now a big crowd of Fritz are running back to us. There must be a hundred of them captured by our advancing companies. Three of our men are detailed to take them back, and do so growling hard at being picked on for the job.

Into a little thick green wood and we're in an enemy camp. Transport carts and wagons are here in dozens. Dead Fritz everywhere and about thirty wounded are lying under a big shady tree. Fritz with little red crosses on their arms are bandaging the wounded. An immaculately clad Fritz officer, who we reckon is a doctor, stands in front holding up a white handkerchief. Two more of our men are left to guard these wounded Fritz and we root and forage about the huts looking for more, but find none. We come across a canteen and load ourselves up with all manner of tinned food, though we don't know what it is. An officer lumping a bag of cigar boxes, laughs at us. 'If you chaps were given an extra pound of gear to carry you'd think you were killed, yet you've loaded yourselves up with a hundredweight of stuff and you'll be lucky if you can eat half of it.'

That doesn't stop us from taking all we can get, though, and we move on out of the wood, heavily laden but happy. She's a decent war at last.

'Here's water!' And we are mobbing around some big wooden water tanks, drinking all we can get. Men fill their steel helmets and pour the water over their red-hot heads and sluice the wonderful cold water over hot, smoke-grim faces.

'Come here, Sir!' a man calls, and I follow an officer up to a little sentry box and we look in. A Fritz officer is in it, dead; hanged by a white cord around his neck. The sight is horrible, especially the bulging eyes and the swollen, protruding tongue.

We are out in the open again and almost level with our advance company when a runner comes rushing up to the O.C. and shouts, 'Enemy guns in the gully there,' pointing, and is running ahead again to rejoin his own company.

'This way.' And the O.C. leads off for the gully. Just a hundred and fifty yards ahead we see a dozen Fritz bustling around a field gun that has four horses harnessed to it. The gun is moving! They'll get away with it if we're not quick!

'Fire at them!' Our men pause and fire. A couple of Fritz gunners fall, but one man is riding one of the leading horses and getting the four horses of the team into a gallop up the side of the gully. Snow and Longun fire, and rider goes down amongst his now galloping horses, but the terror-stricken animals keep galloping on as they climb the gully dragging the gun after them.

'Shoot the horses! Quick!' And Longun and I drop on a knee to fire. *Crack!* And Longun's rifle rings out and dust kicks up ten feet ahead of the horses. I fire at the shoulder of the nearest leader, he stumbles to his knees, half rises and is down upon his side kicking viciously. The other three are rearing and plunging about as they become tangled up with the fallen horse.

'Shake it up! Shoot the other leader! They're going to bolt!' And again Longun fires and again he misses. Before anyone else can fire there comes a joyous shout, 'They're stopping, Sir!' And the team has stopped all tangled up now.

The O.C. shouts to Longun and Snow, 'Unhitch those horses, and tie 'em up somewhere.' And as Longun passes me he hisses, 'You flamin' mongrel, Nulla, you shot that horse!' And now I know why his two shots at less than a hundred and fifty yards went so wide of their mark.

Not a minute ago he and Snow riddled the man riding the horse and half an hour before that he had bayoneted one of those machine-gunners back there, yet he deliberately fired wide and risked them bolting with a gun rather than shoot a horse.

'Come on, they're getting into the dugouts!' And we rush into the gully where eight or ten gunners disappeared down some dugouts. A few of us pause at the first dugout and yell down it, and calls of '*Kamerad!*' float up from its black depths. Again we yell and three Fritz come up holding their hands high. We call down again but there's no answer so two Mills grenades are thrown down. *Whung! Whung!* and the muffled bursts come up. Our sergeant goes down with an electric torch to make sure the dugout is empty so we wait till he comes up.

A commotion at the next dugout. A shot and another rings out, a scream and we look and see a Fritz doubled over the bayonet that one of our men has through him. The bayonet snaps back and the Fritz sags to the ground to die beside another enemy gunner someone has just shot.

'Came up fighting, the cows,' we're told as we race up to where the two enemy men lie, dying in agony. A man of our platoon is being held up by two men and we see that a bullet has drilled his two cheeks.

'Come up and surrender! Hands up! *Kamerad! Compre?*' is yelled down the dugout and three more come up to surrender. The sergeant and his torch go down again. We hear him shouting in the dugout and another Fritz comes rushing up the steps with the sergeant booting him along. He is a gibbering, raving lunatic.

'*Kill der Kaiser! Kill der officer!*' he keeps on shouting in his terror.

'Here, put this between your teeth and shut up.' And a man gives him a big cigar, but the fear-mad poor beggar commences to eat the cigar. Then he spits and splutters and we laugh at him as he is grabbed by another Fritz and pulled across to where a man is guarding the other prisoners.

Longun and Snow are back leading three fine horses, which they tie up to a couple of trees in the gully. Longun comes up to me. 'I'm bloomin' glad you shot that horse or they'd have got away with the gun. It's no use, I couldn't have done it, but of course I know that someone had to stop them.'

As an after thought he adds, 'And I wasn't flamin' well straight enough to do it,' and goes off grinning.

The gully has been left behind us. In all we've rounded up nearly three hundred prisoners and are steadily moving on. Out in the front, our other companies and the six tanks are moving ever ahead, leaving us to round up and collect prisoners and war material.

Our guns are still being galloped up, the horses unhitched, the guns fired. Still the great advance moves ever onwards. Still the guns, transport and field cookers follow the advancing men. Still the perfect organisation of our machine-like advance is unhurried and unruffled. Confident of success, each unit is doing its allotted job in the great stunt.

Now we are on the rim of a great gully full of fog, smoke and dust. Enemy shells are bursting in dozens in the misty gully below as our O.C. leads straight down into the inferno and up the far side. With nerves tensed, we're walking straight down into the shellfire; fuel for the furnace.

I see Clem's startled face turned to me, and hear his, 'Nulla, I've got the breeze up.'

'So've I, Clem; So has everyone,' I call back to him, and the first shell has burst very close to us, but the men do not pause. Now we're in the gully, ducking and flinching along its great rocky depths as the enemy shells screech, flash and explode with shuddering roars all around us.

Bang! A roaring, flashing detonation and a shell bursts two yards ahead. The sergeant is down, yelling in pain as he clutches at a great open gash in his leg. Someone yells and stretcher-bearers are racing across from the next platoon to attend to him, whilst shells keep up a nerve-racking roar from end to end of the gully.

'How's she, Serg?' I pause beside him, but he just rolls over in terrible agony and his voice comes faint and far through the din as he says, 'Go on, keep going. Lead on. General direction straight ahead.' And the bearers are with him as I set out to lead our little crowd up the gully side to escape the devil's inferno.

Now we're out of the gully and rounding up more prisoners. Just ahead of them is a small wood into which our artillery is pouring a devastating barrage. Two tanks are crawling about, rattling their guns as Fritz has been putting up a stand here.

'Look at that Fritz.' And a scraggy Fritz rises from the ground twenty yards outside of the little wood and rushes straight into that awful barrage, jumping and dancing as he goes.

'Fox-trotting to his own funeral.' Darky laughs as the Fritz reaches the edge of the wood and disappears into its flashing, smoking depths.

'They're running out!' And eight or nine Fritz leave the far side of the wood and make a dash to get away from us. A Lewis gunner drops his gun across the shoulder of a mate, rips and rattles the Lewis into action and the little group of running men are writhing in the dust.

'More of 'em coming out!' And nearly fifty terror-stricken poor wretches run out of the wood with hands held up to the men of our first wave who pass through them, and we are up to them, collecting them and sending a couple of men to march them back. An aeroplane flies over, sees the surrender and drops flares which glow red in the smoky morning sky, and our shells no longer rain upon the wood.

The first wave is moving on and we are now in the wood mopping it up. Through a cloud of acrid, throat-scorching shell fumes, we move about searching for hidden enemy. The place is littered with Fritz dead. Trees, men and war material are smashed into torn and twisted fragments. We root out forty terror-stricken wretches. They're pitiful to see. With twitching hands and bulging, blood-shot eyes, they continually fidget and flinch, unable to remain still. Fear-haunted men, they remind us of penned cattle that ever mill under the smell of blood.

On we go towards where a machine-gun had been holding up the advance until one of our tanks waddled around it and spoke its hot leaden message of blood and death. A badly wounded Fritz is lying on a stretcher. Tied to his tunic is a leaf of a field notebook upon which is written: 'This is a brave man. Respect his decorations.'

We see the wounded Fritz is still wearing several decorations and hear that his legs are almost severed by machine-gun bullets. The men with him say he worked his gun right until one of our Lewis guns got a burst into him and that he wouldn't surrender whilst ever he was conscious enough to fire his own gun.

We are again moving on. Fritz continues to fire at us, but our luck is holding and very few are being hit.

Swish, swish, shish, and enemy bullets flip amongst us. A man is down. He staggers to his feet, runs round and round in a circle moaning, 'Oh, my head! My head!'

The two companies in front are stringing out. Spades are out and the men are digging in, so we know we've reached our objective, the Red Line.

We look at the time. Just twenty minutes past ten. We have been two hours and twenty minutes on our 4500-yard advance from the 3rd Division's Green Line position. A wonderful advance.

Our trench is taking shape under the hundreds of spades flashing in the morning sun, the men working in a lather of perspiration. What we have we mean to hold, so we dig on, almost too weary to lift the spades.

Men are coming through from behind. We know these are the crow-eaters, the 46th Battalion men, who are to 'leap-frog' us here on the Red Line and advance another thousand yards to the Blue Line.

The 48th men have gone on away ahead. Out on the left we see a great wave of movement – the cavalry galloping through to clean up the enemy flying before our big advance. Then word is in that the Blue Line has been taken and that the 46th are digging in there.

Now we hear that our battalion has captured four hundred prisoners, thousands of pounds worth of war material, three big howitzer guns, fifteen smaller howitzers, seven whizz-bang guns, some trench mortars and about twenty machine-guns. The officers reckon we've put up a record, as although our haul is so great our casualties are less than fifty.

Night, and we have relieved the 48th in their Blue Line position in front of Proyart. Our line runs to the Warfusée–Aubercourt Road. The battalion cooks have broken records, and dixies of red-hot stew have been sent around the line. We did great justice to that stew, for we've had a very solid day of hot, heavy toil.

Daylight has dawned. The night has been very still and quiet, but we have been getting stirred up this morning by some Fritz aeroplanes. Our own planes have been busy, too, and some decent air-scraps have been staged up in the blue. Yesterday and today our planes have been busy dropping ammunition and other stuff behind our front line. It's a great idea and saves men being detailed to go and carry it up.

Today is 9th August and we are still on the Blue Line we took over from the 48th yesterday afternoon when we moved forward. Our patrols have been half a mile out in front today to find Fritz has gone well back.

Night has come and we are moving forward to advance our line across strange ground into unknown country. Nothing happens and we are in our new position and in line with the battalions on either flank. Through the night we dig and the morning of 10th August is upon us as we steadily work on all day consolidating our new line.

Night again and the hour of our relief is almost here when a Fritz gas bombardment starts. We have our gear ready to move out and are sitting around in our gas respirators, breathing through the rubber valve. Half suffocated, we sit in the darkness, our noses nearly squeezed off by the nose clips of the respirators, thinking the things we'd like to say about this gas if we only dared remove these stifling respirators.

Movement. Men coming up through the gas shells from behind; the 33rd Battalion men who are to relieve us. They're in the trench and we're climbing out in the midst of a hail of gas shells. Heads in gas respirators, we silently move through the bombardment as the gas shells *phut, phut, phut* into the ground. Their little quick flashes dot the darkness of the night like so many dancing fire-flies. Little clouds of smoke that we know are gas drift along amongst us. On we go hoping that we won't stop a gas shell for men in breath- and smoke-fogged goggles can't see far through the blackness of the horrible night.

We have come some way and are being halted. An officer has his respirator off – we see him, reef ours off and joyfully fill our lungs with real air again. We get counted and checked off. We are all here and have successfully come through the gas shells. On through the night we move. Here and there we pass dead Fritz and an odd unburied khaki form. The hot night air is blowing off dead men, so we aren't losing any time in getting back.

After a couple of miles we're now on some road. Word is passed that we may smoke, so we light up. Those of us who have cigarettes in tins are set, but the blokes who carried theirs in the packets reckon they can smell gas in them, so we share out our untainted ones.

We have done a good march and at last reach our destination, Sailly-Laurette. We crawl off into sheds, rooms and fowlhouses to sleep what's left of the night. Very quietly we get rid of our gear, have a meal that's waiting for us and get to sleep. We're too tired and worn out for skylarking or the usual arguments.

The men have had a strenuous few days under boiling heat. The night marches to our two assembly positions, then the 3000 yards to the Green Line followed by our attack across 5000 yards of enemy territory during the big attack of the 6th. That afternoon we dug in and that night did another move of nearly a mile to take over the Blue Line from the 48th. On the night of the 8th and the 9th we again worked trench digging. Another advance on the night of the 9th and all that night and all today digging, forever digging. But that is over now. Just another stunt carried out, another tour of the line over, so now to sleep away what few hours are left of the night.

A little tired talking, a little twisting and wriggling as tired men settle down, a little rubbing and scratching and all is quiet. An Australian battalion just back from a wonderful victory has casually taken to its well-earned rest in billets that a chain gang would despise!

Never mind, the little red fowl lice of old Sailly-Laurette will surely feast well tonight, so into it, you little crawlers, into it, whilst your luck's in!

And here's to sleep, sleep, sleep!

SEVENTEEN

Following Fritz

It's the evening of 13th August and we are to go back into the front line tonight after only two days' rest. It's pretty rough, but at least we won't get flabby and fat from easy living.

We've had two nice quiet days at Sailly-Laurette, swimming in the Somme and lolling about as if we owned the war, and two nights of being constantly wakened by lice working up from below and enemy aerial bombs from above.

It's very dark now and we are moving on for the line in platoons. We've had a rough trot, too, as Fritz planes are dropping bombs on these roads all day and night for two days. The heavy droning song of the engines of bombers is constantly floating to and fro through the black void above.

Now and again a great black moving mass takes shape out of the darkness and we pause and stand still, hoping our luck will hold, for there, just above us, a great black Angel of Death zips and zooms. The plane glides on. There comes a mighty *swosh, swishing* of air, a vivid flash shoots up from the ground ahead and the night is shattered by an awful roar as the great bomb explodes. To right and left, in front and behind, we catch the sound of bombs bursting.

Nearing the forward area we halt to wait for a guide to take us into the line. On through the night he leads and we plod after him, passing old trenches all overgrown by grass, blood-fed no doubt. In our trench somewhere in a reserve line, we begin to get settled down, but know little about it and care less. Slowly the night has drifted by and now it is day and we are having a look about. The O.C. is here warning us that we are to attack the enemy either tonight or in the morning.

'Ah, is that the joke? Two hop-overs in a week.'

'Yes, I'm afraid so. This will be a far tougher proposition than it was on the 8th, for the enemy's resistance is strengthening as he is now very close to the Hindenburg Line.'

The day draws to a close and still we are very hazy as to when and where we are to attack. All we know is that we are in some old trenches to the south-east of Harbonnières.

Fritz is shelling us with some heavy stuff and the odd call goes up for stretcher-bearers as men get hit. We crouch low on the duckboarded floor of these old 1916 trenches with wooden walls, and feel the vibrations of the shell bursts travel along them. In front and behind we hear the shells go *swoosh, bang!* into the soft ground as silent and tensed we cower down, helpless, under the roaring rain of flashing shells. A shell is into the trench very close to us. There comes an awful roar, the night leaps into flame for a second and all is black again.

'Anyone hurt?' is called.

No answer, but the rattling of the duckboards of the trench as a wave of vibration shivers their ancient timbers. Snow slips along to investigate and is back.

'No one about, but she left a hole big enough to bury a mule in.'

Whish, Bang! Another shell lands only a few feet away, just around the next bend of the trench. *Clatter, clat, clat* on the duckboards and a badly scared officer rushes round the bend. He fails to see Longun crouching on the floor of the trench and comes an awful cropper, head over heels, over Longun. A rattle of equipment on the duckboards, the thud of two falling bodies, two grunts, half a dozen fierce oaths and old Longun and the officer are sorting themselves out and getting up.

'Strike me flamin' fat! What's your bloomin' joke?' Longun seems somewhat upset.

'Joke be hanged! What the blazes do you mean squatting there on your haunches, fair in a man's road!' The officer is grieved as he gingerly rubs a tender split lip that has kissed an extra hard duckboard.

The shells come and deep in the soft earth they burst. On the hard duckboards they crash in shuddering, snapping roars. Suddenly another awful maddening explosion is almost onto us. A six-foot length of duckboard sails clean out of the trench to land with a soft little thud amongst the daisy-covered mounds behind the trench.

'Hey, Fritz, send that back when you've done with it,' someone laughs who would have been stilled forever had that shell been six-feet closer. We blow and spit the shell fumes out and wait on.

A dozen more shells thud and roar around us and then the shelling is over. The wounded have been carried back. Five poor smashed wretches have been gathered up and carried away for burial. So long, boys!

Daylight has dawned and word is through that the proposed attack has been cancelled. We take our disappointments very well as the O.C. warns us that we move forward to the front line near Lihons after dark tonight. We gather our gear and march out, picking up the guides from the front line. We move forward in absolute silence and in small parties as Fritz is only fifty yards from our front line. Being in an old French trench system, trenches lead everywhere, mostly into the Fritz lines.

'Easier to get lost than not. Men are continually taking the wrong trench and wandering slap up against enemy posts. You'll have to be very careful in effecting the relief,' he concludes.

We stealthily creep forward through the night behind a 3rd Battalion guide who is leading us in. We sincerely hope he knows his way. All is very still ahead. The guide pauses and looks about him.

'Getting ready to get lost,' someone whispers and the guide turns and tells us that it's about three hundred yards to the line. On he leads us. There are old, dilapidated and broken trenches everywhere with flowers, grass and shrubs growing over them. Into two-year-old shell holes we slip, over grass-covered grave mounds we stumble, until some steel helmets show beneath us and we are at our front line at last. The 3rd Battalion men tell us all they know and fade away into the night. We have taken over another front line to have and to hold.

All night long we wait, for we don't know where Fritz is or where we are for that matter. We're told that Fritz is fifty yards away, that a dozen saps lead for his line into ours and that he was continually bombing along them. Somehow we don't feel very sleepy tonight. We'd far sooner be awake to welcome Fritz if he happens to call, so we decide to postpone our sleep until such time as we know where we are.

Daylight is here; the morning of 16th August, 1918, and all's quiet with no enemy shelling as the lines are too close for the artillery to do much strafing. Now and then an odd sniper lets go or an occasional *minenwerfer* comes *whoofing* and roaring about.

Darky and I get sent back along an old trench to find coils of phone wire at a dump back over the hill somewhere. We move along the trench half doubled over to dodge Fritz snipers. We're interested in these old trench systems dug and held by the French over two years ago, so have a good look about as we go along.

We find several old enemy helmets, now rusted and broken. They are Prussian Guard helmets – we know by the big metal double-eagle design on the front of them that is no longer worn in the front line. Our chaps haven't seen them since Pozières and Mouquet Farm, though we've bumped the Prussian Guard a few times since.

We're now down behind a little hill and into a valley where we can walk upright again. We poke along the valley, having a look at the old battleground. Graves everywhere. British graves carrying neat little wooden crosses giving particulars of the men laid to rest; dozens and dozens of French graves marked '*Mort pour la patrie*' and carrying little tin rosettes painted in the tricolour of France; many Fritz graves bearing the sad inscription '*Hier ruht in Gott*' and particulars as to name and regiment. Once enemy soldiers, they now lie in a common sleeping ground with the men they fought and killed.

Here is the grave of a British soldier with the inscription in Fritz '*Ein unbekannter Engländer*'. A fallen Tommy over whose rough grave a neat cross has been erected by foreign hands, the hands that killed him. Tommy and Fritz; friends in death though enemies in life. Where's the logic in it? Civilisation upside down!

Darky and I move on out of the valley of death. It's just another 'corner of a foreign field that is forever England', and France and Fritz too. What of the superior intelligence of the human creature? Egotism pure and simple. More myth than enduring achievement.

We have found the wire, delivered it to the signallers and are back in our trench having a go to bomb Fritz with rifle grenades. Another night has gone by and it's daylight again, 17th August. Snow is on watch and the rest of us are sleeping when, suddenly, 'Stand to!' is roared out and we are on our feet and diving for our rifles and what bombs we have. Up along the trench, dozens of bombs are exploding in a continuous crackle. An odd machine-gun burst rips out. Rifles fire into the din. Flying above the rim of a distant sap we can see Fritz stick-bombs, twisting and twirling through the air. Little black dots are flying from our trench; Mills grenades being thrown at Fritz now attacking our posts.

The commotion dies down. The attack has been beaten off, but we're stirred up and ready for surely they'll come again. The day drags on. Twice more Fritz sends bombing parties against our posts and twice more we send them rushing back, leaving their dead behind. Ours is a tough crowd to hunt, as Fritz is finding to his sorrow.

Early evening brings more enemy attacks and more defeats for him. We hear that one of our officers and three men rushed an enemy outpost, but were all wounded. Their mates then bombed the Fritz outpost, scattered it and got our wounded safely in.

After four days we're to be relieved tonight and glad to get out of it again.

'Young Nulla about here, men?' And the O.C. is with us. I wander up and get told to make back to battalion H.Q. at Harbonnières and guide in the relief for D Company. The O.C. tells me, 'It's the 48th that's to take over here tonight. Pick up the D Company relief and wait near the dump in the gully for the guides from the line posts.'

I pack up my gear, place it where it will be handy for me to get tonight and make back along an old grassy trench until I reach the little gully where Dark and I collected the phone wire. Then I steer off in the direction of Harbonnières, having a good look about so I'll know my way back after dark. I don't want to get lost when I have two hundred 48th blokes to guide in. On I go, passing some support trenches and a few of our trench-mortar fellows with their guns hidden in old trenches and shell holes.

I bump some guns of the artillery and notice that the gun crews are standing in their action positions ready to fire with great heaps of uncovered shells. Suddenly our guns are belching out a tremendous roar. Little 18-pounders are snapping and yapping like a team of stirred-up Poms, whilst from away in the distance comes the throaty, deep-chested barking as our heavy guns join in.

An artillery officer comes over and enquires if I'm from the forward areas and asks what sort of a time we're having up there. I tell him and ask about the barrage and learn it is supporting the Canadian Corps now about to attack out on the right of the Australian position. I've heard all I want and hurry away before the enemy guns get busy pelting shells about here amongst these batteries, as they surely will when they realise that an attack is being launched against their infantry lines.

On I go. Suddenly all our guns go mad and Fritz shells begin bursting a couple of hundred yards behind me. I hurry along and soon double the distance between me and the Fritz shells, though a few big ones still burst at odd points around. For half an hour the barrage crashes and shudders in an unending roar and then dies down as I reach my destination. I report as their guide and the 48th colonel closely questions me as to conditions.

A phone rings. A signaller approaches the colonel.

'A priority call for you, Sir.' And the colonel goes to the phone. A few minutes go by. The 48th adjutant and officers are getting the men up on their feet and warning them to be ready to move forward at once if needed. A captain is speaking to his N.C.O.s and men. 'The 45th in the front line is being very heavily shelled. Looks as if an enemy attack is to be launched. We're to be ready to move in to reinforce that battalion at a moment's notice.'

He asks me about all the reserve and support trenches and the approaches to the line. I tell him that I thought Fritz couldn't shell the front line as our posts are only fifty yards from his trenches.

'Well if you were back in the line now you'd know whether he could shell it or not. Your crowd is getting it good and solid, lad. Fritz has probably withdrawn his front-line garrison before his guns opened.'

I wait around with the 48th men. Away up in front we hear the drumming of shells ripping and tearing into the front line where I have just left my mates. I wonder how they are faring under the shelling and hope for the best. Half an hour more goes by before the shelling ceases and all is normal again on the 45th Battalion's front.

It is well after dark and I am guiding the 48th men up to our lines. We are at the gully and the guides from our posts are here picking up the reliefs for the various posts, though the relief isn't to be effected for another hour.

A 48th major comes up to me. 'I'd like to have a look over the line before the battalion goes in. A few of us will go up with you now if you're ready.' And half a dozen officers and N.C.O.s are ready to make the trip up. On through the pitch-black night we go along old unoccupied trenches that twist through the tortured land and show where the recent bombardment has been pounding.

Whizz! Bang! Crash! Crash! as shells burst and flash all around our little party. Smoke floats along the trench. Dust and clods of earth clatter down everywhere. The darkness is stabbed on every hand by vivid lightning-like flashes that leap from the ground with mighty, shuddering roars. Under foot we feel the ground rumble and vibrate. Over our ducking heads, shell fragments whizz and hum through the air as along the trench we hurry, fearful lest a shell get amongst us at any step. Fingers of death are clutching through the night.

The barrage is coming down thicker and thicker. Four wounded men come reeling along like rudderless ships, as they hurry on seeking safety for their bleeding, broken bodies. A sergeant leaves our party to guide them back to the 48th medical officer.

On we go for another twenty yards amidst the shuddering, jolting, *crash, crash, crashing* of the barrage; through the mad, dancing bonfires of the flame-shot night, through flame and fear. Surely we can't last much longer! Surely our issue must come at any moment now! We are stumbling along a deep grass-green trench when my foot treads on something soft and springy in the trench floor. I stumble as if walking on a half-inflated football, peer down and see I have trodden on a man's stomach. The 48th officers are up to me. A torch flashes and its fleeting beam shows a headless and legless Australian body lying amongst the lank grass underfoot.

A few steps more and an officer gives a breathless sigh as he sidesteps something else in the grass, something round, something gruesome even to a war-hardened officer – the mangled head of the man whose body lies a few yards back. Still on we go with shells crashing and thudding all around us. Over six or seven dead trench-mortar men we step. On, walking on torn, bleeding, shattered humanity. On, not knowing what's to happen next.

Shoo! Zonk! Crash! The trench wall is tottering, and smoke and fumes are smothering our party. A cloud of dust leaps upwards from almost underfoot. The trench is rocking and swelling. The roar of the explosion has almost stunned us. I feel I am floating away, chasing the roof of my head as it soars up into the blackness above the trench. My leg is paining terribly. I grab at the pain. My pants are split just behind the knee. My hand gropes to locate the wound. My fingers encounter something hard, a red-hot something, a great hot shell fragment that has ripped through the stout cloth and is burning my knee. I tear it out and suck burnt fingers and then find that the leg wound is only skin deep but a bad burn.

'Lend a hand here!' someone calls and we run back to the rear of the little party. A sergeant, white-faced and wild-eyed is excitedly gasping out in queer whistling breath as he sways in an officer's arms. We see that he is coughing up great clots of congealed blood as he tries to speak. We lower him down, but his head is falling limply from side to side and we know he is dead.

'How much further to your trench?' comes the major's anxious question. He's as unstrung and nervous as the rest of us.

'About fifty yards,' I answer, and with the little party behind me I make a mad rush onwards. We are into the front line and out of the fiercest of the shelling which we now see is chiefly on the saps behind the line. I guide the party along to where my O.C. has his headquarters in an old boarded-up dugout. We all crowd in and sit here silent, listening to the thudding of the shells. At every close shell burst the candle splutters and is out and the O.C. is kept busy lighting it again.

The shelling has stopped and the 48th major and his officers are informed as to the position here. For half an hour we sit in the dugout and then the O.C. takes the 48th officers away on an inspection of the line. Time drifts on: the officers are back. More 48th officers are here now and a party of signallers are taking over the phone in the dugout.

I am sent on a message and see that most of our posts have been relieved. I gather my gear from our old post noting that my mates have been relieved and have gone out. Now back at the big dugout, our O.C. tells me that he is remaining in the line until daylight to point out the enemy dispositions and outposts to the 48th, and says he'd like me to remain with him.

Dawn, and the O.C. and I make back from the line. We're now out in the open taking a short cut back to the reserve lines near Harbonnières to rejoin the battalion. Behind us all is quiet. Gone are the crashing shells that heralded the dawn, gone is the morning strafe, but best of all is the fact that the long dark night is gone. Gone with its panics and pains, its death and darkness, its nerve-racking 'mad-minute' bombardments. Gone is another tour of the line. Four days and nights of unrelaxed vigil in a line only fifty yards from the enemy and we are making back to rest, wash and refresh our weary old frames.

We are walking on across the ground fought over on the 8th, just twelve days ago. What tales of daring were done here only a dozen days ago! But now gone are the men who fought and won through, but the men who fought and fell are here still. In khaki and in grey they rest upon the open field, waiting for the spade of the burying parties to turn the end upon their poor, broken bodies.

Still on across the old battle ground we make our way, while in the far distance behind us, we hear our shells bursting on enemy positions, and away in the distant sky can be seen the pink-tinged brickdust rising as a shroud over villages now being shelled into rubble and rubbish.

Now we're crossing some old enemy trenches as fast as we can, for dead men are on every side. Poor fallen wretches rotting under the fierce August sun. They are sickening to behold. They cannot be escaped whilst ever a man is in possession of his sense of sight and smell. On every side are up-turned faces greeny-black in putrefaction and great, swollen, distorted bodies. Sightless, dull, dust-filled eyes. If they would only close! But no, they remain open – and move! Open, gaping mouths are surely moving too! We're sick in every fibre as we hurry on past open eyes and open mouths. Past eaten-out eye-sockets and mouths that are a seething mass of feasting grubs. We're in the land of rotting men in the year of Our Lord, 1918.

Suddenly we pause as we see an enemy barrage burst all around a battery of guns. Ten, a dozen shells fall. Men are racing about amidst the guns. The shelling stops. Another 'mad-minute' barrage, but it has caught a Tommy battery fair and square. We walk over to see if anything can be done, but we can do nothing. The gunners are gathering up their dead and wounded. Half a dozen have been killed. Looking on these freshly killed faces we read fear, repose, shock, pain.

We hop-in and help the gunners reef the planks away from a blown-in dugout. A young Tommy officer, a pink-faced lad of nineteen, comes rushing up out of the dugout and 'Bang! went sixpence of my four and nine,' he laughs, half hysterically, as he brushes blood and brains from his tunic front. The battery major and two signallers have been killed in the dugout from which this unstrung lad has been rescued.

The blown-up battery is far behind and we are back in the reserve lines not very far from Harbonnières. I mooch around, find my mates and crawl into their little possie. We talk as I clean up a mess tin of cold stew that Longun has saved for my breakfast.

We settle down to sleep. From along the trench there comes singing:

When this bloomin' war is over
Oh! How happy I shall be,
When I get my civvy clothes on
No more soldiering for me.

'Shut up, you noisy goat, an' let a man get to sleep,' we hear the singer being advised as we drop off to sleep, well and truly worn out.

✕

We've been in these reserve trenches for five days now doing hard salvage work around the old enemy positions, broken by a wonderful hot bath and change of underclothing at the divisional baths at Harbonnières. All that is over and we are to be relieved tonight, so things aren't as bad as they could be. Today is 24th August and we've been in the very forward areas since the 4th, so we're all very glad to know that we move out tonight.

Night now, and we're ready to move out as soon as our relief turns up to take over these reserve lines. We sit around yarning and as usual our yarns turn to arguments and some skylarking goes on.

Nearly midnight now. The relief isn't here but a heavy Fritz gas barrage is. We sit in our gas respirators unable even to curse except in thought, half stifled, sucking the smelly rubber valve of the helmet. Sweat pours from our faces. We crave fresh air and are sorely tempted to get a breath of cooling breeze upon our perspiring faces. It's too risky so we sit listening to the *phut* of gas shells bursting for an hour as we sit under the drifting gas. A few men have somehow become casualties to the deadly fumes and have been carried out.

At last the long hour is over. Out of our respirators at last as French troops come to relieve us and we're marching back to get into buses for somewhere or other. On through the black night we trudge. A few odd shells are bursting about, which make us nervy for somehow it would be pretty stiff to stop an issue now just as we are almost out of it all. A long line of motor buses are waiting for us so we hand up our rifles, scramble over the tailboard and in a cloud of dust they crawl away into the night.

Across a few small roads and we are on the Amiens to St Quentin road and on through old Villers-Bretonneux. The buses leave the main road and we jolt along rough side roads until we reach Vaux-en-Amiénois where we climb out and, following the billeting officer, reach our allotted billets and drop to sleep. Back out of the line at last until the next time.

We've had a week at Vaux-en-Amiénois and are very comfortably quartered in good billets. Things are quiet and peaceful here. Old Farmer and Yacob are back with us after eighteen months in England, the lucky beggars.

Some fun here last night when Longun and Dark landed in with about four dozen bottles of splendid wine. They wouldn't say where they landed the supply from, but at about the tenth bottle they told us the secret in great confidence. It appears they spotted some Tommies carefully raking the earth back from what we thought was a man's grave and then saw them haul out a bottle, so they lay low until the Tommies had gone then sneaked up and opened the grave and found a great box of bottles. They took the wine but left the box for the Pommies and carefully placed in it a dead dog that a lorry had killed a day or two ago. Longun laughed and called it ingenuity. Won't those clever Tommy gunners storm when they find nothing but dead dog to drink? Ingenuity!

7th September and we are in some rough shelters in the remains of Biaches. We've stayed a couple of days in the village, which has been shelled clean off the map – absolutely obliterated – then move to Stable Wood near Cartigny, marching across miles of country from which Fritz has just been chased.

We are crossing a river by means of an old bridge our engineers have just re-erected – for as Fritz retreated they blew up all the bridges – then on across country that is all valleys and roads and big, timbered gullies. The hillsides are splotched with white patches where enemy trenches and gun emplacements have been dug recently. We pass enemy guns, wagons, carts, limbers and gear everywhere and notice how Fritz has salvaged all old iron. Wagons have been stripped of their iron rims, wire has been taken from fences, iron gates from cottage homes. Tons and tons of old iron are heaped up everywhere ready for despatch to the munitions factories of Fritzy. Ready for shell-making.

At last we are at Stable Wood and sink down, tired out, into little bits of shelters. It's nearly dark, but we find a game of two-up and collect a few francs when Snow does a decent run of heads. That's the way things generally break with us. As soon as we get well cashed-up from a win, we go straight into the line where we can't spend our winnings and then lose it all and more with it as soon as we reach a village where we can find use for a few extra francs.

A quiet night has gone. Morning again, and we are to march to Estrées this afternoon.

'Any of you men care for a walk up to Péronne and Mont St Quentin? We're going up to have a look around.' And Longun and I join in with a couple of officers and a few men and set off to see what can be seen up where the 14th Brigade did their stunt a few days ago.

About three miles we go and are on the old battleground in front of Péronne. The scene is the usual one of shell holes and dead men. We come to an opening in the enemy barbed wire and count fourteen dead in the narrow lane between the wires where enemy guns have been trained upon this gap. Heaps and heaps of equipment show that many others have been wounded.

Across a great open plain we move past still forms showing the black and green colour patches of our 53rd Battalion. That battalion's attack here was beaten off by Fritz machine-guns and we understand when we see the ground they were sent across; ground devoid of all cover, under direct frontal fire.

Crossing a little ditch of water we reach a great earthen mound in front of Péronne town where enemy machine-guns were fired. Hundreds of empty cartridge shells are scattered around each position. No wonder Fritz stopped our men. We move on and an Australian machine-gunner shows us where the 54th entered the town and took most of it. In little side streets we find barricades of bullet-riddled furniture behind which Fritz had taken his rear-guard stand before being pushed out.

On through crumbling walls and fallen houses and we are out in the open on our way for Mont St Quentin. For a couple of miles we push on across well fought over ground and reach Mont St Quentin, which is just a great hill, pock-marked by shell holes and capped by stunted trees now slashed and broken. Shot-torn walls of houses and shattered trees are everywhere.

'The 3rd Brigade took this place on the 31st August. Driven out by Fritz, they retired to Elsa Trench and next day, the 24th Battalion, under cover of a barrage, retook it for keeps,' an officer explains.

We explore about and just down under the ridge we find Elsa Trench, a great wide, open trench with pretty flower-decked rims, but many Australians of the red and white diamond colour patch are still lying hidden amongst the flowers and long grass. In front is an open plain, then an enemy trench and another open stretch leading to the high walls that surround the tree-covered dome of old Mont

St Quentin. We explore along Elsa Trench and find dead men of our 21st and 23rd Battalions as well as 24th Battalion men.

'Better make back now.' And we hit out across the open for our camp near Cartigny. Back in Stable Wood, the men are falling in and after a few hours' marching, camp in the open near Estrées. It's a miserable night lying in the open under steady soaking rain, wet and fed up with everything.

Morning here at last, and we spend the day lying low and being instructed about the coming attack that we are to make in a day or so.

Night finds us once more on the move. As we are getting very close to the line we move in through the darkness. Our guns are very aggressive of late and our batteries seem to have an abundance of shells. For six weeks now we've been at Fritz hammer and tongs, while British, French and Americans have been putting over attack after attack, winning success after success. We feel that surely we have them on the run now, though we are quite aware that the big thrust may end soon as we are almost back to his great Hindenburg Line, the last stronghold of the Fritz army in France.

The battalion is near Pœuilly where we settle down to sleep, for in a week's time, we are to attack the great Hindenburg Outpost Line. We've just taken over some dugouts in a great railway cutting in the support line near Vendelles, but that name means nothing to us.

Daylight finds us being instructed in what we have ahead, stretcher-bearers are making preparations, extra ammunition is being issued and two water bottles per man as well as a spade to lump along. Extra machine-gun magazines are being loaded, iron rations and field dressings being checked over, gas respirators inspected and tested. Then more instructions about how we're to carry out the stunt and finally we get a couple of hours to ourselves with letter writing, two-up, or a few games of poker, rummy or sevens.

The afternoon wears on. Fritz planes come often, flying very low, and we wonder if they smell a rat. Now and again one of our Lewis guns lets go at the enemy planes and we watch our tracer bullets flitting towards the plane, but it just flies away.

Our big howitzers are firing on and off. Above us we hear a great fifteen-inch shell shuffling across the sky like a train moving slowly across the floor of heaven – a funeral train for someone.

3.30 a.m. and a breakfast of hot stew. We move off in drizzling rain, one behind the other, to the assembly position for our hop-over. Overhead, the enemy planes. A big bank looms up out of the mist and we spread out under it and rest. We are on our assembly position and see the tape line extending along the bank.

'We have half an hour to wait for zero hour, men.' The O.C. comes along amongst us. 'Everyone clear as to instructions? Anyone want to know anything?'

'Yes, Sir. Could you sing us "Just before the Battle, Mother",' Longun requests, but only gets an amused grin out of the O.C.

The men are very quiet. With only half an hour to go there's much to think of besides skylarking. Down comes the rain again. As we huddle into our wet clothes a voice comes singing through the rain.

Somewhere the sun is shining,
Somewhere a little rain.
Somewhere a heart is pining . . .

And cutting across the rain-muffled voice of the singer there comes the jolting crash of three big enemy shells bursting just behind us. *Thud! Crash!* And from the trembling earth there leaps three great spouts of smoke-capped mud. Shell fragments strike around me. Nearby, a stretcher-bearer reels back against the muddy bank, fighting to remain on his feet, but slowly sinks down over a bleeding smashed thigh. Our first casualty of the hop-over.

'One in, who'll make it two?'

Again the shells crash near and in defiance of the shelling, a dozen men have joined voices with the singer and lustily we finish our song.

Somewhere a soul is drifting,
Further and further apart,
Somewhere my love lies dreaming,
Somewhere a broken heart.

Time drags slowly on. In various ways we pass through the suspense of waiting for zero hour. How'll he treat us out in the open? That's what none of us ask, but what we'd all like to know.

'Soon be moving now, boys.' Our platoon officer is with us.

'Are we to go through this Le Verguier joint, Fred?' Longun asks the officer. Gone is the parade ground 'Sir'. Men and officer are no longer separated by parade-ground discipline or the gulf of rank. That chasm has been bridged by the bond of mateship. Officers and men are united in a common test that will be carried through. Officers and men will fight and fall side by side in the mateship of men. The differences of rank, creed and calling have been swept aside by that splendid comradeship of men in battle.

'No, we don't go through Le Verguier, unless we get lost,' comes the officer's reply.

'Fall in, men,' our platoon officer's words come not as command, but more as a request. Orders and commands are unnecessary now. Directions and guidance are necessary certainly, but our men will do their job as men. Each man is going into the attack a thinking individual and not merely just a cog in a driven wheel.

We're fixing our heavy loads upon our backs, loading our rifles and getting ready to push off in a few minutes towards the enemy. It's just after five o'clock on the morning of 18th September. The rain is easing off as we await zero hour.

'All ready? Everything clear?' Our officer is getting nervy under the suspense of waiting. No doubt he fully appreciates the responsibility that is his this day.

'Yes, Sir.' The reply is friendly and respectful.

'Too right. We're set. Let her go!'

That's what we all wish now. 'Let her go!' Anything to break the suspense, though the men are outwardly as calm and casual as ever. The suspense of waiting to go over has always been a trial, camouflage it how you may. It's not that we so much fear what we'll meet, bad and all as it generally is. There's a something our being shrinks from. With some it's the fear that they may show the fear they'll so surely feel. Others inwardly shudder at the thought of experiencing the agonising pain of a maimed, mangled body. Others again realise the fact that they may very soon be face to face with their maker. Many more fear death as death. None of us relishes the very serious risk of going west. But whatever our thoughts, or fears or misgivings, we all are more or less anxious to get it over, for from bitter experience we know that thinking only makes things worse.

Eyes are glued to watches. Three minutes to go! Two minutes to go! Barely a minute! A tense silence, a tightening of jaws, or little fixing of equipment that have already been fixed a dozen times. Right on the tick of 5.20 a.m. comes the tremendous crash of a hundred batteries blazing into action in one awful all-shattering roar of explosion. Through the grey fog, the whole countryside is a dancing, flashing glow of jumping light. Hills and trees show up clearly against a flaming, quivering fire.

No order has been heard. Probably none has been given, but we are up over the bank, steadily moving forward in artillery formation. Behind us our guns are roaring in a fury of hate. Fog enshrouds us all and we can see but a few yards ahead.

Now we're in a gully, thick with mist and smoke. On we go walking blind. Ahead of us we can pick out the sounds of enemy shells disputing our progress. On and up to a tape line, which we know is the line from which the 48th jumped off when the barrage began. A few minutes' halt till the platoons are in line, for some have lost touch in the fog.

Again we're moving forward, half deafened by the unceasing roar of our barrage. Our officer keeps his eyes glued to his watch and advances slowly. We must go slowly for we are to keep 500 yards behind our 48th Battalion forming the first wave of the attack.

A few bullets are swishing around us. We know what it is. The bullets fired at the 48th are coming through to us.

'Don't wish those 48th coves any harm, but I wish to cripes they'd do something about stopping a few of these cussed bullets.' Darky laughs as he jerks his face back from some bullets that flit and whizz by uncomfortably close.

Now we are in a great broken gully of smoking mist. Platoons have split into sections and a corporal is leading ours while the men are calling and joking in laughing shouts. On we go, now climbing out of the gully. *Whizz! Bang! Bang! Bang!* And we jump as enemy shells burst around us. A couple land very close. Dust is peppered on us. Still we move on. *Whonk! Bang!* A big shell lands fair amongst us! Longun and Yacob fall on top of me as the explosion sends us flying. We're up, quiet and white-faced, but no one has been hit. We've all had a narrow escape.

On we advance under a heavy barrage. Everything is going wrong. We can't see any of our other sections. All we can see is smoke and fog and the burst of enemy shells landing all over the gully. Every few minutes we stop, as some new men bringing up the rear of our section keep getting behind. Two of them are throwing themselves down at every close shell burst and this keeps delaying us until they catch up. We haven't seen any of our other sections for some time, and advancing over a tangle of small gullies across unknown country, unable to see more than twenty yards through the fog, and with enemy shells falling everywhere but right on us, we're lucky if we're not lost.

'You, Nulla! Go to the rear and keep those men closed up! Blast 'em!' the little corporal yells, as again we have to wait for the rear files to catch up. Back I go, and we're once more advancing somewhere. At least we trust we are advancing, for in this fog and smoke we could be going anywhere.

Now we're making better progress. The new men are keeping closed up now and becoming used to the shell bursts. *Whizz! Bang!* And we jump, startled out of our senses as a small shell bursts in a flash right under our feet! I swallow dust and smoke, see flames shoot up from amongst the men and the man ahead of me sags down over the still-smoking shell hole. Two men run back to the fallen man. In a daze, I stoop and turn him over, but his whole side is blown away. He's dead. Killed before he's even seen a front line or an enemy soldier.

'Keep going! Shake it up!' I yell to the other two new men who are dazed and startled. We catch up to the rest of the section and nervously move along through enemy shells, expecting another to get amongst us at any moment.

Men loom up out of the fog ahead. They are coming our way. Running fast through the bursting shells, holding their hands above their heads. Fritz prisoners coming back. We know they have been captured by the 48th Battalion out ahead somewhere, so we're going in the right direction anyway. Fritz, about thirty of them, rush past with a 48th man hunting them along. He tells us we are almost to the first objective now and goes on to get himself and the prisoners back beyond the shelled area.

We see another group, make over and find our platoon commander and a dozen men here. They know no more about where they are than we do.

'Come on,' calls an officer, 'we're lagging behind the battalion.' And we double along to catch up. Wounded and dead men are on the ground; men of the 48th and many Fritz. The shelling is now much lighter. Another little gully is before us and we run through it and up its fog-shrouded side to catch up with our own battalion. A little shed is just in front and beyond it we can dimly see a few scattered farm buildings through the fog. The shed is only forty yards from us as through the lifting fog we race for it.

'Get down, you mad cows!' And without waiting, we all dive down beside a 48th Battalion man lying under a little bank from which is growing a thick hedge.

'Want to get your flamin' eyes open. Fritz in that farm not thirty yards away,' says the man.

Our officer questions him and we hear that his section rushed the shed and found it empty, but when they moved for the farm house, a dozen rifles opened on them and they were forced to retire into the shed. The man laughs. 'Six of our blokes are in the shed and a dozen or more Fritz are in the house. None of 'em's game to come out. Both sides got the wind up.'

'Looks like a double-barrelled siege.' Dark laughs.

Our officer is worried.

'Where's your battalion? Why haven't they mopped up this place?'

'Out in the flamin' fog somewhere. I slipped out of the shed to find a party to surround the house. The moppers-up should be somewhere about. Thought you were them.'

'Well, what are you doing here still?'

'Just waiting to see what crops up next.'

'Why didn't you make back and find your moppers-up?'

'Can't walk too well.'

'What, are you hit?'

'I'm okay, but got a blasted bullet through each leg, high up. Think me flamin' hips are broken. You coves go on, work round somehow. I'll sit here till things cool down a bit. Not going out through that to risk a nasty wound.' And he points to where the enemy shells are bursting in the gully we just crossed. *Not going to risk a nasty wound*, and he with both legs shot through. Hard as the hobs of hell some of these fellows.

'We'll give the house a rattle up. Get ready to give her five rounds rapid,' the officer directs. Rifles come up. Off go the safety catches.

'Crawl up to the hedge and get set.' And we wriggle up as close to the hedge as we can without exposing ourselves, for the fog is lifting rapidly.

'Ready? Fire!' And twenty rifles thrust through the hedge. *Crack, crack, crackety, crack, crack!* Doing rapid fire at the old white-washed building. Cordite fumes float over us and we're slipping another clip into our magazines.

A hundred bullets have ripped and torn through the building. A yell goes up from the shed and six 48th blokes charge the house. Screams mingle with the shouts of the charging men and six or eight Fritz rush out with hands up yelling for mercy. The 48th blokes are busy ratting them; pockets are ripped open and watches and all manner of souvenirs collected from the startled Fritz.

Our officer turns to the wounded man. 'I'll send help for you. We must push on.' And we are running past the mixed-up crowd of scared Fritz and laughing 48th men.

Now we are passing more prisoners making back. Droves of them. Men of the 48th are moving everywhere. On we go and find the rest of our company resting near a wood. Maps are consulted and the O.C. says it's Cambrieres Wood. For a little while we rest here and a wounded officer of the 48th comes back from ahead and says they took the first objective at six thirty, ten minutes ago.

Up and moving again. We've had a good spell and regained the wind knocked out of us by the long climb and the enemy barrage we've been through. We hear that many men have been hit in the advance so far. A long, sunken road is before us. We drop down under it and rest again. Word drifts along that we are just behind the line captured by the

48th and are to remain here till eight o'clock when we head off to our own objective, the Red Line. We've followed the 48th for 2000 yards and now we are soon to advance a further 3000 yards. All is quiet. Out ahead we hear our shells exploding on the enemy positions against which we are so soon to advance.

'Fall in.' We get into our positions.

'Come on.' And we are moving forward again. Men are ahead. We come up to them, the 48th Battalion busy digging in, consolidating their objective.

Now we are out in front. Ahead is a long dust cloud, shot with the flashing bursts of shells. Closer and closer we move to that line. Closer still, and we're almost up to our barrage. The barrage moves forward, us following. Odd enemy shells crash near, but our luck's in. On we move ever following our barrage. Its accuracy is marvellous. Hundreds of shells bursting in a long, straight line ahead. Hundreds of shells steadily creeping forward still in line. Our artillery's creeping barrage is perfect. Full of confidence we follow.

Enemy shells are falling thicker now. Every now and again a fleeting shower of machine-gun bullets is sprayed over our advancing line. Men are falling here and there. Stretcher-bearers are busy. White bandages are flashing in the brightening day as the bearers are busily engaged bandaging our wounded.

The O.C. is beckoning. I run over to him.

'I'm going along the line. Might have to send a message back. Better come with me.' And away we make along our advancing line. A line of faces we know so well. Gay, care-free faces, laughing faces, quiet faces, calm faces, excited faces, tired faces, fed-up faces, a few nervous apprehensive faces and hundreds of happy-go-lucky, don't give-a-hang faces.

On we go to our left till we reach the end of the line and see the 13th Battalion men extending away to our left. We turn and make back. Dozens of enemy are surrendering to our advancing wave. Poor, broken wretches who have been overrun by our creeping barrage.

Away to the right of our line we go and find the Royal Sussex Regiment carrying on the advance. We turn, race back and resume our old positions with our sections. Still the advance moves on. Still the shells creep forwards. Still we follow their dusty, smoking line.

Fritz are rising shivering from little holes in the ground, surrendering in fear. They seldom attempt to dispute our progress. We're collecting dozens of them. They don't show any fight. A dozen Fritz rise from in front of us in a bunch yelling '*Kamerad!*' We're up to them and busy ratting them for souvenirs. They have surrendered from a great round concrete machine-gun emplacement that they could have held for hours as they have two machine-guns here. We despise them. Too cowardly to fight and too frightened to run. Surrendered an almost impregnable position without firing a shot. The morale of the enemy seems down to zero.

On we go, capturing more and more Fritz; cringing, crawling, cowardly fellows, those we meet now. Poor broken-spirited beggars, they've had the pluck knocked out of them. Attacked here for weeks on end, trouble brewing in their own country, up against it in every way, no wonder they sling it in. Many of them are just kids; poor, frightened, skinny little codgers of fifteen to seventeen, a pathetic sight in their big, round, silver-rimmed spectacles. Clad in men's uniforms that flap all over their under-nourished young bodies, there's nothing of the man about them except the rifle they've flung away.

A great valley is below. We must cross its shrub-dotted depths. Enemy machine-guns are firing from the shrubs. Our barrage is sweeping across the valley, but many Fritz will be left unhurt as the line of bursting shells creeps up on the further side of the great valley. Towards the valley we rush. 'Look at the guns!' And our barrage has jumped twenty yards, and through the smoke ahead, we spot several enemy field guns. A dozen Fritz are rushing about while a big Fritz officer is waving at his men. They're running, and before we can fire they've dropped over a bank and are lost to sight, yet they'll have a job to get away for they're between us and the barrage.

On we race to capture the field guns. *Crack! Crack!* Rifles are firing in our faces. The corporal of our section bowls head over heels and is rolling and rolling in agony, clutching a shattered shoulder. We drop on one knee and fire at the rim of the bank behind which the Fritz disappeared, for we know the firing is coming from them.

Our rifles ring out at the rim of the bank. Enemy rifles crack in reply. From over on our right we see one of our other sections working in behind the mound, trying to get in towards the enemy.

Darky stands upright amidst the bullets, waves the attacking section forward and roars at us, 'Five rounds rapid!' And our rifles are pumping lead at the enemy position. Fritz is no longer replying, our rapid fire has put him under cover.

'Cease fire!' yells Dark. We stop and reload. A man of our section is on his back. A glance tells us he is dead. None of us saw him fall. A nasty shock.

The attacking section is right at the guns. Past the guns they race, jumping down the little bank! Yells and shouts come from behind it. We rush on and see the end of a fierce bayonet scrap. Our men have met a group of Fritz who have mixed it with them. Three of our chaps are on the ground, dead or wounded. Half a dozen enemy forms are down writhing in the grass. Two others turn and run. Several rifles snap out and the running men go down, toppling into shapeless heaps. A fresh yell as three more Fritz come rushing up from a dugout. Our men charge them. Again rifles bark. A Fritz fires, another of our men down. *Crack! Crack!* and two of the three Fritz fall, shot at ten-foot range. A terrible scream of mortal agony cuts through the crashing of the barrage and we see one of our fellows savagely bayonet the Fritz who has just shot one of our men. The bayonet flashes. Thrust, thrust, thrust! Three times driven through the poor screaming wretch before his body hits the ground.

'Give it to 'em! Stonker the stinkin' cows!' Our men, mad with blood lust, are yelling and looking for more to bayonet.

'They're killing men! Oh my God! They're killing men!' A new reinforcement man moans in horror at the killing he is powerless to stop.

'Of course they're killing 'em. Same as the flamin' Huns did to our coves over there. Expect 'em to be cuddlin' an' kissin' 'em?' Longun snaps in disgust at the man's moaning.

Soon the man will probably be as accustomed to this game as the rest of us. He isn't to be blamed, for it's just the reaction of a sensitive soul face to face with the awful reality of hand-to-hand fighting. Yet what did he expect to find when he joined an infantry battalion of the 4th Division, or any division for that matter? Just another of these coves who looks too deep, another chap to learn that the best philosophy is to see the surface only.

Our platoon officer comes rushing up. Two stretcher-bearers are here already. Our little corporal rolls over on to a stretcher, waves to us, and is carried away grinning through his pain.

The officer is shouting to our section, 'Lead on! Catch up to the barrage! Shake it up!' He realises that we've lost ground in taking these guns.

'You, Nulla, keep twenty paces ahead of the section until you're through the wood. Keep well ahead so that you'll see any machine-gun posts first. Mustn't let the section walk on to a hidden gun.' And away he tears to place himself ahead of the other section, whilst I rush out twenty yards ahead of our section and lead on.

The officer's words ring in my ears: 'Mustn't let the section walk on to a hidden gun.' He didn't say anything about not letting me walk on to a hidden gun.

Now we are running. Fritz is surrendering in droves. We leave them for our mopping-up parties to gather up, and rat and race on, and soon we're in line with the rest of the advance, following along after the barrage. Away beyond the barrage we catch glimpses of men running; Fritz bolting before our barrage reaches them. We are continually dropping on one knee and firing, or just standing and blazing away at those running men.

Enemy bullets are coming thicker now. A machine-gun fires at us and we fire back in its direction. Now the barrage has swept up to its position. Shells are bursting all about it. It'll be smashed to ribbons. The barrage lifts beyond the gun. A man drops, two more, another and the enemy gun has survived the shelling and is at us again! On we race to get round it . . . its savage *chut-chut-chut* putting the breeze fair up us. Madly we tear on, several more men dropping.

'There they go!' And four Fritz leave their gun and race to get back by attempting to run through our barrage. They don't reach it. We all fire at them and they drop, bullet-riddled. Brave men who deserved a better fate.

Into another wood we go. More enemy guns here. Twenty Fritz gunners surrender so there's no fight. A white flag is waving nearby.

We run over and see a Fritz officer, a doctor in his shirt sleeves, busily attending about forty wounded. We leave them and hurry along.

Another little wood over on our right. Six of our chaps run into it. Enemy shells land in it in a roar of flame, dust and smoke. The little stunted trees begin to leap skyward under the bursting shells. Four of our men come flying out, yelling hard, and pointing to the wood they've just left.

Two bearers run for the wood carrying a stretcher. Without a pause they charge straight into the jumping, flaring hell that but a few minutes ago was a peaceful little green wood. Fair into the awful shell bursts the two bearers run. Now they are moving through smoke, flying earth and screeching shell fragments. We watch two brave men going to their doom in an endeavour to rescue a couple of wounded men who are by now probably dead. A shell is right on to the bearers! The great explosion seems to leap from under their feet!

'He's got 'em!' And the two bearers are thrown yards by the shell burst.

'They're goners!'

No, they're on their feet, finding their stretcher. On into the wood they go. Straight on into the terrific shellfire. It's impossible for men to live in there. The bearers disappear deep into the shell-tossed wood and we give them up.

'Here they come!' Like two drunken men they stagger out of the smoke, reeling from side to side, but between them carrying their stretcher, a wounded man on it! We see the bearers place him on the ground some distance from the wood.

'They're goin' back in again!'

'Cripes, but that's guts if you like!' And sure enough the two bearers are going back into the wood, going back running! We see them enter that inferno of roaring, crashing flame, both flung down by the force of the explosion of a mighty shell, see them rise and stagger on a few yards only to be blown to the ground again.

Now they are lost to sight behind a wall of belching smoke, stabbing flame and shattering roar. We've forgotten the advance, forgotten the Fritz, forgotten all in our anxiety for two brave men. There comes an emotionally cracked call of, 'God! They're coming out!' And two blotches take shape in the smoke, and the dim figures of our two bearers stagger and lurch out of the smoke, grimly hanging on to their stretcher. They've got their man! Their second man! Clear of the danger they carry him and gently lower the stretcher. Bearers as gentle as they are brave. We've seen something to think about in the past few minutes.

Moving forward again. Still following the barrage, still making splendid headway, still capturing men, guns and territory.

We're halting on the downward slope of a great hill. Officers are sending strong patrols out in front and setting the rest of us digging in. We've reached our objective, advanced our 3000 yards since passing the 48th on their objective, and now we're digging in on the Red Line . . . 5000 yards from our last front line. Fritz is being hunted back in a tearing hurry and in a tearing hurry we are following him, following up every advantage and stirring the possum in him properly.

Hard at it digging in. Each man is going his hardest to dig a little hole just big enough to get into. We know that the smoke barrage now being put down out in front can't last long. Soon Fritz will realise that the advance has stopped. Then he'll come creeping back and we can expect fireworks. Already an enemy machine-gun is on to us.

Still hard at it we work, each man digging to save his life. More and more bullets coming over. Men being wounded, but the majority are down in their healthy dug holes now.

A couple of hours pass. We each have a hole dug four or five feet deep and stand in it and enlarge it. Tonight we shall link them up to form a trench. Working on we look about. Below is a great valley and rising on the further side is a big hill held by Fritz. We hear that the 46th is to take that hill sometime today.

On we work. Enemy bullets are now continually biting into the earth thrown up by our digging, but we are safe from bullets at least, whilst ever we remain in these deeply dug narrow holes.

'Is Nulla here?' And our company O.C. is walking along the line.

'Yes, Sir.' From the bottom of my own private funk hole.

He looks down on me and grins. 'Fritz will have his work cut out to get you there.' And I gladly realise that too. It would take a shell dropped straight down to get me. I'm quite set and happy, but the happiness does not last long for the O.C. says, 'Think you'd better shift up to the company H.Q., there's only one signaller left.'

I thoroughly blast H.Q. and the one signaller left and the other three or four who got themselves wounded, but gather up my gear and wander along to the company H.Q. joint where I find the telephone set up in a wide open trench. A dirty old Fritz waterproof sheet is stretched over it to give some protection against a shower, for that's about all it would stop.

The signaller here is very pleased to see me, far more pleased than I am to see him and his useless great phone possie. But no time for regrets for we have to get a wire run back to where battalion H.Q. now is. The sig has a coil of wire. We fasten one end of it to a bayonet stuck in the ground and, carrying the reel between us, set out to run the wire back to our battalion H.Q. somewhere below the ridge.

Up in the open now and running along, paying out as we go, going flat out, for an enemy machine-gun is having a go at us. Firing from the top of the distant hill, straight across the valley, its bullets aren't hitting within thirty yards of us, but that's about a hundred yards too close for our liking so we race along to get below the rise ahead.

A tremendous *swosh, swosh, swoshing* of rushing air overhead. The thudding *crash, crash, crashing* of shells bursting on the great hill beyond the valley and our barrage is on to the enemy positions! Hundreds of men are coming towards us . . . the 46th Battalion coming up to cross the Red Line we're holding and to capture their objective out ahead somewhere. A few shouts, jokes and calls and the 46th crowd has gone on to do their stunt.

For fifty yards we run the wire out when *Crash! Crash!* Down comes an enemy barrage all around us! The very ground is thudding and jumping. Great rising walls of smoke and dust clouds are leaping to engulf us. *Bang! Bang! Bang!* Shells and more shells are spitting flashing flame, fear and death everywhere about us. We feel the wire is no longer resisting and know it is out between us and our phone possie. *Whooo! Zonk! Bang!* And the sig goes head first to the ground as a shell lands almost under him.

Cr–up! Anxiously we look upward! A big black puff of smoke is floating high above us. *Cr–up! Cr–up! Cr–up!* Three more shrapnel shells burst above us. Shells are reefing and tearing great columns of dust from the ground on all sides. Still that shrapnel bursts above!

'Holy whoever!' And I'm yelling and jumping in pain. I grab my right hand . . . it's on fire. A black shrapnel pellet is protruding from the back of my hand. I grab it. It's red hot, but I pull it out, exposing a deep, bleeding hole.

'Come on, Jim! I've had enough. I'm selling out!' And nursing my bleeding hand I am racing away to get out of the barrage. Jim leaves the coil where I dropped it and is trying to catch up to me.

'What's up? Where're you hit?' he is calling as he races along after me – well after me – as I fly from that barrage . . . the wind right up.

For a hundred yards we rush on and are beyond the enemy barrage. We pause and examine the crack I've got. My fourth wound but it's not very serious. I've had two worse, far worse.

'What about the wire, Jim? Will we slip back and get it?'

'No, leave it there. Blast it! We'll get some more at H.Q.' So on we go and find the H.Q. down in a half-finished dugout some Fritz gunners were once making. Jim lands another coil of wire and gets connected up with the battalion phone and is ready to lay the wire back to our own company phone, but I tell him I'll be with him in a few minutes. He tries to persuade me to go out as a wounded case, but I can't well leave him to watch the phone day and night and mend wires as well for the three or four days we're sure to be in the line. It's my bad luck that four or five signallers who came in should have been wounded, for I wouldn't be signalling at all only that we're so short-handed.

The H.Q. has a regimental aid post here and I get a bottle of extra strong iodine poured around the wound, most of it working in and stinging like billyo, making me more miserable still. The doctor's orderly ties me up like a wounded soldier and Jim and I get the wire run back to our phone and establish communication just in time, for H.Q. are very keen for information as to how the 46th are faring in their stunt.

Time has dragged on. The 46th are now digging in on their objective. Some gas shells came over a while back and cut our wire and Jim had to go out in his gas respirator and mend the break.

Night now. We're all jumpy for Fritz has been seen out in front between our lines and the 46th. Word is back that the 46th have captured an enemy patrol and learned that Fritz is massing for a counter-attack and we all know that the 46th is to do a further advance tonight. Anything can happen so we're all very much on the alert.

The night is dragging on. We hear that one of our listening posts had a bomb fight with one of our own patrols and that an officer, a sergeant and two men were wounded. Fritz machine-guns are continually spraying along our position where the men are busy now connecting up the funk holes to form a trench. Enemy shells keep bursting about the position here and we see the flashes of our shells bursting away on the distant hill, somewhere ahead of the 46th position.

Our barrage is down again. We stand to for an hour or more whilst the 46th do an extra stunt out ahead and advance their line a little further. Dozens of wounded 46th blokes pass through on their way back. They tell us that they attacked the enemy positions and found them crammed full of Fritz waiting to stage a big counter-attack. They captured at least five hundred, they think.

A man comes through from the rear with Australian mail. We get a bundle of letters for our section, but have to wait till daylight to read them. That's the most annoying experience of the stunt so far.

Morning dawns. The morning of 19th September. We're all standing-to, reading our letters as we do so. Broad daylight and we're testing out the many field glasses we souvenired yesterday. My pair is especially good, but then I got them from a big Fritz artillery officer.

Word is through that in yesterday's advance the 45th took over 300 prisoners, half a dozen field guns and sixteen machine-guns. Our total casualties were less than seventy so we have done exceptionally well. The record of the whole 4th Division is great as the division, numbering 3000 men, captured 2500 prisoners, dozens of guns and killed or wounded hundreds of Fritz. The Hindenburg Outpost Line has been taken and the door is now open for breaking the Hindenburg Line. We've got Fritz on the run and no doubt we'll keep close on his heels. Our division's achievements have been wonderful and our losses extremely light, less than five hundred.

'You're a flamin' lucky cow, Nulla.' Old Longun is here with me and tells me that Fritz landed a 5.9-inch shell fair in the hole I had dug for my occupation.

'Burst a shell absolutely in it and blew a hole big enough to bury a cart in. If you'd been in it we'd have been picking you up on blotting paper now,' he goes on.

I'm lucky all right. Still, I'd feel far luckier if my hand wasn't so stiff and sore. The thought of tetanus always puts the breeze up me.

×

I've just had a trip back over the hill to mend a break in our wire. There's an officer dead in a shell hole over there who met his death in a most unusual way. It appears he was left wounded and crippled in a shell hole and that one of our tanks backed onto him and burnt him to death with its exhaust.

I go for a walk along our position. The men dug in all yesterday afternoon and all last night, and now have a very decent trench.

×

Night again. Jim is on the phone and the rest are watching out over the top of our trench, for the 46th out in front are doing some sort of a stunt and we have been warned Fritz may work in behind them and attack our position.

Our shells are whizzing and whirring overhead. We see flames of bursting shells stabbing through the darkness away out ahead. Enemy machine-gun bullets are ripping into the wet dirt along our parapet, so we're having a rotten time looking over the top. Heads pop up. Eyes take a searching sweep into the darkness ahead and down we bob again.

Along the trench, heads going up and down like chickens cleaning up hot soup. Now and again a call goes up for stretcher-bearers as a bullet finds its billet.

On our post we are taking it in turns to look over. The man on my left is looking over the top. Bullets smack into the parapet and he ducks down cursing hard and earnestly. A little pause and he laughs nervously and looks over again.

Now he jumps down. It's my turn and, taking a grip upon myself,

I force my head up until my eyes just clear the parapet. No bullets are coming near me so, getting gamer, I have a good look about out in front. Suddenly my head seems to be floating far away through a black, soundless void. Now it is floating on water. Cold water, into which my face is sinking, sinking, sinking. From miles away above me a voice calls down through the water, 'Some poor cow's got it through the tin lid.'

My mind is working. I somehow realise I'm the 'poor cow' the voice spoke of and begin to struggle. I'm underwater. I'm swallowing water. I can't breathe. My head is above water. Flop, and my face falls through blackness into water again.

'Steady, son, we've got you.' Hands are lifting me from the water. My reason returns and I know I am being lifted from a waterhole in the floor of the trench. Our platoon officer and some men have placed me on a fire-step.

'How d'you feel?'

'Let's see it.' And I jump! My forehead is being lifted! I've sagged back on the step, but feel better except that my head is bursting. Men tie a field dressing around my forehead and soon I am back to normal.

The men are interested in my tin hat. A torch flashed on the floor of the trench and I see my old steel helmet carries a bright copper streak from the top of the dome down to the brim. The brim is creased and bent. A man shows me a great rugged piece of steel that is hanging down from the underside of the tin hat.

'That stuck in your forehead. The tip of it came out through your eyebrow. Look where the bullet travelled down. Cripes, you're lucky!' And I see that a copper-clad enemy machine-gun bullet has travelled from the top of my helmet to the brim and then been guided off. My life undoubtedly saved by my old tin lid!

'How are you? Feel up to going out now?' our officer is asking.

I feel my forehead. It is very sore. I know my eye is swollen. The old hand wound is very sore now. I'll go out. I've had enough. *Swish, swish, swish,* the bullets fly in a stream overhead. I'm not going out through them.

'No, Sir. I'll stay on. I'm right.' I don't tell him that I'm too frightened to make out through those streaming bullets, but he probably knows.

'We can do with you on the phone here if you can stick it out. Slip in under the sheet and have a sleep.'

I make under the old Fritz ground-sheet. Now I'm down beside the phone on a heap of gear and empty sandbags and dropping to sleep despite headache, eye ache and hand ache. Almost two days and two nights since I've shut my eyes, so, despite all, here's for a sleep whilst my luck's in. Over I roll, craving sleep, sleep, just sleep, and soon I find it. Sleep, sleep, sleep.

EIGHTEEN
'Fini la Guerre'

'Stand to!' Far and faint through my sleep-fogged brain I catch the call and am awake. Jim is here on the phone and tells me that I've been asleep for hours, ever since I stopped that Fritz bullet on my steel helmet. I mooch out of our miserable shelter and speak to the men. They tell me that half my face and right eye are black, but I feel good after my long sleep.

The O.C. sends me to the stretcher-bearers to have my two little wounds re-dressed. They work plenty of strong iodine into my hand wound and forehead and I return to our company H.Q. all done out in fresh bandages.

Night of the 20th September and Jim has been asleep all day whilst I've been on the phone. Things are very quiet. We're been in support for three days and are to be relieved tomorrow night.

Slowly the long night drags on and Jim and I take turns on the phone. For hours we sit under the old waterproof sheet with our head-phones strapped on before going off duty in the trench to yarn and argue somewhere behind the village of Jeancourt. Fritz is keeping us aware that we're still at war by continually drilling our parapet with machine-gun bullets and with his whizz-bang shells, while his Taube aeroplanes are making themselves a nuisance dropping bombs on our positions.

Daylight again and our men are lying along the trench sleeping. We are to be relieved after dark so another stunt is nearly over and we're extra glad to get out. The trench is sloppy from some showers we had yesterday and last night. Clay is plastered all over us. The men are tired out, dirty, sleepy and hungry. Fritz has been pelting a lot of whizz-bangs all afternoon and Jim and I have had three trips each out mending the phone wires. My hand is very swollen and I'm still worried about tetanus. Somehow tetanus and gas always put the breeze up me and come first on the list of a thousand modes of death I hope to be spared from.

It's well after dark now. The relief is due at any minute and we are quite ready to shove off; the sooner the better.

'Here they come!' And men are emerging from the gloom behind the trench. Half a dozen Tommies are almost to our trench. *Whizz! Bang! Bang! Bang!* And a shower of Fritz shells are bursting around us again. A mad stampede as the Tommies charge for its protection. A rip, a tear, a thud, and a big heavy Tommie cove comes feet first through the waterproof sheet of our shelter. A grunt from the Tommy and a stream of fierce oaths from Jim as the Tommy joker lands fair on top of him. We laugh as they disentangle.

Jim is grieved and cranky as he picks up the phone from the floor of the miserable shelter and readjusts his headphones. The poor Tommy isn't taking much notice of Jim. He's too busy taking notice of Fritz whizz-bangs now snapping and barking so dangerously about the trench.

The relief has been effected. Our men have gone out and the 5th Battalion of the Leicester Regiment has taken over the position. The O.C., Jim and I, have just left the trench. We were delayed whilst the O.C. showed some Tommy officers all he knew about the position. On across the open we go. All is quiet and still, with a bright moon shining – a lovely night.

We're half a mile back now. Just the three of us, making back from the line. We are uneasy, for an enemy Taube is flying over us and we fear that he can see us.

On we go half expecting his machine-gun bullets to bite through us at any minute, but still the plane doesn't fire, though he keeps on circling us. We can see every strut on the machine as it swoops low over us in the bright moonlight.

Suddenly, we are down with enemy bullets smacking into the ground all around. The air is alive with the *phit, phit, phit* of bullets that swish and sweep over us. Above the roar of the plane's engine we hear the muffled *chut-chut-chuting* of its machine-gun. A roaring swoop and the great Taube has dived low and is circling away.

'Come on!' And the three of us are racing on, flat out to get away before the Taube can turn. Forty, fifty, sixty yards we run and *smack, smack, smack,* the bullets are spraying around us again. Down to the ground we drop with bullets hitting everywhere. We can see the flame leaving the muzzle of the gun as the plane roars by again. The gun stops. The plane has lost us.

'Keep down till he goes away. Got too close for my liking that time.' And our officer is wiping dirt from his eyes.

'Put a burst fair under my nose!' He laughs in a rather mirthless sort of way.

We remain very still as again the great plane is swooping over us, but his gun is silent. He can't see us. The plane has flown on and is now very slowly circling around two hundred yards away to our right.

Up and moving forward again. The plane is taking no notice of us. A little dark wood is just ahead and we make for it. A wide road, glistening white in the moonlight, is between us and the wood. As we walk on to it, sparks leap from underfoot as bullets sweep and swish viciously by smacking into the hard road before they *ping* and *whine* away into the night. Like madmen we race across it, charging for the shelter of the little wood just ahead.

'Run! Run!' The enemy plane is coming at us, flat out. Riding on a wave of roaring sound it is almost on to us. The bullets sweep and swish around. We hear that faint *chut-chut* and catch a glimpse of sparking flashes of its gun. Into the wood, and thick bushes are smacking against our faces, branches are buffeting and slapping us as we charge headlong through its black unknown depths.

'Don't stop! Make for the far side of the wood!' our O.C. shouts.

Flop! and we're down, wriggling against the butt of a tree where we curl ourselves up into a ball against it. Bombs are *swosh, swosh, swoshing* through the air. *Zonk! Bong! Bong! Bong!* and bursting in the wood just behind us! A roar and the Taube is over us and away.

A hurried, mingled *swooshing* from just ahead as a dozen bombs burst in a bunch twenty yards beyond the wood, sending great bomb fragments twisting and twirling as they burr away into the night. It's all quiet again.

'Well, that's that!' The O.C. laughs as we scramble up, listening to the plane now humming away into the night. We count eighteen bomb holes in a bunch. As Jim leads off, the O.C. points to Jim's back where a brand new mess tin is shining in the moonlight.

'See you get a cover for that mess tin before we come in again. No wonder the Taube could pick us out so easily.'

After some time, we follow a road quite lost, but the O.C. seems to know where he is making for, so we don't worry much for we're going back from the line and that's all we're interested in just at present.

Men are on the side of the road and we are back with the battalion again having a hot meal so we get our mess tins, find the cookers and get an issue of red-hot stew with plenty of meat and maconochie rations in it. The tea is good, too, so we have a good meal here by the roadside in the middle of the night, our first hot meal in four days.

After half an hour's spell we fall in and the battalion marches away along the road past the usual stream of traffic, moving up and back from the front until we reach a camp of huts at Tincourt, arriving at 3 a.m. Each platoon is allotted a hut. Exhausted, equipment and rifles are thrown anywhere and we drop off to sleep, dead weary and utterly worn out. An officer comes round with a rum issue and we all come to life in a great hurry, polish it off, go back, get down on the hard boards and are asleep at once.

'Come on! Show a leg here!' Broad daylight and our sergeant is waking us for breakfast. Later in the morning, the mail is given out. I have landed a parcel from my old high school at Bathurst and one from my grandmother and aunt at Carlton, so our little crowd is set. We eat tinned pears and smoke Australian cigarettes. I find a nice pair of knitted mittens in my parcels and, not wanting to lug them all over France for another two months, I give them to Clem, for he gave me his rum issue this morning. He's a teetotaller and as such is well worth cultivating. We could do with quite a lot more teetotallers in our platoon.

Clem tries the mittens on. 'Do me, thanks Nulla. They'll come in handy for the winter. It gets very cold over here, I believe.' And Clem goes away to put the mittens in his already over-loaded haversack. A man's expectation of life is pretty good when he will carry extra weight about for two months before it is needed.

After spending all day in the huts at Tincourt watching the rain, we're on the move again marching fifteen miles to Assevillers near Péronne. Here, scattered about, are old trenches, a few dirty huts and dugouts which the men try to fix up. While Farmer and Yacob are helping Snow make a dugout habitable, Longun, Darky and I sleep out under a clump of bushes, for these old Fritz positions are generally lousy and smelly.

It's 6 a.m. and breakfast is over. We're marching into the village of Hesbécourt to get into motor lorries as the battalion is going out for a bit of a spell. After a three-hour wait, we board the lorries and move off along the St Quentin road towards Amiens. For hours we ride along in the jolting lorries and at last get out at a village we hear is Fluy. Here we find a very decent billet so we're set, especially given the furphies say we're out for a real spell this time.

We've had half an hour fixing up the billet and ourselves when 'Fall-in!' is shouted up the stairs by a sergeant who is too tired to climb them.

'What the devil's the matter now!'

'Bet they've made a mistake and put us in the wrong village. Knew the billets were too good for us.'

'It's all right. Fritz has broken through again. He always does as soon as our turn comes for a bit of a rest.'

We stamp down the stairs and fall-in.

The sergeant comes along. 'Go up and get all your stuff and fall in for kit inspection. Shake it up!'

Up the stairs we climb, pull our bunks to pieces, roll our blankets, get all our gear and fall in again. The officers come round with the quartermaster who checks our stuff and makes a list of shortages before we lump it back upstairs to our billets.

Night, and all we get is a mess tin of black tea, but no food as our transport with the field cookers hasn't turned up. We go to sleep cranky and hungry.

Morning, and no food. Darky and I make off and find a village called Revelles where we buy a few loaves of bread from the French people. We wander about and get a shirt full of apples and Dark's tin hat holds ten new laid eggs, but we didn't buy the apples or the eggs. We borrowed them till the weather breaks. We reach our billet and the section has a good dinner.

I've had a few bike rides over to the battalion at Pissy after mail for the men. On one trip I discovered that some fellow had souvenired my bullet-dented helmet and probably sent it home to Aussie to show his narrow escape. Word is through that Turkey has asked for peace. We hope it's right, though it won't make much difference to us here we suppose.

A couple of days have gone by and it's 8th November. Yesterday we did a march in full equipment up through Fluy, a few hours' bayonet fighting and ended the day by scoring a hot bath and clean underclothing. Our uniforms were disinfected, turned inside out and ironed to scorch the chats to death, but no one burst out crying over that.

Today we've been put through some 'Bull Ring' concentrated training. Our blankets have just been handed in to be put on the train for the forward area tonight. We're going back into the front line again. Our six weeks' rest is over.

Night of 8th November and we are all sitting and shivering in our billets. Word is just through that our move has been postponed for twenty-four hours, but our blankets have already gone on ahead somewhere, so there's nothing to do but sleep, or try to sleep, without them.

Slowly the cold night is passing. A group of us are sitting by the fire as it's too cold to sleep without our blankets. Longun is mooching round the ring of men crouched close to the fire, but can't find a place to squeeze in. I feel him quietly take the signaller's pliers from my belt and see his quiet grin as he fades into the darkness beyond the fire's warm glow.

'Supposed to grip these Mills bombs like this, aren't you?' And Longun's back, standing behind us and waving a Mills about in the approved manner.

'Hey, you haven't got the pin out of that bomb, have you?' I anxiously ask. The new men turn, startled at the bomb Longun's messing about with.

'Yeah, it's out, but I won't drop her.' And he turns the bomb over a few more times when *Clang!* he's dropped it, flop in front of the sitting men.

'Look out!' And men are falling over backwards and clambering away down the stairs in a mad, headlong rush. A dozen new men fly from the room leaving a dozen seats vacant near the fire. We grin and edge in closer as Longun helps himself to a front-row seat. He picks up the bomb, remarking, 'Wonder if Mr Mills knows all the uses of his old grenade?'

Of course we enjoy the joke and the fire. Slowly the new men drift back. An old army joke has been put over them. Their education has been improved, but somehow they don't seem as grateful to old Longun as they might be and he won't lose any warmth over that.

Daylight dawns again very cold and so are we after a blanketless night. Word has just come that the move to the front has been postponed another 18 hours so we're in for another freezing night, shivering and telling yarns.

It's the morning of 10th November and word is here that the Kaiser has abdicated. Rumours of peace are floating around, but we no longer worry over rumours these days. Then another freezing night and we are at 11th November when word comes that we are to entrain for the front early tomorrow morning.

The French people are going clean mad today as they reckon the war is over. Every French man, woman and child is racing around waving flags and wine bottles and telling us, '*Fini la guerre, Monsieur.*' Rumours and furphies are going everywhere. The division signallers are supposed to have intercepted a wireless message saying that an armistice has been signed today. Then we hear that Fritz has sued for peace, but that General Foch has announced he won't entertain any peace proposals until the Allies have crossed the Rhine.

The bugle is blowing 'fall in' and we line up. Our O.C. gets rid of a few stray frogs from his throat and says, 'A message is just through, men, to say that hostilities ceased at eleven o'clock this morning. That means that the war is over, and –'

'Hooray!' we all yell, very much doubting him. Surely wars don't end like this.

He grins hard. 'I regret to announce that the message is unofficial.' And we give him three more 'hoorays', real full-blooded ones.

'The battalion entrains at daylight tomorrow for the front. Now just break off and get your rifles and bayonets and fall in here for some bayonet fighting exercises,' the O.C. instructs us, and we set off up the stairs for our rifles. The men are somewhat worked up about the peace rumours, for the French civilians seem quite certain the war is over.

Farmer wants to know if we think there's anything in the peace rumours. We don't, and tell him so.

'Yes, the war's over all right. All over the flamin' place. We'll know all about how much it's over by tomorrow night.' And we go off and get nearly two hours' solid bayonet fighting drill.

Night, and the civilians are having a great time. They can't understand why we won't believe the war is over, but a lot of our blokes join in the celebrations and render assistance by helping the Froggies get drunk, and keep drunk.

Again we sit and shiver the night away. Our fourth night without blankets. There's only one discussion tonight and that's the persistent rumours that the war is over. Long into the cold night we argue, each of us so wishing and hoping the rumours were only true. But what's the use of wishing and hoping, for tomorrow we push off for the line again, the line with its dangers and death. The talking falls and fades as one by one we get off into a cold, broken sleep.

Reveille is sounding. It's 4 a.m. on the 12th November. We tidy up our billet, get breakfast, save some warm tea for shaving water and pack up our equipment. We fall in and the battalion marches away from Pissy for the line again. On we march till we reach Ailly-sur-Somme where we climb onto a long train of waiting cattle trucks, which waits till twelve o'clock before the whistle blows and we move off.

A French boy, then another, runs on to the little platform. They have Paris editions of the London daily papers for sale. A few men jump out and buy papers. The men shout and wave the papers. We read the great inch type headlines. We've seen enough, seen that in print which we can hardly believe, seen that which the optimists ever hoped to see! The

French boys are doing a roaring trade. More and more men buy papers, calling out to mates back in the trucks. Calling a message of life!

'*Papier! Fini la guerre!*' screech the boys, and eight hundred men are leaping down from the moving train. Papers are snatched from the boys. Papers are being handed out everywhere. The boys are reaping a harvest. No change is being given, none expected. All we want is the official confirmation of the rumours we hardly dared to believe.

The war is over! *Deo gratias!*

We're back in the train and jolting along. Papers have been read. We've convinced our innermost selves that the war is over, that we've seen it through, that we'll really again see our own people and our own homes that have seemed so hopelessly distant of late.

The train grinds on. Sitting in the rocking, lurching cattle trucks amongst the grime and grit, we read the glad news. We read of how the people of Paris, of London, of the whole Allied world went head-over-heels, riding on a surge of bottled-up emotion so suddenly uncorked by the news of the armistice.

Our men are as calm as ever. We, to whom the screeched '*Fini la guerre*' of the newsboys really mean the most, are taking our release from all that war has meant very calmly and casually.

'If the news of this armistice affair was sent all over the world yesterday morning, it's flamin' queer that a battalion only fifty miles from the line couldn't have been officially advised.'

'It's not a fair go. Corps and divisional H.Q. must have known all about it.'

'Perhaps they'd forgotten where we were.'

'They'd have flamin' soon remembered if Fritz had broken through again.'

All through the cold afternoon the train crawls slowly on towards the line that we no longer dread, past Tincourt and on into the darkening night. After a night on the cold train, it stops in the early morning.

'Come on, get out!' And we wake up and climb down to hear that we are at our journey's end. We're at Roisel from where commenced the great enemy advance last March; that great, sweeping push we helped to stop up near Dernancourt.

The battalion has formed up and away we march for a mile, where we stop and take possession of some dirty old dugouts. Quietly we spend the day here. A few hands of poker, a game or two of rummy and giving our few francs a flutter in a two-up game, then night is down, cold and damp.

A cold night goes by and the morning of 14th November sees us cramped up in little open trucks of a light railway in the cold, biting wind. We pull up at Bellicourt, a few miles behind the line just vacated by Fritz. Off again and on into the wind to Brancourt-le-Grand where we spill our frozen frames out of the trucks. From here, a cold, freezing march of three miles to Fresnoy-le-Grand where we spend a week of drill, ceremonial parades, inspections, washing equipment and dolling ourselves up like real soldiers. The afternoons have been far better with plenty of inter-company football matches and we cleaned up a few francs in bets.

22nd November and we're on the march again, this time to Coblenz on the Rhine as part of the Army of Occupation. Now we're well into territory held for a long time by the enemy. We see men approaching from along the road towards us. They are in absolute rags and tatters, their clothes a mixture of old, torn uniforms, British, French and Fritz. The fellows are filthy. The poor wretches are staggering as they walk from sheer weakness, for they're just skin and bone, scarecrows on legs.

A tall, gaunt figure sways towards us from the bunch of scarecrows. 'Can you spare us a coupla tins of bully beef? I belonged to the 19th Battalion. Got knocked and taken prisoner at Fleurbaix in July sixteen. There's two other Aussies in the mob.'

We look at him and his mates. Prisoners of war. Poor, half-starved wretches. All dirty yellow skin, hollow cheeks and sunken, hopeless eyes. Food and cigarettes are being handed out everywhere. Handed out to be clutched at by long, claw-like, grasping fingers that shake. How we pity these poor beggars! How we thank our lucky stars we escaped the ordeal of being prisoners of war. We look upon fellow men reduced to skin-clad skeletons and are sickened.

The fellows bite like starved dogs. Animal hunger shows in their every movement. They say they were left behind to fend for themselves when Fritz retreated. Now they're in no one's care, but just have to depend upon getting food from passing battalions until some organised effort is made to collect and care for them.

An A.M.C. doctor comes along and takes the poor wretches away and we're nearly as glad as they are.

On we go and reach St Souplet where we doss for the night. Worn out from our long tramp along slushy roads, we have our meal and drop to sleep, utterly done up.

Daylight again and we're on the march once more. For twenty miles we march in drizzling rain. Mud and slush is deep underfoot. Streams of motor lorries are passing all day, which shower us with dirty, sloppy water, and plaster sheets of mud over us as their great wheels churn through the muddy shell holes of the broken road. We plod along, heads down, backs strained under a 90-pound load as equipment straps cut into our sore shoulders. And still the traffic slushes by. We swear and wipe it off and slog on.

At last we reach Le Favril and gladly get in a night's rest. Morning of 24th November is here, about ten hours too soon. We have to do what we can to clean our equipment and uniforms. The day passes slowly. A few of us have been for a walk to Maroilles and Landrecies, two nearby towns, but there wasn't much to see there except scores of sore-eyed little Franco–Fritz waifs and strays, the flotsam and jetsam tossed aside by the great wave that surged ever onwards across this corner of France for four years. A wave that has now ebbed back beyond the Rhine, leaving its unwanted debris behind. We've had a peep behind just another curtain of war and have seen some backstage effects that will take more than a Peace Treaty to clean up. Thank God the war wasn't fought in our country!

Our fourth day at Avesnes-sur-Helpe and we're all dolled up and marching away somewhere to be inspected by the King and Prince of Wales. On through bitter cold winds blowing off the snow-covered ground we are lined up along a roadside waiting for the King and Prince to come along. As far as we can see, Australian battalions are lining the road in the cold, blowing wind.

An hour goes by bringing more wind but no King. Men are stamping frozen feet and blowing through numbed fingers. A group breaks off and gets a little game of two-up going, but a patriotic officer rushes up and hunts the men back into their ranks in a tearing hurry.

'Come on, take a pull to yourselves,' the officer yells. 'Look funny if the King came along and caught you fellows playing two-up.'

'Oh, I dunno. The old codger might give his few francs a bit of a flutter.' And the men drift back and pass nasty remarks about a little group of British Tommies who are very steadily 'standing-at-ease' just along from us. The sight of this good soldier stuff generally gets our goat.

Another half hour drags by. The men are sauntering about, thoroughly blasting everything from the King to their own ill luck at being here. How the wind is howling! All our respect and patriotism have been blown away two hours ago. In little groups the men are slipping away to a nearby estaminet and cleaning up what bottled cheer old madame has.

A movement starts surging down our lines. Men cheering loud and long.

'Come on, into your places. The King is coming!' our officers are yelling.

'An' about flamin' time too!' And we get into line in a hurry to have an eyeful of him.

'Hip, hip, hooray!'

'Hoop-ran!'

'Hooray!'

The cheering is closer. The next platoon is cheering now. We crane our necks and from around the next bend two fine horses canter, carrying two great useless military police running the gauntlet of a whole brigade. And how we cheer those military Johns and whistle at them. Mad with rage they pass on and we laugh at the tuning up we gave them, for we get a bit of our own back.

'The King is coming! Properly "at ease" everywhere!'

Motor cars are coming slowly down the road behind half a dozen mounted men cantering ahead.

'D Company, 'shun!' And our officers out in front are standing at the salute, one eye on the approaching King and the other watching us to see if we are on our best behaviour. Of course we are. Some of the men are even standing properly at 'attention'. Others are standing anyhow, casually having a look at our King.

The cars are here. We spot the Prince of Wales. We know the boyishly self-conscious, slightly retiring face beneath the red, braided cap of a staff officer. The Prince is a sort of cobber of ours, though we haven't told him so yet, but we think he knows that already.

Here's the King! A little man, mostly beard and overcoat. A friendly, manly face is creased in sympathetic wrinkles as he smiles at us freezing here in the snow. The big, silent car glides slowly by and some cove calls, 'How's it for a loan of your overcoat, King?' and gets promptly roared up by the sergeant major. No shouts, no cheers, and our King has gone by.

'Hip, hip, hooray!'

'Hip, hip, hooray!' is ringing out from down along the road where the little handful of Tommies are loyally cheering their passing King. Now our mob is cheering, cheering hard, cheering the Tommies' effort, and the King is past.

Long live the King. Our crowd didn't shout and cheer, yet we somehow feel that the King didn't expect it.

⨯

It's 13th December and we are marching out of old Avesnes where we've had a peaceful fortnight or so, though a jolly cold one. All day we march and reach billets in Sivry-Rance, a little old town in Belgium where the Belgian people are very friendly as we're the first Aussies they've seen.

On the march again. For three more days we push on into Belgium. The night before last at Boussu-lez-Walcourt, last night at St Aubin, and now we've just reached a lovely town, Hastière, on the Meuse. As the Aussies aren't going to the Rhine after all, we're to remain here until demobilised. Hastière with its friendly, hospitable people will do us, for we're sure of a quiet, peaceful time here under ideal surroundings until our turn comes for demobilisation.

⨯

It's 22nd February, 1919, and we've just reached Florennes from

Hastière where we had a very enjoyable two months. There's not so many of us left now as nearly all the 1914 and 1915 men have left for demobilisation. Our turn is coming and may the happy day roll along with all speed. After a night in Florennes we are marching out again, through Nalinnes to our destination, Thy-le-Chateau, where we again find ourselves amongst more very friendly people. We attend civilian churches, visit and play cards with the Belgian people and enjoy the fine hospitality these poor war-wretched people so freely offer.

We've been seeing something of neighbouring towns, Thuillies, Somzée and Gourdinne, and some of us have slipped off on civilian bicycles to our old haunts at Hastière and on to Dinant, Namur and Charleroi with just an odd trip to Brussels. Not long now and we'll be on the move we all want, the move for old Aussie. Soon we'll be going home.

Today a letter from the Prof who is to join our draft when we reach England, so the seven of us will be reunited for the voyage home. Our little crowd has weathered the storm. We've been lucky where so many better men have gone under. Of the two hundred and fifty men and two officers of our reinforcement, just nineteen are left with the battalion now, and practically every man of this nineteen has been wounded on more than one occasion. Of our two officers, one was invalided home, badly smashed up two years ago and our other, killed during our last stunt in the line whilst lying wounded waiting for a stretcher to carry him out. Just the luck of the game. Our reinforcement has been through the mill that has taken full toll of the fine Australian lads who made it up, now so sadly broken.

It's early April 1919. The cold winter is giving way to spring. We're still at Nalinnes, but our equipment has been handed in and we are on a draft due to leave for England any day now. We've been doing a lot of slipping off to see our Belgian friends in Thy-le-Chateau and Hastière, as discipline is very elastic now for anyone who plays the game and we appreciate the spin we're being given.

9th April and we're at Charleroi and are to entrain for the base camps sometime today. Last night, Snow and I stayed at a hotel in Charleroi as we couldn't quite stand another night on the hard boards of the great factory where our draft is camped. We're getting fussy these days.

We're now marching through Charleroi to entrain. People in hundreds line the hard, cobbled streets to see us march out. They're giving us a send off as we leave their country and we appreciate their kindly interest. The Belgians are showing that they realise the bond now existing between their land and ours, a bond cemented by blood.

Our train has pulled out. We're in the usual cattle trucks, but well cared for now as our Comforts Fund has provided chocolates and smokes. Rations are good and plentiful and each truck has a fire brazier and a bag of coal with straw on the floor for our comfort. We travel on through Mons and Arras, so close to old Bullecourt, well remembering having been here exactly two years ago. The blood of Bullecourt – shall we ever forget it?

The train moves on, crawling all night through France. Daylight, 10th April, and our train has pulled into Romescamps where cups of good tea and hot soup are being freely offered and gratefully accepted. France is paying what she can of her debt, as Belgium has done, paying it in the best coin – practical help that we can appreciate.

Our journey is over. We're at the big Australian General base depot at Le Havre. Things are good here too. Five blankets, a hot bath, a shave, plenty of cigarettes and good food, soon puts us in fine fettle and at peace with the world and our own army heads too. Four days at the base where rifles and equipment are handed in, clothing fumigated, and we're ready to say the old *au revoir* to France, for we embark tomorrow for England.

It's 15th April, our last day in France, and teeming rain. All morning we sit in the huts watching the rain and thinking. Somehow there's a sadness behind our apparent gladness at leaving France, for we're not only leaving France but leaving dozens of fine mates who fell whilst we lived through it all.

'Fall in, the draft.' And we march away into motor cars and get whizzed off towards the harbour of Le Havre, not waiting about the wharf, but straight onto a big ship.

Now the transport is moving away from the wharf, away from France, we're off, but no, the ship is stopping. For five long hours the ship rides at anchor and finally, at 5 p.m., digs her nose into the channel and we're really away. The grey waters of the choppy Channel turn dull and murky. Dusk engulfs us. Now it is very dark. The ship steams on for hours. Lights show ahead and at midnight the ship stops. We're in the outer harbour of Southampton and are at anchor till morning.

All night we walk the cramped ship or just sit and sleep. It's cold and we're hungry, but what does it matter for behind us lies France, the Fritz and the war, whilst ahead is England, Aussie and hope. So we eventually all drop to sleep hoping, ever hoping, and a silent, happy peace descends upon the transport of sleeping men. Men back from the war. Men coming home, home, home.

NINETEEN

A Dinner to the Troops

It's 25th April, 1919, and we're over in England thawing out a bit and waiting, ever waiting, for the longed-for order that will send our draft to embark for Aussie and home. We've seen our fair share of the war, though, and come out alive, thanks to God's goodness and our own good luck.

We give our luck some credit and suppose there's something in what writers call the 'luck of life'. We joke and speak of our luck and attribute much of the daily good or evil to the fact that our luck was in, or out.

We don't openly speak of being preserved by the Grace of God, for somehow in the A.I.F. it doesn't seem the thing to dwell too much upon religious convictions. It isn't done, not openly at any rate. With luck it's far different. We can wax free about luck, shower it with praise, blame it for our own short-sighted madness or make it responsible for any bravery. When a man's modesty forbids him accepting the praise his actions have so well merited, he passes it off to his luck. Or, if he has been so careless over little things as to throw his hat down in Piccadilly Circus and defy six big military policemen to touch it, and gets landed in Warwick Square gaol for being drunk, disorderly and A.W.L., he's not to blame in the least . . . his luck was out, that's all.

But religion, or luck, or both, we're going home to our own kith and kin. We find it hard to believe that we shall soon be amongst our own people in our own land. As the full realisation of all that 'going home' really means becomes clearer, so does the waiting become harder and the longing turns to yearning as the long, cold tail-end of our last European winter slowly warms into the glorious flower-decked greenery of English lanes and hedges of springtime.

We're spending the morning being inoculated. We don't know or much care what the inoculation is for or against. Way back in our marmalade days we were interested in inoculations and knew just what each one was supposed to guard us against, but after the first few dozen we lost interest, and count.

Our little crowd is last to be done. We've seen to that by hanging back, for we know from past experience that the first batches done are swooped upon by spare sergeants and corporals for work details.

At last we get landed and in we go, baring our left arms. The medical officer's orderly dabs iodine on each man's arm. This orderly joker is silent and sour, but he somehow attracts Longun who becomes friendly and asks, 'What's this inoculation for, Dig?'

The orderly gets a burst of wit and tells Longun, 'To guard against the prevailing epidemic of catching Pommy brides.' We grin at Longun and wait. Longun gazes long and unlovingly in that orderly's face and screws his long neck to get a side view, too, and in a friendly sort of tone tells the orderly, 'You should be thankful that your face has saved you the necessity of being inoculated.'

Of course we enjoy Longun and laugh. Longun passes on. The orderly becomes flustered and dabs iodine on Darky's flannel instead of his arm.

'Steady up!' sneers Dark. 'Don't you think a man's singlet's dirty and smelly enough without havin' stinkin' iodine plastered all over it?'

We laugh some more and the doctor does his stuff on each man's arm. Snow is the last to be done. In goes the needle and Snow gives a twitch and closes his right hand hard upon a lighted cigarette he has been smuggling along. He gives a bounce, opens his hand in a mighty hurry, stamps quite a good cigarette nearly through the floor and makes a dash for the door in a nasty frame of mind, but he's got to go back again as he's getting away with the doctor's needle still stuck in his hide.

The quack grins, rescues his needle, gives Snow another dab of good strong iodine upon the burnt palm and asks Snow if he's glad the war is over and grins some more.

We get back to our hut to find great activity. The men are cleaning boots, shaving or having a go to remove stew stains from tunics. We wonder what's gone wrong, but are told that the local town corporation has invited our draft to a smoko dinner tonight. We're told, 'Today's Anzac Day, don't you know?' We didn't know, or care much either.

Snow, who's been away somewhere cooling down, comes in and gives us the dinkum oil about the dinner. It is to be in the town hall, a real ding-dong sit-down dinner with free beer laid on, free cigarettes and Tommy mess orderlies to wait on us. All the civilian heads of the town are to be there and the old general commanding the depot is the guest of honour. We're the guests of the town and the colonel of the Tommy mob down the road is to be the chairman.

Snow is well up in it. He had to buy our O.C.'s little batman three big beers before he learnt all the particulars. He becomes pretty popular. We ask if the mess orderlies will be in livery and when our cars will call and if we are to wear dinner suits and enquire of Snow as to the correct tie to wear.

⤫

Fall in sounds and we make a rush to be ready by the time the sergeant-major will be along to enquire if we're all deaf or dead or something, and if we didn't hear the bugle.

Eventually we fall in. The sergeant-major gives us, ''shun' and 'stand-at-ease' half a dozen times in case we have forgotten it, but we can do it still, though it's four years since we first learnt it. The S.M. inspects us, then the O.C. gives us a little lecture on our behaviour at the coming dinner. We're told we have to uphold the honour of Australia tonight, before British officers and the gentlemen of the town, and that a very serious view will be taken of any larrikinism. At this the O.C. looks hard at our section to see if we're paying attention to his warning. We're not, but he doesn't know that and we don't tell him. We're like that mostly. We have to be.

The O.C. now inspects us in case the eagle-eyed S.M. has missed spotting any unbuttoned pockets or cigarette bumpers behind our ears. He must be feeling good for he compliments us upon our appearance and says we're a credit to the fine battalion to which we belong.

The band strikes up. We 'form-fours', 'right-turn' and 'quick-march' after the band. Ahead of us march the O.C. and the S.M. carrying useless little canes. We don't begrudge them their canes for we remember when these two marched ahead of us carrying in their hands not canes but their lives, and leading us not to a sit-down dinner but to assault Fritz trenches or pill-boxes, or those deadly machine-gun nests from which so many of our mates collected their R.I.P.

Some of us remember, too, when these two were just diggers in the ranks following on after other leaders who have since passed on. Some home to Australia, maimed in body and spirit, soured and seared, or happy to have got out of it all at any cost. Others who found their last long resting place in the slimy Somme mud, or amid the utter desolation that is Flanders. Others still whose remains lie shattered and scattered in the hundred tiny graves that house all that is left of the man who caught the burst of a 9.2.

A final flourish from the band and we're at the town hall. We halt and see our O.C. salute the Tommy colonel and be introduced to other officers and civilians.

We file into a flag-bedecked hall and take our seats at long tables tastefully laden with good cheer. We sit down and talk.

A commotion and the heads file in and prop themselves up behind the chairs of the official table. Then 'Party . . . 'shun' and we hop to attention. In this Snow's a bit unlucky. He's been gazing into his empty glass and dreaming of better things to come when the order gives him such a shock that he knocks his chair over, makes a big noise and a far bigger one trying to rescue it.

We're just nicely 'shunned' when in comes our old general, all smiles and medals, shakes hands with everyone in the room, except the two hundred and fifty of us. Perhaps he doesn't see us.

We are told to 'sit down, men', and we do. The chairman, the Tommy colonel, makes a fine speech and introduces our old general, as if we don't know all we want to know about the old beggar. Then he introduces the mayor and we clap him.

He next introduces the president of the Red Cross Society and we clap him too. Several spare persons and blokes carrying bowler hats are next introduced and likewise clapped. The colonel says we'll get a start on and has 'much pleasure in introducing the mess orderlies with the beer', and we cheer him and he looks happy and sits down and we make a start on the dinner.

We are uprising and drink several toasts. We also drink many more for practice in between the uprisings. We listen to the speeches more or less, generally less. We're having great fun as we have a good pianist and after each speech we have a song just to forget what the speaker wants us to remember.

The colonel raps louder than usual and we give him more attention than usual. He has 'the great honour and pleasure of calling upon the Australian Divisional Commander, our distinguished guest here tonight, to say a few words. Gentlemen, the General.'

The old general rears up like a cavalry charger on parade and goes into action straight away. He doesn't tell us what wonderful soldiers we are. Perhaps he doesn't know, or if he does, he leaves that to the Tommy officers. In about a dozen words he is back on Gallipoli with the British 29th Division on his left, and trouble and Turks on the other three sides. Away he goes, but we don't try to follow him, as we are otherwise engaged.

It's a great speech although the old general does spend most of his time between raising an imaginary hat to the 29th Division and a real whisky glass, fully charged, to himself. We sit back and enjoy our old general. We're proud of him, for the first time in the war. We wish we could have an Anzac Dinner with the old boy every day.

The dinner goes on, so does our old general, and on and on and on.

Longun yanks his six feet of skinniness upright and wants to know, 'Where on earth has the flamin' mess orderly got himself to with our jug of beer?' In the interests of peace, we beckon the orderly over and get Longun's glass refilled.

Longun promptly empties it, but is still grieved and wants the orderly fellow to tell him, 'Where the devil have you been to, anyway?' and doesn't give the poor beggar time to answer before he glares at him and demands, 'Did you think you could hatch a flamin' circus out of the bloomin' jug? Been away somewhere sittin' on it have you?'

Longun cools down a bit and tells the orderly, 'Here, fill this rat of a glass again and don't get losin' yourself with the beer in case we happen to want another.' And when the chap fills the glass Longun tells all and sundry, 'You'd think he had to pay for it himself, the way he's hangin' on to it.' Longun doesn't trust anyone where beer or poker is concerned.

Longun begins to take an interest in Yacob and advises him to 'shove the puddin' on the spoon with your fork, not your dirty great thumb. Do you want to disgrace us?'

The Prof becomes interested in Yacob too, and wants to know, 'Hadn't the invention of the fork reached Russia in your time, Yacob?'

But Yacob only shows his nicotine teeth in a silly sneer and we grin some more. Dark comes to old Russia's aid, and orders, 'Leave the Bolshie alone, you lot o' goats.'

'Order! Order at that table down there, men!'

We settle down again. Some to pay attention to the general, others to their dinner. Just then down comes the old man's glass, *plonk* into the colonel's jelly and cream. The colonel reaches to save his jelly and the general to rescue his glass, which comes up with its ground floor well lathered in jelly and cream. The colonel rises to knock the plaster off the glass. He succeeds in knocking it off all right, fair into the lap of the President of the Red Cross Society. Doesn't the president bounce! You'd think he didn't like jelly and cream.

Excitement is great and our old general so far forgets himself as to sit down. Then we clap him! How we clap! Out of appreciation and thankfulness . . . mostly thankfulness. The old general doesn't seem quite to realise this. He takes it for an encore and begins to clear his nearly drowned vocal chords for a fresh affliction upon us.

The chairman comes to the rescue. He beats the general to his feet and in a big voice and bigger hurry announces, with a wave at the pianist, 'We'll be upstanding and sing "Back Home in Tennessee".'

The song ends and we sit down. The fat parson says 'very good' three times in case we didn't hear him, or believe him, the first time. Still it must have been pretty decent sort of singing for the parson to say that, for we haven't given him any particular reason to tell a lie just to please us. We diggers are far more generous. We don't mind telling a lie, or a few dozen, just to please our padre.

We stand up and drink a few more toasts, have a few more songs, pay less and less attention to the speeches that come on, and our dinner draws to its close.

Our O.C. gets up and makes a pretty poor sort of a speech thanking the town for the feed, though he doesn't call it a feed . . . officers don't. Anyway he has brains enough to realise he's not a general, or a Billy Hughes, so cuts the agony short by calling upon, 'My men (that's us) to show their appreciation by giving three hearty cheers.'

We give three beauts. 'One for the umpire,' some fellow shouts, and we let it go . . .

'Hoop-rah!' And we are getting a bit out of hand and boisterous when 'God Save the King' is struck up and we stand to attention, just like real soldiers.

Our dinner is over. We're told to 'file out quickly and fall in outside'. Out we go, all but Darky and Longun. Darky wanders about filling his pockets with stray cigarettes and peanuts, whilst Longun seeks out the lance-corporal in charge of the mess orderlies and asks if he wants any help to carry the spare beer back to the canteen or the pub or wherever it's supposed to go.

The lance-jack doesn't want any help. He doesn't want Longun, either, but a Tommy lieutenant does and asks Longun to 'lend a hand – move this piano, my man'.

'Certainly, Sir. I'll get a coupla men to help,' replies Longun and rushes out and tells the sergeant-major to 'send four men in to shift the flamin' goanna'.

Snow and three other blokes get sent back in to grunt and strain under a heavy piano whilst Longun helps Dark to clean up the few peanuts he salvaged. The furniture removalists come back and we march off through the silent town back to our camp huts.

We reach the camp, troop into our huts, climb out of our clothes, hang them up on the floor, and drop down into our bunks.

And thus another day of army life peters out to the man-sized snores of Farmer and the wheezy whistle of Yacob's slumber song.

TWENTY

Till the Boys Come Home

Time has moved on. We've had no end of medical inspections, route marches and physical jerks to keep us fit and well.

Our fourteen days demobilisation furlough is over. Also an extra four days' leave and wonderful trips to various towns in the U.K. Great times in London and there's a more wonderful time to come for very soon now we're going home. Delay after delay has held us back, but now word is here that our draft, Quota 30 we're called, is to sail from Devonport on the *Beltana* on 30th May, just a week ahead.

Days drift by. Visits to a big race meeting at Salisbury, concerts, picture shows, letter writing and looking up digger friends in the various camps fill in our time. It's 1st June, 1919, but we don't sail for another two days. Another delay has held us up. Our little crowd is mooching about the huts trying to fill in time somehow. A game of two-up is in progress and Longun and I are winning well. An officer drifts along to the game and Dark, very friendly like, asks him, 'Goin' to have a spin, Sir?'

'No, you fellows want to take a bit of a pull. Playing two-up here today! Surely you know it's Sunday. Get round behind the huts if you must play.'

'What day is it behind the huts, Sir?' Dark asks, but the officer buzzes off so we get into an empty hut, fix a blanket on the floor and finish the game.

Monday 2nd June, and we are on a train bound for Plymouth.

We reach Exeter and the Lady Mayoress is on the platform with dozens of pretty girls who fill us up with tea and buns whilst each man gets a little souvenir card of our call at Exeter.

Snow is doing pretty well with a little girl when the engine whistles and he casually tells her, 'Oh well, see you again,' as he climbs aboard to do a twelve-thousand-mile voyage away from her. Snow must reckon he's a pretty long-sighted sort of a cove.

We're at Plymouth. It is half-past three in the afternoon and we march straight from the train on to the wharf and aboard the *Beltana*. I knew a whole heap of people in Plymouth and Saltash when I was in hospital in October, 1916, so spend half an hour unsuccessfully trying to get the afternoon off to do some visiting.

Night. The ship is still at the wharf. Will we never get away? Our little crowd is on B deck. We're back in the old hammocks. Six weeks of troopship life is ahead of us, and then?

Daylight is here. 3rd June, King's birthday, a red-letter day on the harbour. Nine o'clock comes around and the ship slowly moves away from the wharf and anchors in what the sailors call Plymouth Sound. We spend the morning taking it easy, exploring the canteen and the Y.M.C.A. library that is on the ship for our comfort. I collect four good books, two in my own name and two in Yacob's, and give them to the Prof to mind whilst I nose around the ship some more.

Plymouth Sound is full of ships. The warships are all decked out in dozens of flags in celebration of the King's birthday. The *Mahia* passes close by as she steams into the wharf to collect our Quota 33.

Afternoon now. Mail leaves the ship in half an hour and Snow, who's been busy all day writing to his spare girls in various parts of Blighty, rushes over to where we're playing a few hands of show poker and asks, 'Hey, Dark, got one of those snapshots to spare that you had taken?'

'What d'you want it for anyway?'

'That girl up in Wolverhampton wants a photo of me, and I've got none to send. One of yours will do just as well.'

'Like blazes it will! Any rate I've got none left now. Get one of Nulla's.' And he grins at me.

'Want to cruel a man's pitch? I told her I was a good-lookin' sort of a bloke.' And he buzzes off to put the acid on Yacob for a photo in order that his lonely soldier correspondent may have just another photo for her collection.

The ship is moving. Slowly across the harbour we glide past some British battleships with hundreds of sailors lining the rails. As we pass each ship we cheer and cheer the Jack Tars; we kick up a wonderful noise, a whole boatload of noise. Suddenly from the nearest warship there floats three great cheers, three real British cheers, as the sailors, guided by an officer, let it go in perfect unison. We've heard some fine effects this past few years, but never anything to come up to this organised cheering of a British battleship.

Night is here now. We have passed through the line of cheering warships and the high coast of England slips on to the horizon and fades from view as the murk of night comes down upon us. Hammocks are being hung on the troop decks while up on deck, heads are already being hung over the railings as men are turning green about the gills.

We've had a week at sea now. Times are good as is the food and we have very little drill to worry us. There are plenty of books to read and we have two bands and a concert party on board. The sea has been calm and we've had only two inoculations so far. Many of us are attending educational lectures held under the A.I.F. Education Scheme and are probably learning something else to forget.

Into our second week at sea now. The Canary Islands were passed a day or two ago and we're just in the tropics. The days are very hot, but the sea is becoming unsettled and the old *Beltana* is doing over three hundred miles a day. Day after day goes by, just one sweltering hot day after another. Now and again we run into a storm or a day or so of strong wind and heavy seas, but monotony is constant.

13th June, and we've just finished going mad in our celebrations, for today we crossed the equator and ducked all and sundry, except the few nurses who are on board somewhere.

Open-air concerts are held every night now. By means of lantern slides, the words of popular songs are thrown on the screen and we join in the singing.

Towards evening we get an issue of cigarettes and socks from the Comforts Fund. Getting rid of surplus supplies evidently, and the boys get wondering if there was any surplus rum left over from the war, but Darky reckons, 'You can't have surplus rum when you've got an overdose of bloomin' quartermasters.' And we sadly suppose he's right.

Monday 16th June. Had a bit of a row on the troopdeck during breakfast when the men discovered that the sausages contained a liberal flavouring of the rotten cheese we handed back to the Q.M. yesterday. Time is going on. Father Goodman has given a lecture on 'France from Napoleon to 1870', and the 'Beltana Buskers' have staged some good concerts.

The romantically inclined coves are up on deck every night now pointing to a bunch of about a thousand stars low down on the horizon and saying, 'See that star? It's one of the stars of our old Southern Cross. The bosun pointed it out to us the other night,' whilst other lying jokers reckon, 'Yes, I can pick it all right. Good old Southern Cross.'

Seventeen days out of England. An albatross has been flying round the ship all day and we hear we're in wireless communication with Cape Town and with the *Rio Negro* carrying Quota 28 home. The men are discussing the wonders of wireless and Longun reckons he's going to 'rip up a wireless fence to keep the flamin' cockatoos off the old man's corn'.

Another two days have gone by and we've been in sight of land all day and are to reach Cape Town this evening.

The night of 25th June and we're on deck watching a couple of lighthouses that are our last link with Cape Town where we had three wonderful days with plenty of shore leave. The harbour was very busy too. The *Mahia* came in yesterday. Then a troopship, the *Willochra*, was there with a load of Fritz internees, and the *Euripides* with passengers from Aussie to Blighty.

We enjoyed Cape Town, but in a calmer, maturer manner than when we bubbled over on our wild day there three years ago on our way to the war. Perhaps we've had such a surfeit of excitement and seen so many strange places since those far-away days that we've become somewhat blasé.

Perhaps the thought that we're so near home and all that that means has blunted the edge off our wildness. Perhaps we are better behaved because the slackening of the usual discipline has given us the opportunity for indulging our wildness, and what's the use of mucking up when it's not against authority? Or perhaps we've just got more sense, or is it that the past three years have quietened us down more than we realise?

We're into cold weather now and the starboard portholes are kept closed at night. A cold wind is blowing from the starboard, blowing from the Great Ice Barrier so it seems. Debates every night now, so we hear a lot about Free Trade and Protection, State Control versus Private Enterprises, Taxing Bachelors and other high-sounding arguments. Lectures are laid on too. Father Goodman has given us two on the Light Horse in Palestine and one about Sinai.

Well into July now and very cold, sleety weather, so men are lying in their hammocks arguing. The argument turns to why we enlisted. We hear the old one about enlisting whilst drunk, but know that is all lies and rot, just so much camouflage to hide the real reason.

No one ever seems to admit that he enlisted out of love of country, or because he thought his loved ones were in danger. Somehow it seems that most of us enlisted because our mates did. That men were driven to enlist by that urging spirit of pulling together that is really mateship undefined. A man enlists because his mates do, not because he wants to bayonet and bomb other men.

There's a parallel between civilian and army life. A man doesn't go into a pub to get drunk, yet when he gets there he does as other men are doing and ends up three sheets to the wind. In the army it's the same, for although a man doesn't go into a stunt with the deliberate intention of killing his fellow man, yet put a bayonet or bomb into his hand and he'll do as his mates are doing and use them to the full.

Darky tells us he enlisted because he was impelled by love of country and pride and race to do so, and gets called a hero and is howled down.

Longun says, 'I enlisted because I was a bloomin' coward and too flamin' frightened to face the things they were saying about coves who didn't enlist.' And he too is disbelieved. Many of us realise that our own enlistments were brought about by a blending of the reasons given by Dark and Longun.

Of course we vow we'll never enlist again, yet we know that if ever the boys are on the job again, many vows will be swept aside by the thunder of marching feet, the marching feet of old mates. Mateship transcends reason. That has been proved on the battlefield time after time. Mateship is born or renewed when the country calls and that is how it should be and how it ever must be. Mateship.

Sunday 13th July and we're eighteen days out from Cape Town without sighting land. Apples were issued out today but we didn't go them. We've been well cared for on this trip as the Comforts Fund and the Y.M.C.A. have done much to make things better and happier for us.

Talk turns to some of our doings in France. Snow recalls the night he and Yacob sneaked off to tap the milk supply of a cow the British Officers' mess kept tethered in an old garden. They got the cow bailed up and Snow milked her and told Yacob to let her out. Yacob let her out all right. Let her head out before he took the leg-rope off and didn't she bellow and kick! She kicked the side out of the old shed and, bellowing loudly, careered madly down the village street with a great plank still hanging to her kicking leg. Every Tommy officer within miles woke up and came to see what was biting their cow, so Snow had to hide the great dixie till the hubbub quietened down a bit. He had to leave it hidden till nearly daylight and when he went to collect it he found a mangy yellow kitten drowned in it and somehow we never fancied milk again.

Darky is lying in his hammock curling his great toes around the ropes and laughing at some memory of a by-gone day. Well into the night we yarn. The talking fades away and one by one the men become lost in thought as the tendrils of clinging memories fasten upon mates who fought and frolicked their happy-go-lucky way through the fun and fury of war until their day came to go under. Our voices are no longer heard. The troop deck is wrapped in the hushed silence of flooding memories, as men's minds traverse the battlefields of France seeking silent commune with brave spirits now laid in their lonely graves in that foreign land.

Almost home. Our ship has anchored at Melbourne and we're to go overland to Sydney. Back home at last! For the past five days we've been in touch with our own homeland. First sight of Kangaroo Island then anchoring out near Semaphore for a night. The train trip from the Outer Harbour to Adelaide where we had two days on shore amongst Australian people before the short voyage from Adelaide to Melbourne. Today we join the train that will carry us north over the Murray to our own homes in old New South.

Two o'clock Saturday afternoon, 19th July, and our train is moving off from Melbourne, a cheering, friendly, laughing Melbourne.

'We hop-off at zero hour tomorrow morning and take Sydney,' a chap jokes. Tomorrow, Sunday, will see us at old Sydney. Right through the piece it's been a case of going into the line on Sunday, and even now we are still going our last stunt on a Sunday. But what a different stunt it will be this Sunday! And that Sunday is tomorrow!

We're now at Albury changing trains and are being shepherded into a big hospital train full of beds for our night journey through our own state. Northward we go. Station after station flits by, each with its little cheering crowd to yell a welcome home as we steam by, waving and calling from every window and door. There's little sleep tonight.

Daylight. Men dressing with care. Those who will so soon be greeting us are worthy of the best we can produce. Moss Vale and breakfast of boiled sausages and toast; back in the train and off on the last stage of our advance on Sydney.

We're running through the outer suburbs now. Every suburban train we pass is screeching a welcome. Front gardens and backyards are filled with happy, waving people. Hundreds of nippers are perched upon paling fences shouting and grinning their little welcomes.

Flags are fluttering ahead. We're running into a flag-bedecked platform at Central and the train glides to a standstill. We grab our kit bags and file down the platform to a barrier. An officer calls our names and each man is handed a leave pass. On towards the barrier we move and we're through and into a motor car and being whisked away along streets lined with thousands of cheering people.

The car stops near the Domain. We get out. A laneway is open before us, a laneway fenced with friendly faces. Down that lane we move towards the Anzac Buffet.

On we move. Faces search ours. Faces that are so easily read. Bright happy faces that bubble over with excitement. Bright eyes that dance again as they recognise a returning brother or a bloke who is something more than a brother.

Dozens of little kiddie faces everywhere, perched on adults' shoulders or poking through between the iron railings, they look upon us with wide, wondering eyes and one little chap of five or six echoes his disappointment. 'Hey, where's ya rifle and machine-gun, Mister?'

We laugh at the eager mite, but feel sorry that we've let him down. What's the use of a war to a kid if he can't see a few weapons displayed?

The lane is narrowing now. We move through hundreds of anxious faces that show anxiety and disappointment as people fail to find the one man they are so anxiously looking for. Here and there are the sad, hopeless faces of those who know they will never welcome their own returning boy. Their cross is heavy today.

In on us they crowd. Men and women in all degrees of mental excitement from sorrow to joy. Eyes that cry and eyes that laugh. Young girls crying when they should be laughing, brave women laughing who really should be crying.

Still on we make our way. 'Hey, Blue, strike me pink, but here's Longun and Dark and Nulla. Whato, Longun? How goes it, Nulla? Hey there, Dark! Thought you were stonkered years ago, you lot o' bloomin' ole cows.' And we recognise two of the boys from our old reinforcement who left us on the Somme in the 1916 winter. Decked out in their Sunday best, it's hard to reconcile their get-up with that of old mates, for somehow the civvy clothes seem out of keeping.

A few more yards and 'Ah, there, Nulla!' a man in uniform is calling me. I see the colour patch of the trench-mortar crowd and recognise a great friend of our family.

'Whato! Lin!' I call and he shoves his broad shoulders through the crowd and has me by the hand.

'Your mother is just beyond the crowd there on the other side of the buffet. Keep a stiff upper lip for her sake. Stick it out, old man.' And he shoves me on my way.

My mother is here, waiting to give me her lonely welcome, a welcome I so look forward to and so shrink from meeting, for our cup of sorrow, my own and my mother's, is full and it will take that 'stiff upper lip' that Lin has just advised to prevent it from brimming over.

Good old Lin. The practical help of a digger is being extended to a mate in trouble.

Again my name comes and another digger, a cousin, is shouting to me across a sea of heads that wave mistily before my eyes, eyes striving desperately to fight back the tears of a great and crushing sorrow that my home-coming must renew afresh in kindred, sorrowing hearts.

'Hey there! Nulla!'

And there comes a call I haven't heard for years, but which I pick out instantly, and my brother, now out of uniform, is calling to me. I spot him standing about the twelfth row back.

'Here, Bill, catch this!' I call to break the tension and wave my great heavy kit bag towards him. A dozen hands reach for the bag and back to Bill it sails on a magic carpet of helping hands as the crowd seizes on to the bag in their eagerness to be of some assistance.

Now I'm inside the buffet, tea and cakes are offered. I don't want any. I've got enough to swallow as it is. A sergeant is asking my name and number and writing them down, as mechanically I answer him.

'Ever been wounded?'

'Yes.'

'How many times?'

'Five.'

'What wound marks do you carry?'

Mechanically I tell him a few. Outward woundings seem of very little account compared with the inward wound the hand of Death has so very lately dealt our family.

As I move on a lady says, 'That boy seems queer. Wonder if he has shell shock?'

No, not shell shock, but just a lonely boy trying hard to fight down his sorrow for the sake of that grief-torn mother he must meet at any step now.

I'm beyond the buffet at last and find my mother, but dozens of friends and relatives surround us and a wild rush sets in, mercifully allowing no time for brooding.

On across the Domain we all surge. My grandmother is here waiting to swell the welcome. Brothers, sisters, aunts and cousins flocking around. Heaps of girls I know and plenty I don't are shaking hands and laughing as they rush in and kiss me. I'm being kissed by girls I've never seen before and it's not too bad either. This part of the welcome is pretty decent. In fact, now I wouldn't mind coming home from a war every day.

Across Hyde Park we stream. Oxford Street is before us and we all climb aboard a tram.

'Fares, please.'

'Here, half a tram load to Coogee,' one of the men calls and we're on our way.

A relative's home at Coogee. More relatives and friends to see. All day long people dropping in. All day long I am kept busy shaking hands and being kissed and told how well I look. Night, bright lights and music. Friends departing. Enquiries about last trams. More music, an extra final cup of tea and I'm in bed back in Aussie. Back home in Aussie!

Now to sleep, but who wants to sleep? So now to think.

Memories are crowding my mind. It has been wonderful today but nothing has driven from my sorrowing mind, the heart-breaking realisation that I'll never get the warm, friendly grip of welcome from my own proud father. The dear father, whom I loved as few men ever loved a father, has been called to his Eternal Home just a few short weeks ago. The very bottom has fallen out of my homecoming. May God rest his dear soul. My father and my mate.

I'm back amongst my own people. Back to take up the threads of the civilian life I had barely begun when I left to become a link in the chain of the A.I.F. What lies ahead I don't know. Plans, dreams, much to be attempted, perhaps much to be done.

Behind memories, memories of mates of war, old mates of the happy-go-lucky, never-say-die philosophy. Memories of real men we've known. Men who were mates. Men we've helped and men who have so often helped us.

Where are our old mates now? Our mates who slogged along with us through the black, clinging Somme mud, that awful Somme mud that so clung to tired legs. Men who faced and broke the unbreakable Hindenburg Line at Bullecourt, who climbed with us side by side through the shell-fed smoke and dust of Messines Ridge, who somehow did their job through the all but impassable shell-ploughed mud that was Passchendaele. Our mates of Péronne, of Hollebeke, of Dernancourt and Villers-Bretonneux, of Hamel, Proyart and Lihons.

The brightest memory of the lot is that I have known real men. Men with the cover off. Men with their wonderful nobility of character, of mateship, revealed. It's a glorious memory to have. To have known men as men. That is something that does not come to everyone.

The war is over. The trial was long and severe. The prize was worth it, though, when measured in the mateship of men. My mates! Memories of men! Memories of mates! Men who were mates and mates who were men.

C'est la guerre!

EPILOGUE

Will Davies

In 1921, Edward Lynch enrolled in Sydney Teachers College, graduating two years later, after which he was sent to Goulburn as a young teacher. In June 1923 he married Yvonne Peters and in the years following they had five children, who are still alive today. He then spent many years teaching along the Murrumbidgee and, when World War II came in 1939, joined the militia. In 1942 he transferred to the regular army, was promoted to Captain and was Officer Commanding the NSW Jungle Training School (Lowana). After the war he returned to teaching until his retirement. He died on 12 September 1980.

GLOSSARY

A.I.F.	Australian Imperial Forces
A.A.M.C	Australian Army Medical Corps
A.M.C.	Army Medical Corps
A.W.L	Absent Without Leave
Blighty	Britain
block	defended barricade in a trench
bosun	boatswain; a warrant officer on board ship
'Boys of the Dardanelles'	popular song after Gallipoli campaign
brown	penny
buckshee	army rations or something given away free
Bull Ring	training area at Étaples, general training ground
bully beef	tinned meat common in Allied armies
chats	body lice
clink	gaol
clobber	hit, struck, taken out
C.O.	Commanding Officer
cobber	friend, mate
colour patches	distinctive shoulder badges indicating a division, brigade, battalion or unit within the A.I.F.
cove	man, bloke
C.S.M.	Company Sergeant Major
demijohn	large earthenware container with a small neck, often used to hold rum
detrain	unloading from a train

digs	accommodation of some form
dixie	metal container for eating food
dodger	bread
double	run or walk 'double time'
duckboard	wooden decking
18-pounders	the British empire field artillery gun, firing an 18-pound shell
field dressing	bandage carried by all troops
fire step	step in the side of the trench to raise a man to a firing position
floppin'	swearword of the time, a euphemism for 'fucking'
Fritz	common name for a German
funk hole	hole in the side of a trench for sleeping and protection
furphy	horse-drawn cast iron water tank around which stories were told, hence the term 'furphy', a tall story, rumour or lie
furlough	leave to allow travel
gas	various poisonous gases used by both sides during the war
gas respirator	gas-mask used to prevent inhaling poisonous gas during a gas attack
'get a Blighty'	getting wounded badly enough to be sent to England
G.S. wagon	General Service wagon, horse-drawn dray
hop-over	climbing out of the trench to attack the enemy line
H.Q.	headquarters
Jack Tars	sailors of the Royal Navy
Jerry	German
Kamerad!	German word meaning 'comrade', used when wishing to surrender
K.I.A.	killed in action
kruger	coin from South Africa equal to about two shillings
Lewis gun	American-designed lightweight machine-gun
lift	the artillery would 'lift' from one map reference to another at predetermined times so that

	following, attacking infantry, could assault the enemy trench
limber	two-wheeled cart used to carry stores or ammunition
L.P.	listening post, usually out in no-man's-land to give warning of an enemy attack
Maconochie	a mixture of tinned meat and vegetables
M.G.	machine-gun
M.I.A.	missing in action
Mills bomb	British-issue hand grenade
Minenwerfer	German trench mortar
mooching	hanging around, waiting, wasting time
mopping up	eliminating remaining enemy pockets of resistance after the main attack has gone through
N.C.O.	Non-Commissioned Officer
no-man's-land	the dangerous land between two opposing trench lines
O.C.	Officer Commanding
O.P.	observation post
O.R.s	other ranks
pannikins	metal containers for food
parados	the rear edge of a trench (the opposite of a parapet)
parapet	built up front edge of a trench, which protected men
pill-box	concrete machine-gun emplacement
pioneers	infantry troops trained and equipped to perform light engineering tasks
platoon	army unit of thirty men under a lieutenant and sergeant
plum duff	tinned plum pudding supplied to troops
possie	position
puttees	cloth strips wound around the legs from below the knee to the top of the boot
Q.M.	Quartermaster
Qui vive	'on the qui vive', on the alert
R.A.M.C.	Royal Army Medical Corps
R.A.P.	Regimental Aid Post
respirator	gas mask

reveille	dawn wake-up bugle call
route march	hard marching between two points
S.A.A.	small arms ammunition
salient	prominent or projecting part of the line often protruding out from the main front line
Sam Browne	leather belt worn as part of an officer's uniform
sap	trench dug towards the enemy from which more trenches radiate out each side
S.B.s	stretcher-bearers
scabbard	metal sheath for a bayonet
scran	food
screw picket	twisted metal post to hold up barbed wire
section	ten men usually under the command of a corporal
sigs	signallers who used field telephones
S.M.	Sergeant Major
S.O.S. barrage	barrage put down on pre-designated map references in case of attack
sprat	sixpence or five cents
S.R.D.	Service Rum – Dilute. This rum came in a concentrated form and needed to be watered down before drinking.
stand to	stand ready for the enemy, usually at dawn and dusk
start line	the line from where an attack commences
Stokes mortar	British small trench mortar
stonker	hit, knocked over
strafe	fired upon by shells or machine-guns
strides	pants, trousers
stunt	action or attack on the enemy
tapes	cotton tapes laid down to designate the starting line for an attack
Taube	German fighter aircraft
Tommy	British soldier, deriving from 'Tommy Atkins'
two bob	two shillings or twenty cents
W.I.A.	wounded in action
wire	barbed wire

wiring party	group of men who put up barbed wire
yarns	talking, chatting, discussion
Y.M.C.A	Young Men's Christian Association

ACKNOWLEDGEMENTS

There are a number of people who have made the publication of this manuscript possible. First, my thanks to Edward Lynch's grandson Mike Lynch for not only introducing me to the story and the Lynch family, but also taking on the enormous task of re-typing the original manuscript of 180,000 words and making this available to me for the edit.

My thanks also to the rest of Edward Lynch's family: in particular his daughter Shirley and granddaughter Jane Harrison, who has kindly provided me with permission to edit and publish her grandfather's story. My thanks also to David Campbell, who scanned the original typed manuscript and made this available to Edward Lynch's family, enabling the grandchildren to make use of it in their HSC.

I would also like to thank the ongoing support of my wife, Heather, my boys, and a number of friends who know my passion for history and the importance of getting this book completed. To Bill Gammage, who put me straight on the integrity of the story and the author's original words, a special thanks. To my publisher, Jane Palfreyman, and to the editor, Sophie Ambrose, for their support and advice, and to the staff at the Australian War Memorial, especially Patricia Sabine and Anne Bennie, who have assisted with photographic research and clearance, and Dr Peter Stanley and Peter Burness.